Stock Investing
For Canadians

5th Edition

by Andrew Dagys, CPA, CMA, and Paul Mladjenovic, CFP

for
dummies®
A Wiley Brand

Stock Investing For Canadians For Dummies®, 5th Edition

Published by: **John Wiley & Sons, Inc.**, 111 River Street, Hoboken, NJ 07030-5774, www.wiley.com

Copyright © 2019 by John Wiley & Sons, Inc., Hoboken, New Jersey

Published simultaneously in Canada

For general information on our other products and services, please contact our Customer Care Department within the U.S. at 877-762-2974, outside the U.S. at 317-572-3993, or fax 317-572-4002. For technical support, please visit https://hub.wiley.com/community/support/dummies.

Wiley publishes in a variety of print and electronic formats and by print-on-demand. Some material included with standard print versions of this book may not be included in e-books or in print-on-demand. If this book refers to media such as a CD or DVD that is not included in the version you purchased, you may download this material at http://booksupport.wiley.com. For more information about Wiley products, visit www.wiley.com.

Library of Congress Control Number: 2018961131

ISBN 978-1-119-52194-5 (pbk); ISBN 978-1-119-52188-4 (ePub); ISBN 978-1-119- 55361-8 (epdf)

Manufactured in the United States of America

C10006052_111218

Table of Contents

Introduction

Stock Investing For Canadians For Dummies, 5th Edition, has been an honour for us to write. We are grateful we can share our thoughts, information, and experience with such a large and devoted group of Canadian readers. This edition is by far our most important one because so much has changed by way of brand new markets and jurisdictions that stock investors can now invest in. In today's global investing landscape, the opportunities for great gains (and even greater losses) have reached an extreme. In some ways, our current market reminds us of Dickens's famous novel opener: "It was the best of times, it was the worst of times . . ."

In terms of the negative realities that face us now — economic uncertainty, high personal and national debt, terrorism, war, job and political instability, rising inflation, and so on — these seem like the worst of times. Yet when we think of the opportunities represented by new, mobile, and emerging financial technologies to improve investing and risk management, we are encouraged. Financial innovations such as robo-advisors that use artificial intelligence, and digital currency that has value and trades on exchanges much like stocks, have captured the imagination, and finances, of the stock markets. Rising stock markets like Asia, new market segments like medical cannabis, and new types of exchange-traded funds have opened up exciting stock-investing opportunities for Canadians. It's clear these can also become the best of times.

At the time of this writing and by most measures of performance, the combined value of U.S. and Canadian stocks has reached record levels. A powerful combination of easy money printed and doled out by governments and raw but powerful demographics and economics have not only sustained these high levels, but also impacted the value of the real estate sector — a sector that is well-represented in the market where stocks are bought and sold.

Exactly what can or should Canadian stock investors do? How can Canadians seize the opportunities in financial technology, including cryptocurrency? How can investors know whether a dip is around the corner or a recovery in stock values in areas like commodities is imminent? As with so many of life's lessons, being successful at stock investing takes diligent effort, experience, and knowledge. We can definitely help you understand stock-investing fundamentals and avoid some of the big mistakes others have already made. We can also help you better understand and hopefully not repeat any past stock-investing mistakes you yourself may have made.

In this edition, for the very first time, we introduce you to financial instruments, tools, and platforms with wild names like Ethereum, Bitcoin, blockchain, and robo-advisors. Of course, we start and will always focus on the core of this book — stocks. It is our pleasure and purpose to help you succeed!

In the face of all of this uncertainty, today's most effective stock investors will be those who are nimble, prepared to make quick decisions, and perceptive to changes that are relevant to stock investing. This book helps you get to that state and shows you how to make important connections to the events and drivers that move stocks in one direction or another.

In all the years that we've counselled and educated investors, the single difference between success and failure, between gain and loss, boils down to one word: *knowledge*. Welcome to this book — and welcome to the intriguing and exciting world of stock investing!

About This Book

The stock market has been a cornerstone of the Canadian investor's passive wealth-building program for more than a century and continues in this role. Recent years have been one wild roller-coaster ride for stock investors. Fortunes have been made and lost. Even with all the media attention, all the talking heads on radio and television, and the reams of books promising great profits, the investing public is still exposed to things like world recessions, corporate scandals, and other market-moving events. With just a little more knowledge and a few wealth-preserving techniques, more investors could have held onto their hard-earned stock market fortunes. This book gives you an early warning on those megatrends and events that will affect your stock portfolio.

This book is designed to give you a realistic approach to making money in stocks. It can help you succeed not only in up markets but also in down markets. It provides the essence of sound, practical stock-investing strategies and insights that have been market-tested and proven over nearly 100 years of stock market history. We don't expect you to read it cover to cover, although we'd be delighted if you read every word. Instead, this book is primarily designed as a reference tool. Feel free to read the chapters in whatever order you choose.

Stock Investing For Canadians For Dummies, 5th Edition, is different from the "get rich with stocks" titles that have crammed the bookshelves in recent years. It doesn't take a standard approach to the topic; it doesn't assume that stocks are a sure thing and the be-all, end-all of wealth building. In fact, at times in this book, we tell you when *not* to invest in certain types of stocks. We rest confident that this is our best edition ever.

Foolish Assumptions

We figure you've picked up this book for one or more of the following reasons:

>> You're a beginner and want a crash course on stock investing that's an easy read.

>> You're already a stock investor, and you need a book that allows you to read only those chapters that cover specific stock investing topics of interest to you.

>> You need to review your own situation with the information in the book to see whether you missed anything when you invested in that hot stock your brother-in-law recommended.

>> You need a great gift. When Uncle Gus is upset over his poor stock picks, give him this book so he can get back on his financial feet. Be sure to get a copy for his broker, too. (Odds are the broker was the one who made those picks to begin with.)

Icons Used in This Book

Useful icons appear in the margins of this book; here's what they mean.

REMEMBER

When you see this icon, we're reminding you about some information to always keep stashed in your memory, whether you're new to investing or an old pro.

TECHNICAL STUFF

The text attached to this icon may not be crucial to your success as an investor, but it may enable you to talk shop with investing gurus and better understand the financial pages of your favourite business publication or Web site.

TIP

This icon flags a particular bit of advice that may just give you an edge over other investors.

WARNING

Pay special attention to this icon, because the advice can prevent headaches, heartaches, and financial aches.

Beyond the Book

In addition to the material in the print or digital book you're reading right now, *Stock Investing For Canadian For Dummies*, 5th Edition, comes with other great content available online. To get the Cheat Sheet, simply go to www.dummies.com and search for "Stock Investing For Canadians For Dummies Cheat Sheet" in the Search box.

Where to Go from Here

You may not need to read every chapter to make you more confident as a stock investor, so feel free to jump around to suit your personal needs. Because every chapter is designed to be as self-contained as possible, it won't do you any harm to cherry-pick what you really want to read. But if you're like us, you may still want to check out every chapter because you never know when you may come across a new tip or resource that will make a profitable difference in your stock portfolio. We want you to be successful so we can brag about you in the next edition.

1

The Essentials of Stock Investing

IN THIS PART . . .

Get to know the basics, preparing to buy stocks, and figuring out how to pick good ones.

Tally up your personal balance sheet and cash flow statement and set some personal financial goals.

Come up with strategies to match your investing goals.

Look at different types of risk, understand volatility, and balance risk versus return.

Know similarities and differences between ETFs and mutual funds and the basics of indexes.

Chapter **1**

Surveying the World of Stock Investing

For Canadians who are new to stock investing, the stock market must certainly look both enticing and scary at the same time. Since we wrote the last edition, the world-leading U.S. stock market has gone nowhere but up. During this time, the much smaller but still exciting Canadian stock market has gone up too, though nowhere near as much. No matter where you invest, or what level the stock market is at today, the decision to buy or sell is never easy.

We wrote much of this 5th Canadian Edition as the United States, Canada, and the rest of the world were wondering if international military tensions would escalate, or whether international economic trade agreement disputes would lead to financial turbulence or even an economic abyss. (Events such as these directly affect stock investing because our world and our financial markets are more interrelated and connected than ever.) Too many folks are pining for the good 'ol days of the 80s and 90s, when choosing winning stocks was easier than finding aliens in *Star Wars.* Today's stock market is more than a little puzzling . . . but it can still be rewarding. And it can be better understood. We can only promise you that if you read this book seriously and apply its fundamental lessons, you'll do *much* better than the average investor. Just keep in mind that patience and discipline count now more than ever.

The purpose of this book is not only to tell you about the basics of stock investing but also to let you in on solid investment strategies that can help you profit from the stock market. Before you invest, you need to understand the fundamentals of stock investing, which we introduce in this chapter. Then we give you an overview of how to put your money where it will count the most. We even point you to some emerging and exciting areas that represent great opportunities. But first things first.

Understanding the Basics

The basics of stock investing are so elementary that few people recognize them. When you lose track of the basics or first principles, you lose track of why you invested to begin with. Part 1 of this book helps you grasp these basics:

>> Knowing the risk and volatility involved: Perhaps the most fundamental (and therefore most important) concept to grasp is the risk you face whenever you put your hard-earned money in an investment such as a stock. In fact, very few investors have the risk tolerance to invest 100 percent in stocks. They generally invest in a balanced, diversified portfolio composed of multiple stocks, fixed income, and other assets. This important asset allocation decision (how many stocks, bonds, and other assets you should own) helps determine the overall risk of your total portfolio.

Related to risk is the concept of volatility: Volatility refers to a condition in which there is rapid movement in either direction in the price of a particular stock (or other investment); investors use this term especially when there's a sudden drop in price in a relatively short period of time. Fixed income investments (bonds, bank certificates of deposit, etc.) tend to be less volatile than stocks. Find out more about both risk and volatility in Chapter 4.

>> **Assessing your financial situation:** You need a firm awareness of your starting point and where you want to go. Chapter 2 helps you take stock of your current financial status and your goals, two fundamental building blocks that need to be in place and understood before you invest in stocks.

>> **Understanding approaches to investing:** You want to approach investing in a way that works best for you. Chapter 3 discusses investment time horizons, as well as purpose- and style-driven approaches to investing.

>> **Seeing what exchange-traded funds have to offer:** Exchange-traded funds are like mutual funds, but are growing in popularity much faster than mutual funds because they can be traded like stocks. See Chapter 5 for the lowdown on Canadian and other exchange-traded funds.

REMEMBER

The bottom line in stock investing is that you shouldn't immediately send your money to a Canadian brokerage account or go to a website and click "buy stock." The first thing you should do is find out as much as you can about what stocks are, key stock-investing principles, and how to use this knowledge to achieve your wealth-building goals.

REMEMBER

Before you continue, we want to get straight exactly what a stock is. *Stock* is a type of security or financial instrument that indicates ownership in a corporation and represents a claim on a part of that corporation's assets and earnings. The two primary types of stocks are common and preferred:

>> **Common stock:** Common stock (the type we cover throughout this book) entitles the owner to vote at shareholders' meetings and receive any dividends that the company issues.

>> **Preferred stock:** Preferred stock doesn't usually confer voting rights, but it does include some rights that exceed those of common stock. Preferred stockholders, for example, have priority in certain conditions, such as receiving dividends before common stockholders in the event that the corporation goes bankrupt. Additionally, preferred stocks operate similarly to a bond for those investors who seek stable income. However, you should be aware that bondholders generally hold priority over both common and preferred stockholders. (In this book, we mostly cover common stock.)

In addition to common stock, in this new Canadian edition we also cover exchange-traded funds because they can be a very valuable part of the Canadian stock investor's portfolio (see Chapter 5 for more details on exchange-traded funds).

Preparing to Buy Stocks

Gathering information is critical in your stock-investing pursuits. You should gather information on your stock picks two times: before you invest and after. Obviously, you should become more informed before you invest your first dollar, but you also need to stay informed about what's happening to the company whose stock you buy as well as about the industry and the general Canadian and world economies. All too many Canadians don't make it a habit to check up on their stock holdings, which is risky business. To find the best information sources to stay on top of your stocks, check out Chapter 6.

When you're ready to invest, you need a Canadian brokerage account, and you may even need some advice about things like portfolio allocation options. How do you know which broker to use? What type of portfolio best aligns with your financial goals and risk appetite? Chapter 7 provides some answers and resources to help you choose brokers and advisors that serve your needs.

Knowing How to Pick Winners

When you get past the basics, you can get to the meat of stockpicking. Successful stockpicking isn't mysterious, but it does take some time, effort, and analysis. And the effort is worthwhile because stocks are a convenient and important part of most investors' portfolios. Read the following sections and be sure to leapfrog to the relevant chapters to get the inside scoop on hot stocks.

Recognizing stock value

Imagine that you like eggs and you're buying them at the grocery store. In this example, the eggs are like companies, and the prices represent the prices that you would pay for the companies' stock. The grocery store is the stock market. What if two brands of eggs are similar, but one costs $2.99 a carton and the other costs $3.99? Which would you choose? Odds are that you'd look at both brands, judge their quality, and, if they're indeed similar, take the cheaper eggs. The eggs at $3.99 are overpriced. The same is true of stocks. What if you compare two companies that are similar in every respect but have different share prices? All things being equal, the cheaper price has greater value for the investor.

But the egg example has another side. What if the quality of the two brands of eggs is significantly different, but their prices are the same? If one brand of eggs is stale, of poor quality, and priced at $2.99 and the other brand is fresh, of superior quality, and also priced at $2.99, which would you get? We'd take the good brand because they're better eggs. Perhaps the lesser eggs are an acceptable purchase at $1.99, but they're definitely overpriced at $2.99. The same example works with stocks. A poorly run company isn't a good choice if you can buy a better company in the marketplace at the same — or a better — price.

REMEMBER

Comparing the value of eggs may seem overly simplistic, but doing so does cut to the heart of stock investing. Eggs and egg prices can be as varied as companies and stock prices. When considering stocks, however, *relative valuation* (how undervalued or overvalued the stock is relative to the overall market index) is generally more important than absolute price. As a Canadian investor, you must make it your job to find the best value for your investment dollars. (Otherwise, you get egg on your face. You saw that one coming, right?)

Understanding how market capitalization affects stock value

REMEMBER

You can determine a company's value (and thus the value of its stock) in many ways. The most basic way is to look at the company's market value, also known as market capitalization (or market cap). *Market capitalization* is simply the value you get when you multiply all the outstanding shares of a stock by the price of a single share. Calculating the market cap is easy; for example, if a company has 1 million shares outstanding and its share price is $10, the market cap is $10 million.

Small cap, mid cap, and large cap aren't references to headgear; they're references to how large a company is as measured by its market value. Here are the five typical stock categories of market capitalization used in major North American stock markets, defined from smallest to largest:

>> **Micro cap (less than $250 million):** These stocks are the smallest, and hence the riskiest, available. (There's even a subsection of micro cap called nano cap, which refers to stocks under $50 million).

>> **Small cap ($250 million to $1 billion):** These stocks fare better than the micro caps and still have plenty of growth potential. The key word here is "potential."

>> **Mid cap ($1 billion to $10 billion):** For many investors, this category offers a good compromise between small caps and large caps. These stocks have some of the safety of large caps while retaining some of the growth potential of small caps.

>> **Large cap ($10 billion to $50 billion):** This category is usually best reserved for conservative stock investors who want steady appreciation with greater safety. Stocks in this category are frequently referred to as blue chips. CIBC and Imperial Oil Ltd. fit into this category.

>> **Ultra cap (more than $50 billion):** These stocks are also called mega caps and obviously refer to companies that are the biggest of the big. Stocks such as Alphabet (formerly Google), Amazon, and Apple are examples. Not many stocks in Canada make it to this size, but some names that do include the Royal Bank of Canada and the Toronto-Dominion Bank.

REMEMBER

From a safety point of view, a company's size and market value do matter. All things being equal, large cap stocks are considered safer than small cap stocks. However, small cap stocks have greater potential for growth. Compare these stocks to trees: Which tree is sturdier, a giant redwood tree or a small maple tree that's just a year old? In a great storm, the redwood holds up well, whereas the smaller tree has a rough time. But you also have to ask yourself which tree has more opportunity for growth. The redwood may not have much growth left, but the small maple tree has plenty of growth to look forward to.

For beginning investors, comparing market cap to trees isn't so far-fetched. You want your money to branch out without becoming a sap.

REMEMBER

Although market capitalization is important to consider, don't invest (or not invest) based solely on it. It's just one of many measures of value. As a serious investor, you need to look at numerous factors that can help you determine whether any given stock is a good investment. Keep reading — this book is full of information to help you decide.

Sharpening your investment skills

Canadian investors who analyze a company well can better judge the value of its stock, and profit from buying and selling it. Your greatest asset in stock investing is knowledge (and a little common sense). To succeed in the world of stock investing, keep in mind these key success factors:

>> **Understand why you want to invest in stocks.** Are you seeking appreciation (capital gains) or income (dividends)? Look at Chapters 8 and 9 for information on these topics.

>> **Timing your buys and sells does matter.** Terms like "overbought" and "oversold" can give you an edge when you're deciding whether to purchase or sell a stock. Technical analysis is a way to analyze securities through their market activity (past prices and volume) to find patterns that suggest where those investments may be headed in the short term. For more information, see Chapter 10.

>> **Do some research.** Look at the company whose stock you're considering to see whether it's a profitable business worthy of your investment dollars. Chapters 11 and 12 help you scrutinize companies using some basic financial analysis and research approaches and tools.

>> **Understand and identify what's up with "The Big Picture."** It is a small world after all, and you should be aware of how the world can affect your stock portfolio. Everyone from the bureaucrats in Europe to the politicians in the U.S. Capitol or Canadian Parliament can affect a stock or industry like a match in a dry haystack. Chapters 13, 14, and 15 give you lots of guidance on cool megatrends; exciting sector, industry, and international opportunities; and, yes, the Big Picture (both economic and political).

>> **Use investing strategies like the pros do.** In other words, how you go about investing can be just as important as what you invest in. We're very big on strategies such as trailing stops and limit orders, and fortunately today's technology gives you even more tools to help you grow or protect your money. Chapters 16, 17, and 18 highlight techniques for investing to help you make more money from your stocks.

- >> **Consider Bitcoin and alternative cryptocurrencies.** Buying stocks doesn't always mean that you must buy common shares. Equities such as stocks come in different forms. Contrary to their name, *cryptocurrencies* are more like stocks and equities than currencies. Chapter 19 has comprehensive and exciting information about Bitcoin and its kissing-cousin cryptocurrencies. We're confident you will enjoy it.

- >> **Do as others do, not as they say.** Sometimes, what people tell you to do with stocks is not as revealing as what people are actually doing. This is why we insist on looking at company insiders before we buy or sell a particular stock. To find out more about insider buying and selling, read Chapter 20.

- >> **Keep more of the money you earn.** After all your great work in getting the right stocks and making the big bucks, you should know about keeping more of the fruits of your investing. We cover Canadian taxes related to stock investing in Chapter 21.

Every chapter in this book offers you valuable guidance on some essential aspect of the fantastic world of stocks. The fundamental knowledge you pick up and apply from these pages has been tested over nearly a century of stock picking. The investment experience of the past — the good, the bad, and some of the ugly — is here for your benefit. Use this information to make a lot of money (and make us proud!). And don't forget to check out the appendixes, where we provide a wide variety of Canadian-oriented investing resources and financial ratios as well!

STOCK MARKET CONFUSION

Have you ever noticed a stock going up even though the company is reporting terrible results? How about seeing a stock nosedive despite the fact that the company is doing well? What gives? Well, judging the direction of a stock in a short-term period — over the next few days or weeks — is almost impossible.

Yes, in the short term, stock investing is irrational. Just think about how volatile Blackberry has been over the last two decades! The price of a stock and the value of its company seem disconnected and crazy. The key phrase to remember is "short term." A stock's price and the company's value become more logical over an extended period of time. The longer a stock is in the public's view, the more rational the performance of the stock's price. Now that we know what Blackberry's corporate strategy is today, as well as its smaller but important role in the smartphone ecosystem, we begin to better understand yesteryear's highs and lows. Blackberry's current valuation begins to make sense to us.

Chapter 2

Taking Stock of Your Financial Situation and Goals

Yes, you want to make the big bucks. Or maybe you just want to get back the big bucks you lost in stocks during *a recent market correction* (a short period of falling prices usually accompanied by lots of volatility). (Canadian investors who followed the guidelines from previous editions of this book did much better than the crowd!) Either way, you want your money to grow so that you can have a better life. But before you make reservations for that Caribbean cruise you're dreaming about, you have to map out your action plan for getting there. Stocks can be a great component of most wealth-building programs, but you must first do some homework on a topic that you should be very familiar with — yourself. That's right. More than ever before, you need to understand your current financial situation and clearly define your financial goals as the first steps to successful and careful investing.

Here's an example. We met an investor who had a million dollars' worth of Procter & Gamble (PG) stock, and he was nearing retirement. He asked us whether he should sell his stock and become more growth-oriented by investing in a batch of *small cap* stocks (stocks of a company worth $250 million to $1 billion; refer to Chapter 1 for more information). Because he already had enough assets to retire on at that time, we said that he didn't need to get more aggressive. In fact, we told him that he had too much tied to a single stock, even though it was a solid, large company. What would happen to his assets if problems arose at PG? A diversified stock portfolio should include multiple stocks (more than 20) from various sectors and countries. Telling him to shrink his stock portfolio and put that money elsewhere — by paying off debt, adding a Guaranteed Investment Certificate from a Canadian bank, and/or buying a U.S. treasury bill (a fixed-income security) for diversification, for example — seemed obvious.

This chapter is undoubtedly one of the most important chapters in this book. At first, you may think it's a chapter more suitable for some general book on personal finance. Wrong! Unsuccessful investors' greatest weakness is not understanding their financial situations and how stocks fit in. Often, we counsel people to stay out of the stock market if they aren't prepared for the responsibilities of stock investing, such as regularly reviewing corporate financial statements and the actual progress of the companies they invest in.

REMEMBER

Investing in stocks requires balance. Investors sometimes tie up too much money in stocks, putting themselves at risk of losing a significant portion of their wealth if the market plunges. This is especially dangerous for the many Canadians who hold on to excessive personal debt, which has been rising nationally over the years. Then again, other Canadian investors place little or no money in stocks and therefore miss out on excellent opportunities to meaningfully grow their wealth. Canadians should make stocks a part of their investment portfolios, but the operative word is *part*. Most investors hold a balanced portfolio, composed of stocks, bonds, and other assets. You should let stocks take up only a *portion* of your money. A disciplined investor also has money in bank accounts, investment-grade bonds, precious metals, and other assets that offer growth or income opportunities. Diversification is the key to minimizing risk. (For more on risk, see Chapter 4. We even touch on volatility there.)

Establishing a Starting Point by Preparing a Balance Sheet

Whether you already own stocks or are looking to get into the stock market, you need to find out about how much money you can afford to invest. No matter what you hope to accomplish with your stock investing plan, the first step you should take is to figure out how much you own and how much you owe. To do this, prepare and review your personal balance sheet. A *balance sheet* is simply a list of your assets, your liabilities, and what each item is currently worth so you can arrive at your net worth. Your *net worth* is total assets minus total liabilities. (We know these terms sound like accounting mumbo jumbo, but knowing your net worth is important to your future financial success, so just do it.)

Composing your balance sheet is simple. Pull out a pencil and a piece of paper. For the computer savvy, a spreadsheet software program accomplishes the same task. Gather all your financial documents, such as bank and brokerage statements and other such paperwork — you need figures from these documents. Then follow the steps that we outline in the following sections. Update your balance sheet at least once a year to monitor your financial progress (is your net worth going up or down?).

Note: Your personal balance sheet is really no different from balance sheets that giant companies prepare. (The main difference is a few zeros, but you can use our advice in this book to work on changing that.) In fact, the more you find out about your own balance sheet, the easier it is to understand the balance sheet of companies in which you're seeking to invest. See Chapter 11 for details on reviewing company balance sheets.

Step 1: Have an emergency fund

First, list cash on your balance sheet. Your goal is to have a reserve of at least three to six months' worth of your gross living expenses in cash and cash equivalents. The cash is important because it gives you a cushion. Three to six months' worth is usually enough to get you through the most common forms of financial disruption, such as losing your job.

If your monthly expenses (or *outgo*) are $2,000, you should have at least $6,000, and probably closer to $12,000, in a secure, CDIC-insured, interest-bearing bank account (or another relatively safe, interest-bearing vehicle such as a Canadian money market fund). Consider this account an emergency fund, not an investment. Don't use this money to buy stocks.

Too many Canadians don't have an emergency fund, meaning that they put themselves at risk. Walking across a busy and snowy street while wearing a blindfold is a great example of putting yourself at risk. Investors often do the financial equivalent. All too many Canadian investors pile on tremendous debt, put too much into investments (such as stocks) that they don't truly understand, and have little or no savings left over to cushion any unwanted financial surprises. One of the biggest problems during this past decade was that North American savings were sinking to record lows while debt levels were reaching new heights. After the Tech Wreck that began in 2000 and the global financial crisis of 2008, interest rates were so low that many Canadians couldn't resist the urge to borrow money! People then sold many stocks because they needed funds for — you guessed it — paying bills, mortgages, and other debt.

Resist the urge to start thinking of your investment in stocks as a savings account generating more than 20 percent per year. This is dangerous thinking! If your investments tank, or if you lose your job, you'll have financial difficulty and that will affect your stock portfolio (you may have to sell some stocks in your account just to get money to pay the bills). An emergency fund helps you through a temporary cash crunch.

Step 2: List your assets in decreasing order of liquidity

Liquid assets aren't references to beer or cola (unless you're Molson or Cott). Instead, *liquidity* refers to how quickly you can convert a particular *asset* (something you own that has value) into cash. If you know the liquidity of your assets, including investments, you have some options when you need cash to buy some stock (or pay some bills). All too often, people are short on cash and have too much wealth tied up in *illiquid* investments such as real estate. *Illiquid* is just a fancy way of saying that you don't have the immediate cash to meet a pressing need. (Hey, we've all had those moments!) Review your assets and take measures to ensure that enough of them are liquid (along with your illiquid assets).

TIP

Listing your assets in order of liquidity on your balance sheet gives you an immediate picture of which assets you can quickly convert to cash and which ones you can't. If you need money *now*, you can see that cash in hand, your chequing account, and your savings account are at the top of the list. The items last in order of liquidity become obvious; they're things like real estate and other assets that can take a long time to convert to cash.

Table 2-1 shows a hypothetical list of assets in order of liquidity. Use it as a guide for making your own asset list using more appropriate figures that better reflect your actual personal financial situation.

TABLE 2-1   **Listing Personal Assets in Order of Liquidity**

Asset Item	Market Value	Annual Growth Rate %
Current assets		
Cash on hand and in chequing	$150	
Bank savings accounts and certificates of deposit	$5,000	2%
Stocks	$2,000	11%
Mutual funds	$2,400	9%
Exchange-traded funds	$240	
Total current assets	**$9,790**	
Long-term assets		

Asset Item	Market Value	Annual Growth Rate %
Auto	$1,800	–10%
Residence	$150,000	5%
Real estate investment	$125,000	6%
Personal stuff (such as jewelry and collectibles)	$4,000	
Total long-term assets	**$280,800**	
Total assets	**$290,590**	

Here's how to make sense of the information in Table 2-1:

>> **The first column describes the asset.** You can quickly convert *current assets* to cash — they're more liquid; *long-term assets* have value, but you can't necessarily convert them to cash quickly — not very liquid.

>> *Note:* We have stocks listed as short-term in the table. Because a stock can be sold and converted to cash very quickly, it's a good example of a liquid asset. (However, that's not the main purpose for buying stocks.)

>> **The second column gives the current market value for that item.** Keep in mind that this value isn't the purchase price or original value; it's the amount you'd realistically get if you sold the asset in the current market at that moment.

>> **The third column tells you how well that investment is doing compared to one year ago.** If the percentage rate is 5 percent, that item is worth 5 percent more today than it was a year ago. You need to know how well all your assets are doing. Why? So you can adjust your assets for maximum growth or sell assets that are losing money and are overvalued. Assets that are doing well should be kept (consider increasing your holdings in these assets), and assets that are down in value should be scrutinized to see whether they're candidates for removal. Perhaps you can sell them and reinvest the money elsewhere. In addition, the realized loss has tax benefits (see Chapter 21).

TIP

>> Figuring the annual growth rate (in the third column) as a percentage isn't difficult. Say that you buy 100 shares of the stock Gro-A-Lot Corp. (GAL), and its market value on December 31, 2012, is $50 per share for a total market value of $5,000 (100 shares x $50 per share). When you check its value on December 31, 2013, you discover that the stock is at $60 per share for a total market value of $6,000 (100 shares x $60). The annual growth rate is 20 percent. You calculate this percentage by taking the amount of the gain ($60 per share less $50 per share = $10 gain per share), which is $1,000

TIP

(100 shares times the $10 gain), and dividing it by the value at the beginning of the time period ($5,000). In this case, you get 20 percent ($1,000 ÷ $5,000).

>> What if GAL also generates a dividend of $2 per share during that period — now what? In that case, GAL generates a total return of 24 percent. To calculate the total return, add the appreciation ($10 per share x 100 shares = $1,000) and the dividend income ($2 per share x 100 shares = $200) and divide that sum ($1,000 + $200, or $1,200) by the value at the beginning of the year ($50 per share x 100 shares, or $5,000). The total is $1,200 ÷ $5,000, or a growth rate of 24 percent.

>> **The last line** lists the total for all the assets and current market value.

Step 3: List your liabilities

Liabilities are the bills that you're obligated to pay. Whether it's a credit card bill or a mortgage payment, a liability is an amount of money you have to pay back eventually (usually with interest). If you don't keep track of your liabilities, you may end up thinking that you have more money than you really do.

Table 2-2 lists some common liabilities. Use it as a model when you list your own. You should list the liabilities according to how soon you need to pay them. Credit card balances tend to be short-term obligations, whereas mortgage payments not due this year are long-term.

TABLE 2-2 **Listing Personal Liabilities**

Liabilities	Amount	Paying Rate %
Credit cards	$4,000	15%
Personal loans	$13,000	10%
Mortgage	$100,000	8%
Total liabilities	**$117,000**	

Here's a summary of the information in Table 2-2:

>> **The first column** names the type of debt. Don't forget to include student loans and auto loans if you have them.

>> Never avoid listing a liability because you're embarrassed to see how much you really owe. Be honest with yourself — doing so helps you improve your financial health.

REMEMBER

>> **The second column** shows the current value (or current balance) of your liabilities. List the most current balance to see where you stand with your creditors.

>> **The third column** reflects how much interest you're paying for carrying that debt. This information is an important reminder about how debt can be a wealth zapper. Credit card debt can have an interest rate of 17 percent or even more in Canada, and to add insult to injury, it isn't even tax-deductible. Using a credit card to make even a small purchase costs you if you don't pay off the balance each month. Within a year, a $50 sweater at 17 percent costs almost $60 when you add in the potential interest you pay.

TIP

If you compare your liabilities in Table 2-2 and your personal assets in Table 2-1, you may find opportunities to reduce the interest you pay. Say, for example, that you pay 15 percent on a credit card balance of $4,000 but also have a personal asset of $5,000 in a bank savings account that's earning 2 percent in interest. In that case, you may want to consider taking $4,000 out of the savings account to pay off the credit card balance. Doing so saves you $520; the $4,000 in the bank was earning only $80 (2 percent of $4,000), while you were paying $600 on the credit card balance (15 percent of $4,000).

TIP

If you can't pay off high-interest debt, at least look for ways to minimize the cost of carrying the debt. The most obvious ways include the following:

>> **Replace high-interest cards with low-interest cards.** Many Canadian credit card companies offer incentives to consumers, including signing up for cards with better though still high rates (recently under 12 percent) that can be used to pay off ridiculously high-interest cards (typically 20 to 22 percent or higher in Canada). These companies are robbing us and we're helping them do it when we use these cards.

>> **Replace unsecured debt with secured debt.** Credit cards and personal loans are *unsecured* (you haven't put up any collateral or other asset to secure the debt); they have higher interest rates because this type of debt is considered riskier for the creditor. Sources of *secured debt* (such as home equity line accounts and brokerage accounts) provide you with a means to replace high-interest debt with lower-interest debt. You get lower interest rates with secured debt because it's less risky for the creditor — the debt is backed up by collateral (your home or your stocks).

>> **Replace variable-interest debt with fixed-interest debt.** Think about what would happen if Canadian mortgage rates go up more than expected. If you have a mortgage, your monthly payments on a variable-rate mortgage could go up drastically. If you can't lower your debt, at least consider making it fixed and predictable at some point.

WARNING

During the last few years, Canadian personal debt as a percentage of the national GDP (gross domestic product) was rising at a disturbing rate. The Bank of Canada recently sounded a warning bell about this. Make a diligent effort to control and reduce your debt; otherwise, the debt can become too burdensome. If you don't control it, you may have to sell your stocks just to stay liquid. Remember, Murphy's Law states that you *will* sell your stock at the worst possible moment! Don't go there.

Step 4: Calculate your net worth

Your *net worth* is an indication of your total wealth. You can calculate your net worth with this basic equation: Total assets (Table 2-1) less total liabilities (Table 2-2) equal net worth (net assets or net equity).

Table 2-3 shows this equation in action with a net worth of $173,590 — a very respectable number. For many Canadians, just being in a position where assets exceed liabilities (a positive net worth) is great news. Use Table 2-3 as a template and model to analyze your own financial situation. Your mission (if you choose to accept it — and you should) is to ensure that your net worth increases from year to year as you progress toward your financial goals (we discuss financial goals later in this chapter).

TABLE 2-3

Figuring Your Personal Net Worth

Totals	Amounts ($)	Increase from Year Before
Total assets (from Table 2-1)	$290,590	+5%
Total liabilities (from Table 2-2)	($117,000)	–2%
Net worth (total assets less total liabilities)	**$173,590**	**+3%**

Step 5: Analyze your balance sheet

After you create a balance sheet (based on the steps in the preceding sections) to illustrate your current finances, take a close look at it and try to identify any changes you can make to increase your wealth. Sometimes, reaching your financial goals can be as simple as refocusing the items on your balance sheet (use Table 2-3 as a general guideline). Here are some brief points to consider:

I OWE, I OWE, SO OFF TO WORK I GO

Debt is one of the biggest financial problems in North America and across the world today. Companies and individuals holding excessive debt (to buy assets or finance growth) contributed to the stock market's massive decline in 2009 and the resultant Great Recession that followed. If individuals would manage their personal liabilities more responsibly, the general Canadian and world economy would be much better off. Even when the Canadian or American economy looks strong, sooner or later there is a day of reckoning. This may mean working longer and harder than you had hoped. Remember: Stock prices may go up and down, but debt stays up until it is either paid down or the debtor files for bankruptcy. As of the time of this writing, the American and Canadian national debts combined stood at around $24 trillion— which means that consumers, businesses, and governments will continue to be financially challenged during this decade. Yes, the North American stock markets will be affected!

TIP

>> **Is the money in your emergency (or rainy day) fund sitting in an ultra-safe account and earning the highest interest available?** Bank money market accounts or money market funds are recommended. Another safe type of investment is a Government of Canada or provincial Treasury bill. Bank deposits are backed by the federal government's Canada Deposit Insurance Corporation (CDIC) up to $100,000. Shop around for the best rates.

>> **Can you replace depreciating assets with appreciating assets?** Say that you have two stereo systems. Why not sell one and invest the proceeds? You may say, "But I bought that unit two years ago for $500, and if I sell it now, I'll get only $300." That's your choice. You need to decide what helps your financial situation more — a $500 item that keeps shrinking in value (a *depreciating asset*) or $300 that can grow in value when invested (an *appreciating asset*).

>> **Can you replace low-yield investments with high-yield investments?** Maybe you have $5,000 in a bank certificate of deposit (CD) earning 3 percent. You can certainly shop around for a better rate at another bank, but you can also seek alternatives that can offer a higher yield, such as Guaranteed Investment Certificates (GICs) or short-term bond funds. Just keep in mind that if you already have a GIC and you withdraw the funds before maturity, you may face a penalty (such as losing some interest).

>> **Can you pay off any high-interest debt with funds from low-interest assets?** If, for example, you have $5,000 earning 2 percent in a taxable bank account, and you have $2,500 on a credit card charging 17 percent (which is not tax-deductible), you may as well pay off the credit card balance and save on the interest.

>> **If you're carrying debt, are you using that money for an investment return that's greater than the interest you're paying?** Carrying a loan with an interest rate of 8 percent is acceptable if that borrowed money is yielding more than 8 percent elsewhere. Suppose that you have $6,000 in cash in a Canadian brokerage account. If you qualify, you can actually make a stock purchase greater than $6,000 by using margin (essentially a loan from the broker). You can buy $12,000 of stock using your $6,000 in cash, with the remainder financed by the broker. Of course, you pay interest on that margin loan. But what if the interest rate is 6 percent and the stock you're about to invest in has a dividend that yields 9 percent? In that case, the dividend can help you pay off the margin loan, and you keep the additional income. Remember, however, that buying on margin or incurring leverage can work against you if your stock falls in value. (For more on buying on margin, see Chapter 17.)

>> **Can you sell any personal stuff for cash?** You can replace unproductive assets with cash from garage sales and auction websites.

>> **Can you use your home equity to pay off consumer debt?** Borrowing against your home has more favourable interest rates.

WARNING

Paying off consumer debt by using funds borrowed against your home is a great way to wipe the slate clean. What a relief to get rid of your credit card balances! Just don't turn around and run up the consumer debt again. You can get overburdened and experience financial ruin (not to mention homelessness). Not a pretty picture on a snowy and windy Canadian day.

The important point to remember is that you can take control of your finances with discipline (and with the advice we offer in this book).

Funding Your Stock Program

If you're going to invest money in stocks, the first thing you need is . . . money! Where can you get that money? If you're waiting for an inheritance to come through, you may have to wait a long time, considering all the advances being made in healthcare lately. (What's that? You were going to invest in healthcare stocks? How ironic.) Yet, the challenge still comes down to how to fund your stock program.

Many Canadians can reallocate their investments and assets to do the trick. *Reallocating* simply means selling some investments or other assets and reinvesting that money into something else (such as stocks or bonds). It boils down to deciding what investment or asset you can sell or liquidate. Generally, you want to consider reallocating or selling investments and assets that give you a low return on your money (or no return at all). If you have a complicated mix of investments and assets, you may want to consider reviewing your options with a financial planner. Reallocation is just part of the answer; your cash flow is the other part.

Ever wonder why there's so much month left at the end of the money? Consider your cash flow. Your *cash flow* refers to what money is coming in (income) and what money is being spent (outgo). The net result is either a positive cash flow or a negative cash flow, depending on your cash management skills. Maintaining a positive cash flow (more money coming in than going out) helps you increase your net worth. Negative cash flow ultimately depletes wealth and wipes out your net worth if you don't turn it around immediately.

The following sections show you how to calculate and analyze your cash flow. The first step is to do a cash flow statement. With a cash flow statement, you ask yourself three questions:

>> **What money is coming in?** In your cash flow statement, jot down all sources of income. Calculate net income for the month and then for the year. Include everything: salary, wages, interest, dividends, and so on, after taxes. Add them all up and get your grand total for income.

>> **What is your outgo?** Write down all the things that you spend money on. List all your expenses. If possible, categorize them as essential and nonessential. You can get an idea of all the expenses that you can reduce without affecting your lifestyle. But before you do that, make as complete a list as possible of what you spend your money on.

>> **What's left?** If your income is greater than your outgo, you have money ready and available for investing. No matter how small the amount seems, it definitely helps. We've seen fortunes built when people started to diligently invest as little as $25 to $50 per week or per month. If your outgo is greater than your income, you'd better sharpen your pencil. Cut down on nonessential spending, or increase your income. If your budget is a little tight, hold off on investing until your cash flow improves.

TIP

Don't confuse a cash flow statement with an income statement (also called a *profit and loss statement* or an *income and expense statement*). A cash flow statement is simple to calculate because you can easily track what cash goes in and what goes out. Income statements are a little different (especially for businesses) because they take into account things that aren't technically cash flow (such as depreciation or amortization). Chapter 11 has more about income statements.

Step 1: Tally up your income

Using Table 2-4 as a worksheet, list and calculate the money you have coming in. The first column describes the source of the money, the second column indicates the monthly amount from each respective source, and the last column indicates the amount projected for a full year. Include all income, such as wages, business income, dividends, interest income, and so on. Then project these amounts for a year (multiply by 12) and enter them in the third column.

TABLE 2-4

Listing Your Income

Item	Monthly $ Amount	Yearly $ Amount
Salary and wages		
Interest income and dividends		
Business net (after taxes) income		
Other income		
Total income		

REMEMBER

Your total income is the amount of money you have to work with. To ensure your financial health, don't spend more than this amount. Always be aware of and carefully manage your income.

Step 2: Add up your outgo

Using Table 2-5 as a worksheet, list and calculate the money that's going out. How much are you spending, and on what? The first column describes the source of the expense, the second column indicates the monthly amount, and the third column shows the amount projected for a full year. Include all the money you spend: Credit card and other debt payments; household expenses, such as food, utility bills, and medical expenses; and nonessential expenses such as video games and elephant-foot umbrella stands.

TABLE 2-5

Listing Your Expenses (Outgo)

Item	Monthly $ Amount	Yearly $ Amount
Payroll and related taxes		
Rent or mortgage		
Utilities		

Item	Monthly $ Amount	Yearly $ Amount
Food		
Clothing		
Insurance (medical, auto, homeowners, and so on)		
Telephone		
Real estate taxes		
Auto expenses		
Charity		
Recreation		
Credit card payments		
Loan payments		
Other		
Total outgo		

REMEMBER

You may notice that the outgo doesn't include items such as payments to a RRSP plan and other Canadian tax savings vehicles. Yes, these items do affect your cash flow, but they're not expenses; the amounts that you invest (or your employer invests for you) are essentially longer-term assets that benefit your financial situation versus point-in-time expenses that generally don't help you build wealth. To account for an RRSP, simply deduct it from the gross pay (in Table 2-4) before you calculate the preceding worksheet (Table 2-5). If, for example, your gross pay is $2,000 and your RRSP contribution is $300, then use $1,700 as your income figure.

Step 3: Create a cash flow statement

Okay, you're near the end. The next step is creating a cash flow statement so that you can see (all in one place) how your money moves — how much comes in and how much goes out and where it goes.

Plug the amount of your total income (from Table 2-4) and the amount of your total expenses (from Table 2-5) into the Table 2-6 worksheet to see your *cash flow*. Do you have positive cash flow — more coming in than going out — so that you can start investing in stocks (or other investments), or are expenses overpowering your income? Doing a cash flow statement isn't just about finding money in your financial situation to fund your stock program. First and foremost, it's about your financial well-being. Are you managing your finances well or not?

TABLE 2-6

Looking at Your Cash Flow

Item	Monthly $ Amount	Yearly $ Amount
Total income (from Table 2-4)		
Total outgo (from Table 2-5)		
Net inflow/outflow		

Step 4: Analyze your cash flow

Use your cash flow statement in Table 2-6 to identify sources of funds for your investment program. The more you can increase your income and decrease your outgo, the better. Scrutinize your data. Where can you improve the results? Here are some questions to ask yourself:

>> How can you increase your income? Do you have hobbies, interests, or skills that can generate extra cash for you?

>> Can you get more paid overtime at work? How about a promotion or a job change?

>> Where can you cut expenses?

>> Have you categorized expenses as either "necessary" or "nonessential"?

>> Can you lower your debt payments by refinancing or consolidating loans and credit card balances?

>> Have you shopped around for lower insurance, telephone, or Internet service rates?

>> Have you analyzed your tax withholdings in your paycheque to make sure that you're not overpaying your taxes (just to get your overpayment back next year as a refund)?

Another option: Finding investment money in tax savings

According to very recent Canadian and U.S. Tax Foundation studies, the average Canadian or American citizen pays more in taxes than for food, clothing, and housing combined. Sit down with your tax advisor to try to find ways to reduce your taxes. Starting a home-based business, for example, is a great way to gain new income and increase your tax deductions, resulting in a lower tax burden. Your tax advisor or professional accountant (CPA) can make recommendations that may work for you. Chapter 21 covers taxes in detail.

Setting Your Sights on Financial Goals

Consider stocks as tools for living, just like any other investment — no more, no less. Stocks are among the many tools you use to accomplish something — to achieve a goal. Yes, successfully investing in stocks is the goal that you're probably shooting for if you're reading this book. However, you must complete the following sentence: "I want to be successful in my stock investing program to accomplish _____." You must consider stock investing as a means to an end.

REMEMBER

Know the difference between long-term, intermediate-term, and short-term goals, and then set some of each (see Chapter 3 for more information).

>> Long-term goals refer to projects or financial goals that need funding more than ten years from now.

>> Intermediate-term goals refer to financial goals that need funding five to ten years from now.

>> Short-term goals need funding less than five years from now.

REMEMBER

Stocks, in general, are best suited for long-term goals such as these:

>> Achieving financial independence (think retirement funding)

>> Paying for future college or university costs

>> Paying for any long-term expenditure or project

Some categories of stock (such as conservative or large cap) may be suitable for intermediate-term financial goals. If, for example, you'll retire six years from now, conservative stocks combined with some quality fixed income investments can be appropriate. If you're optimistic (or *bullish*) about the stock market and confident that stock prices will rise, go ahead and invest. However, if you're negative about the market (you're *bearish*, or you believe that stock prices will decline), you may want to wait until the economy starts to forge a clear path. To help you figure out some megatrends, flip to Chapter 13, which is quite an exciting chapter.

REMEMBER

In recent years, investors have sought quick, short-term profits by trading and speculating in stocks. Lured by the fantastic returns generated by the stock market in the dot-com and Internet 2.0 eras (about when Facebook and Google came to town), investors saw stocks as a get-rich-quick scheme. Understanding the differences among *investing*, *saving*, and *speculating* is very important. Which one do you want to do? Knowing the answer to this question is crucial to your goals and aspirations. Investors who don't know the differences tend to get burned. The following will help you distinguish among these actions:

>> *Investing* **is the act of putting your current funds into securities or tangible assets in order to gain future appreciation, income, or both.** You need time, knowledge, and discipline to invest. The investment can fluctuate in price but has been chosen for long-term potential.

>> *Saving* **is the safe accumulation of funds for a future use.** Savings don't fluctuate and are generally free of financial risk. The emphasis is on safety and liquidity.

>> *Speculating* **is the financial world's equivalent of gambling.** An investor who speculates is seeking quick profits gained from short-term price movements in a particular asset or investment. In recent years, many folks have been trading stocks (buying and selling in the short term with frequency), which is in the realm of short-term speculating.

These distinctly different concepts are often confused, even among so-called financial experts. For more on the distinctions between investing and speculating (and trading too!), go to Chapter 17.

The Shape of Equities: Stocks, ETFs, and Mutual Funds

In Chapter 1 we introduced you to a basic definition of stocks. Moving a bit ahead, and to help you make sense of the following discussion regardless of your age, we briefly want to introduce you to the concept of *equities*. Equities include stocks, of course, but they also include other financial instruments like exchange-traded funds, much more commonly referred to as ETFs. In fact, ETFs are such important kissing cousins to pure stocks that we discuss ETFs in even more depth in Chapter 5. In fact, we refer to them throughout this book. More on ETFs in a moment.

Understanding equities and their subset components will help set the stage for you to figure out how much you should actually invest in stocks and their blood relatives, as a percentage of your total investment portfolio. Let's explore and probe equities and some of these components next.

REMEMBER

Equities, which technically represent ownership interests or stakes in a company, really refer to stocks at the very root level. They also refer to shares. Equities even refer to other financial instruments you can invest in such as equity mutual funds and equity-oriented ETFs. What we're really saying to you is that it's very likely that a rose by any other name is still an equity.

So, if you own an equity financial instrument such as the ones we've described here, you're actually entitled to a proportionate share of any company profits. That entitlement may come in the form of dividends, if the company chooses to have a policy to try to pay out dividends. In addition, you're also entitled to participate in any growth in the value of the company you invested in. This is the compelling feature of equities and stocks in general: the chance to make outsized returns. Welcome to the stock market!

Mutual fund equities

Mutual funds — investment vehicles consisting of a pool of funds and contributions collected from multiple investors — may be part of the equity family. Mutual funds invest the cash funds they have and contributions they get into financial instruments such as stocks, bonds, money market instruments, and other liquid (easily disposable) assets. To the extent that mutual funds mainly hold stocks, they're considered to be equity investments as well and are commonly called *stock* mutual funds. If you have a pension plan that holds stock mutual funds, you're already a stock investor. Congratulations!

Exchange-traded fund (ETF) equities

Another potential equity is the ETF, which typically falls into one of three essential categories. However, there are many other subcategories. The three main categories are:

>> **Broad market ETFs** that give you exposure to multiple key sectors in a given country. These ETFs typically track the main benchmark equity index of that country's stock market.

>> **Sector ETFs** that provide you with exposure to a specific sector of the economy and essentially represent a way of stock investing by theme.

>> **Beta or factor-based ETFs** that are special creatures employing rules-based algorithms and investment strategies that define the types of financial instruments to be included in the ETF. Huh?

ETFs can be sliced and diced in dozens of ways — and in fact they are. For example, they can be dividend-focused, stability-oriented, or blue chip (reliable)-focused funds. To the extent that ETFs hold stocks, they're also equities, and the principles of stock investing we set out in this book continue to hold true. We show you more about ETFs in Chapter 5, but in the meantime keep in mind that this $ 3.5 trillion class of equities deserves your attention in the context of your investing options.

Canadians in Their 20s and 30s: Setting the Foundations

In the preceding sections, we laid the foundation of stock investing by showing you the importance of knowing your current financial status as well as your financial goals. We defined equities, a key definition you need to know as a stock investor. Another key piece to this particular puzzle, before moving on to other essentials of stock investing, is understanding how your age will influence your stock-investing decisions.

Canadians in their 20s and 30s are a logical place to begin. This cohort enjoys a tremendous luxury in addition to being young, which is way cool — they have a long-term time frame before retirement comes into the picture. If you're young, the amount of funds you can allocate to stock investing is a lot greater than if you are an older Canadian. That's because you can ride any stock market corrections and storms that will come along from time to time. In fact, stock market turbulence creates an ideal opportunity to buy low and sell high, or just buy low and hold for now. The younger you are, the more opportunities you have to rinse and repeat this dynamic process. That's a lot better than ending up at the cleaners.

Another luxury a young Canadian stock investor can enjoy is the development of a mindset with a focus on investment planning, a critical success factor in stock investing. *Planning* in this case means taking the time to really learn and master the fundamentals of stock investing, and to learn from mistakes. If you do so, the invariable hiccups and slumps in stock prices won't jeopardize your entire stock portfolio because you will have a longer time frame to recoup any losses, and a more confident and less fearful mindset. As long as you embrace the reality, opportunity, and risks presented by stock market volatility, this is the time in life to invest a bit more aggressively.

From what you learned so far, with a better understanding of your net assets, cash inflows and outflows, and personal goals and investment return expectations, you're now poised to make better sense of your investing options. These options include equities, explored previously, as well as bonds, real estate, and other areas you can park your very hard-earned cash into. And this is where age is very relevant, because the younger you are, the more risk you can tolerate and the more compounding of returns you can take advantage of. This is where we begin the even more fun part of our stock-investing journey.

Determining the right allocation to stocks and other equities

Whatever age you may be, most of the principles we lay out in this book will apply. In other words, this book is age-agnostic. However, one important exception is how age relates to your risk tolerance and appetite and therefore how much you devote to stocks. Age is so important that we added this chapter section to help guide you.

TIP

One key concept we want to impress on you is simple: the younger you are — say, in your 20s and 30s — the more risk you can afford to take on. In fact, *failure* to seize an opportunity to make outsized returns, due especially to the power of compounding and reinvested returns, is itself a risk.

In this section we outline some general guidelines for optimal equity-asset allocations relative to your young age. We introduce the concepts of passive and aggressive investing, and taxation, although you'll hear more about those things in later chapters as well.

GROWTH POTENTIAL OF STOCKS

Data shows that over the past century, if you owned equal amounts of every U.S. stock excluding the smallest 20 percent, you would have earned average annual growth of over 11 percent, for an inflation-adjusted real return of just over 8 percent. On the other hand, bonds averaged just over 4 percent, or real returns of 1 percent. Even over ten-year times frames, the results are very similar. To add color to the math, if you began with $100,000 in bonds, this would have yielded just under $30,000 in real returns after 20 years. By comparison, that same $100,000 invested in stocks would have grown to well over $400,000. It's not even close. In Chapter 8, we discuss investing for growth in detail and know that you will find value in it.

To be sure, stocks are riskier than bonds, but that's over shorter time frames, when you're likely to run into significant price volatility. Long-term history shows time and again that dips in the stock market are invariably made up after some time passes.

A prevailing view, and these are just judgement calls, is that Canadians in their 20s and 30s should have about 75 percent in equities and the balance in fixed-income investments such as bonds. If this is held in a Tax-Free Savings Account, or TFSA, the ratio in equities should be even higher. We introduce you to TFSAs in the context of stock investing in the next section.

Because younger Canadians can afford, time-wise, to take a more aggressive and less risk averse stance on stocks, they're more prone to look for growth stocks and stories. They're likely, even more than older investors, to be familiar with stocks of growing technology companies like Twitter, Amazon, Spotify, Blackberry, and Apple. However, we advise anyone in this age cohort not to put an excessive amount of money into one particular area. In other words, it's important to diversify, especially if you're just learning the stock-investing ropes.

When it comes to choosing one type of equity instrument over another, we're definitely not big fans of equity mutual funds as compared to stocks or ETFs. Mutual funds do not typically generate high growth. They also come with higher and often hidden fees that eat into your returns. They're more expensive than ETFs. Although they're less volatile during downturns, they often defeat the purpose of growth investing. Equity ETFs, on the other hand, at least offer you better growth prospects. Equity mutual funds may bury you in a sea of fees and offer you low-end returns.

Start off by investing in big picture themes

The Internet of Things. Cannabis and marijuana. Stock markets in China and the rest of Asia. The blockchain. Autonomous cars. These are but a few of the themes, concepts, and stories that drive investment world headlines today. In Chapter 13, we provide you with insights on how to seize investment opportunities in some of these new domains. We also discuss even more traditional but growing areas or sectors like healthcare, travel, real estate, and resources that are presented in other chapters as well.

But if you're in the 20s to 30s, your most significant investments likely to compete with and complement stock investing are investments in real estate and your education, including educating yourself in stock investing.

Home sweet home

In much the same way that equity investing does not have to be restricted to pure stock investing, what with the availability of alternatives like equity ETFs and mutual funds, real estate investing can vary as well. For example, you might invest in a home, condominium, or commercial or residential investment property. Yet, once again, the stock market offers alternatives to even these traditional investment opportunities. In Chapter 9 we introduce you to real estate investment trusts (REITs), which are traded on Canadian and U.S. stock exchanges and relate to all types of real estate — even prisons! With the current low Canadian interest rates, if you're not in one of the major overpriced real estate markets like Toronto, Vancouver, or New York, it can make good personal and financial sense to purchase real estate. After all, it's your home. But even if you do in fact live in a high-rent city with crazy real estate prices, you can invest in property through the REIT option. The stock market has something for everyone. But it has to be navigated carefully, and we provide you with the compass to navigate the market's choppy waters.

Learning and personal development

Perhaps the most important investment is the investment you make in your education. The best annuity in the world is one powered and inspired by the knowledge you build within your head and intellect. God provided you with brains. We're proud to do our part by providing you with knowledge about the stock market you may not have known about or considered in the past. This book contains proven, tried, and tested investing and financial fundamentals. You won't be disappointed, no matter what your current knowledge level is. Your 20s and 30s are an ideal time to get that knowledge.

Your Tax-Free Savings Account (TFSA) as a tax-free stock investing account

Although we don't want to get ahead of ourselves with a discussion of the tax impact of stock-investment decisions, which we fully cover in Chapter 21, we do believe that one tax-smart strategy needs a basic introduction. It's the Tax-Free Savings Account, better known to Canadians as the TFSA. The TFSA was designed by the government with stocks top of mind. TFSAs are presented in the context of age because the more time and risk appetite you have to invest in stocks, the more conducive a TFSA will be to your investment portfolio structure.

As you will see again in Chapter 21, on taxes, you may not only invest in stocks but also in Guaranteed Investment Certificates (GICs), bonds, mutual funds, simple cash, and more. The key tax and total return advantage is that a TFSA allows you to invest in eligible investments and lets those savings grow tax free throughout your lifetime. For example, dividends, capital gains, and interest earned in a TFSA are tax free for life. You can take out your accumulated TFSA savings from your account at any time, and for any reason. This tax-free growth also means that all withdrawals are tax free.

REMEMBER

While you can save for any personal goal you want (such as a new car, home, or vacation), TFSAs are absolutely ideal for *growth* stocks, which we discuss in Chapter 8 and elsewhere in this book. Stocks grow in two key ways: via capital gains (if the stock value rises) and via dividends (assuming the stock you hold within the tax-free account pays dividends, which is something we discuss in depth in Chapter 9).

Whether you're just beginning to build your financial portfolio or just placing all your savings in a TFSA as you begin to pay off your new mortgage, credit card, auto loan, and/or student loans, just remember that you really have two stock-allocation decisions. The first decision is how much of your overall net investable cash to allocate to stocks and other equities. The other allocation decision is to determine whether you want this to be inside or outside of a tax-smart savings account like a TFSA.

Invest in your company registered pension or retirement savings plan

Before we leave you young Canadians in this part of the book — and by the way, we wish we were as young as you — consider your registered pension plans. These tax and savings plans are primarily your Registered Retirement Savings Plan (RRSP) as well as your company registered pension plan. Most Canadians strive to make or match employer contributions into one or both of these savings vehicles. So, in addition to TFSAs, be mindful of these latter plans as you consider your total portfolio and percentage allocation to stocks. Like TFSAs, RRSPs and employer pension plans exist to help to set you up for a stable financial future. We discuss RRSPs and more in Chapter 21.

Canadians in Their 40s

If you're in the 40+ age bracket, you're in or are approaching your peak earning years and are likely reducing personal debt. As a result you may have a bit more to sock away into stocks. If that's not your reality, this is the ideal time to take stock investing very seriously. You still have plenty of time to take advantage of the potential for much better growth than bonds or just plain old cash can offer. This assumes you have embraced a longer-term mindset, which is a luxury you can still have in your 40s. This section explores reasonable allocations to stocks we see in industry all the time, as well as potential tax and pension options and strategies you should be aware of.

Exploring common investment portfolio allocations to stocks

As Canadian stock investors get older, the asset-allocation equation typically begins to shift toward fixed investments like bonds. However, this recalibration over time still depends on your existing risk tolerance or appetite, and that in turn is driven by your goals and financial plans and needs.

If you're in your 40s and consider yourself to be risk averse — a deeper discussion of conservative, aggressive, and other approaches to stock investing follows in Chapter 3 — you may be comfortable with a 50 percent to 60 percent stock and 50 percent to 40 percent bond allocation range. If you're a more aggressive investor in this age bracket, you may very well be at ease with a 70 percent to 80 percent stock allocation, if not more.

Yet another perspective is "time to retirement" in that if you have 25 years to retire, then 85 percent can be in stocks, and if you have 15 years, that rule of thumb figure for stocks versus bonds goes down to about 70 percent. In the current low interest rate environment, where your potential for outsized fixed income returns is limited, a reasonable rule of thumb promoted by the investment industry is that you should invest 75 percent of your assets in stocks and 25 percent in bonds in your 40s.

The point we want to drive home with these examples or conventions is much more substantive — your allocation depends on several variables over and above just age. These additional variables include risk tolerance, interest rates, time to retirement, market conditions, and investor acumen, something we will help you sharpen as you read this book. The other key point we drive home throughout this book is that the more assets you allocate to stock holdings, the more volatile your stock-investing experience will be, both on the upside and on the downside. We will set you up to maximize the number of your upside experiences.

Always keep in mind that investment diversification — which is really risk mitigation or risk management — is not just a binary or "black and white" stock-versus-bond equation or debate. There are many shades of grey for you to exploit, and we teach you how in this book. As we've mentioned, equities include not just stocks but also exchange-traded funds. They include real estate investment trusts. Diversify even more deeply, still within equities per se, by holding not just domestic stocks, ETFs, and REITs but also international equivalents. We discuss international stock investing and particularly mature Asian stock markets in Chapter 14. These lower-fee and easy-to-trade ETF and REIT alternatives are things you must absolutely know about and are great ways to keep more money in your hands than in the hands of sometimes expensive advisors.

Taxes, company pensions, and Registered Retirement Savings Plans (RRSPs)

It's always a good idea to park as much as you can in a pension plan. But that's a lot easier said than done. Competing priorities, and associated costs related to marriage, buying a home, travel, healthcare, and just plain old living life, all stand in the way of pension planning. Yet, for many Canadians in their 40s, this is the exact time when some extra cash can be found. Perhaps a raise, a bequest, or a seriously dented mortgage balance has found its way to you. If so, you may find yourself in a great position to invest in an existing or new pension plan, and — as importantly — to make stocks a key part of that plan.

If you're lucky, you have a company pension plan that invests on your behalf, likely in lots of stocks. If you are really lucky, that pension plan is of the *defined benefit* variety, but we digress. Even with such a plan, consider investing more within a Registered Retirement Saving Plan, or RRSP. We cover RRSPs and the tax implications and fun new rules (okay, they're not really fun) in Chapter 21. Our key message to you here is that if you have not yet saved within your employer's pension plan, or don't have that option, start thinking about RRSPs now.

REMEMBER

RRSPs are a future-oriented "forced" savings vehicle with a tax structure that benefits you (you get a deduction in high tax-bracket years and are taxed on RRSP withdrawals in later and lower tax-bracket retirement years). In contrast, TFSAs are more mid-range in terms of planning horizons. Within RRSPs, and as your stock-investing expertise and comfort grows, you can look at more company- and industry-specific stocks and away from themes.

50+ Canadian Stock Investors

As Canadians move into their 50s, stock-investing decisions should be geared towards "safer" stocks (that is, ones that are financially stable, and less cyclical and volatile) and dividend-paying stocks. We discuss dividend-paying stocks in Chapter 9, a key chapter for 50+ Canadian stock investors.

Fifty and 60-plus year-old Canadians may still be in their peak earning years, but as far as their investment time horizon is concerned, their peak investing years are behind them. At the same time, though, what with the average life expectancy in Canada pushing into the mid-80s, Canadian stock investors still need to consider their investment portfolios. Sitting still can be hazardous to financial health. The goal in your late 50s and 60s is to have an investment portfolio that will sustain you throughout your retirement years.

To be sure, if you are in your 60s, you want to calibrate your portfolio away from stocks and more toward an income stream. But recall what we said in the previous section, namely that equities come in different shapes, sizes, and, more importantly, risk profiles. Again, and more specifically, you can lower your stock-investing risk and still stay in stocks by considering exchange-traded funds as well as real estate investment trusts. In your 50+ years, don't just hold domestic equities, but consider some stable international equities as well. Dividend-paying stocks and international stock investing are extremely important for 50+ investors, and we dedicate Chapters 9 and 14 just for that.

Revisiting your allocation to stocks

The 50+ age zone is the time to examine your retirement goals and desired retirement lifestyle. You can't do that in a vacuum. Consider your existing income flows, projected income streams, and your tax situation, including special tax rules for older Canadians. Just because you're older is not a reason to take your foot off the investing accelerator. Rather, it's more of a time to pay special attention to hazard signs. You've learned a lot about investing by this time, so you don't have to throw that knowledge away. Warren Buffet doesn't. Even if you're older and are new to stock investing, growth is still a consideration. Equities are still a very real alternative.

A typical rule of thumb for those in their 50s and 60s is to have about half of your portfolio in equities and the rest in fixed-income financial instruments such as bonds. Remember that *equities* refer to stocks, ETFs, and equity mutual funds. Also recall that if, for example, you have 15 years to retirement, one of several rules of thumb is that the ratio of equities versus bonds can be 70 percent. There is no "golden year" rule.

If you're a savvy and careful stock investor, you may want to invest as much as 75 percent in equities and 25 percent in fixed-income financial instruments, again depending on other variables already mentioned in this chapter. Decades ago, a half-and-half ratio of equities to bonds was reasonable and very effective. That's when interest rates were high and heavily rewarded savers. Today, interest-rates are much lower, so finding significant, guaranteed fixed-income returns is very difficult.

A final variable to consider when determining your investment allocation to stocks is the nature, extent, and timing of your withdrawal of investment resources. What will you sell first — your house, cottage, or other assets? Will you continue to work part-time past your retirement age? In addition, when do you expect to draw from your Canadian government entitlements such as Canada Pension Plan (CPP) or Old Age Security (OAS)? This is where tax-planning and stock-investing decisions have to be integrated — things that are beyond the scope of this book. These more complex considerations will also drive your decisions regarding allocations to stocks at this stage of life.

REMEMBER

For all stock-allocation decisions for all stages of like, don't just look at one investment or savings account in isolation. Be mindful of your big picture. Look at your entire investment portfolio. Consider company pensions, RRSPs, TFSAs, and government retirement annuities you're entitled to. As one Canadian bank commercial reminds us: "You may be richer than you think!" If so, you can continue to delve into the exciting and potentially rewarding realm of stock investing, with an even greater allocation than you think.

Taxes, registered pensions, and Registered Retirement Income Funds (RRIFs)

Our final comment to you if you're over 50 is to remember the importance of taxes and financial planning. While extreme tax planning is beyond the intent of this book, we're happy to point you to the relevant (stock-investing) basics of Canadian taxation in Chapter 21. In that chapter we even discuss Registered Retirement Income Funds (RRIFs), which allow you to withdraw some of your registered savings in a tax-smart way.

As for other retirement-planning decisions regarding estate planning, income splitting, foreign taxes, and the use of TFSAs versus RRSPs to park your money, you should seek the specialized expertise of a professional. But if you have a simpler portfolio, see Chapter 7, which introduces you to the latest innovation in financial technology, called *robo-advisors*.

Chapter **3**

Common Approaches to Stock Investing

" nvesting for the long term" isn't just some perfunctory investment slogan. It's a culmination of proven stock market experience that goes back many decades. Unfortunately, investor buying and selling habits have deteriorated in recent years due to impatience. Today's investors think that the short term is measured in days, the intermediate term is measured in weeks, and the long term is measured in months. Yeesh! No wonder so many Canadians are complaining about lousy investment returns. Investors have lost the profitable art of patience!

What should you do? Become an investor with a time horizon greater than one year (the emphasis is on "greater"). Give your investments time to grow. Everybody dreams about emulating the success of someone like Warren Buffett, but few emulate his patience (a huge part of his investment success).

Stocks are tools you can use to build your wealth. When used wisely, for the right purpose and in the right environment, they do a great job. But when improperly applied, they can lead to disaster. In this chapter, we show you how to choose the right types of investments based on your short-term, intermediate-term, and long-term financial goals. We also show you how to decide on your purpose for investing (growth or income investing) and your style of investing (conservative or aggressive).

...ching Stocks and Strategies with Your Goals

Various stocks and investment approaches are out there. The key to success in the stock market is determining how much to allocate to stocks and then matching the right kind of stocks with the right kind of investment situation. You must choose the stocks and the asset allocation approach that match your goals. (Chapter 2 has more on defining financial goals.)

Before investing in a stock, ask yourself, "When do I want to reach my financial goal?" Stocks are a means to an end. Your job is to figure out what that end is — or, more important, when it is. Do you want to retire in ten years or next year? Must you pay for your kid's university education next year or 18 years from now? The length of time you have before you need the money you hope to earn from stock investing determines what stocks you should buy and how you can best achieve your financial goals. Table 3-1 gives you some guidelines for choosing the kind of stock best suited for the type of investor you are and the financial goals you have.

TABLE 3-1   Investor Types, Financial Goals, and Stock Types

Type of Investor	Time Frame for Financial Goals	Type of Stock Most Suitable
Conservative (worries about risk)	Long term (more than 10 years)	Large cap stocks and mid cap stocks
Aggressive (high tolerance to risk)	Long term (more than10 years)	Small cap stocks and mid cap stocks
Conservative (worries about risk)	Intermediate term (5 to 10 years)	Large cap stocks, preferably with dividends
Aggressive (high tolerance to risk)	Intermediate term (5 to 10 years)	Small cap stocks and mid cap stocks
Short term	Less than 5 years	Stocks are generally not suitable for the short term, unless they're limited to a small part of a balanced portfolio. Instead, look at vehicles such as savings accounts, Guaranteed Investment Certificates, and money market funds.
Very short term	Less than 1 year	Stocks? Don't even think about it! Well . . . you *can* invest in stocks for less than a year, but seriously, you're not really investing — you're either trading or speculating. Instead, use savings accounts and money market funds.

TIP

Dividends are payments made to a stockholder (unlike interest, which is payment to a creditor). Dividends are a great form of income, and companies that issue dividends tend to have more stable stock prices, as well. For more information on dividend-paying stocks, see the section "Steadily making money: Income investing," later in this chapter, and also see Chapter 9 for more on investing for income, including dividends.

REMEMBER

Table 3-1 gives you general guidelines, but not everyone fits into a particular profile. Every investor has a unique situation, set of goals, and level of risk tolerance. The terms large cap, mid cap, and small cap refer to the size (or market capitalization, also known as market cap) of the company. All factors being equal, large companies are safer (less risky and volatile) than small companies. For more on market caps, see the section "Investing for Your Personal Style," later in this chapter, as well as Chapter 1.

Investing for the Future

REMEMBER

Individual stocks can be either great or horrible choices, depending on the time period you want to focus on. Generally, you can plan to invest in stocks for the short, intermediate, or long term. These sections outline which stocks are most appropriate for each term length.

Investing in quality stocks becomes less risky as the time frame lengthens. Stock prices tend to fluctuate daily, but they tend to trend up or down over an extended period of time. Even if you invest in a stock that goes down in the short term, you're likely to see it rise and possibly exceed your investment if you have the patience to wait it out and let the stock price appreciate.

Focusing on the short term

Short term generally means five years or less. Short-term investing isn't about making a quick buck — it refers to when you may need the money. Every person has short-term goals. Some are modest, such as setting aside money for a vacation next month or paying for medical bills. Other short-term goals are more ambitious, such as accruing funds for a down payment to purchase a new home in downtown Winnipeg within six months. Whatever the expense or purchase, you need a predictable accumulation of cash soon. If this sounds like your situation, stay away from the stock market!

WARNING

Because stocks can be so unpredictable in the short term, they're a bad choice for short-term considerations. We get a kick out of market analysts on TV saying things such as, "At $25 a share, XYZ is a solid investment, and we feel that its stock should hit our target price of $40 within six to nine months." You know that an eager investor hears that and says, "Gee, why bother with 1 percent at the bank when this stock will rise by more than 50 percent? I'd better place a trade through an online broker." It may hit that target amount (or surpass it), or it may not. Most of the time, the stock doesn't reach the target price, and the investor is disappointed. The stock can even go down! Do not rely on analyst forecasts! (We discuss online brokers in Chapter 7, and how to trade stocks in Chapters 17 and 18.)

The reason that target prices are frequently missed is because figuring out what millions of investors will do in the short term is difficult. The short term can be irrational because so many investors have so many reasons for buying and selling that it can be difficult to analyze. If you invest for an important short-term need, you can lose very important cash quicker than you think.

TECHNICAL STUFF

During the bull market still in progress at the time of this writing, Canadian investors watched as some high-profile stocks, especially U.S. stocks, went up 20 to 50 percent in a matter of months. Hey, who needs a savings account earning a measly interest rate when stocks grow like that! Of course, when the bear market eventually "opens for business" — and it will — those same stocks may very well test 50 to 70 percent price drops. A savings account earning a measly interest rate from a bank suddenly wouldn't seem so bad.

REMEMBER

Short-term stock investing is unpredictable. Stocks — even the best ones — fluctuate in the short term. In a negative environment, they can be very volatile. No one can accurately predict the price movement (unless one has some inside information). You can better serve your short-term goals with stable, interest-bearing investments like Guaranteed Investment Certificates (GICs) at your bank. See Table 3-1 for suggestions about your short-term strategies.

Considering intermediate-term goals

Intermediate term refers to the financial goals you plan to reach in five to ten years. For example, if you want to accumulate funds to put money down for investment in real estate six years from now, some growth-oriented investments may be suitable. (We discuss growth investing in more detail later in this chapter, and in Chapter 8.)

Although some stocks may be appropriate for a two- or three-year period as part of a larger balanced portfolio, not all stocks are good intermediate-term investments. Some stocks are fairly stable and hold their value well, such as the stock of large or established dividend-paying companies. Canadian bank, pipeline, and utility stocks come to mind. Other stocks have prices that jump all over the place, such as those of untested companies that haven't been in existence long enough to develop a consistent track record. Junior mining and technology stocks such as blockchain stocks often fall here.

If you plan to invest in the stock market to meet intermediate-term goals, consider large, established companies or dividend-paying companies in industries that provide the necessities of life (like the food and beverage industry, pipelines, or electric utilities). In today's economic environment, we strongly believe that stocks attached to companies that serve basic human needs should have a major presence in most Canadian stock portfolios. They're especially well-suited for intermediate investment goals and are also very well represented in the Canadian stock market.

Just because a particular stock is labelled as being appropriate for the intermediate term doesn't mean you should get rid of it by the stroke of midnight five years from now. After all, if the company is doing well and going strong, you can continue holding the stock indefinitely. The more time you give a well-positioned, profitable company's stock to grow, the better you'll do.

Preparing for the long term

Stock investing is best suited for making money over a long period of time. Usually, when you measure stocks against other investments in terms of five to (preferably) ten or more years, they excel. Even investors who bought stocks during the depths of the Great Depression saw profitable growth in their stock portfolios over a ten-year period. In fact, if you examine any ten-year period over the past 50 years, you see that stocks beat out other financial investments (such as bonds or bank investments) in most periods when measured by total return (taking into account reinvesting and compounding of capital gains and dividends)!

Of course, your work doesn't stop at deciding on a long-term investment. You still have to do your homework and choose stocks wisely, because even in good times, you can lose money if you invest in companies that go out of business. Part 3 of this book shows you how to evaluate specific companies and industries and alerts you to factors in the general economy that can affect stock behaviour. Appendix A provides plenty of resources you can turn to.

REMEMBER

Because so many different types and categories of stocks are available, virtually any Canadian with a long-term perspective should add some stocks to his investment portfolio. Whether you want to save for a young child's university fund or for future retirement goals, carefully selected stocks have proven to be a superior long-term investment.

Investing for a Purpose

When someone asked the lady why she bungee jumped off the bridge that spanned a massive ravine, she answered, "Because it's fun!" When someone asked the fellow why he dove into a pool chockfull of alligators and snakes, he responded, "Because someone pushed me." You shouldn't invest in stocks unless you have a purpose that you understand, like investing for growth or income. Keep in mind that stocks are just a means to an end — figure out your desired end and then match the means. The following sections can help.

TIP

Even if an advisor pushes you to invest, be sure that advisor gives you an explanation of how each stock choice fits your purpose. We know of a very nice, elderly lady who had a portfolio brimming with aggressive-growth stocks because she had an overbearing broker. Her purpose should've been conservative, and she should've chosen investments that would preserve her wealth rather than grow it. Obviously, the broker's agenda got in the way. (To find out more about dealing with brokers and advisors, go to Chapter 7.)

Making money quickly: Growth investing

When investors want their money to grow (versus just trying to preserve it), they look for investments that appreciate in value. Appreciate is just another way of saying grow. If you bought a stock for $8 per share and now its value is $30 per share, your investment has grown by $22 per share — that's appreciation. We know we would appreciate it.

Appreciation (also known as *capital gain*) is probably the number-one reason people invest in stocks. Few investments have the potential to grow your wealth as conveniently as stocks. If you want the stock market to make you loads of money (and you can assume some risk), head to Chapter 8, which takes an in-depth look at investing for growth.

WARNING

Stocks are a great way to grow your wealth, but they're not the only way. Many investors seek alternative ways to make money, but many of these alternative ways are more aggressive than stocks and carry significantly more risk. You may have heard about people who made quick fortunes in areas such as commodities (like wheat, pork bellies, or precious metals), options, and other more-sophisticated investment vehicles. Keep in mind that you should limit these riskier investments to only a small portion of your portfolio, such as 5 or 10 percent of your investable funds, and you should always understand the type of security (stock, bond, and so on) you're invested in. Experienced investors, however, can go higher.

Making money steadily: Income investing

Not all investors want to take on the risk that comes with making a killing. (Hey . . . no guts, no glory!) Some people just want to invest in the stock market as a means of providing a steady income and preserving wealth. They don't need stock values to go through the ceiling. Instead, they need stocks that perform well consistently.

If your purpose for investing in stocks is to create income, you need to choose stocks that pay dividends. Dividends are typically paid quarterly to stockholders on record as of specific dates. How do you know if the dividend you're being paid is higher (or lower) than other vehicles (such as bonds)? The following sections help you figure it out.

Distinguishing between dividends and interest

Don't confuse dividends with interest. Most people are familiar with interest because that's how you grow your money over the years in the bank. The important difference is that interest is paid to creditors, and dividends are paid to owners (meaning shareholders — and if you own stock, you're a shareholder because shares of stock represent ownership in a publicly traded company).

REMEMBER

When you buy stock, you buy a piece of that company. When you put money in a bank (or when you buy bonds), you basically loan your money. You become a creditor, and the bank or bond issuer is the debtor; as such, it must eventually pay your money back to you with interest.

Recognizing the importance of an income stock's yield

When you invest for income, you have to consider your investment's after-tax yield and compare it with the alternatives. The yield is an investment's payout expressed as a percentage of the investment amount. Looking at the yield is a way to compare the income you expect to receive from one investment with the expected income from others. Table 3-2 shows some comparative yields.

TABLE 3-2   **Comparing the Yields of Various Investments**

Investment	Type	Amount	Pay Type	Payout	Yield
Smith Co.	Stock	$50/share	Dividend	$2.50	5.0%
Jones Co.	Stock	$100/share	Dividend	$4.00	4.0%
Acme Bank	Bank GIC	$500	Interest	$25.00	5.0%
Acme Bank	Bank GIC	$2,500	Interest	$131.25	5.25%
Acme Bank	Bank GIC	$5,000	Interest	$287.50	5.75%
Brown Co.	Bond	$5,000	Interest	$300.00	6.0%

REMEMBER

To calculate yield, use the following formula:

yield = payout ÷ investment amount

For the sake of simplicity, the following exercise is based on an annual percentage yield basis, before tax (compounding would increase the yield).

Jones Co. and Smith Co. are typical dividend-paying stocks. Looking at Table 3-2 and presuming that both companies are similar in most respects (including risk) except for their differing dividends, how can you tell whether the $50 stock with a $2.50 annual dividend is better (or worse) than the $100 stock with a $4.00 dividend? The yield tells you.

Even though Jones Co. pays a higher dividend ($4.00), Smith Co. has a higher yield (5 percent). So, if you have to choose between those two as an income investor, choose Smith Co. Of course, if you truly want to maximize your income and don't really need your investment to appreciate a lot, you should probably choose Brown Co.'s bond because it offers a yield of 6 percent.

REMEMBER

Dividend-paying stocks can increase in value and to different extents. They may not have the same growth potential as growth stocks, but at the very least, they have a greater potential for capital gain than GICs or bonds. Dividend-paying stocks (good for investing for income) are covered in Chapter 9.

Investing for Your Personal Style

Your investing style isn't a blue-jeans-versus-three-piece-suit debate. It refers to your approach to stock investing. Do you want to be conservative or aggressive? Would you rather be the tortoise or the hare? Your investment personality greatly depends on your purpose and the term over which you're planning to invest (see the previous two sections). The following sections outline the two most general investment styles.

Conservative investing

Conservative investing means you put your money in something proven, tried, and true. You invest your money in safe and secure places, such as banks and government-backed securities. But how does that apply to stocks? (Table 3-1 gives you suggestions.) If you're a conservative stock investor, you want to place your money in companies that exhibit some of the following qualities:

>> **Proven performance:** You want companies that have shown increasing sales and earnings year after year. You don't demand anything spectacular — just a strong and steady performance.

>> **Large market size:** You want to invest in large cap companies (short for large capitalization). In other words, they should have a market value exceeding $5–$25 billion. Conservative investors surmise that bigger is safer.

>> **Proven market leadership:** Look for companies that are leaders in their industries, with excellent senior management.

>> **Perceived staying power:** You want companies with the financial clout and market position to weather uncertain market and economic conditions. What happens in the economy or who gets elected to the House of Commons shouldn't matter.

REMEMBER

As a conservative investor, you don't mind if the companies' share prices jump (who would?), but you're more concerned with steady growth and less risk over the long term. (Risk, in stock investing, is introduced in Chapter 4.)

Aggressive investing

Aggressive investors can plan long-term or look over only the intermediate term, but in any case, they want stocks that resemble jack rabbits — those that show the potential to break out of the pack.

If you're an aggressive stock investor, you want to invest your money in companies that exhibit some of the following qualities:

>> **Great potential:** Choose companies that have superior goods, services, ideas, or ways of doing business compared to the competition.

>> **Capital gains possibility:** Don't even consider dividends. If anything, you dislike dividends. You feel that the money dispensed in dividend form is better reinvested in the company. This, in turn, can spur greater growth.

>> **Innovation:** Find companies that have innovative technologies, ideas, or methods that make them stand apart. Innovation is critical.

REMEMBER

Aggressive Canadian investors usually seek out small capitalization stocks, known as small caps, because they can have plenty of potential for growth. Take the tree example, for instance: A giant redwood may be strong, but it may not grow much more, whereas a brand-new sapling has plenty of growth to look forward to. Why invest in big, stodgy companies when you can invest in smaller enterprises that may become the leaders of tomorrow? Aggressive investors have no problem buying stock in obscure businesses because they hope that such companies will become another Apple or McDonald's. Find out more about growth investing in Chapter 8.

Chapter **4**

Recognizing Risk and Volatility

anadian stock investors face many risks, most of which we cover in this chapter. The simplest definition of risk for investors is "the possibility that your investment will lose some (or all) of its value." Yet you don't have to fear risk if you understand it and plan for it. You must understand the oldest equation in the world of investing — risk versus return. This equation states the following:

> If you want a greater return on your money, you need to accept more risk. If you don't want to accept more risk, you must expect a lower rate of return.

This point about risk is best illustrated from a moment in one of our investment seminars. One of the attendees told us that he had his money in the bank but was dissatisfied with the rate of return. He lamented, "The yield on my money is pitiful! I want to put my money somewhere where it can grow." We asked him, "How about investing in common stocks? Or what about growth-oriented exchange-traded funds? They both have a solid, long-term growth track record." He responded, "Stocks? ETFs? I don't want to put my money there. It's too risky!" Okay, then. If you don't want to accept and tolerate more risk, don't complain about earning less on your money. Risk (in all its forms) has a bearing on all your money concerns and goals. That's why understanding risk before you invest is so important.

This man — as well as the rest of us — needs to remember that risk is not a four-letter word. (Well, it is a four-letter word, but you know what we mean.) Risk is present no matter what you do with your money. Even if you simply stick your money in your mattress, risk is involved — several kinds of risk, in fact. You have the risk of fire. What if your house burns down? You have the risk of theft. What if burglars find your stash of cash? You also have relative risk. (In other words, what if your relatives find your money?)

Be aware of the different kinds of risk that we describe in this chapter, so you can easily plan around them to keep your money growing. And don't forget risk's kid brother . . . volatility! Volatility is about the rapid movement of buying or selling, which, in turn, causes stock prices to rise or fall rapidly. Technically, volatility is considered a "neutral" condition, but it's usually associated with the rapid downward movement of stock because this causes anxiety and means a sudden loss for investors.

Exploring Different Kinds of Risk

Think about all the ways an investment can lose money. You can list all sorts of possibilities. So many that you may think, "Holy cow! Why invest at all?"

Don't let risk frighten you. After all, life itself is risky. Just make sure that you understand the different kinds of risk that we discuss in the following sections and throughout this book before you start navigating the investment world. Risk can be mitigated. We'll show you some of the ways you can manage risk, through approaches like diversification, asset allocation, brokerage order tactics, financial statement analysis, and much more. Be mindful of risk and find out about the effects of risk on your investments and personal financial goals.

Financial risk

The financial risk of investing is that you can lose your money if the company whose stock or bond you purchase loses money or goes belly up. This type of risk is the most obvious because companies do go bankrupt.

REMEMBER

You can greatly enhance the chances of your financial risk paying off by doing an adequate amount of research and choosing your stocks carefully (which this book helps you do — see Part 3 for details on picking winners). Financial risk is a real concern even when the economy is doing well. Some diligent research, a little planning, and a dose of common sense help you reduce your financial risk.

In the stock investing mania of the late 1990s, millions of investors (along with many well-known investment gurus) ignored some obvious financial risks of many then-popular stocks. Investors blindly plunked their money into stocks that were bad choices. Consider investors who put their money in Nortel — if Canadians even remember that name anymore — and held on. This company had no profit and was in debt. It eventually went bankrupt! Blackberry, formerly known as Research In Motion, almost went belly up and remains a shadow of its former self.

Technology and other high risk stocks littered the graveyard of stock market catastrophes during the Tech Wreck of 2000–2001 and during the Great Recession of 2008–2009 because investors didn't see (or didn't want to see?) the risks involved with companies that didn't offer a solid record of results (profits, good cash flows, growing sales, and so on). When you invest in companies without a proven track record, you're not investing, you're speculating.

Investors who did their homework regarding the financial conditions of companies represented by Internet technology stocks discovered that these companies had the hallmarks of financial risk — high debt, low (or no) earnings, and plenty of competition. They steered clear, avoiding tremendous financial loss. Investors who didn't do their homework were lured by the status of these companies and lost their shirts. But some investors found gems, including names like eBay, Amazon, and Priceline. The homework they did allowed them to seize great opportunities if they held on to those stocks over the rough periods. Today, brand new companies are emerging in the blockchain, medical cannabis, and other emerging industries, and the lessons learned in the past can provide you with great insights into today's stock investing decisions. Chapter 13 and 19 deal with emerging industries and opportunities.

Of course, the individual investors who lost money by investing in these trendy, high-profile companies don't deserve all the responsibility for their tremendous financial losses; some high-profile analysts appearing on television or in online media, or commenting in newspapers also should have known better. The time periods we discuss in this section may someday be case studies of how euphoria and the herd mentality (rather than good, old-fashioned research and common sense) ruled the day (temporarily). The excitement of making potential fortunes gets the best of people sometimes, and they throw caution to the wind. Historians may look back at those days and say, "What *were* they thinking?" Achieving true wealth takes diligent work and careful analysis.

REMEMBER

In terms of financial risk, the bottom line is . . . well . . . the bottom line! A healthy bottom line means that a company is making money. And if a company is generating cash (not just paper profits), you can make money by investing in its stock. However, if a company isn't making money, you won't make money if you invest in it. Profit and cash generation is the lifeblood of any company. See Chapter 11 for the scoop on determining whether a company's bottom line is healthy.

Interest rate risk

REMEMBER

You can lose money in an apparently sound investment because of something that sounds as harmless as "interest rates have changed." Interest rate risk may sound like an odd type of risk, but in fact, it's a common consideration for investors. Be aware that interest rates change on a regular basis, causing some challenging moments. Banks set interest rates, and the primary institutions to watch closely are the Bank of Canada and the U.S. Federal Reserve (the Fed), which are both national central banks. The Bank of Canada and the Fed raise or lower their interest rates, actions that, in turn, cause Canadian and U.S. banks to raise or lower their interest rates accordingly. Interest rate changes affect consumers, businesses, and, of course, investors.

Here's a generic introduction to the way fluctuating interest rate risk can affect investors in general: Suppose that you buy a long-term, high-quality corporate bond and get a yield of 6 percent. Your money is safe, and your return is locked in at 6 percent. Whew! That's 6 percent. Not bad, huh? But what happens if, after you commit your money, interest rates increase to 8 percent? You lose the opportunity to get that extra 2 percent interest. The only way to get out of your 6 percent bond is to sell it at current market values and use the money to reinvest at the higher rate.

The only problem with this scenario is that the 6 percent bond is likely to drop in value because interest rates rose. Why? Say that the investor is Barb and the bond yielding 6 percent is a corporate bond issued by Lucin-Muny (LM). According to the bond agreement, LM must pay 6 percent (called the *face rate* or *nominal rate*) during the life of the bond and then, upon maturity, pay the principal. If Barb buys $10,000 of LM bonds on the day they're issued, she gets $600 (of interest) every year for as long as she holds the bonds. If she holds on until maturity, she gets back her $10,000 (the principal). So far so good, right? The plot thickens, however.

Say that she decides to sell the bonds long before maturity and that, at the time of the sale, interest rates in the market have risen to 8 percent. Now what? The reality is that no one is going to want her 6 percent bonds if the market is offering bonds at 8 percent. What's Barb to do? She can't change the face rate of 6 percent, and she can't change the fact that only $600 is paid each year for the life of the bonds. What has to change so that current investors get the *equivalent* yield of 8 percent? If you said, "The bonds' value has to go down" ... bingo! In this example, the bonds' market value needs to drop to $7,500 so that investors buying the bonds get an equivalent yield of 8 percent. (For simplicity's sake, we left out the time it takes for the bonds to mature.) Here's how that figures.

New investors still get $600 annually. However, $600 is equal to 8 percent of $7,500. Therefore, even though investors get the face rate of 6 percent, they get a yield of 8 percent because the actual investment amount is $7,500. In this example, little, if any, financial risk is present, but you see how interest rate risk presents itself. Barb finds out that you can have a good company with a good bond yet still lose $2,500 because of the change in the interest rate. Of course, if Barb doesn't sell, she doesn't realize that loss. (For more on the how and why of selling your stocks and other financial instruments using brokers, check out Chapter 17.)

Bond funds fluctuate in price daily; the portfolio manager is regularly turning over the portfolio (buying and selling bonds in the fund), and market interest rates are constantly fluctuating. Be aware that interest rates (at the time of writing) are near record lows, so even investing in a bond fund can have significant short-term risk if rates rise rapidly. This differs somewhat from bank deposits and investments (GICs, Term Deposits, and so on), which pay the specified interest yield as long as they are held to maturity.

REMEMBER

Historically, rising interest rates have had an adverse effect on stock prices. We outline several reasons why in the following sections. Because the Canadian and U.S. economies are heavily indebted, rising interest rates are an obvious risk that threatens both stocks and fixed-income securities (such as bonds).

Hurting a company's financial condition

Rising interest rates have a negative impact on companies that carry a large current debt load or that need to take on more interest-sensitive debt, because when interest rates rise, the cost of borrowing money rises, too. Ultimately, the company's profitability and ability to grow are reduced. When a company's profits (or earnings) drop, its stock becomes less desirable, and its stock price falls.

Affecting a company's customers

A company's success comes from selling its products or services. But what happens if *increased* interest rates negatively impact its customers? The financial health of a company's customers directly affects ability to grow sales and earnings.

Affecting investors' decision making considerations

When interest rates rise, investors start to rethink their investment strategies, resulting in one of two outcomes:

>> Investors may sell any shares in interest-sensitive stocks that they hold. Interest-sensitive industries include electric utilities, real estate, and the financial sector. Although increased interest rates can hurt these sectors, the reverse is also generally true: Falling interest rates boost the same industries. Keep in mind that interest rate changes affect some industries more than others.

>> Investors who favour increased current income (versus waiting for the investment to grow in value to sell for a gain later on) are definitely attracted to investment vehicles that offer a higher yield. Higher interest rates can cause investors to switch from stocks to bonds or bank certificates of deposit.

Hurting stock prices indirectly

High or rising interest rates can have a negative impact on any investor's total financial picture. What happens when an investor struggles with burdensome debt, such as a second mortgage, credit card debt, or *margin debt* (debt from borrowing against stock in a brokerage account)? He may sell some stock to pay off some of his high-interest debt. Selling stock to service debt is a common practice that, when taken collectively, can hurt stock prices.

As this book goes to press, the U.S. stock market and the Canadian and U.S. economies are in a bull market and growth phase that has lasted a decade. However, the debt that fueled much of this economic growth and momentum poses perhaps the greatest challenge since the Great Depression. Specifically, some North American financial institutions hold more than 600 trillion dollars' worth of derivatives. These can be very complicated and sophisticated investment vehicles that can backfire "real fast." Derivatives have, in fact, sunk some large organizations (such as Bear Stearns and Lehman Brothers), and investors should be aware of them. Just check out the company's financial reports. (Find out more in Chapter 12.)

REMEMBER

Because of the effects of interest rates on stock portfolios, both direct and indirect, successful investors regularly monitor interest rates in both the general economy and in their personal situations. Although stocks have proven to be a superior long-term investment (the longer the term, the better), every investor should maintain a balanced portfolio that includes other investment vehicles. A diversified investor has some money in vehicles that do well when interest rates rise. These vehicles include Canadian money market funds and other variable-rate investments whose interest rates rise when market rates rise. These types of investments add a measure of safety from interest rate risk to your stock portfolio. (We discuss diversification in detail later in this chapter.)

REMEMBER

Closely related to interest rate risk is the concept of credit risk. Some companies loan money to other organizations. In this case, the lending company expects to receive interest revenue from the borrowing company. *Credit risk* is the risk of the lending company losing all or part of the principal or interest amount if the borrower fails to repay the loan or otherwise doesn't meet a contractual obligation. Be sure to review the company's financial reports. (We show you how in Chapter 12.)

Market risk

People talk about *the market* and how it goes up or down, making it sound like a monolithic entity instead of what it really is — a group of millions of individuals making daily decisions to buy or sell stock. No matter how modern our society and economic system, you can't escape the laws of supply and demand. When masses of people want to buy a particular stock, it becomes in demand, and its price rises. That price rises higher if the supply is limited. Conversely, if no one's interested in buying a stock, its price falls. Supply and demand is the nature of market risk. The price of the stock you purchase can rise and fall on the fickle whim of market demand.

Millions of investors buying and selling each minute of every trading day affect the share price of your stock. This makes it impossible to judge which way your stock will move tomorrow or next week. This unpredictability and seeming irrationality are why stocks aren't appropriate for short-term financial growth.

Markets are volatile by nature; they go up and down, and investments need time to grow. Market volatility is an increasingly common condition that we have to live with (see the section "Getting the Scoop on Volatility" later in this chapter). Canadians should be aware of the fact that stocks in general (especially in today's marketplace) aren't suitable for short-term (one year or less) goals (refer to Chapters 2 and 3 for more on short-term goals). Despite the fact that companies you're invested in may be fundamentally sound, all stock prices are subject to the gyrations of the marketplace and need time to trend upward.

WARNING

Investing requires diligent work and research before putting your money in quality investments with a long-term perspective. Speculating is attempting to make a relatively quick profit by monitoring the short-term price movements of a particular investment. Investors seek to minimize risk, whereas speculators don't mind risk because it can also magnify profits. Speculating and investing have clear differences, but investors frequently become speculators and ultimately put themselves and their wealth at risk. Don't go there!

Consider the married couple nearing retirement who decided to play with their money in an attempt to make their pending retirement more comfortable. They borrowed a sizable sum by tapping in to their home equity to invest in the stock market. (Their home, which they had paid off, had enough equity to qualify for this loan.) What did they do with these funds? You guessed it; they invested in the high-flying and speculative stocks of the day. Within eight months, they lost almost all their money.

WARNING

Understanding market risk is especially important for people who are tempted to put their nest eggs or emergency funds into volatile investments such as growth stocks (or even exchange-traded funds that invest in growth stocks or similar aggressive investment vehicles). Remember, you can lose everything.

Inflation risk

Inflation is the artificial expansion of the quantity of money so that too much money is used in exchange for goods and services. To consumers, inflation shows up in the form of higher prices for goods and services. Inflation risk is also referred to as *purchasing power risk*. This term just means that your money doesn't buy as much as it used to. For example, a dollar that bought you a sandwich in 1980 barely bought you a candy bar a few years later. For you, the investor, this risk means that the value of your investment (a stock that doesn't appreciate much, for example) may not keep up with inflation.

Say that you have money in a bank savings account currently earning 1 percent. This account has flexibility — if the market interest rate goes up, the rate you earn in your account goes up. Your account is safe from both financial risk and interest rate risk. But what if inflation is running at 5 percent? At that point, you're losing money.

At the time of this writing, inflation is re-emerging, albeit slowly, as a real and serious concern, and it should not be ignored. We touch on inflation in Chapter 15.

Liquidity risk

Lots of stocks exist out there, good and bad, that aren't really in the national spotlight. They are the stocks of companies that many Canadians may not have heard about. In many cases, these stocks, while listed on stock exchanges, don't trade heavily in terms of the number of shares exchanging hands on a daily basis. When this happens, it's referred to as *low trading volume*. *Liquidity risk* is the risk of a stock investor being unable to readily trade (buy or sell) a stock at a desired price that is considered fair in value. This means that you can be exposed to price volatility, which may or may not result in a loss for you. We show you how to manage this risk in Chapter 17, where we discuss brokerage order techniques such as placing price limits on sell orders.

Foreign exchange risk

Canadian stock investors shouldn't limit their stock investing to Canadian stocks and Canadian stock exchanges. In fact, we insist you do not. Why? Because the Canadian stock market typically represents less than 4 percent of the world stock markets in terms of size. Therefore, diversifying your stock investing into U.S., and to some extent Asian and other foreign markets is very important. We discuss diversification in more detail later in this chapter, and we diversified our discussion with brand new content in Chapter 14 which deals with Asian-Pacific stock markets.

Here's the problem: Although international diversification minimizes one type of risk (putting all of your eggs in one basket), it exposes Canadian stock investors to another risk — *foreign exchange risk*, which is the risk of losses when currency exchange rates fluctuate. However, currencies can move up or down, so just be aware that, yes, you can lose money on exchange rates. On the other hand, if rates move in your favour, you can make additional money too. Also be aware that foreign exchange risk may be reduced through hedging strategies, which may reduce your foreign currency exposure.

Tax risk

REMEMBER

Canadian taxes (such as income tax or capital gains tax) don't affect your stock investment directly, but taxes can obviously affect how much of your money you get to keep. Because the entire point of stock investing is to build wealth, you need to understand that taxes take away a portion of the wealth that you're trying to build. Taxes can be risky because if you make the wrong move with your stocks (selling them at the wrong time, for example), you can end up paying higher taxes than you need to. Because Canadian tax laws change frequently, tax risk is part of the risk-versus-return equation as well.

It pays to gain knowledge about how taxes can impact your wealth-building program before you make your investment decisions. Chapter 21 covers the impact of Canadian taxes in greater detail. In that chapter you'll see that stocks have much more favorable tax treatment than interest-bearing financial instruments like bonds.

Political and governmental risks

If companies were fish, politics and federal government policies (such as taxes, laws, and regulations) would be the pond. In the same way that fish die in a toxic or polluted pond, politics and government policies can kill companies. Of course, if you own stock in a company exposed to political and governmental risks, you need to be aware of these risks. For some companies, a single new regulation or law is enough to send them into bankruptcy. For other companies, a new law can help them increase sales and profits. We see this type of turbulence happening today in Canada with seemingly endless pipeline debates and protests.

What if you invest in companies or industries that become political targets? You may want to consider selling them (you can always buy them back later) or consider putting in stop-loss orders on the stock (see Chapter 17). For example, over quite a few decades, tobacco and oil companies were, and still continue to be, targets of political firestorms that batter their stock prices when critical events occur — like deaths, spills, and elections. Whether you agree or disagree with the political and ethical machinations of today is not the issue. As an investor, you have to simply ask yourself in a very dispassionate and black and white way, "How do politics affect the market value and the current and future prospects of my chosen investment?" After and only after you answer that initial question, by all means superimpose your values, as that is every bit as important as stock price impact.

Taking the preceding point a step further, we'd like to remind you that politics and government have a direct and often negative impact on the economic environment. And one major pitfall for investors is that many misunderstand even basic economics. Considering all the examples we could find in recent years, we could write a book! Or . . . uh . . . simply add it to this book. Chapter 15 goes into greater detail to help you make (and keep) stock market profits just by understanding rudimentary (and quite interesting) economics. (Don't worry; the dry stuff will be kept to a minimum!)

Personal risks

Frequently, the risk involved with investing in the stock market isn't directly related to the investment; rather, it's associated with the investor's circumstances.

Suppose that investor Ralph puts $15,000 into a portfolio of common stocks. Imagine that the market experiences a drop in prices that week and Ralph's stocks drop to a market value of $14,000. Because stocks are good for the long term, this type of decrease usually isn't an alarming incident. Odds are that this dip is temporary, especially if Ralph carefully chose high-quality companies. Incidentally, if a portfolio of high-quality stocks *does* experience a temporary drop in price, it can be a great opportunity to get more shares at a good price. (Chapter 17 covers orders you can place with your broker to help you do that.)

Over the long term, Ralph will probably see the value of his investment grow substantially. But what if Ralph experiences financial difficulty and needs quick cash during a period when his stocks are declining? He may have to sell his stock to get some money.

This problem occurs frequently for investors who don't have an emergency fund to handle large, sudden expenses. You never know when your company may lay you off or when your basement may flood, leaving you with a huge repair bill. Car accidents, medical emergencies, and other unforeseen events are part of life's bag of surprises — for any Canadian.

REMEMBER

You probably won't get much comfort from knowing that stock losses are tax deductible — a loss is a loss (see Chapter 21 for more on taxes). However, you can avoid the kind of loss that results from prematurely having to sell your stocks if you maintain an emergency cash fund. A good place for your emergency cash fund is in either a bank savings account or a money market fund. Then you aren't forced to prematurely liquidate your stock investments to pay emergency bills. (Chapter 2 provides more guidance on having liquid assets for emergencies.)

Emotional risk

WARNING

What does emotional risk have to do with stocks? Everything. Emotions are important risk considerations because investors are human beings. Logic and discipline are critical factors in investment success, but even the best investor can let emotions take over the reins of money management and cause loss. For stock investing, you're likely to be sidetracked by three main emotions: greed, fear, and love. You need to understand your emotions and what kinds of risk they can expose you to. If you get too attached to a sinking stock, you don't need a stock investing book — you need a therapist!

Paying the price for greed

In 1998–2000, millions of investors threw caution to the wind and chased highly dubious, risky technology stocks. The dollar signs popped up in their eyes (just like slot machines) when they saw that easy street was lined with stocks that were doubling and tripling in a very short time. Who cares about price/earnings (P/E) ratios and cashflows when you can just buy stock, make a fortune, and get out with millions? (Of course, *you* care about making money with stocks, so you can flip to Chapter 11 and Appendix B to find out more about P/E ratios and the importance of cashflows.)

Unfortunately, the lure of the easy buck can easily turn healthy attitudes about growing wealth into unhealthy greed that blinds investors and discards common sense. Avoid the temptation to invest for short-term gains in dubious hot stocks instead of doing your homework and buying stocks of solid companies with strong fundamentals and a long-term focus, as we explain in Part 3.

Recognizing the role of fear

Greed can be a problem, but fear is the other extreme. People who are fearful of loss frequently avoid suitable investments and end up settling for a low rate of return. If you have to succumb to one of these emotions, at least fear exposes you to less immediate loss.

Also, keep in mind that fear is frequently a symptom of lack of knowledge about what's going on. If you see your stocks falling and don't understand why, fear will take over, and you may act irrationally. That's what happened during the Great Recession, which was triggered by a real estate bubble gone bad but also resulted in a panicked stock market meltdown. When stock investors are affected by fear, they tend to sell their stocks and head for the exits and the lifeboats. When investors see their stock go down 20 percent, what goes through their heads? Experienced, knowledgeable investors realize that no bull market goes straight up. Even the strongest bull goes up in a zigzag fashion. Conversely, even bear markets don't go straight down; they zigzag down. Out of fear, inexperienced investors sell good stocks when they see them go down temporarily (the *correction*), whereas experienced investors see that temporary downward move as a good buying opportunity to add to their positions.

INVESTMENT LESSONS FROM SEPTEMBER 11

September 11, 2001, was a horrific day that is burned in our minds and won't be forgotten in our lifetime. The acts of terrorism that day took more than 3,000 lives and caused untold pain and grief. Fast-forward nearly two decades and we can add dozens more instances of modern-day horror shows produced by fanatics. Are we as investors being desensitized?

A much less important after-effect of any act of terrorism is the hard set of lessons that investors learn from days like that. Terrorism reminds us that risk is more real than ever and that we should never let our guard down. What lessons can investors learn from this and similar events? Here are a few pointers:

- **Diversify your portfolio.** Of course, the events of September 11 were certainly surreal and unexpected. Stocks plummeted. But before the events occurred, investors should have made it a habit to assess their situations and see whether they had any vulnerabilities. Stock investors with no money outside the stock market are always more at risk. Keeping your portfolio diversified is a time-tested strategy that's more relevant than ever before. (We discuss diversification later in this chapter.)

- **Review and reallocate.** Subsequent acts of terrorism exported to France and elsewhere in Europe and abroad triggered declines in the overall market, but specific tourism-related industries, such as airlines and hotels, were hit particularly hard. In addition, some industries, such as defence and food, saw stock prices rise. Monitor your portfolio and ask yourself whether it's overly reliant on or exposed to events in specific sectors. If so, reallocate your investments to decrease your risk exposure.

- **Check for signs of trouble.** Techniques such as trailing stops (explained in Chapter 17) come in handy when your stocks plummet after unexpected events. Even if you don't use these techniques, you can make it a regular habit to check your stocks for signs of trouble, such as debts or P/E ratios that are too high. If you see signs of trouble, consider selling.

Looking for love in all the wrong places

Stocks are dispassionate, inanimate vehicles, but people can look for love in the strangest places. Emotional risk occurs when investors fall in love with a stock and refuse to sell it, even when the stock is plummeting and shows all the symptoms of getting worse. Emotional risk also occurs when investors are drawn to bad investment choices just because they sound good, are popular, or are pushed by family or friends. Love and attachment are great in relationships with people but can be horrible with investments. To deal with this emotion, investors have to deploy techniques that take the emotion out. For example, you can use brokerage orders (such as trailing stops and limit orders; see Chapter 17), which can automatically trigger buy and sell transactions and leave out some of the agonizing. Hey, disciplined investing may just become your new passion!

Getting the Scoop on Volatility

How often have you heard a financial commentator on TV say, "Well, it looks like a volatile day as the markets plunge 700 points. . . ." Oh dear . . . pass us the antacid! Volatility has garnered a bad reputation because roller coasters and weak stomachs don't mix — especially when your financial future seems to be acting like a kite in a tornado.

People may think of volatility as "risk on steroids," but you need to understand what volatility actually is. Technically, it isn't really good or bad (although it's usually associated with bad movements in the marketplace). *Volatility* is the movement of an asset (or the entire market) very quickly down (or up) in price due to large selling (or buying) in a short period of time.

Volatility tends to be more associated with the negative due to crowd psychology. People are more likely to act quickly (sell!) due to fear than to other motivators (such as greed; refer to the section "Emotional risk" for more info). More people are apt to run for the exits than to the entrance, so to speak.

TIP

Not all stocks are equal with regard to volatility. Some can be very volatile, whereas others can be quite stable. A good way to determine a stock's volatility is to look at the beta of the stock. *Beta* is a statistical measure that attempts to give the investor a clue as to how volatile a stock may be. It's determined by comparing the potential volatility of a particular stock to the market in general. The market (as represented by, say, the Standard & Poor 500 or any other broad stock market index) is assigned a beta of "1." Any stock with a beta greater than 1 is considered more volatile than the general stock market, whereas any stock with a beta of less than 1 is considered less volatile. If a stock has a beta of 1.50, for example, it's considered 50 percent more volatile than the general market. Meanwhile, a stock with a beta of 0.85 is considered 15 percent less volatile than the general stock market.

Therefore, if you don't want to keep gulping down more antacid, consider stocks that have a beta of less than 1. The beta can be found easily in the stock report pages that are usually provided by major financial websites such as Yahoo! Finance Canada (ca.finance.yahoo.com) and MarketWatch (www.marketwatch.com). (See Appendix A for more financial websites.)

Minimizing Your Risk

Now, before you go crazy thinking that stock investing carries so much risk that you may as well not get out of bed, take a breath. Minimizing your risk in stock investing is easier than you think. Although wealth-building through the stock market doesn't take place without some amount of risk, you can practice the following tips to maximize your profits and still keep your money secure.

Gaining knowledge

REMEMBER

Some people spend more time analyzing a restaurant menu to choose a $10 entrée than analyzing where to put their next $5,000. Lack of knowledge constitutes the greatest risk for new investors, so diminishing that risk starts with gaining knowledge. The more familiar you are with the stock market — how it works, factors that affect stock value, and so on — the better you can navigate around its pitfalls and maximize your profits. The same knowledge that enables you to grow your wealth also enables you to minimize your risk. Before you put your money anywhere, you want to know as much as you can. This book is a great place to start — check out Chapter 6 for a rundown of the kinds of information you want to know before you buy stocks, as well as the resources that can give you the information you need to invest successfully.

Staying out until you get a little practice

If you don't understand stocks, don't invest! Yeah, we know this book is about stock investing, and we think that some measure of stock investing is a good idea for most people. But that doesn't mean you should be 100 percent invested 100 percent of the time. If you don't understand a particular stock (or don't understand stocks, period), stay away until you do. Instead, give yourself an imaginary sum of money, such as $100,000, give yourself reasons to invest, and just make believe (a practice called *simulated stock investing* or *trading*). Pick a few stocks that you think will increase in value, track them for a while, and see how they perform. Begin to understand how the price of a stock goes up and down, and watch what happens to the stocks you choose when various events take place. As you find out more about stock investing, you get better at picking individual stocks, without risking — or losing — any money during your learning period.

TIP

A good place to do your imaginary investing is at a website such as Investopedia's simulator (www.investopedia.com/simulator). You can design a stock portfolio and track its performance with thousands of other investors to see how well you do.

WHY MORE VOLATILITY?

People will always gasp at the occasional big up or down day, but volatility is more prevalent overall today than, say, 10 or 20 years ago. Why is that? Several contributing factors exist:

- First of all, today's investor has the advantages of cheaper commissions and faster technology. Years ago, if investors wanted to sell, they had to call their brokers — usually during business hours. On top of that, the commission was usually high. That discouraged a lot of rapid-fire trading. Today, Canadian online trading is not only cheaper (around $10 with certain holding minimums) but also anyone can do it from home with a few clicks of a mouse on a website literally 24 hours a day, seven days a week.

- A growing trend is the use of high-frequency trading, which involves the use of financial technologies such as trading computer algorithms to rapidly trade securities. High-frequency traders can contribute to volatility in a big way. You may recall the Flash Crash of May 6, 2010, as well as several other incidents after that where high-frequency traders withdrew from the market en masse. Several stock exchanges now have controls to curtail excessive amounts of this type of trading, which still occurs in a significant way today.

- In addition, large organizations — ranging from financial institutions to government-sponsored entities such as sovereign wealth funds — can make large trades or huge amounts of money either nationally or globally within seconds. The rapid movement of large amounts of money both in and out of a stock or an entire market means that volatility is high and likely to be with us for a long time to come.

- Lastly, the world is now more of a global marketplace, and our markets react more to international events than in the past. With new technology and the Internet, news travels farther and faster than ever before.

Putting your financial house in order

Advice on what to do before you invest could be a whole book all by itself. The bottom line is that you want to make sure that you are, first and foremost, financially secure before you take the plunge into the stock market. If you're not sure about your financial security, look over your situation with a financial planner. (You can find more on financial planners in Appendix A.)

REMEMBER

Before you buy your first stock, here are a few things you can do to get your finances in order:

>> **Have a cushion of money.** Set aside three to six months' worth of your gross living expenses somewhere safe, such as in a bank account or money market fund, in case you suddenly need cash for an emergency (refer to Chapter 2 for details).

>> **Reduce your debt.** Overindulging in debt continues to be a serious personal economic problem for many Canadians. Recently, the Bank of Canada raised warning signals about the personal levels of debt held by many individuals in this country (refer to Chapter 2).

>> **Make sure that your job is as secure as you can make it.** Are you keeping your skills up to date? Is the company you work for strong and growing? Is the industry that you work in strong and growing?

>> **Make sure that you have adequate insurance.** You need enough insurance to cover your needs and those of your family in case of illness, death, disability, and so on.

Diversifying your investments

WARNING

Diversification is a strategy for reducing risk by spreading your money across different investments. It's a fancy way of saying, "Don't put all your eggs in one basket." But how do you go about divvying up your money and distributing it among different investments? The easiest way to understand proper diversification may be to look at what you *shouldn't* do:

>> **Don't put all your money in one stock.** Sure, if you choose wisely and select a hot stock, you may make a bundle, but the odds are tremendously against you. Unless you're a real expert on a particular company, having small portions of your money in several different stocks is a good idea. As a general rule, the money you tie up in a single stock should be money you can do without.

>> **Don't put all your money in one industry or country.** We know people who own several stocks but their stocks are all in the same industry. Again, if you're an expert in that particular industry, it can work out. But just understand that

you're not properly diversified. If a problem hits an entire industry, you may get hurt. Similarly, and as we mention earlier in this chapter, don't have all of your stock holdings in the stock market of one country.

>> **Don't put all your money in one type of investment.** Stocks may be a great investment, but you need to have money elsewhere. Bonds, bank accounts, treasury securities, real estate, and precious metals are perennial alternatives to complement your stock portfolio. Some of these alternatives can be found in mutual funds or exchange-traded funds (ETFs). An *exchange-traded fund* is a fund with a fixed portfolio of stocks or other securities that tracks a particular index but is traded like a stock. By the way, we really love ETFs and think that every serious investor should consider them; see Chapter 5 for more information.

REMEMBER

Okay, now that you know what you *shouldn't* do, what *should* you do? Until you become more knowledgeable, follow this advice:

>> **Keep only 5 to 10 percent (or less) of your investment money in a single stock.** Because you want adequate diversification, you don't want overexposure to a single stock. Aggressive investors can certainly go for 10 percent or even higher, but conservative investors are better off at 5 percent or less.

>> **Invest in various industries and hold several stocks in each industry (four or five stocks, and no more than ten, in each).** Which industries? Choose industries that offer products and services that have shown strong, growing demand. To make this decision, use your common sense (which isn't as common as it used to be). Think about the industries that people need no matter what happens in the general economy, such as food, energy, and other consumer necessities. See Chapter 13 for more information about analyzing sectors and industries.

Weighing Risk against Return

How much risk is appropriate for you, and how do you handle it? Before you try to figure out what risks accompany your investment choices, analyze yourself. Here are some points to keep in mind when weighing risk versus return in your situation:

>> **Your financial goal:** In five minutes with a financial calculator, you can easily see how much money you're going to need to become financially independent (presuming financial independence is your goal). Say that you need $500,000 in ten years for a worry-free retirement and that your financial assets (such as stocks, bonds, and so on) are currently worth $400,000. In this scenario, your

assets need to grow by only 2.25 percent per year, on average, to hit your target. Getting investments that grow by 2.25 percent safely is easy to do because that's a relatively low rate of return.

REMEMBER

The important point is that you don't have to knock yourself out trying to double your money with risky, high-flying investments; some run-of-the-mill bank investments will do just fine. All too often, investors take on more risk than is necessary. Figure out what your financial goal is so that you know what kind of return you realistically need. Flip to Chapters 2 and 3 for details on determining your financial goals.

>> **Your investor profile:** Are you nearing retirement, or are you fresh out of university? Your life situation matters when it comes to looking at risk versus return. If you're just beginning your working years, you can certainly tolerate greater risk than someone who is facing retirement. However, if you're within a few years of retirement, risky or aggressive investments can do much more harm than good. (Refer to Chapter 2 for more on investing within your age cohort.)

>> **Asset allocation:** We never tell retirees to put a large portion of their retirement money into a high-tech stock or other volatile investment. But if they still want to speculate, we don't see a problem as long as they limit such investments to 5 percent of their total assets. As long as the bulk of their money is safe and sound in secure investments (such as Canadian Treasury bills), we know we can sleep well (knowing that *they* can sleep well!).

REMEMBER

Asset allocation beckons back to diversification, which we discuss earlier in this chapter. For people in their 20s and 30s, having 75 percent of their money in a diversified portfolio of growth stocks (such as mid cap and small cap stocks; refer to Chapters 1 and 2) is acceptable. For people in their 60s and 70s, it's not acceptable. They may, instead, consider investing about 20 percent or so of their money in stocks (mid caps and large caps are preferable). Check with your financial advisor to find the right mix for your particular situation.

BETTER LUCK NEXT TIME!

A little knowledge can be very risky. Consider the true story of one "lucky" fellow who played the California lottery in 1987. He discovered that he had a winning ticket, with the first prize of $412,000. He immediately ordered a Porsche, booked a lavish trip to Hawaii for his family, and treated his wife and friends to a champagne dinner at a posh Hollywood restaurant. When he finally went to collect his prize, he found out that he had to share first prize with more than 9,000 other lottery players who also had the same winning numbers. His share of the prize was actually only $45! Hopefully, he invested that tidy sum based on his increased knowledge about risk. (That story always cracks us up.)

Chapter **5**

Investing in Canadian Exchange-Traded Funds

When it comes to stock investing, there's more than one way to do it. Buying stocks directly is good; sometimes, buying stocks indirectly is equally good (or even better) — especially if you're risk averse. Buying a great stock is every stock investor's dream, but sometimes you face investing environments that make finding a winning stock a hazardous pursuit. Prudent stock investors should consider adding Canadian and U.S. exchange-traded funds (ETFs) to their wealth-building arsenal.

We first introduced you to ETFs in Chapter 2 when we discussed equities and the age appropriateness of ETFs at various stages of life. By way of reminder, an exchange-traded fund (ETF) is basically a mutual fund that invests in a fixed basket of securities but with a few twists. In this chapter, we show you how ETFs are similar to (and different from) mutual funds, we provide some pointers on picking ETFs, and we note the fundamentals of stock indexes (which are connected to ETFs).

Comparing Exchange-Traded Funds and Mutual Funds

For many folks and for many years, the only choice besides investing directly in stocks was to invest indirectly through mutual funds. After all, why buy a single stock for roughly the same few thousand dollars that you can buy a mutual fund for and get benefits such as professional management and diversification?

For small investors, mutual fund investing isn't a bad way to go. Investors participate by pooling their money with others and get professional money management in an affordable manner. But mutual funds have their downsides too. Many, in fact. Mutual fund fees, which include management fees and sales charges (referred to as *loads*), eat into gains, and investors have no choice about investments in a mutual fund. Whatever the fund manager buys, sells, or holds on to is pretty much what the investors in the fund have to tolerate. Investment choice is limited to either being in the fund . . . or being out.

But now, with ETFs, investors have greater choices than ever, a scenario that sets the stage for the inevitable comparison between mutual funds and ETFs. The following sections go over the differences and similarities between ETFs and mutual funds.

The differences

Simply stated, in a mutual fund, securities such as stocks and bonds are constantly bought, sold, and held (in other words, the fund is actively managed by a third-party portfolio manager). An ETF holds similar securities, but the portfolio typically isn't actively managed. Instead, an ETF usually holds a fixed basket of securities that may reflect an index or a particular industry or sector (see Chapter 13). (An index is a method of measuring the value of a segment of the general stock market. It's a tool used by money managers and investors to compare the performance of a particular stock to a widely accepted standard; see the later section "Taking Note of Indexes" for more.)

For example, an ETF that tries to reflect the S&P/TSX 60 will attempt to hold a securities portfolio that mirrors the composition of the S&P/TSX 60 Index as closely as possible. Here's another example: A water utilities ETF may hold the top 15 or 20 publicly held water companies. (You get the picture.)

REMEMBER

Where ETFs are markedly different from mutual funds (and where they're really advantageous, in our opinion) is that they can be bought and sold like stocks. In addition, you can do with ETFs what you can generally do with stocks (but can't usually do with mutual funds): You can buy in share allotments, such as 1, 50, or 100 shares more. Mutual funds, on the other hand, are usually bought in dollar amounts, such as 1,000 or 5,000 dollars' worth. The dollar amount you can initially invest is set by the manager of the individual mutual fund. Did we forget to say that mutual funds can really rip you off in so many ways?

Here are some other advantages of ETFs: You can put various buy/sell brokerage orders on ETFs (see Chapter 17), and many ETFs are optionable (meaning you may be able to buy/sell put and call options on them; we discuss these options in Chapter 23). Mutual funds typically aren't optionable.

In addition, many ETFs are marginable (meaning that you can borrow against them with some limitations in your brokerage account). Mutual funds usually aren't marginable in Canada or the U.S. (although it is possible if they're within the confines of a stock brokerage account). To find out more about margin, check out Chapter 17.

REMEMBER

Sometimes an investor can readily see the great potential of a given industry or sector but is hard-pressed to get that single really good stock that can take advantage of the profit possibilities of that particular segment of the market. The great thing about an ETF is that you can make that investment very easily, knowing that if you're unsure about it, you can put in place strategies that protect you from the downside (such as stop-loss orders or trailing stops). That way, you can sleep easier!

The similarities

Even though ETFs and mutual funds have some major differences, they do share a few similarities:

>> First and foremost, ETFs and mutual funds (MFs) are similar in that they aren't direct investments; they're "conduits" of investing, which means that they act like a connection between the investor and the investments.

>> Both ETFs and MFs basically pool the money of investors and the pool becomes the "fund," which in turn invests in a portfolio of investments.

>> Both ETFs and MFs offer the great advantage of diversification (although they accomplish it in different ways).

>> Investors don't have any choice about what makes up the portfolio of either the ETF or the MF. The ETF has a fixed basket of securities (the money manager overseeing the portfolio makes those choices), and, of course, investors can't control the choices made in a mutual fund.

For those investors who want more active assistance in making choices and running a portfolio, the MF may very well be the way to go. For those who are more comfortable making their own choices in terms of the particular index or industry/sector they want to invest in, the ETF is a much better venue.

Choosing an Exchange-Traded Fund

Buying a stock is an investment in a particular company, but an ETF is an opportunity to invest in a block of stocks. In the same way a few mouse clicks can buy you a stock at a stock brokerage website, those same clicks can buy you virtually an entire industry or sector (or at least the top-tier stocks).

For investors who are comfortable with their own choices and do their due diligence, buying a winning stock is a better (albeit more aggressive) way to go. For those investors who want to make their own choices but aren't that confident about picking winning stocks, getting an ETF is definitely a better way to go.

You had to figure that choosing an ETF wasn't going to be a coin flip. You should be aware of certain considerations, some of which are tied more to your personal outlook and preferences than to the underlying portfolio of the ETF. We give you the info you need on bullish and bearish ETFs in the following sections.

TIP

Picking a winning industry or sector is easier than finding a great company to invest in. Therefore, ETF investing goes hand in hand with the guidance offered in Chapters 13 and 14, which are "big picture" and thematic in nature.

Main types of ETFs

You may wake up one day and say, "I think the stock market or a special segment of it will do very well going forward from today," and that's just fine if you think so. Maybe your research on the general economy, financial outlook, and political considerations make you feel happier than a starving man on a cruise ship. But you just don't know (or don't care to research) which stocks would best benefit from the good market moves yet to come. No problem! That's because in the following sections, we cover the primary types of ETFs you can choose from. ETFs represent one of the best examples of what is often referred to as *story investing*.

Major market equity index ETFs

Why not invest in ETFs that mirror a general major market index such as the U.S. S&P 500 or Canadian S&P/TSX 60? This type of index ETF tracks the overall market. Other index ETFs track a specific subset of the overall market, such as small capitalization stocks or large capitalization stocks. Subset indexes also exist for sectors such as technology, oil and gas, and consumer goods. The slicing and dicing can go further — much further, in fact, as each year passes and the ETF industry continues to grow.

Index ETFs typically include equities. The equities may be from Canada, the U.S., elsewhere in North America, or they may be global or international in scope. (We discussed the nature of equities in Chapter 2.) Perhaps the ETF is a combination of all of the above. The bottom line is *anything goes,* so don't worry too much about the categories. What's important is *what* the ETF contains by way of underlying securities, and the stories those stocks and other securities tell.

An index-based ETF tries to earn the return of the market or subset of the market that it seeks to mimic, less the fees. American ETFs such as SPY construct their portfolios to track the composition of the S&P 500 as closely as possible. Canadian ETFs such as the Horizons AlphaPro Managed S&P/TSX 60 ETF track component stocks within the S&P/TSX 60 Index. As they say, why try to beat the market when you can match it? It's a great way to go when the market is having a good rally. (See the later section "Taking Note of Indexes" for the basics on indexes.)

When the S&P 500 and the S&P/TSX 60 were battered in late 2008 and early 2009, the respective U.S. and Canadian ETFs, of course, mirrored that performance and hit the bottom in March 2009. But from that moment on and well into the time of the writing of this book, the S&P 500 (and the ETFs that tracked it like the iShares Core S&P 500 ETF) did really well. The ETFs that tracked the S&P/TSX 60 did reasonably well during this same period. It paid to buck the bearish sentiment of early 2009. Of course it did take some contrarian gumption to do so, but at least you had the benefit of the full S&P 500 stock portfolio, which at least had more diversification than a single stock or a single subsection of the market.

ETFs that include dividend-paying stocks

ETFs don't necessarily have to be tied to a specific industry or sector; they can be tied to a specific type or subcategory of stock. All things being equal, what basic categories of stocks do you think would better weather bad times: stocks with no dividends or stocks that pay dividends? (We guess the question answers itself, pretty much like "What tastes better: apple pie or barbed wire?") Although some sectors are known for being good dividend payers, such as utilities (and there are some good ETFs that cover this industry), some ETFs cover stocks that meet a specific criteria.

You can find ETFs that include high-dividend income stocks (typically 4 percent or higher), as well as ETFs that include stocks of companies that don't necessarily pay high dividends but do have a long track record of dividend increases that meet or exceed the rate of inflation.

Given these types of dividend-paying ETFs, it becomes clear what is good for what type of stock investor:

>> If we were stock investors who were currently retired, we'd probably choose the high-dividend stock ETF, along with a bond ETF. Dividend-paying stock ETFs are generally more stable than those stock ETFs that don't pay dividends and, for most Canadians, are important vehicles for generating retirement income.

>> If we were in pre-retirement (some years away from retirement but clearly planning for it), we'd probably choose the ETF with the stocks that had a strong record of growing the dividend payout, along with a bond ETF. That way, those same dividend-paying stocks would grow in the short-term and provide better income down the road during retirement.

For more information on dividends, flip to Chapters 6 and 9. We cover investing according to age in Chapter 2.

Currency ETFs

Currency ETFs are designed to track the performance of a single currency in the foreign exchange market against a benchmark currency or basket of currencies. The way ETFs do this is quite exotic and beyond the scope of this book. But in short, the ETFs consist of cash deposits, debt instruments denominated in a certain currency, and futures or swap contracts.

Currency markets used to be the playground of experienced traders. However, exchange traded funds kicked open the doors of foreign exchange to Canadian investors. Through a stock market gateway, currency ETFs are used by Canadians who look for exposure to the foreign exchange market, seek diversification, and prefer to transact outside of the complex and cumbersome futures or foreign exchange market.

Fixed-income ETFs

Fixed-income or *bond* ETFs are still in their infancy. However, they may have a role during times of instability. They are a form of ETF that exclusively invests in fixed-income financial instruments. These holdings can be a portfolio of corporate or government bonds or a combination of the two. They can employ different strategies such as high yield only, and can hold within the ETF long-term or short-term maturity financial instruments. These are called *maturity-themed ETFs*. Take note that the ETF itself has no maturity, and bond ETFs are passively managed. Fixed-income ETFs trade like stock ETFs on a major exchange.

TIP

Keep in mind that dividend-paying stocks generally fall within the criteria of "human need" investing because those companies tend to be large and stable, with good cash flows, giving them the ongoing wherewithal to pay good dividends.

To find out more about ETFs in general and to get more details on the ETFs we mention (Horizons AlphaPro Managed S&P/TSX 60 ETF, SPY, PBJ, and SH), go to websites such as etf.stock-encyclopedia.com and www.etfdb.com. Many of the resources in Appendix A also cover Canadian and foreign ETFs. A great way to see if ETFs exist to fit a theme you have in mind is to simply search for the term in your favorite search engine. For example, if you are intrigued by artificial intelligence, use the search term "ETFs for artificial intelligence." On our first attempt we not only came up with a long list of results of ETFs, but we also found news on ETFs like Horizons Active A.I. Global Equity ETF (MIND) — cool ticker symbols like "MIND."

Alternative ETFs related to a strategy

What are alternative ETFs? In a nutshell, they're anything that doesn't fit nicely into the equity or other types of ETFs we've covered so far. Some ETFs cover industries such as food and beverages, water, energy, and other things that people will keep buying no matter how good or bad the economy is. Without needing a crystal ball or having an iron-willed contrarian attitude, a stock investor can simply put money into stocks — or in this case, ETFs — tied to human need.

Another type of alternative strategy is to focus on a sector such as commodities. Sub-sectors may include oil and gas, agriculture, sugar, coffee, precious metals, livestock — just about anything! This is where stock investor creativity can pay off.

ETFs may also be thematic by focusing, for instance, on stocks of growth companies, or stocks of value companies. We cover some of the more common approaches to stock investing in Chapter 3.

To give you a better sense of the wide array of Canadian ETFs that are out there, check out the following list of ETFs trading on the Canadian stock exchange:

» BMO Agriculture Commodities Index ETF

» BMO Base Metals Commodities Index ETF

» Canadian Russell 2000 Index Fund

» Canadian Small Cap Index Fund

- **CDN MSCI Emerging Markets Index Fund**
- **CDN MSCI World Index Fund**
- **Claymore Global Monthly Advantaged Dividend ETF**
- **Claymore Oil Sands Sector ETF**
- **COMEX Gold ETF**
- **Horizons Absolute Return Global Currency ETF**
- **Horizons Canadian Dollar Currency ETF**
- **Horizons US Dollar Currency ETF**
- **Horizons**
- **iShares CDN MidCap Index Fund**
- **iShares CDN REIT Sector Index Fund**
- **S&P/TSX Capped Financials Inverse ETF**
- **U.S. Dollar Bear Plus ETF**

Bearish ETFs

Most ETFs are bullish in nature because they invest in a portfolio of securities that they expect to go up in due course. But some ETFs have a bearish focus. Bearish ETFs (also called short ETFs) maintain a portfolio of securities and strategies that are designed to go the opposite way of the underlying or targeted securities. In other words, this type of ETF goes up when the underlying securities go down (and vice versa). Bearish ETFs employ securities such as put options (and similar derivatives) and employ strategies such as going short (see Chapter 17).

Take the S&P/TSX 60, for example. If you were bullish on that index, you might choose an ETF such as Horizons AlphaPro Managed S&P/TSX 60. If you were bearish, you could invest in the Horizons BetaPro S&P/TSX 60 Inverse ETF, which seeks investment returns that fully correspond to the inverse of the S&P/TSX 60 Index.

If you were bearish on the US S&P 500 index because of Fiscal Cliff and other concerns and wanted to seek gains by betting that it would go down, you could choose an ETF such as the ProShares Short S&P 500 ETF (SH).

You can take two approaches on bearish ETFs:

>> **Hoping for a downfall:** If you're speculating on a pending market crash, a bearish ETF is a good consideration. In this approach, you're actually seeking to make a profit based on your expectations. Those folks who aggressively went into bearish ETFs during early or mid 2008 made some spectacular profits during the tumultuous downfall during late 2008 and early 2009.

>> **Hedging against a downfall:** A more conservative approach is to use bearish ETFs to a more moderate extent, primarily as a form of hedging, whereby the bearish ETF acts like a form of insurance in the unwelcome event of a significant market pullback or crash. We say "unwelcome" because you're not really hoping for a crash; you're just trying to protect yourself with a modest form of diversification. In this context, diversification means that you have a mix of both bullish positions and, to a smaller extent, bearish positions.

Taking Note of Indexes

For stock investors, ETFs that are bullish or bearish are ultimately tied to major market indexes. You should take a quick look at indexes to better understand them (and the ETFs tied to them).

Whenever you hear the CBC or other media commentary, or the scuttlebutt at the local watering hole about "how the market is doing," it typically refers to a market proxy such as an index. You'll usually hear them mention "the Dow" or perhaps the "S&P/TSX 60." There are certainly other major market indexes, and there are many lesser, yet popular, measurements such as the Dow Jones Transportation Average. Indexes and averages tend to be used interchangeably, but they're distinctly different entities of measurement.

Most people use these indexes basically as standards of market performance to see whether they're doing better or worse than a yardstick for comparison purposes. They want to know continually whether their stocks, ETFs, mutual funds, or overall portfolios are performing well.

In Canada, the TSX (www.tmx.com) is now Canada's main exchange for the trading of equities. The S&P/TSX 60 Index includes 60 large capitalization stocks for Canadian equity markets. The index is market-capitalization weighted (weighted for company stock market value), weight-adjusted for things like share float (shares readily available to the public), and also balanced across ten industry sectors. The following list shows the current lineup of 60 stocks tracked on the S&P/TSX 60:

Agnico-Eagle Mines Ltd.	AEM
Alimentation Couche-Tard Inc. Class B	ATD.B
ARC Resources Ltd.	ARX
Barrick Gold Corporation	ABX
BlackBerry Limited	BB
Bombardier Inc. Class B	BBD.B
BCE Inc.	BCE
Bank of Montreal	BMO
Bank of Nova Scotia	BNS
Brookfield Asset Management Inc. Class A	BAM.A
Cameco Corporation	CCO
Canadian Imperial Bank of Commerce	CM
Canadian Natural Resources Limited	CNQ
Canadian National Railway Company	CNR
Canadian Pacific Railway Limited	CP
Crescent Point Energy Corp.	CPG
Canadian Tire Corporation, Limited	CTC.A
CCL Industries Inc. Unlimited Class B	CCL.B
Cenovus Energy Inc.	CVE
CGI Group Inc. Class A	GIB.A
Constellation Software Inc.	CSU
Dollarama Inc.	DOL
Emera Incorporated	EMA
Encana Corporation	ECA
Enbridge Inc.	ENB
First Quantum Minerals Ltd.	FM
Fortis Inc.	FTS

Franco-Nevada Corporation	FNV
George Weston Limited	WN
Gildan Activewear Inc.	GIL
Husky Energy Inc.	HSE
Imperial Oil Limited	IMO
Inter Pipeline Ltd.	IPL
Kinross Gold Corporation	K
Loblaw Companies Limited	L
Manulife Financial Corporation	MFC
Magna International Inc.	MG
Metro Inc.	MRU
National Bank of Canada	NA
Nutrien Ltd.	NTR
Open Text Corporation	OTEX
Pembina Pipeline Corporation	PPL
Power Corporation of Canada	POW
Restaurant Brands International Inc.	QSR
Rogers Communications Inc.	RCI.B
Royal Bank of Canada	RY
Saputo Inc.	SAP
Shaw Communications Inc. Class B	SJR.B
Sun Life Financial Inc.	SLF
SNC-Lavalin Group Inc.	SNC
Suncor Energy Inc.	SU
TELUS Corporation	T
Teck Resources Limited	TCK.B
Toronto-Dominion Bank	TD
Thomson Reuters Corporation	TRI
TransCanada Corporation	TRP

(continued)

(continued)

Valeant Pharmaceuticals International, Inc.	VRX
George Weston Limited	WN
Waste Connections Inc.	WCN
Wheaton Precious Metals Corp.	WPM
Yamana Gold Inc.	AUY

Even though the S&P/TSX 60 Index contains the "big guns" as its constituent companies, it's the S&P/TSX Composite Index that's the headline benchmark Canadian index, and the one you hear on the radio about the most. It represents about 70 percent of the total market capitalization on the Toronto Stock Exchange (TSX) with about 250 companies out of the total 1,500 companies that make up the Toronto Stock Exchange. (We discuss stock exchanges shortly, in the "Looking to Stock Exchanges for Answers" section of Chapter 6.)

2

Before You Jump In

Obtain investment information and apply it to your investments

See what brokers do, how they can help you, and how to choose them.

Understand growth stocks, small caps, and other speculative investments.

Know the fundamentals of income stocks.

Find out about technical analysis and use trends and charts in your investing decisions.

IN THIS CHAPTER

» Using Canadian and other stock exchanges to get investment information

» Applying accounting and economic know-how to your investments

» Keeping up with financial news

» Deciphering stock tables and interpreting dividend news

» Recognizing good (and bad) investing advice

Chapter **6**

Gathering Information

K nowledge and information are two critical success factors in stock investing. (Isn't that true about most things in life?) Canadians who plunge head-
long into stocks without sufficient knowledge of the stock market in general,
and current information in particular, quickly learn the lesson of the eager diver
who didn't find out ahead of time that the pool was only an inch deep (ouch!). In
their haste not to miss so-called golden investment opportunities, investors too
often end up losing money.

REMEMBER

Opportunities to *make* money in the stock market will always be there, no matter
how well or how poorly the Canadian and world economies are performing in
general. There's no such thing as a single (and fleeting) magical moment, so don't
feel that if you let an opportunity pass you by, you'll always regret that you missed
your one big chance.

For the best approach to stock investing, build your knowledge and find quality
information first so you can make your fortune more assuredly. Before you buy,
you need to know that the company you're investing in is

>> Financially sound and growing

>> Offering products and services that are in demand by consumers

>> In a strong and growing industry (and general economy)

Where do you start, and what kind of information do you want to acquire? Keep reading.

Looking to Stock Exchanges for Answers

Before you invest in stocks, you need to be completely familiar with the basics of stock investing. At its most fundamental, stock investing is about using your money to buy a piece of a company that will give you value in the form of appreciation or income (or both). Fortunately, many resources are available to help you find out about stock investing. Some of our favourite places are the websites of stock exchanges themselves.

Stock exchanges are organized marketplaces for the buying and selling of stocks (and other securities). The New York Stock Exchange (NYSE), Nasdaq, and the Toronto Stock Exchange (TSX) are the premier North American stock exchanges. They provide a framework for stock buyers and sellers to make their transactions. The Toronto and New York exchanges, like all others, make money not only from a cut of every transaction but also from fees (such as listing fees) charged to companies and brokers that are members of their exchanges.

REMEMBER

The Toronto Stock Exchange, often referred to as the TSX, is one of the world's larger stock exchanges by market capitalization. It offers a range of businesses from Canada and abroad. The TSX, like the NYSE and Nasdaq, offers a wealth of free (or low-cost) resources and information on its websites for all stock investors.

There are peripheral exchanges to be mindful of as well. Formerly known as the American Stock Exchange, NYSE American is an exchange designed for growing companies. In Canada, other exchanges you may see in some newspaper business sections or online include the following:

>> **TSX Venture Exchange:** This is a public venture capital stock market for emerging innovative companies that are not yet big enough to be listed on larger exchanges like the TSX.

>> **Canadian Securities Exchange (CSE):** Considered to be an alternative stock exchange for entrepreneurs, it is an option for companies looking to access Canadian capital markets. The CSE lists hundreds of micro-cap equities, government bonds, and other financial instruments.

>> **Montreal Exchange (MX):** The MX is low profile in that it's a derivatives exchange — a place to trade futures contracts and options.

>> **NASDAQ Canada:** This is a subsidiary of the NASDAQ Stock Market in the U.S. Its purpose is to ensure Canadian investors quick availability of all key information of all Nasdaq securities and the ability for companies to raise capital more efficiently.

>> **Aequitas NEO Exchange:** The NEO Exchange, or NEO, aims to help companies and investors by creating a better trading and listing experience (for example, with free stock quotes and faster listing times).

REMEMBER

On the U.S. side, the Dow Jones Industrial Average (DJIA) is the most widely watched index worldwide (although technically it's not an index, it's still used as one). It tracks 30 widely owned, large cap stocks, and it's occasionally rebalanced to drop (and replace) a stock that's not keeping up. The Nasdaq Composite Index covers a cross-section of stocks from Nasdaq. It's generally considered a mix of stocks that are high-growth (riskier) companies with an over-representation of technology stocks. The S&P 500 Index tracks 500 leading, publicly traded companies considered to be widely held.

Go to the NYSE, Nasdaq, and TSX websites to find useful resources such as these:

>> Tutorials on how to invest in stocks, common investment strategies, and so on

>> Glossaries and free information to help you understand the language, practice, and purpose of stock investing

>> A wealth of news, press releases, financial data, and other information about companies listed on the exchange or market, usually accessed through an on-site search engine

>> Industry analysis and Canadian and foreign news

>> Stock quotes and other market information related to the daily market movements of Canadian and other stocks, including data such as volume, new highs, new lows, and so on

>> Free tracking of your stock selections (you can input a sample portfolio or the stocks you're following to see how well you're doing)

TIP

What each exchange/market offers keeps changing and is often updated, so explore them periodically at their respective websites:

>> **Nasdaq:** www.nasdaq.com

>> **New York Stock Exchange:** www.nyse.com

>> **Toronto Stock Exchange:** www.tmx.com

Recently, the federal and provincial governments have been planning to create a national securities regulator, like the Securities and Exchange Commission in the U.S. (despite trying and failing to do this in the past). The objective is to create a single Canadian securities watchdog, rather than have a dozen or so separate securities regulators in the provinces and territories. Stay tuned to the resources we mention in this chapter for further developments.

Grasping the Basics of Accounting and Economics

Stocks represent ownership in companies. Before you buy individual stocks, you want to understand the companies whose stock you're considering and find out about their operations. It may sound like a daunting task, but you'll digest the point more easily when you realize that companies work very similarly to the way you work. They make decisions on a daily basis just like you.

Think about how you grow and prosper as an individual or family, and you see the same issues with businesses and how they grow and prosper. Low earnings and high debt are examples of financial difficulties that can affect both people and companies. You can better understand companies' finances by taking the time to pick up some information in two basic disciplines: accounting and economics. These two disciplines, discussed in the following sections, play a significant role in understanding the performance of a firm's stock.

Accounting for taste and a whole lot more

Accounting. Ugh! But face it: Accounting is the language of business, and believe it or not, you're already familiar with the most important accounting concepts! Just look at the following three essential principles:

>> **Assets minus liabilities equals net worth.** In other words, take what you own (your *assets*), subtract what you owe (your *liabilities*), and the rest is yours (your *net worth*)! Your own personal finances work the same way as Microsoft's (except yours have fewer zeros at the end). Refer to Chapter 2 to figure out how to calculate your own net worth.

A company's balance sheet shows you its net worth at a specific point in time (such as December 31). The net worth of a company is the bottom line of its asset and liability picture, and it tells you whether the company is *solvent* (has the ability to pay its debts without going out of business). The net worth of a successful company grows regularly. To see whether your company is successful, compare its net worth with the net worth from the same point a year earlier. A firm that had a $4 million net worth last year and has a $5 million net worth this year is doing well; its net worth has gone up 25 percent ($1 million) in one year.

» **Income minus expenses equals net income.** In other words, take what you make (your income), subtract what you spend (your expenses), and the remainder is your *net income* (or *net profit* or *net earnings* — your gain).

A company's profitability is the whole point of investing in its stock. As it profits, the business becomes more valuable, and in turn, its stock price becomes more valuable. To discover a firm's net income, look at its income statement. Try to determine whether the company uses its gains wisely, either by reinvesting them for continued growth or by paying down debt.

» **Do a comparative financial analysis.** That's a mouthful, but it's just a fancy way of saying how a company is doing now compared with something else (like a prior period or a similar company).

If you know that the company you're looking at had a net income of $50,000 for the year, you may ask, "Is that good or bad?" Obviously, making a net profit is good, but you also need to know whether it's good compared to something else. If the company had a net profit of $40,000 the year before, you know that the company's profitability is improving. But if a similar company had a net profit of $100,000 the year before and in the current year is making $50,000, then you may want to either avoid the company making the lesser profit or see what (if anything) went wrong with the company making less.

Accounting can be this simple. If you understand these three basic points, you're ahead of the curve (in stock investing as well as in your personal finances). For more information on how to use a company's financial statements and reports to pick good stocks, see Chapters 11 and 12.

Understanding how economics affects stocks

Economics. Double ugh! No, you aren't required to understand "the inelasticity of demand aggregates" (thank heavens!) or "marginal utility" (say what?). But having a working knowledge of basic economics is crucial (and we mean crucial) to your success and proficiency as a stock investor. The stock market and the economy are joined at the hip. The good (or bad) things that happen to one have a direct effect on the other. The following sections give you the lowdown.

Getting the hang of the basic concepts

REMEMBER

Alas, many Canadian investors get lost on basic economic concepts (as do some so-called experts that you see on TV). We owe our personal investing successes to our status as students of economics. Understanding basic economics helps us (and will help you) filter the financial news to separate relevant information from the irrelevant in order to make better investment decisions. Be aware of these important economic concepts:

>> **Supply and demand:** How can anyone possibly think about economics without thinking of the ageless concept of supply and demand? *Supply and demand* can be simply stated as the relationship between what's available (the supply) and what people want and are willing to pay for (the demand). This equation is the main engine of economic activity and is extremely important for your stock investing analysis and decision making process. Do you really want to buy stock in a company that makes elephant-foot umbrella stands if you find out that the company has an oversupply and nobody wants to buy them anyway?

>> **Cause and effect:** If you pick up a prominent news report and read, "Companies in the table industry are expecting plummeting sales," do you rush out and invest in companies that sell chairs or manufacture tablecloths? Considering cause and effect is an exercise in logical thinking, and believe us, logic is a major component of sound economic thought.

When you read Canadian and U.S. business news, play it out in your mind. What good (or bad) can logically be expected given a certain event or situation? If you're looking for an effect ("I want a stock price that keeps increasing"), you also want to understand the cause. Here are some typical events that can cause a stock's price to rise:

- **Positive news reports about a company:** The news may report that the company is enjoying success with increased sales or a new product. Blackberry's introduction of new security software services to underserved or new markets like autonomous cars is a perfect example of how news can move the price of a stock one way or another.

- **Positive news reports about a company's industry:** The media may be highlighting that the industry is poised to do well.

- **Positive news reports about a company's customers:** Maybe your company is in industry A, but its customers are in industry B. If you see good news about industry B, that may be good news for your stock.

- **Negative news reports about a company's competitors:** If the competitors are in trouble — say, due to their deficient customer service and poor overall reputation — their customers may seek alternatives to buy from, including your company.

>> **Economic effects from government actions:** Political and governmental actions have economic consequences. As a matter of fact, nothing (and we mean nothing!) has a greater effect on investing and economics than government. Government actions usually manifest themselves as taxes, laws, or regulations. They also can take on a more ominous appearance, such as war or the threat of war. Government can willfully (or even accidentally) cause a company to go bankrupt, disrupt an entire industry, or even cause a depression. Government controls the money supply, credit, and all public securities markets. For more information on political effects, see Chapter 15.

Gaining insight from past mistakes

Because most investors ignored some basic observations about economics during the Great Recession, they subsequently lost trillions in their stock portfolios during 2008–2009. Even today, the U.S. and Canada are experiencing the greatest expansion of total debt in history, coupled with a record expansion of their respective money supplies. To be sure, part of this government behavior has fueled the recent bull market. But our question to you is when will this "fun" stop? We try to help you answer this.

Of course, you should always be happy to earn double-digit annual returns with your investments, but such a return can't be sustained and encourages speculation. This artificial stimulation by the Fed, and to a certain extent by the Bank of Canada, resulted and continues to result in the following:

>> More and more people depleted their savings. After all, why settle for 1–3 percent in a Canadian chartered bank when you can get 20 percent in the stock market?

>> More and more Canadians bought on credit. If the economy is booming, why not buy now and pay later? Canadian consumer credit recently hit record per capita highs.

>> More and more Canadians borrowed against their homes. Why not borrow and get rich now? "I can pay off my debt later" was at the forefront of these folks' minds at the time.

>> More and more companies sold more goods as consumers took more vacations and bought SUVs, electronics, and so on. Companies then borrowed to finance expansion, open new stores, and so on.

>> More and more Canadians made lower and lower down payments, simply because they could. "Why shouldn't I own a house too?" they asked. The risk profile of Canadian homeowners got so bad that recently the Canada Mortgage and Housing Corporation imposed a minimum percentage down payment limit before it would write any new mortgages.

>> More and more companies went public and offered stock to take advantage of the increase in money that was flowing to the markets from banks and other financial institutions.

In summary, the economic cycle as it relates to stocks goes something like this: North American spending starts to slow down because consumers and businesses become too indebted. This slowdown in turn causes the sales of goods and services to taper off. Companies are left with too much overhead, capacity, and debt because they expanded too quickly. At this point, businesses get caught in a financial bind. Too much debt and too many expenses in a slowing economy mean one thing: Profits shrink or disappear. To stay in business, companies have to do the logical thing — cut expenses. What's usually the biggest expense for companies? People! Many companies start laying off employees. As a result, consumer spending drops further because more people were either laid off or had second thoughts about their own job security.

Because people had little in the way of savings and too much in the way of debt, they had to sell their stock to pay their bills. Stocks drop. This rinse and repeat trend is one major reason that stocks can fall for an extended period.

The lessons from years past are important ones for investors today:

>> Stocks aren't a replacement for savings accounts or GICs. Always have some money in the bank.

>> Stocks should never occupy 100 percent of your investment funds.

>> When anyone (including an expert) tells you that the economy will keep growing indefinitely, be skeptical and read diverse sources of information.

>> If stocks do well in your portfolio, consider protecting your stocks (both your original investment and any gains) with stop-loss orders. (See Chapter 17 for more on these strategies.)

>> Keep debt and expenses to a minimum.

>> If the U.S. and Canadian economy is booming, a decline is sure to follow as the ebb and flow of the economy's business cycle continues.

At the time of this writing, the U.S. is grappling with the double-edged sword of debt ceiling and fiscal cliff talks in Congress. In fact, the world economies, including the eurozone economies, continue to struggle. In the U.K., the situation is so dire that the British hired Canada's own Bank of Canada Governor Mark Carney away from us so that he could help fix the U.K. economy! Then it was hit with Brexit, and even more uncertainty ensued.

Staying on Top of Financial News

Reading the financial news can help you decide where or where not to invest. Many newspapers, magazines, and websites offer great coverage of the financial world. Obviously, the more informed you are, the better, but you don't have to read everything that's written. The information explosion in recent years has gone beyond overload, and you can easily spend so much time reading that you have little time left for investing. In the following sections, we describe the types of information you need to get from the financial news.

The most obvious publications of interest to stock investors are the two Canadian national dailies — the *National Post* (www.nationalpost.com) and *The Globe and Mail* (www.theglobeandmail.com). Other useful publications include *The Wall Street Journal* and *Investor's Business Daily*, U.S. newspapers that also cover world financial news. These leading publications report the news and stock data on a regular basis. Some other leading websites are CBS's MarketWatch (www.marketwatch.com) and Bloomberg (www.bloomberg.com), which include Canadian company news and information. The websites of all of these information providers can also give you news and stock data within minutes of a transaction.

TIP

Appendix A of this book provides more information on stock investing and related resources, along with a treasure trove of some of the best publications and websites to assist you.

KNOW THYSELF BEFORE YOU INVEST IN STOCKS

If you're reading this book, you're probably doing so because you want to become a successful investor. Granted, to be a successful investor, you have to select great stocks, but having a realistic understanding of your own financial situation and goals is equally important. We recall one investor who lost $10,000 in a speculative Canadian resource stock. The loss wasn't that bad because he had most of his money safely tucked away elsewhere. He also understood that his overall financial situation was secure and that the money he lost was "play" money — the loss wouldn't have a drastic effect on his life. But many investors often lose even more money, and the loss does have a major, negative effect on their lives. You may not be like the investor who can afford to lose $10,000. Take time to understand yourself, your own financial picture, and your personal investment goals before you decide to buy stocks. Refer to Chapter 2 for guidance.

Figuring out what a company's up to

REMEMBER

Before you invest, you need to know what's going on with the company. When you read about a company, either in the firm's literature (its annual report, for example) or in media sources, be sure to get answers to some pertinent questions:

>> **Is the company making more net income than it did last year?** You want to invest in a company that's growing, with sustainable cashflows.

>> **Are the company's sales greater than they were the year before?** Keep in mind that you won't make money if the company isn't making money.

>> **Is the company issuing press releases on new products, services, inventions, or business deals?** All these achievements indicate a strong, vital company.

Knowing how the company is doing, no matter what's happening with the Canadian, U.S., or world economy, is obviously important. To better understand how companies tick, and to identify their strengths and weaknesses, see Chapters 11 and 12.

Discovering what's new with an industry

As you consider investing in a stock, make a point of knowing what's going on in that company's industry. If the industry is doing well, your stock is likely to do well, too. But then again, the reverse is also true.

Yes, we've seen investors pick successful stocks in a failing industry, but those cases are exceptional. By and large, succeeding with a stock is easier when the entire industry is doing well. As you're watching the news, reading the financial pages, or viewing financial websites, check out the industry to ensure that it's strong and dynamic. See Chapter 13 for information on analyzing existing and emerging sectors and industries.

Knowing what's happening with the economy

No matter how well or how poorly the overall economy is performing, you want to stay informed about its general progress. It's easier for the value of stock to keep going up when the economy is stable or growing. The reverse is also true: If the economy is contracting or declining, the stock has a tougher time keeping its value. Here are some basic items to keep tabs on:

>> **Gross domestic product (GDP):** The GDP is roughly the total value of output for a particular nation, measured in the dollar amount of goods and services. It's reported quarterly, and a rising GDP bodes well for your stock. When the GDP is rising 3 percent or more on an annual basis, that's solid growth. If it rises but is less than 3 percent, that's generally considered less than stellar (or mediocre). A GDP under zero (a negative number) means that the economy is shrinking (heading into recession).

>> **The index of leading economic indicators (LEI):** The LEI is a snapshot of a set of economic statistics covering activity that precedes what's happening in the economy. Each statistic helps you understand the economy in much the same way that barometers (and windows!) help you understand what's happening with the weather. Economists don't just look at an individual statistic; they look at a set of statistics to get a more complete picture of what's happening with the economy.

Chapter 15 goes into greater detail on economics and its effect on stock prices.

Seeing what politicians and government bureaucrats are doing

Being informed about what public officials are doing is vital to your success as a stock investor. Because federal, provincial, and local governments pass literally thousands of laws, rules, and regulations every year, monitoring the political landscape is critical to your success. The news media report what the prime minister and Parliament are doing, so always ask yourself, "How does a new law, tax, trade treaty like NAFTA, or regulation affect my stock investment?"

TIP

Some great organizations inform the Canadian public about tax laws and their impact, such as the Canadian Taxpayers Federation (www.taxpayer.com). Laws being proposed or enacted by the U.S. federal government can be found through the Thomas legislative search engine, which is run by the Library of Congress (www.loc.gov).

Checking for trends in society, culture, and entertainment

As odd as it sounds, trends in society, popular culture, and entertainment affect your investments, directly or indirectly. For example, a CTV or *Maclean's* headline such as "The Greying of Canada — More People Than Ever Before Will Be Senior Citizens" gives you some important information that can make or break your stock portfolio. With that particular headline, you know that as more and more people age, companies that are well positioned to cater to that growing market's wants and needs will do well — meaning a successful stock for you.

Keep your eyes open for emerging trends in society at large by reading and viewing the media that cover such matters (*Time* magazine, CNN, Business News Network (BNN), and so on). What trends are evident now? Can you anticipate the wants and needs of tomorrow's society? Being alert, staying a step ahead of the public, and choosing stocks appropriately gives you a profitable edge over other investors. If you own stock in a solid company with growing sales and earnings, other investors eventually notice. As more investors buy up your company's stocks, you're rewarded as the stock price increases.

Reading and Understanding Stock Tables

The stock tables in major business publications such as *The Wall Street Journal* and *Investor's Business Daily* are loaded with information that can help you become a savvy investor — *if* you know how to interpret them. You need the information in the stock tables for more than selecting promising investment opportunities. You also need to consult the tables after you invest to monitor how your stocks are doing. The *National Post* (www.nationalpost.com) and *The Globe and Mail* (www.theglobeandmail.com) also produce stock tables for a selection of mostly Canadian equities in their print editions. As well, they let you check just about any stock (U.S. or Canadian) in their online editions.

Looking at the stock tables without knowing what you're looking for or why you're looking is the equivalent of reading *War and Peace* backwards through a kaleidoscope — nothing makes sense. But we can help you make sense of it all (well, at least the stock tables). Table 6-1 shows a sample stock table. Each item gives you some clues about the current state of affairs for that particular company. The sections that follow describe each column to help you understand what you're looking at.

TABLE 6-1 **A Sample Stock Table**

52-Wk High	52-Wk Low	Name (Symbol)	Div	Vol	Yld	P/E	Day Last	Net Chg
21.50	8.00	SkyHighCorp (SHC)		3,143		76	21.25	+0.25
47.00	31.75	LowDownInc (LDI)	2.35	2,735	5.9	18	41.00	−0.50
25.00	21.00	ValueNowInc (VNI)	1.00	1,894	4.5	12	22.00	+0.10
83.00	33.00	DoinBadly Corp (DBC)		7,601			33.50	−0.75

Every newspaper's financial tables are a little different, but they give you basically the same information. Updated daily, these tables aren't the place to start your search for a good stock; they're usually where your search ends. The stock tables are the place to look when you own, or are about to own, a stock or know what you want to buy, or possibly sell, and you're just checking to see the most recent price.

52-week high

The column in Table 6-1 labelled "52-Wk High" gives you the highest price that particular stock has reached in the most recent 52-week period. Knowing this price lets you gauge where the stock is now versus where it has been recently. SkyHighCorp's (SHC) stock has been as high as $21.50, whereas its last (most recent) price is $21.25, the number listed in the "Day Last" column. (Flip to the later section "Day last" for more on understanding this information.) SkyHigh-Corp's stock is trading very high right now because it's hovering near its overall 52-week high figure.

Now, take a look at DoinBadlyCorp's (DBC) stock price. It seems to have tumbled big time. Its stock price has had a high in the past 52 weeks of $83, but it's currently trading at $33.50. Something just doesn't seem right here. During the past 52 weeks, DBC's stock price has fallen dramatically. If you're thinking about investing in DBC, find out why the stock price has fallen. If the company is strong, it may be a good opportunity to buy stock at a lower price. If the company is having tough times, avoid it. In any case, research the firm and find out why its stock has declined. (Chapters 11 and 12 provide the basics of researching companies.)

52-week low

The column labelled "52-Wk Low" gives you the lowest price that particular stock reached in the most recent 52-week period. Again, this information is crucial to your ability to analyze stock over a period of time. Look at DBC in Table 6-1, and you can see that its current trading price of $33.50 in the Day Last column is close to its 52-week low of $33.

Keep in mind that the high and low prices just give you a range of how far that particular stock's price has moved within the past 52 weeks. They can alert you that a stock has problems, or they can tell you that a stock's price has fallen enough to make it a bargain. Simply reading the 52-Wk High and 52-Wk Low columns isn't enough to determine which of those two scenarios is happening. They basically tell you to get more information before you commit your money.

Name and symbol

The "Name (Symbol)" column is the simplest in Table 6-1. It tells you the company name (usually abbreviated) and the stock symbol assigned to the company.

TIP

When you have your eye on a Canadian or other stock for potential purchase, get familiar with its symbol. Knowing the symbol makes it easier for you to find your stock in the financial tables, which list stocks in alphabetical order by the company's name (or symbol, depending on the source). Stock symbols are part of the language of stock investing, and you need to use them in all stock communications, from getting a stock quote at your broker's office to buying stock over the Internet.

Dividend

Dividends (shown under the "Div" column in Table 6-1) are basically payments to owners (stockholders). If a company pays a dividend, it's shown in the dividend column. The amount you see is the annual dividend quoted for one share of that stock. If you look at LowDownInc (LDI) in Table 6-1, you can see that you get $2.35 as an annual dividend for each share of stock that you own. Companies usually pay the dividend in quarterly amounts. If you own 100 shares of LDI, the company pays you a quarterly dividend of $58.75 ($235 total per year). A healthy company strives to maintain or upgrade the dividend for stockholders from year to year. (We discuss additional dividend details later in this chapter.)

The dividend is very important to investors seeking income from their stock investments. For more about investing for income, see Chapter 9. Investors buy stocks in companies that don't pay dividends primarily for growth. For more information on growth stocks, see Chapter 8.

Volume

Normally, when you hear the word "volume" on the news, it refers to how much stock is bought and sold for the entire market: "Well, stocks were very active today. Trading volume at the New York Stock Exchange hit 2 billion shares." Volume is certainly important to watch because the stocks that you're investing in are somewhere in that activity. For the "Vol" column in Table 6-1, though, the volume refers to the individual stock.

Volume tells you how many shares of that particular stock were traded that day. If only 100 shares are traded in a day, then the trading volume is 100. SHC had 3,143 shares change hands on the trading day represented in Table 6-1. Is that good or bad? Neither, really. Usually the business news media mention volume for a particular stock only when it's unusually large. If a stock normally has volume in the 5,000 to 10,000 range and all of a sudden has a trading volume of 87,000, then it's time to sit up and take notice.

REMEMBER

Keep in mind that a low trading volume for one stock may be a high trading volume for another stock. You can't necessarily compare one stock's volume against that of any other company. The large cap stocks like IBM or Microsoft typically have trading volumes in the millions of shares almost every day, whereas less active, smaller stocks may have average trading volumes in far, far smaller numbers.

The main point to remember is that trading volume that is far in excess of that stock's normal range is a sign that something is going on with that stock. It may be negative or positive, but something newsworthy is happening with that company. If the news is positive, the increased volume is a result of more people buying the stock. If the news is negative, the increased volume is probably a result of more people selling the stock. What are typical events that cause increased trading volume? Some positive reasons include the following:

>> **Good earnings reports:** The company announces good (or better-than-expected) earnings.

>> **A new business deal:** The firm announces a favourable business deal, such as a joint venture, or lands a big client.

>> **A new product, service, or discovery:** The company's research and development department creates a potentially profitable new product, or the company finds something new and of value, such as oil reserves in a northern territory.

>> **Indirect benefits:** The business may benefit from a new development in the economy, or from a new law passed by Parliament.

Some negative reasons for an unusually large fluctuation in trading volume for a particular stock include the following:

>> **Bad earnings reports:** Profit is the lifeblood of a company. When its profits fall or disappear, you see more volume.

>> **Governmental problems:** The stock is being targeted by government action, such as a lawsuit or an Ontario Securities Commission (OSC) probe.

>> **Liability issues:** The media report that the company has a defective product or similar problem.

>> **Financial problems:** Independent analysts report that the company's financial health or cashflow is deteriorating.

REMEMBER

Check out what's happening when you hear about heavier-than-usual volume (especially if you already own the stock).

Yield

In general, yield is a return on the money you invest. However, in the stock tables, *yield* ("Yld" in Table 6-1) is a reference to what percentage that particular dividend is of the stock price. Yield is most important to income investors. It's calculated by dividing the annual dividend by the current stock price. In Table 6-1, you can see that the yield du jour of ValueNowInc (VNI) is 4.5 percent (a dividend of $1 divided by the company's stock price of $22). Notice that many companies report no yield; because they have no dividends, their yield is zero.

REMEMBER

Keep in mind that the yield reported in the financial pages changes daily as the stock price changes. Yield is always reported as if you're buying the stock that day. If you buy VNI on the day represented in Table 6-1, your yield is 4.5 percent. But what if VNI's stock price rises to $30 the following day? Investors who buy stock at $30 per share obtain a yield of just 3.3 percent (the dividend of $1 divided by the new stock price, $30). Of course, because you bought the stock at $22, you essentially locked in the prior yield of 4.5 percent. Lucky you. Pat yourself on the back.

P/E

REMEMBER

The *P/E ratio* is the ratio between the price of the stock and the company's earnings. P/E ratios are widely followed and are important barometers of value in the world of stock investing. The P/E ratio (also called the *earnings multiple* or just *multiple*) is frequently used to determine whether a stock is expensive (a good value). Value investors find P/E ratios to be essential to analyzing a stock as a potential investment. As a general rule, the P/E should be 10 to 20 for large cap or income stocks. For growth stocks, a greater P/E is generally preferable. (See Chapter 11 and Appendix B for full details on P/E ratios.)

In the P/E ratios reported in stock tables, *price* refers to the cost of a single share of stock. *Earnings* refers to the company's reported earnings per share as of the most recent four quarters. The P/E ratio is the price divided by the earnings. In Table 6-1, VNI has a reported P/E of 12, which is considered a low P/E. Notice how SHC has a relatively high P/E (76). This stock is considered too pricey because you're paying a price equivalent to 76 times earnings. Also notice that DBC has no available P/E ratio. Usually this lack of a P/E ratio indicates that the company reported a loss in the most recent four quarters.

Day last

The "Day Last" column tells you how trading ended for a particular stock on the day represented by the table. In Table 6-1, LDI ended the most recent day of trading at $41. Some Canadian newspapers report the high and low for that day in addition to the stock's ending price for the day.

Net change

The information in the "Net Chg" column answers the question, "How did the stock price end today compared with its price at the end of the prior trading day?" Table 6-1 shows that SHC stock ended the trading day up 25 cents (at $21.25). This column tells you that SHC ended the prior day at $21. VNI ended the day at $22 (up 10 cents), so you can tell that the prior trading day it ended at $21.90.

Using News about Dividends

Reading and understanding the news about dividends is essential if you're an *income investor* (someone who invests in stocks as a means of generating regular income; see Chapter 9 for details). The following sections explain some basics you should know about dividends.

TIP

You can find news and information on dividends in newspapers such as *The Wall Street Journal*, *Investor's Business Daily*, and *Barron's* (you can find their websites online with your favourite search engine, or just check out Appendix A).

Looking at important dates

REMEMBER

In order to understand how buying stocks that pay dividends can benefit you as an investor, you need to know how companies report and pay dividends. Some important dates in the life of a dividend are as follows:

>> **Date of declaration:** This is the date when a company reports a quarterly dividend and the subsequent payment dates. On January 15, for example, a company may report that it "is pleased to announce a quarterly dividend of 50 cents per share to shareholders of record as of February 10." That was easy. The date of declaration is really just the announcement date. Whether you buy the stock before, on, or after the date of declaration doesn't matter in regard to receiving the stock's quarterly dividend (but it will affect your purchase price). The date that matters is the date of record (see that bullet later in this list).

>> **Date of execution:** This is the day you actually initiate the stock transaction (buying or selling). If you call a broker (or contact her online) today to buy a particular stock, then today is the date of execution, or the date on which you execute the trade. You don't own the stock on the date of execution; it's just the day you put in the order. For an example, skip to the following section.

>> **Closing date (settlement date):** This is the date on which the trade is finalized, which usually happens three business days after the date of execution. The closing date for stock is similar in concept to a real estate closing. On the closing date, you're officially the proud new owner (or happy seller) of the stock.

>> **Ex-dividend date:** *Ex-dividend* means *without dividend*. Because it takes three days to process a stock purchase before you become an official owner of the stock, you have to qualify (that is, you have to own or buy the stock) *before* the three-day period. That three-day period is referred to as the "ex-dividend period." When you buy stock during this short time frame, you aren't on the books of record, because the closing (or settlement) date falls after the date of record. See the next section to see the effect that the ex-dividend date can have on an investor.

>> **Date of record:** This is used to identify which stockholders qualify to receive the declared dividend. Because stock is bought and sold every day, how does the company know which investors to pay? The company establishes a cutoff date by declaring a date of record. All investors who are official stockholders as of the declared date of record receive the dividend on the payment date, even if they plan to sell the stock any time between the date of declaration and the date of record.

>> **Payment date:** The date on which a company issues and mails its dividend cheques to shareholders. Finally!

For typical dividends, the events in Table 6-2 happen four times per year.

TABLE 6-2 The Life of the Quarterly Dividend

Event	Sample Date	Comments
Date of declaration	January 15	The date that the company declares the quarterly dividend
Ex-dividend date	February 7	Starts the three-day period during which, if you buy the stock, you don't qualify for the dividend
Date of record	February 10	The date by which you must be on the books of record to qualify for the dividend
Payment date	February 27	The date that payment is made (a dividend cheque is issued and mailed to stockholders who were on the books of record as of February 10)

Understanding why certain dates matter

Three business days pass between the date of execution and the closing date. Three business days also pass between the ex-dividend date and the date of record. This information is important to know if you want to qualify to receive an upcoming dividend. Timing is important, and if you understand these dates, you know when to purchase stock and whether you qualify for a dividend.

As an example, say that you want to buy ValueNowInc (VNI) in time to qualify for the quarterly dividend of 25 cents per share. Assume that the date of record (the date by which you have to be an official owner of the stock) is February 10. You have to execute the trade (buy the stock) no later than February 7 to be assured of the dividend. If you execute the trade right on February 7, the closing date occurs three days later, on February 10 — just in time for the date of record.

But what if you execute the trade on February 8, a day later? Well, the trade's closing date is February 11, which occurs *after* the date of record. Because you aren't on the books as an official stockholder on the date of record, you aren't getting that quarterly dividend. In this example, the February 7–10 period is called the *ex-dividend period*.

TIP

Fortunately, for Canadians who buy the stock during this brief ex-dividend period, the stock actually trades at a slightly lower price to reflect the amount of the dividend. If you can't get the dividend, you may as well save on the stock purchase. How's that for a silver lining?

Evaluating or Ignoring Investment Tips

Psssst. Have we got a stock tip for you! Come closer. You know what it is? Research! What we're trying to tell you is to never automatically invest just because you get a hot tip from someone. Good investment selection means looking at several sources before you decide on a stock. No shortcut exists. That said, getting opinions from others never hurts — just be sure to carefully analyze the information you get. Here are some important points to bear in mind as you evaluate tips and advice from others:

>> **Consider the source.** Frequently, people buy stock based on the views of some market strategist or analyst. People may see an analyst being interviewed on a television financial show and take that person's opinions and advice as valid and good. The danger here is that the analyst may be biased because of some relationship that isn't disclosed on the show.

WARNING

It happens on TV all too often. The show's host interviews analyst U.R. Kiddingme from the investment firm Foollum&Sellum. The analyst says, "Implosion Corp. is a good buy with solid, long-term upside potential." You later find out that the analyst's employer gets investment banking fees from Implosion Corp. Do you really think that analyst would ever issue a negative report on a company that's helping to pay the bills? It's not likely. Don't trust analyst recommendations. Just use them as one of several data points that inform your investment decisions.

» **Get multiple views.** Don't base your investment decisions on just one source unless you have the best reasons in the world for thinking that a particular, single source is outstanding and reliable. A better approach is to scour current issues of independent financial publications, such as *Barron's, Canadian Business, MoneySense,* and other publications (and websites) listed in Appendix A.

IN THIS CHAPTER

» **Finding out what brokers do**

» **Comparing full-service and discount brokers**

» **Selecting a broker**

» **Exploring the types of brokerage accounts**

» **Evaluating the recommendations of brokers**

» **Evaluating robo-advisors**

Chapter **7**

Going for Brokers

W hen you're ready to dive in and start investing in stocks, you first have to choose a broker. It's kind of like buying a car: You can do all the research in the world and know exactly what kind of car you want, but you still need a venue to conduct the actual transaction. Similarly, when you want to buy stock, your task is to do all the research you can to select the company you want to invest in. Still, you need a Canadian — yes, it has to be a Canadian — broker to actually buy the stock, whether over the phone or online. In this chapter, we introduce you to the intricacies of the investor/broker relationship.

For information on various types of orders you can place with a broker, such as market orders, stop-loss orders, and so on, flip to Chapter 17. To see how the latest technology (such as trade triggers) offers some cool possibilities for today's investor, check out Chapter 18.

Defining the Broker's Role

The broker's primary role is to serve as the vehicle through which you either buy or sell stock. When we talk about brokers, we're referring to companies such as TD Waterhouse, BMO InvestorLine, and many other Canadian organizations that can buy stock on your behalf. Brokers can also be individuals who work for such firms. Although you can buy some stocks directly from the companies that issue them, to purchase most stocks, you still need a broker.

REMEMBER

The distinction between institutional stockbrokers and personal stockbrokers is important:

>> **Institutional stockbrokers** make money from institutions and companies through investment banking and securities placement fees (such as initial public offerings and secondary offerings), advisory services, and other broker services.

>> **Personal stockbrokers** generally offer the same services to individuals and small businesses.

Although the primary task of brokers is the buying and selling of securities around the world (the word securities refers to the world of financial or paper investments, and stocks are only a small part of that world), they can perform other tasks for you, including the following:

>> **Providing advisory services:** Investors pay brokers a fee for investment advice. Customers also get access to the firm's research.

>> **Offering limited banking services:** Brokers can offer features such as interest-bearing Canadian and U.S. dollar trading accounts, cheque writing, electronic deposits and withdrawals, and credit/debit cards.

>> **Brokering other securities:** In addition to stocks, brokers can buy bonds, options, exchange-traded funds (ETFs), mutual funds, and other investments on your behalf.

Personal stockbrokers make their money from individual investors like you and us through various fees, including the following:

>> **Brokerage commissions:** This fee is for buying or selling stocks and other securities.

>> **Margin interest charges:** This interest is charged to investors for borrowing against their brokerage account for investment purposes. (We discuss margin accounts in more detail later in this chapter.)

>> **Service charges:** These charges are for performing administrative tasks and other functions. Brokers charge account opening, maintenance, and other fees to investors for Registered Retirement Savings Plans (RRSPs), Registered Education Savings Plans (RESPs), and Tax-Free Savings Accounts (TFSAs).

REMEMBER

Any smaller broker (some individual brokers are now called financial or investment advisors) that you deal with should be a member in good standing of IIROC — the Investment Industry Regulatory Organization of Canada. IIROC is a self-regulatory organization that oversees all member investment dealers. It also watches out for suspicious and questionable trading activity on debt and equity markets in Canada. It sets regulatory and investment industry standards, tries to protect investors' interests, and attempts to strengthen market integrity while maintaining smoothly operating capital markets.

REMEMBER

To further protect your money after you deposit it into a brokerage account, that broker should be one of the more than 200 members of the Canadian Investor Protection Fund (CIPF). CIPF doesn't protect you from losses from market fluctuations; it protects your money, within limits, in case the brokerage firm goes out of business or if your losses are due to brokerage fraud. CIPF's coverage limit is $1 million for any combination of cash and securities. If you have both a general and a retirement account, each account qualifies for $1 million coverage.

To find out whether a broker is registered with these organizations, contact IIROC (www.iiroc.ca) and CIPF (www.cipf.ca).

Distinguishing between Full-Service and Discount Brokers

Stockbrokers fall into two basic categories, which we discuss in the following sections: full-service and discount. The type you choose really depends on what type of investor you are. Here are the differences in a nutshell:

>> **Full-service brokers** are suitable for investors who need some guidance, advice, and personal attention.

>> **Discount brokers** are better for those investors who are sufficiently confident and knowledgeable about stock investing to manage with minimal help (usually through the broker's website).

At your disposal: Full-service brokers

Full-service brokers provide two things: brokerage and advisory services. They try to provide as many services as possible for Canadians who open accounts with them. When you open an account at a brokerage firm, a representative is assigned to your account. This representative is usually called an account executive, a registered rep, or a financial advisor by the brokerage firm. This person usually has a securities licence (meaning that she's registered with IIROC and at a minimum has passed the Canadian Securities Course or an equivalent).

Examples of full-service brokers are HSBC InvestDirect (http://invest.hsbc.ca), RBC Dominion Securities (www.rbcds.com), and TD Waterhouse's (www.td.com) Private Investment Advice service. All brokers now have full-featured websites to give you information about their services. Get as informed as possible before you open your account. A full-service broker is there to help you build wealth, not make you . . . uh . . . broker.

What they can do for you

Your account executive is responsible for assisting you, answering questions about your account and the securities in your portfolio, and transacting your buy and sell orders. Here are some things full-service brokers can do for you:

>> **Offer guidance and advice:** The greatest distinction between full-service brokers and discount brokers is the personal attention you receive from your account rep. You get to be on a first-name basis with a full-service broker, and you disclose much information about your finances and financial goals. The rep is there to make recommendations about stocks and funds that are hopefully suitable for you.

>> **Provide access to research:** Full-service brokers can give you access to their investment research department, which can give you in-depth information and analysis on a particular company. This information can be very valuable, but be aware of the pitfalls. (See the section "Judging Brokers' Recommendations," later in this chapter.)

>> **Help you achieve your investment objectives:** A good rep gets to know you and your investment goals and *then* offers advice and answers your questions about how specific investments and strategies can help you accomplish your wealth-building goals.

>> **Make investment decisions on your behalf:** Many investors don't want to be bothered when it comes to investment decisions. Full-service brokers can actually make decisions for your account with your authorization (this is also referred to as a *discretionary* account). This service is fine, but be sure to require brokers to explain their choices to you.

What to watch out for

Although full-service brokers, with their seemingly limitless assistance, can make life easy for an investor, you need to remember some important points to avoid problems:

>> Brokers and account reps are salespeople. No matter how well they treat you, they're still compensated based on their ability to produce revenue for the brokerage firm. They generate commissions and fees from you on behalf of the company. (In other words, they're paid to sell you things.)

REMEMBER

>> Whenever your rep makes a suggestion or recommendation, be sure to ask why and request a complete answer that includes the reasoning behind the recommendation. A good advisor is able to clearly explain the reasoning behind every suggestion. If you don't fully understand and agree with the advice, don't take it. This is an important discipline we recommend you hone.

>> Working with a full-service broker costs more than working with a discount broker. They always charge extra for the advice. Discount brokers, on the other hand, are paid for simply buying or selling stocks for you and therefore cost less. Also, most full-service brokers expect you to invest at least $5,000 to $10,000 just to open an account, although many require higher minimums.

>> Handing over decision making authority to your rep can be a possible negative because letting others make financial decisions for you is always dicey — especially when they're using *your* money. If they make poor investment choices that lose you money, you may not have any recourse because you authorized them to act on your behalf.

WARNING

>> Some brokers engage in an activity called churning. Churning is basically buying and selling stocks for the sole purpose of generating commissions. Churning is great for brokers but really bad for customers. If your account shows a lot of activity, ask for justification. Commissions, especially by full-service brokers, can take a big bite out of your wealth, so don't tolerate churning or other suspicious activity.

Just the basics: Discount brokers

Perhaps you don't need any hand-holding from a broker (that'd be kinda weird anyway). You know what you want, and you can make your own investment decisions. All you need is a convenient way to transact your buy/sell orders. In that case, go with a discount broker. These brokers let you buy or sell stocks two ways: through the Internet or by phone (touch tone, automated voice prompt, or via a live representative). They don't offer advice or premium services — just the basics required to perform your stock transactions.

Canadian discount brokers, as the name implies, are cheaper to engage than full-service brokers. Because you're advising yourself (or getting advice and information from third parties such as newsletters, hotlines, or independent advisors), you can save on costs you'd incur if you used a full-service broker.

REMEMBER

If you choose to work with a discount broker, you must know as much as possible about your personal goals and needs. You have a greater responsibility for conducting adequate research to make good stock selections, and you must be prepared to accept the outcome, whatever that may be. (See Part 3 for details on researching stock selections.)

For a while, the regular Canadian investor had two types of discount brokers to choose from: conventional discount brokers and Internet discount brokers. But the two are basically synonymous now, so the differences are hardly worth mentioning. Through industry consolidation in Canada, most of the conventional discount brokers today have fully featured websites, while Internet discount brokers have adapted by adding more telephone and face-to-face services. There really are no more pure discount brokers left.

What they can do for you

Discount brokers offer some significant advantages over full-service brokers:

» **Lower cost:** This lower cost is usually the result of lower commissions, and it's the primary benefit of using discount brokers.

» **Unbiased service:** Because they don't offer advice, discount brokers have no vested interest in trying to sell you any particular stock.

» **Access to information:** Established discount brokers offer extensive educational materials at their offices or on their websites. In this regard, they can provide you with valuable passive advice.

What to watch out for

Of course, doing business with discount brokers also has its downsides, including the following:

» **No guidance:** Because you've chosen a discount broker, you *know* not to expect guidance, but the broker should make this fact clear to you anyway. If you're a knowledgeable investor, the lack of advice is considered a positive thing — no interference.

WARNING

» **Hidden fees:** Discount brokers may shout about their lower commissions, but commissions aren't their only way of making money. Many discount brokers charge extra for services that you may think are included, such as issuing a stock certificate or mailing a statement. Ask whether they assess fees for maintaining tax-deferred savings accounts like RRSPs or for transferring stocks and other securities (like bonds) in or out of your account, and find out what interest rates they charge for borrowing through brokerage accounts.

>> **Minimal customer service:** If you deal with an Internet brokerage firm, find out about its customer service. If you can't transact business on its website, find out where you can call for assistance with your order.

Choosing a Broker

Before you choose a broker, you need to analyze your personal investing style (as we explain in Chapter 3), and then you can proceed to finding the kind of broker that fits your needs. It's almost like choosing shoes; if you don't know your size, you can't get a proper fit (and you can be in for a really uncomfortable future).

When it's time to choose a broker, keep the following points in mind:

REMEMBER

>> Match your investment style with a brokerage firm that charges the least amount of money for the services you're likely to use most frequently.

>> Compare all the costs of buying, selling, and holding stocks and other securities through a broker. Don't compare only commissions; compare other costs, too, like margin interest and other service charges (see the earlier section "Defining the Broker's Role" for more about these costs).

>> Use broker comparison services available in financial publications such as *Report on Business* and *Maclean's* (and, of course, their websites) and online sources such as Canoe Money (www.canoe.ca/Canoe/Money).

TIP

Finding brokers is easy. Just search for "Canadian online discount brokers" in your favorite search engine. The search results will also pull up many online articles rating each broker and itemizing their services and fees. Start your search by using the sources in Appendix A, which includes a list of the major brokerage firms.

Discovering Various Types of Brokerage Accounts

When you start investing in the stock market, you have to somehow actually pay for the stocks you buy. Most brokerage firms offer investors several types of accounts, each serving a different purpose. We present three of the most common types in the following sections. The basic difference boils down to how particular brokers view your creditworthiness when it comes to buying and selling securities. If your credit isn't great, your only choice is a cash account. If your credit is good, you can open either a cash account or a margin account. After you qualify for a margin account, you can (with additional approval) upgrade it to do options trades.

REMEMBER

To open an account, you have to fill out an application and submit a cheque or money order, or execute an online bank transfer for at least the minimum amount required to establish an account.

Cash accounts

A cash account (also referred to as a Type 1 account) means just what you'd think. You must deposit a sum of money along with the new account application to begin trading. The amount of your initial deposit varies from broker to broker. Some brokers have a minimum of $10,000; others let you open an account for as little as $500. Once in a while you may see a broker offering cash accounts with no minimum deposit, usually as part of a promotion. Use the resources in Appendix A to help you shop around. Qualifying for a cash account is usually easy, as long as you have cash and a pulse.

With a cash account, your money has to be deposited in the account before the closing (or settlement) date for any trade you make. The closing occurs three business days after the date you make the trade (the date of execution). You may be required to have the money in the account even before the date of execution. Refer to Chapter 6 for details on these and other important dates.

In other words, if you call your broker on Monday, October 10, and order 50 shares of CashLess Corp. at $20 per share, then on Thursday, October 13, you better have $1,000 in cash sitting in your account (plus commission). Otherwise, the purchase doesn't go through.

WARNING

In addition, ask the broker how long it takes deposited cash (such as a cheque) to be available for investing. Some brokers put a hold on cheques for up to ten business days (or longer), regardless of how soon that cheque clears your account (that would drive us crazy!).

TIP

See whether your broker will pay you interest on the uninvested cash in your brokerage account. Some Canadian brokers offer a service in which uninvested money earns money market rates, and you can even choose between a regular money market account and a more exotic municipal bond money market account.

Margin accounts

A margin account (also called a Type 2 account) allows you to borrow money against the securities in the account to buy more stock. Because you can borrow in a margin account, you have to be qualified and approved by the broker. After you're approved, this newfound credit gives you more leverage so you can buy more stock or do short-selling. (You can read more about buying on margin and short-selling in Chapter 17.)

For stock trading, the margin limit is 50 percent. For example, if you plan to buy $10,000 worth of stock on margin, you need at least $5,000 in cash (or securities owned) sitting in your account. The interest rate you pay varies depending on the broker, but most brokers generally charge a rate that's considerably higher than their own borrowing rate.

Why use margin? Margin is to stocks what mortgage is to buying real estate. You can buy real estate with all cash, but using borrowed funds often makes sense because you may not have enough money to make a 100 percent cash purchase, or you may just prefer not to pay all cash. With margin, you can, for example, buy $10,000 worth of stock with as little as $5,000. The balance of the stock purchase is acquired using a loan (margin) from the brokerage firm.

WARNING

Personally, we're not big fans of margin, and we use it sparingly. Margin is a form of leverage that can work out fine if you're correct but can be very dangerous if the market moves against you. It's best applied with stocks that are generally stable and dividend-paying. That way, the dividends help pay off the margin interest.

Option accounts

An option account (also referred to as a Type 3 account) gives you all the capabilities of a margin account (which in turn also gives you the capabilities of a cash account) plus the ability to trade options on stocks and stock indexes. To upgrade your margin account to an option account, the broker usually asks you to sign a statement that you're knowledgeable about options and familiar with the risks associated with them.

TIP

Options can be a very effective addition to a stock investor's array of wealth-building investment tools. A more comprehensive review of options is available in the book *Trading Options For Dummies*, 3rd Edition, by Joe Duarte (Wiley, 2017). We personally do use options (as do our clients and students), and we think they can be a great tool in your wealth-building arsenal. But use them very carefully.

Judging Brokers' Recommendations

Canadians and Americans have become enamoured with a new sport: the rating of stocks by brokers on financial TV channels like BNN and MSNBC. Frequently, these channels feature shows with a dapper market strategist talking up a particular stock. Some stocks have been known to jump significantly right after an influential analyst issues a buy recommendation. Analysts' speculation and opinions make for great fun, and many people take their views very seriously. However, most investors should be wary when analysts, especially the glib ones on TV, make a recommendation. It's often just showbiz. In the following sections, we define basic broker recommendations and list a few important considerations for evaluating them.

Understanding basic recommendations

Brokers issue their recommendations (advice) as a general idea of how much regard they have for a particular stock. The following list presents the basic recommendations (or ratings) and what they mean to you:

>> *Strong buy* and *buy:* Hot diggity dog! These ratings are the ones to get. The analyst loves this pick, and you would be very wise to get a bunch of shares. The thing to keep in mind, however, is that *buy* recommendations are probably the most common because (let's face it) brokers sell stocks.

>> *Accumulate* and *market perform:* An analyst who issues these types of recommendations is positive, yet unexcited, about the pick. This rating is akin to asking a friend whether he likes your new suit and getting the response "It's nice" in a monotone voice. It's a polite reply, but you wish his opinion had been more definitive.

>> *Hold* or *neutral:* Analysts use this language when their backs are to the wall, but they still don't want to say, "Sell that loser!" This recommendation reminds us of a mother telling her children to be nice and to either say something positive or keep their mouths shut. In this case, the rating is the analyst's way of keeping his mouth shut.

>> *Sell:* Many analysts should have issued this recommendation before and even during the early part of the bear markets of 2000–2002 and 2008–2009 but didn't. What a shame. So many investors lost money because some analysts were too nice (or biased?) or just afraid to be honest, sound the alarm, and urge people to sell.

>> *Avoid like the plague:* We're just kidding about this one, but we wish this recommendation was available. We've seen plenty of stocks that we thought were dreadful investments — stocks of companies that made no money, were

in terrible financial condition, and should never have been considered at all. Yet investors gobble up billions of dollars' worth of stocks that eventually become worthless.

Asking a few important questions

Don't get us wrong. An analyst's recommendation is certainly a better tip than what you'd get from your barber or your sister-in-law's neighbour, but you want to view recommendations from analysts with a healthy dose of reality. Analysts have biases because their employment depends on the very companies that are being presented. What investors need to listen to when a broker talks up a stock is the reasoning behind the recommendation. In other words, why is the broker making this recommendation?

Keep in mind that analysts' recommendations can play a useful role in your personal stock investing research. If you find a great stock and then you hear analysts give glowing reports on the same stock, you're on the right track! Here are some questions and points to keep in mind:

>> **How does the analyst arrive at a rating?** The analyst's approach to evaluating a stock can help you round out your research as you consult other sources such as newsletters and independent advisory services.

>> **What analytical approach is the analyst using?** Some analysts use fundamental analysis — looking at the company's financial condition, key financial ratios, and factors related to its success, such as its standing within the industry and the overall market. Other analysts use technical analysis — looking at the company's stock price history and judging past stock price movements to derive some insight regarding the stock's future price movement (see Chapter 10 for more about technical analysis). Many analysts use a combination of the two. Is this analyst's approach similar to your approach, or to those of sources that you respect or admire?

>> **What is the analyst's track record?** Has the analyst had a consistently good record through both bull and bear markets? Major financial publications and websites, such as Barron's (www.barrons.com), MarketWatch (www.marketwatch.com), Canoe Money (www.canoe.ca/Canoe/Money), and the National Post (www.nationalpost.com), regularly track recommendations from well-known analysts and stock pickers. Also check out www.adviceforinvestors.com, which as a subscriber gives you free online access to Investor's Digest of Canada, The TaxLetter, and The Moneyletter. Some other resources for this type of info are in Appendix A.

>> **How does the analyst treat important aspects of the company's performance, such as sales and earnings?** How about the company's balance sheet? The essence of a healthy company is growing sales and earnings coupled with strong assets, low debt and good cashflows. (See Chapter 11 for more details on these topics.)

>> **Is the industry that the company's in doing well?** Does the analyst give you insight on this important information? A strong company in a weak industry can't stay strong for long. The right industry and sector is a critical part of the stock selection process (for more, see Chapter 13).

>> **What research sources does the analyst cite?** Does the analyst quote the federal or provincial government or industry trade groups to support her thesis? These sources are important because they help give a more complete picture regarding the company's prospects for success. Imagine that you decide on the stock of a strong company. What if the provincial government (through agencies like the Ontario Securities Commission) is penalizing the company for fraudulent activity? Or what if the company's industry is shrinking or has ceased to grow (making it tougher for the company to continue growing)? The astute investor looks at a variety of sources before buying stock.

>> **Is the analyst rational when citing a target price for a stock?** When he says, "We think the stock will hit $100 per share within 12 months," is he presenting a rational model, such as basing the share price on a projected price/earnings ratio (see Chapter 11)? The analyst must be able to provide a logical scenario explaining why the stock has a good chance of achieving the cited target price within the time frame mentioned. You may not necessarily agree with the analyst's conclusion, but the explanation can help you decide whether the stock choice is well thought out.

WARNING

>> **Does the company that's being recommended have any ties to the analyst or the analyst's firm?** To this day, the financial industry gets occasional bad publicity because some analysts continue to give shining recommendations on stocks of companies that are doing business with the very firms that employ those analysts. This conflict of interest is probably the biggest reason why analysts can be so wrong in their recommendations. Ask your broker to disclose any conflict of interest.

>> **What school of economic thought does the analyst adhere to?** This may sound like an odd question, and it may not be readily answered, but it's a good thing to know. If we had to choose between two analysts that were very similar except that Analyst A adhered to the Keynesian school of economic thought and Analyst B adhered to the Austrian school, guess what? We'd choose Analyst B because those who embrace the Austrian school have a much better grasp of real-world economics (which means better stock investment choices).

REMEMBER

The bottom line with brokerage recommendations is that you shouldn't use them to buy or sell a stock. Instead, use them as a back-end check to confirm your own up-front research. We know that if we buy a stock based on our own research and later discover the same stock being talked up on the financial shows, that's just the icing on the cake. The experts may be great to listen to, and their recommendations can augment your own opinions, but they're no substitute for your own careful research. We devote Part 3 to researching and picking winning stocks.

Robo-advisors and Fintech

Financial technology, or *fintech,* is a term you'll be hearing about more and more. Fintech represents digital technology and those electronic processes that directly compete with traditional financial services. This is not the only distinction. Your access to fintech is empowered by multiple channels you can use — such as your home computer, smartphone, or tablet — all to give you convenient, fast, and flexible access to mobile banking and stock trading, services that are now entrenched in the Canadian financial industry.

One of the more recent, cooler applications of fintech is the provision of something you've likely heard of already — robo-advisors — also known as *online wealth managers* or *virtual advisers. Robo-advisors* represent great ways for younger Canadians and those new to stock investing to pick stocks and easily sock away some money in a Registered Retirement Savings Plan, Tax Free Savings Account, or other tax-smart financial vehicle or plan.

Currently, robo-advisors are managing hundreds of million dollars in Canada and billions of dollars worldwide. This segment of the financial services industry is growing incredibly fast. One fascinating factoid is that in Canada, robo-advisors are better regulated than many traditional financial advisors! More on that later.

High tech meets equity investing

The term *robo-advisor* can be a bit of a misnomer. That's because there is no robot involved. Instead, it's really a paperless electronic platform powered by brainy artificial intelligence and wild but complex algorithms (formulae). These electronic advisors are not just advisors, but actual businesses. So when you think of a robo-advisor, think of an "advice business" with electronic advisors, in much the same way banks are businesses that employ bankers.

Although the robo-advisor platform is indeed operated by humans behind the scenes, there is no actual carbon-based life form that will select an investment portfolio for you. That's where the *robo* part comes in. Robo-advisors will provide you with a selection of tailored investment portfolios (made up of stocks, but more on that later) that are electronically aligned with your financial needs. Robo-advisors use the results of an online questionnaire you fill out. This in turn allows the robo-advisor to generate and determine your risk tolerance and investment objectives. Once your portfolio is selected, it is periodically and automatically rebalanced should the composition of your portfolio deviate significantly from plan.

Terminating bad investment decisions with artificial intelligence

Robo-advisors are a natural evolution of fintech. We remember when we began to write the *Stock Investing For Canadians For Dummies* series almost two decades ago how the online brokerage revolution allowed you to economically take control of your stock trades with powerful tools and resources. Robo-advice is an extension of fintech into the more non-mechanical and judgmental aspect of investing — the provision of actual advice based on the artificial intelligence of robots programmed with algorithms.

The advantage here is that the algorithms, though of course not guarantees of success, are proven best-case scenarios of stock investing that have been tested over the years. These models are being continuously improved and tweaked. In this way, you get a measure of consistency, expertise, and immediacy in your investment decision making.

Advantages of an inhuman touch

Canadians have no doubt seen a few robo-advisor commercials where the client sits across the desk of a smug stockbroker or investment advisor and asks why results are so poor. The broker or advisor smiles and glibly answers, "Just wait, it's a long-term game." The client replies, "It's not a game. That's my kids' education we're talking about," and is far from smiling. The advisor is still smug.

Robo-advisors have no attitude. They generally don't get tempted by selling higher-commission financial products that don't suit your needs but pay them great commissions. They're not tempted by selling you more than you need or selling you with high frequency to rack up fees and commissions. You don't need us to tell you that the reputation of the entire industry has been harmed by an array of bad apples and unqualified pretenders who work as "advisors."

It's important to point out, however, that the robo-advisor ecosystem is not all about programming stuff and artificial intelligence. It's not all bits and bytes. Invariably, you will communicate and interact with humans through different channels including email, phone or Skype conversations, and computer chat windows.

REMEMBER

Robo-advisors are businesses owned and run by people.

Research has shown that many Canadians actually prefer the robo-advisor option to the traditional approach, especially Millennials. Although the inhuman touch has clear advantages, it's incredibly important to be able to access real people to make sure you understand how the robo-advisor process works. This is, after all, your money at stake!

Although robo-advisors won't be able to match everything that a full-service financial planner or broker could do for you, they will do the lion's share of it — and for much cheaper. The good news is that if, after all this, you still need more advice, you can still use a professionally certified and qualified planner, accountant, or tax expert to help you with estate planning, insurance, and complex tax planning. It's ultimately a question of knowing *when* to use robo-advisors, and this chapter is here to help you.

What can go wrong with a short circuit?

Whenever we deal with artificial intelligence, including robo-advisors, it's a natural instinct to worry a bit. We've seen the headlines of self-driving cars crashing into other vehicles or, worse, people. Yet all great ideas have challenges to learn from and overcome.

From a business governance and practice perspective, you may be surprised to learn that robo-advisors in North America must also follow fiduciary duty standards. Fiduciary standards exist to protect *your* best interests, not the advisor's interests. This reduces conflicts of interest which are rampant in the softly regulated Canadian investment advice industry. (We discuss some of these problems in the preceding section.) But fiduciary duty itself is not the greatest surprise. The real surprise is that robo-advisor fiduciary standards actually exceed the standards governing most investment advisors and financial planners. In a way, this saddens us, but makes the case for considering robo-advisors even more compelling for newbies to stock investing.

WARNING

In Canada, human advisors generally do not have a strict fiduciary duty. In Canada's wishy-washy regulatory landscape, that's too bad. A *fiduciary* (a person) is supposed to, by definition, "prudently and with due care take great care of your investments and represent the highest standard of care in equity or law." Human investment advisors just have to follow a weaker "suitability standard." As Canada's Justin Bieber would say, "What do you mean?" The suitability obligation means making recommendations that are consistent with the best interests of you, the client. Though Canadian advisors are self-regulated, under the softer suitability standard human advisors just have to "reasonably believe" that any recommendations made are "suitable" for clients. There is no specific requirement not to place the advisor's interests below that of the client, as a fiduciary standard requires.

Unlike *The Terminator* series of movies, where the machines run amok, robo-advisors are restricted in the choices they can make. They can't "short-circuit." Their strength lies in the fact they are really good at wielding algorithms to match a predetermined set of standard portfolios, covering all the key equity asset categories, to your specified needs and risk profile. Robo-advisors follow sound investment practices and are not distracted by higher fees they can get if they sell you substandard investment products.

Robo-advisors are as secure as any credit union, investment broker, or even to an extent a Canadian chartered bank. By *secure* we mean two things:

>> **Financially secure:** Like other investment accounts under the custodianship of a member of the Investment Industry Regulatory Organization of Canada (IIROC), your robo-advisor account is eligible for protection of up to $1,000,000 by the Canadian Investor Protection Fund (CIPF). This protection is invoked should the custodian become insolvent. That shouldn't be a problem, as your investment funds are typically held separately in an account in your name at a chartered bank-owned custodian.

>> **Cyber threat secure:** Most robo-advisors use the cyber security standards and measures of Canada's OSFI (Office of the Superintendent of Financial Institutions) and NIST (National Institute of Standards and Technology) to ensure that your sensitive financial and other information is held and processed securely.

Robo-advisors are also transparent and let you see where your money is held. The robo-advisor model has been used around the world for several years now, and at the time of writing robo-advisors manage about $4 billion in assets. They are a growing and trusted investment advice alternative.

Canadian Robo-advisors

There are about 15 robo-advisors operating in Canada today. We expect this number to grow as the popularity of the platform continues to grow. Some of the names, which you may recognize through Canadian TV and radio commercials, are listed in the following table. Almost all of these have been established since 2015, and most but not all operate across Canada.

BMO Smartfolio	Idema Investments	Invisor
Justwealth	ModernAdvisor	Nest Wealth
Questrade Portfolio IQ	RoboAdvisors+	Smart Money Capital Management
Virtual Wealth	WealthBar	Wealthsimple
Virtual Brokers Wealth Management		

Not just for Millennials

We know what you're thinking. Fintech is the plaything of Millennials, and robo-advisors are just for the young. Well, it turns out that both Millennials as well as older Canadians are very much at ease within an online investment advice platform. Both age cohorts interact well with robo-advisor interfaces. How do we know this? Research indicates that the average age of Canadian robo-advisor customers is about 45 years old. In fact, the average age of robo-advisor customers, depending on the robo-advisor, ranges from as low as 34 to as high as 50 years old. In the United States, about half of robo-advisor clients are over 35 years old.

Asset allocation: What is the robo-advisor investing my money in?

Chapter 2 stresses the importance of age, risk appetite, personal goals, return objectives, and other factors in stock investment allocation decisions. With robo-advisors, it's no different. (Again, there is no "robot" — just a simple but very smart computer managed and supported by a person who will execute your portfolio.) We start with *you*. Your robo-advisor journey begins with you telling the robo-advisor (a company) a bit about yourself. Based on that little human-to-robot chat, the robo-advisor will recommend a certain exchange traded fund (ETF) or array of ET funds that will suit your needs. The number of portfolio choices ranges from 5 (which appears to be the current norm) up to 10 or more funds.

Most if not virtually all of Canadian robo-advisors invest your funds in ETFs. Those that don't invest exclusively in ETFs, such as RoboAdvisors+ and Wealth-Bar, also invest in mutual funds, pooled funds, and private funds. Typical and main ETF providers across all of Canada's robo-advisors include BMO, Vanguard, Horizons, iShares, Purpose, and many more ETF providers.

REMEMBER

Each recommended ETF portfolio is usually top-heavy with *stock* equities and bolstered with some non-equities. Stocks within the ETF will come in different flavours. They may be Canadian, U.S., global (outside of Canada and the U.S.), or any combination of stocks. ETFs may also include real estate investment trusts — discussed in Chapter 9 — and other equity asset categories like emerging market equities or sectors like commodities.

Some of the sexier ETFs will delve into concepts like futures, sectors like commodities and cannabis, and themes like growth. The ETFs recommended by your robo-advisor may be capped off with fixed-income (non-equity) components and financial instruments such as high-quality investment-grade bonds, lower-quality but higher-return corporate bonds, and money market funds.

REMEMBER

The allocation possibilities are many and go even further than we've indicated. Your portfolios can be embedded within RRSPs, TFSAs, and (if you're older) RRIFs.

After that comes another key feature: You can, should you choose, turn over the day-to-day management of your portfolio to the robo-advisor. You can even choose between robo-advisor offerings that come with passive asset allocation approaches (where the ETF portfolio mirrors a market index) or active asset management (which focuses on outperforming the stock benchmark indexes by buying and selling securities and not sitting still).

Finally, most robo-advisors can execute free or low-fee automatic portfolio rebalances and tax-loss harvesting — which is a big deal, because these duties can be time consuming, tedious, and costly under the traditional investment advisor model.

What to watch for

The first thing to watch for with robo-advisors is the very thing that is obvious from the previous section: Your investment vehicle choice is essentially limited to ETFs. This is neither a good or bad thing. It simply restricts your potential for outsized returns, unless of course the ETF your robo-advisor recommends is of a higher growth but higher risk variety (for example, emerging market or high technology stock).

The second risk area is that robo-advisors vary in the extent and nature of the "personal touch" advice they provide and the time of day when such advice can be accessed. Some robo-advisors pitch the word *advice* in every second sentence, yet offer very little of it. Again, remember that the robos are there to give you the solution to an algorithmic equation. They give you options and a recommendation. You still have to make a few decisions after that.

Finally, even though robo-advisors are regulated more stringently than human advisors, that regulation deals with governance and business processes. What may *not* be governed, and where your exposure lies, is in the fact that the algorithms may be flawed or even hacked and destroyed at your expense. Speaking of hacking, your personal data may even be stolen. There is no such thing as 100 percent data security.

Fees

Fees are low with robo-advisors, and that is a key appeal. Low fees are possible because robo-advisors don't have to incur the type of office space overhead that financial advisors of similar profile require. Robo-advisors save the most, however, by the fact that they automate so much of their key administrative and operational business processes like registration, monitoring, and reporting to you. The key operational saving stems from the fact that a computer does the thinking and solving for you, not a higher-priced human advisor. If that human advisor is not even qualified or properly trained — and many are not — then you are really getting fleeced.

Every robo-advisor has a distinct fee structure. Some levy a flat rate. Most charge a certain percentage fee. Others utilize a hybrid of flat and percentage fees. Still others charge more (up to 7 percent with Nest Wealth) with lower balances but drastically reduce the fee once you reach higher minimum balances. Some, like WealthBar and Wealthsimple, charge fees that are well below 1 percent across a wide range of portfolio balances.

In general, though, robo-advisor clients often pay fees under 1 percent even if they have a limited amount to invest. Investors who are just beginning their stock-investing journey can open accounts with minimums of $5,000 — and in other cases a lot less. In many cases, robo-advisors that invest in Canada's less-expensive ETFs can charge about one half of a percentage point. One thing that's certain is that they compete as lower-cost alternatives to traditional advisors.

Make no mistake, though: The quality of advice you can get from traditional fee for service advisors, assuming they are experienced and certified, is going to be deeper and broader in scope. It's just that they typically charge at least 2 percent of your portfolio size in total fees. If you have a very large portfolio, that can build to thousands and tens of thousands of dollars in total annual fees.

REMEMBER

Do the fee math before selecting a robo-advisor. (We point you to robo-advisor resources that include summaries of Canada's robo-advice services, fees, and other details in Appendix A.)

Final thoughts

This book is all about stock investing and is written to enable you to do it yourself. It empowers you with the fundamental knowledge and resources to make you a do-it-yourself investor. But there are situations where you may want to have advisors, be they human or robotic, to help you out. It may be when you are starting out. It may be when you are older and have emerging retirement-planning considerations. It may be after you claim an inheritance and suddenly have complex investing decisions to make.

When we wrote the first edition of this book, online investing was just emerging. It unchained you from the monopolistic and often unethical behaviour of some unscrupulous stockbrokers and conflicted brokerage house equity analysts who sold you lots of bad and expensive junk. This section in this edition of our book is simply meant to introduce you to yet another cost-saving revolution in stock investing.

If you don't need or want to use a robo advisor, you don't have to. This book teaches you how to be a do-it-yourself stock investor anyway, or to fill in loose ends. If you are just starting out, we maintain that it's not too difficult to do for yourself what robo-advisors do — build a basic portfolio of index exchange traded funds for essentially no fee. In Chapter 5 we show you how. We can even help you with a cool and perfectly legal hack. Because some robo-advisors provide you with a glimpse of available portfolio options during your introductory consultation with them, you can refer to those options and then go solo. Okay, that's a dirty trick. We admit it.

Chapter **8**

Investing for Long-Term Growth

What's the number-one reason people invest in stocks? To grow their wealth (also referred to as capital appreciation). Yes, some Canadians invest for income (in the form of dividends), but that's a different matter (we discuss investing for income in Chapter 9). Investors seeking growth would rather see the money that could have been distributed as dividends be reinvested in the company so that (hopefully) a greater gain is achieved when the stock's price rises or appreciates. People interested in growing their wealth see stocks as one of the convenient ways to do it. Growth stocks tend to be riskier than other categories of stocks, but they offer excellent long-term prospects for making the big bucks. If you don't believe us, just ask Warren Buffett, Peter Lynch, and other successful, long-term investors.

Although someone like Buffett is not considered a growth investor, his long-term, value-oriented approach has been a successful growth strategy. If you're the type of investor who has enough time to let somewhat risky stocks trend upward or who has enough money so that a loss won't devastate you financially, then growth stocks are definitely for you. As they say, no guts, no glory. The challenge is to figure out which stocks make you wealthier quicker; we give you tips on how to do so in this chapter.

REMEMBER

Short of starting your own business, stock investing is the best way to profit from a business venture. We want to emphasize that to make money in stocks consistently over the long haul, you must remember that you're investing in a company; buying the stock is just a means for you to participate in the company's success (or failure). Why does it matter that you think of stock investing as buying a company versus buying a stock? Invest in a stock only if you're just as excited about it as you would be if you were the CEO in charge of running the company. If you're the sole owner of the company, do you act differently than one of a legion of obscure stockholders? Of course you do. As the firm's owner, you have a greater interest in the company. You have a strong desire to know how the enterprise is doing. As you invest in stocks, make believe that you're the owner, and take an active interest in the company's products, services, sales, earnings, and so on. This attitude and discipline can enhance your goals as a stock investor. This approach is especially important if your investment goal is growth.

Becoming a Value-Oriented Growth Investor

REMEMBER

A stock is considered a growth stock when it's growing faster and higher than the overall stock market. Basically, a growth stock performs better than its peers in categories such as sales and earnings. Value stocks are stocks that are priced lower than the value of the company and its assets — you can identify a value stock by analyzing the company's fundamentals and looking at key financial ratios, such as the price-to-earnings (P/E) and price-to-sales (P/S) ratios. (Company finances are covered in Chapter 11, and ratios are covered in Chapter 11 and Appendix B.) Growth stocks tend to have better prospects for growth in the immediate future (from one to four years), but value stocks tend to have less risk and steadier growth over a longer term.

Over the years, a debate has quietly raged in the financial community about growth versus value investing. Some people believe that growth and value are mutually exclusive. They maintain that large numbers of people buying stock with growth as the expectation tend to drive up the stock price relative to the company's current value. Growth investors, for example, aren't put off by P/E ratios of 30, 40, or higher. Value investors, meanwhile, are too nervous to buy stocks at those P/E ratio levels.

However, you can have both. A value-oriented approach to growth investing serves you best. Long-term growth stock investors spend time analyzing the company's fundamentals to make sure that the company's growth prospects lie on a solid foundation. But what if you have to choose between a growth stock and a value stock? Which do you choose? Seek value when you're buying the stock and analyze the company's prospects for growth. Growth includes but is not limited to the health and growth of the company's specific industry, the economy at large, and the general political climate (see Chapters 13 and 15).

REMEMBER

The bottom line is that growth is much easier to achieve when you seek a one-two punch of solid, value-oriented companies in growing industries. (To better understand industries and sectors and how they affect stock value, see Chapter 13.) It's also worth emphasizing that time, patience, and discipline are key factors in your success — especially in the tumultuous and uncertain stock investing environment of the current world.

TECHNICAL STUFF

Value-oriented growth investing probably has the longest history of success compared to most stock investing philosophies. The track record for those people who use value-oriented growth investing is enviable. Warren Buffett, Benjamin Graham, John Templeton, and Peter Lynch are a few of the more well-known practitioners. Each may have his own spin on the concepts, but all have successfully applied the basic principles of value-oriented growth investing over many years.

Handy Growth Stock Tips

Although the information in the previous section can help you shrink your stock choices from thousands of stocks to maybe a few dozen or a few hundred (depending on how well the general stock market is doing), the purpose of this section is to help you cull the so-so growth stocks to unearth the go-go ones. It's time to dig deeper for the biggest potential winners. Keep in mind that you probably won't find a stock to satisfy all the criteria presented here. Just make sure that your selection meets as many criteria as realistically possible. But hey, if you do find a stock that meets all the criteria cited, buy as much as you can!

For the record, our approach to choosing a winning growth stock is probably almost the reverse method of . . . uh . . . that screaming money guy on TV (we won't mention his name!). People watch his show for "tips" on "hot stocks." The frenetic host seems to do a rapid-fire treatment of stocks in general. You get the impression that he looks over thousands of stocks and says "I like this one" and "I don't like that one." The viewer has to decide. Sheesh.

Verifiably, 80 to 90 percent of our stock picks are profitable. People ask us how we pick a winning stock. We tell them that we don't just pick a stock and hope that it does well. In fact, our respective stock-picking research doesn't even begin with stocks; we first look at the investing environment (politics, economics, demographics, and so on) and choose which industry will benefit. After we know which industry will prosper accordingly, then we start to analyze and choose individual stock(s). We start with the big picture first and methodically drill down to the company level afterwards.

After we choose a stock, we wait. Patience is more than just a virtue; patience is to investing what time is to a seed that's planted in fertile soil. The legendary Jesse Livermore said that he didn't make his stock market fortunes by trading stocks; his fortunes were made "in the waiting." Why?

When we tell you to have patience and a long-term perspective, it isn't because we want you to wait years or decades for your stock portfolio to bear fruit. It's because you're waiting for a specific condition to occur: for the market to discover what you have! When you have a good stock in a good industry, it may take time for the market to discover it. When a stock has more buyers than sellers, it rises — it's as simple as that. As time passes, more buyers find your stock. As the stock rises, it attracts more attention and therefore more buyers. The more time that passes, the better your stock looks to the investing public.

REMEMBER

When you're choosing growth stocks, you should consider investing in a company only if it makes a cash profit (in other words, profits without accounting voodoo) and if you understand how it makes that profit and from where it generates sales. Part of your research means looking at the industry and sector (see Chapter 13) and economic trends in general (which are covered in Chapter 15). Chapter 11 helps you avoid voodoo numbers!

Look for leaders in megatrends

A strong company in a growing industry is a recipe for success. If you look at the history of stock investing, this point comes up constantly. Investors need to be on the alert for megatrends because they help ensure success.

A megatrend is a major development that has huge implications for much (if not all) of society for a long time to come. Good examples are the advent of social media and the blockchain (including cryptocurrency) on the Internet (new technology) and the aging of Canada (demographics). (We cover blockchain and cryptocurrency technology in Chapter 19.) Both of these trends offer significant challenges and opportunities for our Canadian economy. Take the Internet, for example. Its potential for economic application is still being developed and honed. Millions keep flocking to its new and exciting applications for many reasons. And census data tells us that senior citizens (over 65) will be the fastest-growing segment of the Canadian population during the next 20 years. How does the stock investor take advantage of a megatrend?

In this edition, we plan to do what we did in the last edition, which is help you identify current megatrends to make it easier for you to pick winning stocks (you're welcome!). Find out more in Chapter 13.

Compare company growth to industry growth

You have to measure the growth of a company against something else to figure out whether its stock is a growth stock. Usually, you compare the growth of a company with the growth of other companies in the same industry or with the stock market in general. In practical terms, when you measure the growth of a stock against the stock market, you're actually comparing it against a generally accepted benchmark, such as the S&P/TSX60, Dow Jones Industrial Average (DJIA), or the Standard & Poor's 500 (S&P 500). For more on stock indexes, refer to Chapter 5.

TIP

If a company's earnings grow 15 percent per year over three years or more and the industry's average growth rate over the same time frame is 10 percent, then the stock qualifies as a growth stock. You can easily calculate the earnings growth rate by comparing a company's earnings in the current year to the preceding year and computing the difference as a percentage. For example, if a company's earnings (on a per-share basis) were $1 last year and $1.10 this year, then earnings grew by 10 percent. Many analysts also look at a current quarter and compare the earnings to the same quarter from the preceding year to see whether earnings are growing.

REMEMBER

A growth stock is called that not only because the company is growing but also because the company is performing well with some consistency. Having a single year where your earnings do well versus the S&P/TSX60's or the S&P 500's average doesn't cut it. Growth must be consistently accomplished.

Consider a company with a strong niche

TIP

Companies that have established a strong niche are consistently profitable. Look for a company with one or more of the following characteristics:

>> **A strong brand:** Companies such as Coca-Cola, Metro, and Shoppers Drug Mart come to mind. Yes, other companies out there can make soda or sell personal hygiene products, but a business needs a lot more than a similar product to topple companies that have established an almost irrevocable identity with the public.

>> **High barriers to entry:** United Parcel Service, Shopify, and Blackberry have set up tremendous distribution and delivery networks that competitors can't easily duplicate. High barriers to entry offer an important edge to companies that are already established. Examples of high barriers include high capital requirements (like needing lots of cash to start, or significant investment in machinery or infrastructure) or special technology or patented intellectual property that's not easily reproduced or acquired.

>> **Research and development (R&D):** Companies such as Celestica and Pfizer spend a lot of money researching and developing new pharmaceutical products. This investment becomes a new product with millions of consumers who become loyal purchasers, so the company's going to grow. You can find out what companies spend on R&D by checking their financial statements and their annual reports (more on this in Chapters 11 and 12).

Check out a company's fundamentals

REMEMBER

When you hear the word fundamentals in the world of stock investing, it refers to the company's financial condition and related data. When investors (especially value investors) do fundamental analysis, they look at the company's fundamentals — its balance sheet, income statement, cash flow, and other operational data, along with external factors such as the company's market position, industry, and economic prospects. Essentially, the fundamentals indicate the company's financial condition. Chapter 11 goes into greater detail about analyzing a company's financial condition. However, the main numbers you want to look at include the following:

>> **Sales:** Are the company's sales this year surpassing last year's? As a decent benchmark, you want to see sales at least 10 percent higher than last year. Although it may differ depending on the industry, 10 percent is a reasonable, general yardstick.

>> **Earnings:** Are earnings (especially cash, not just paper earnings or estimates like accrued interest revenue) at least 10 percent higher than last year? Earnings should grow at the same rate as sales (or better, which is what would happen if the company improved its cost control).

>> **Debt:** Is the company's total debt equal to or lower than the prior year? The death knell of many a company has been excessive debt.

A company's financial condition has more factors than we mention here, but these numbers are the most important. We also realize that using the 10 percent figure may seem like an oversimplification, but you don't need to complicate matters unnecessarily. We know someone's computerized financial model may come out to 9.675 percent or maybe 11.07 percent, but keep it simple for now.

Evaluate a company's management

The management of a company is crucial to its success. Before you buy stock in a company, you want to know that the company's management is doing a great job. But how do you do that? If you call up a company and ask, it may not even return your phone call. How do you know whether management is running the company properly? The best way is to check the numbers. Financial numbers are the language of business. The following sections tell you the numbers you need to check. If the company's management is running the business well, the ultimate result is a rising stock price.

Return on equity

REMEMBER

Although you can measure how well management is doing in several ways, you can take a quick snapshot of a management team's competence by checking the company's return on equity (ROE). You calculate the ROE simply by dividing earnings by equity. The resulting percentage gives you a good idea whether the company is using its equity (or net assets) efficiently and profitably. Basically, the higher the percentage, the better, but you can consider the ROE solid if the percentage is 10 percent or higher. Keep in mind that not all industries have identical ROEs.

To find out a company's earnings, check out the company's income statement. The income statement is a simple financial statement that expresses this equation: sales (or revenue) minus expenses equals net earnings (or net income or net profit). You can see an example of an income statement in Table 8-1. (We give more details on income statements in Chapter 11.)

TABLE 8-1

Grobaby, Inc., Income Statement

	2012 Income Statement	2013 Income Statement
Sales	$82,000	$90,000
Expenses	-$75,000	-$78,000
Net earnings	$7,000	$12,000

To find out a company's equity, check out that company's balance sheet. (See Chapter 11 for more details on balance sheets.) The balance sheet is actually a simple financial statement that illustrates this equation: total assets minus total liabilities equals net equity. For public stock companies, the net assets are called shareholders' equity or simply equity. Table 8-2 shows a balance sheet for Grobaby, Inc.

TABLE 8-2

Grobaby, Inc., Balance Sheet

	Balance Sheet for December 31, 2012	Balance Sheet for December 31, 2013
Total assets (TA)	$55,000	$65,000
Total liabilities (TL)	–$20,000	–$25,000
Equity (TA minus TL)	$35,000	$40,000

Table 8-1 shows that Grobaby's earnings went from $7,000 to $12,000. In Table 8-2, you can see that Grobaby increased the equity from $35,000 to $40,000 in one year. The ROE for the year 2012 is 20 percent ($7,000 in earnings divided by $35,000 in equity), which is a solid number. The following year, the ROE is 30 percent ($12,000 in earnings divided by $40,000 equity), another solid number. A good minimum ROE is 10 percent, but 15 percent or more is preferred.

Equity and earnings growth

Two additional barometers of success are a company's growth in earnings and growth of equity.

>> Look at the growth in earnings in Table 8-1. The earnings grew from $7,000 (in 2012) to $12,000 (in 2013), a percentage increase of 71 percent ($12,000 minus $7,000 equals $5,000, and $5,000 divided by $7,000 is 71 percent), which is excellent. At a minimum, earnings growth should be equal to or better than the rate of inflation, but because that's not always a reliable number, we like at least 10 percent.

>> In Table 8-2, Grobaby's equity grew by $5,000 (from $35,000 to $40,000), or 14.3 percent ($5,000 divided by $35,000), which is very good — management is doing good things here. We like to see equity increasing by 10 percent or more.

Insider buying

TIP

Watching management as it manages the business is important, but another important indicator of how well the company is doing is to see whether management is buying stock in the company as well. If a company is poised for growth, who knows better than management? And if management is buying up the company's stock en masse, that's a great indicator of the stock's potential. See Chapter 20 for more details on insider buying.

Notice who's buying and/or recommending a company's stock

TIP

You can invest in a great company and still see its stock go nowhere. Why? Because what makes the stock go up is demand — having more buyers than sellers of the stock. If you pick a stock for all the right reasons and the market notices the stock as well, that attention causes the stock price to climb. The things to watch for include the following:

>> **Institutional buying:** Are mutual funds and pension plans buying up the stock you're looking at? If so, this type of buying power can exert tremendous upward pressure on the stock's price. Some resources and publications track institutional buying and how that affects any particular stock. (You can find these resources in Appendix A.) Frequently, when a mutual fund buys a stock, others soon follow. In spite of all the talk about independent research, a herd mentality still exists in Canada.

>> **Analysts' attention:** Are analysts talking about the stock on the financial shows? As much as you should be skeptical about an analyst's recommendation (given the past two stock market debacles like the Tech Wreck and the Great Recession), it offers some positive reinforcement for your stock. Don't ever buy a stock solely on the basis of an analyst's recommendation. Just know that if you buy a stock based on your own research and analysts subsequently rave about it on BNN (www.bnn.ca), your stock price is likely to go up. A single recommendation by an influential analyst can be enough to send a stock skyward.

>> **Newsletter recommendations:** Independent researchers usually publish newsletters. If influential Canadian newsletters are touting your choice, that praise is also good for your stock. Although some great newsletters are out there (find them in Appendix A) and they offer information that's as good as or better than that of some brokerage firms' research departments, definitely don't base your investment decision on a single tip. However, seeing newsletters tout a stock that you've already chosen should make you feel good.

>> **Consumer publications:** No, you won't find investment advice here. This one seems to come out of left field, but it's a source that you should notice. Publications such as Consumer Reports regularly look at products and services and rate them for consumer satisfaction. If a company's offerings are well received by consumers, that's a strong positive for the company. This kind of attention ultimately has a positive effect on that company's stock.

PROTECTING YOUR DOWNSIDE

We become Johnny-one-notes on one topic: trailing stops. (See Chapter 18 for a full explanation of various defensive trading techniques.) Trailing stops are stop-losses that you regularly manage with the stock you invest in. We always advocate using them, especially if you're new to the game of buying growth stocks. Trailing stops can help you, no matter how good or bad the economy is (or how good or bad the stock you're investing in is).

Suppose that you had invested in Research In Motion (now called Blackberry), a classic example of a phenomenal Canadian growth stock that went bad. Really bad. Around the year 2000, when its stock was still riding high, investors were as happy as chocoholics at a Cadbury factory. Along with many investors who forgot that sound investing takes discipline and research, some Research In Motion investors thought, "Downside risk? What downside risk?"

Here's an example of how a stop-loss order would have worked if you had invested in Research In Motion. Pretend you're back in 2000 and you buy Research In Motion at a price of, let's say, $65 per share (we discuss stock splits in Chapter 20) and put in a stop-loss order with your broker at $60. (Remember to make it a GTC, or good-till-cancelled order. If you do, the stop-loss order stays on indefinitely.) As a general rule, we like to place the stop-loss order at 10 percent below the market value (to reduce the stop-loss purchase cost). As the stock goes up, you keep the stop-loss trailing upward like a tail. (Now you know why it's called a "trailing" stop; it trails the stock's price.) When Research In Motion hits $75, your stop-loss changes to, say, $70, and so on. Now what?

When Research In Motion starts its perilous descent, you get out at $70. The new price of $70 triggers the stop-loss, and the stock is automatically sold — you stopped the loss! Actually, in this case, you could call it a "stop and cash in the gain" order. Because you bought the stock at $65 and sold at $70, you pocket a respectable capital gain of $5 (7.6 percent appreciation), less the cost of the stop-loss. Now you safely step aside and watch the stock continue its plunge.

What if the market is doing well? Are trailing stops a good idea? Because these stops are placed below the stock price, you're not stopping the stock from rising indefinitely. All you're doing is protecting your investment from loss. That's discipline! The stock market of 2004 to 2007 was fairly good to stock investors because the bear market that started in 2000 took a break — at least until 2008 when another one started. That bear market was even worse and the drop in stock prices ushered in the Great Recession! Ouch! During a bear market, trailing-stop strategies are critical because a potential decline in the stock price will become a greater risk.

Make sure a company continues to do well

A company's financial situation does change, and you, as a diligent investor, need to continue to look at the numbers for as long as the stock is in your portfolio. You may have chosen a great stock from a great company with great numbers a few years ago, but chances are pretty good that the numbers have changed since then.

WARNING

Great stocks don't always stay that way. A great selection that you're drawn to today may become tomorrow's pariah. Information, both good and bad, moves like lightning. Keep an eye on your stock company's numbers! To help minimize the downside risk, see the sidebar "Protecting your downside" for an example. For more information on a company's financial data, check out Chapter 11.

Heed investing lessons from history

A growth stock isn't a creature like the Loch Ness monster — always talked about but rarely seen. Growth stocks have been part of the financial scene for nearly a century. Examples abound that offer rich information that you can apply to today's stock market environment. Look at past market winners, especially those during the recent bull market, and the bearish markets found between 2000–2010, and ask yourself, "What made them profitable stocks?" We mention these two time frames because they offer a stark contrast to each other. The current bull market is a booming time for stocks, especially U.S. stocks, whereas the years before were very tough and bearish. In fact, Canadian stock market indexes, although higher than before, still lag U.S. indexes at the time of this writing.

REMEMBER

Being aware and acting logically are as vital to successful stock investing as they are to any other pursuit. Over and over again, history gives you the formula for successful stock investing:

>> Pick a company that has strong fundamentals, including signs such as rising sales and earnings and low debt. (See Chapter 11.)

>> Make sure that the company is in a growing industry. (See Chapter 13.)

>> Fully participate in stocks that are benefiting from bullish market developments in the general economy. (See Chapter 15.)

>> During a bear market or in bearish trends, switch more of your money out of growth stocks (such as technology) and into defensive stocks (such as utilities).

>> Monitor your stocks. Hold on to stocks that continue to have growth potential, and sell those stocks with declining prospects.

Exploring Small Caps and Speculative Stocks

Everyone wants to get in early on a hot new stock. Why not? You buy Shlobotky, Inc., at $1 per share and hope it zooms to $98 before lunchtime. Who doesn't want to buy a cheapy-deepy stock today that becomes the next Apple or Walmart? This possibility is why investors are attracted to small cap stocks.

Small cap (or small capitalization) is a reference to the company's market size, as we explain in Chapter 1. Small cap stocks are stocks that have a market value under $1 billion. Investors may face more risk with small caps, but they also have the chance for greater gains. Canada's stock market is replete with small cap stocks.

Out of all the types of stocks, small cap stocks continue to exhibit the greatest amount of growth. In the same way that a tree planted last year has more opportunity for growth than a mature 100-year-old redwood, small caps have greater growth potential than established large cap stocks. Of course, a small cap doesn't exhibit spectacular growth just because it's small. It grows when it does the right things, such as increasing sales and earnings by producing goods and services that customers want.

REMEMBER

For every small company that becomes a Financial Post FP500 firm, hundreds of companies don't grow at all or go out of business. When you try to guess the next great stock before any evidence of growth, you're not investing — you're speculating. Have you heard that one before? Of course you have, and you'll hear it again. Don't get us wrong — there's nothing wrong with speculating. But it's important to know that you're speculating when you're doing it. If you're going to speculate in small stocks hoping for the next Alphabet (Google), use the guidelines we present in the following sections to increase your chances of success.

Knowing when to avoid IPOs

Initial public offerings (IPOs) are the birthplaces of public stocks, or the proverbial ground floor. The IPO is the first offering to the public of a company's stock. The IPO is also referred to as "going public." Because a company going public is frequently an unproven enterprise, investing in an IPO can be risky. Here are the two types of IPOs:

>> **Start-up IPO:** This is a company that didn't exist before the IPO. In other words, the entrepreneurs get together and create a business plan. To get the financing they need for the company, they decide to go public immediately by approaching an investment banker. If the investment banker thinks that it's a

good concept, the banker will seek funding (selling the stock to investors) via the IPO.

>> **A private company that decides to go public:** In many cases, the IPO is done for a company that already exists and is seeking expansion capital. The company may have been around for a long time as a smaller private concern, but now decides to seek funding through an IPO to grow even larger (or to fund a new product, promotional expenses, and so on). Facebook and Groupon are examples of such IPOs.

Which of the two IPOs do you think is less risky? That's right — the private company going public. Why? Because it's already a proven business, which is a safer bet than a brand-new start-up. Some more great examples of successful IPOs in recent years are United Parcel Service and Google (they were established companies before they went public).

Great stocks started as small companies going public. You may be able to recount the stories of Federal Express, Dell, Home Depot, and other great successes. But do you remember an IPO by the company Lipschitz & Farquar? No? We didn't think so. It's among the majority of IPOs that don't succeed.

WARNING

IPOs have a dubious track record of success in their first year. Studies periodically done by the brokerage industry have revealed that IPOs actually decline in price 60 percent of the time (more often than not) during the first 12 months. In other words, an IPO has a better-than-even chance of dropping in price. For Canadian stock investors, the lesson is clear: Wait until a track record appears before you invest in a company. If you don't, you're simply rolling the dice (in other words, you're speculating, not investing!). Don't worry about missing that great opportunity; if it's a bona fide opportunity, you'll still do well after the IPO.

Making sure a small cap stock is making money

REMEMBER

We emphasize two points when investing in stocks:

>> **Make sure that a company is established.** Being in business for at least three years is a good minimum.

>> **Make sure that a company is profitable.** It should show net profits of 10 percent or more over two years or longer.

These points are especially important for investors in small stocks. Plenty of start-up ventures lose money but hope to make a fortune down the road. A good example is a company in the biotechnology industry. Biotech is an exciting area, but it's esoteric, and at this early stage, companies are finding it difficult to use the technology in profitable ways. You may say, "But shouldn't I jump in now in anticipation of future profits?" You may get lucky, but when you invest in unproven, small cap stocks, you're speculating.

Analyzing small cap stocks before investing

The only difference between a small cap stock and a large cap stock is a few zeros in their numbers and the fact that you need to do more research with small caps. By sheer dint of size, small caps are riskier than large caps, so you offset the risk by accruing more information on yourself and the stock in question. Plenty of information is available on large cap stocks because they're widely followed. Small cap stocks don't get as much press, and fewer analysts issue reports on them. Here are a few points to keep in mind:

WARNING

>> **Understand your investment style.** Small cap stocks may have more potential rewards, but they also carry more risk. No investor should devote a large portion of his capital to small cap stocks. If you're considering retirement money, you're better off investing in large cap stocks, exchange-traded funds (ETFs; refer to Chapter 5), investment-grade bonds, bank accounts, and/or mutual funds. For example, retirement money should be in investments that are either very safe or have proven track records of steady growth over an extended period of time (five years or longer).

>> **Check with the SEC and SEDAR.** Get the financial reports that the company must file with the SEC and SEDAR (such as its quarterly reports — see Chapter 12 for more details). These reports offer more complete information on the company's activities and finances. Go to the Securities and Exchange Commission website at www.sec.gov and check its massive database of company filings at EDGAR (Electronic Data Gathering, Analysis, and Retrieval system). Get the financial reports for Canadian public companies through SEDAR (System for Electronic Document Analysis and Retrieval) at www.sedar.com. You can also check to see if any complaints have been filed against the company.

>> **Check other sources.** See whether brokers and independent research services, such as Value Line, follow the stock. If two or more different sources like the stock, it's worth further investigation. Check out Appendix A for further sources of information before you invest.

WARNING

In Chapters 5 and 6, we touch on the TSX Venture Exchange. This is the Canadian stock exchange where you can find lots of small, and risky, development-stage companies. All trading here is executed electronically. Be careful when you invest in one of the many stocks listed on this exchange. You can lose a lot of money before you hit that one diamond in the rough!

Chapter **9**

Investing for Income

I nvesting for income means investing in stocks that provide you with regular cash payments (dividends). Income stocks may not be known to offer stellar growth potential, but they're good for a steady infusion of cash. If you have a lower tolerance for risk, or if your investment goal is anything less than long-term, income stocks are a better bet than growth stocks. Long-term, conservative Canadian investors who need income resources can also benefit from income stocks because of their better track record of keeping pace with inflation (versus fixed-income investments, such as bonds) over the long term.

The bottom line is that we like dividend-paying stocks, and they deserve a spot in a variety of Canadian portfolios. In this chapter, we explain the basics of income stocks, show you how to analyze income stocks with a few handy formulas, and describe several typical income stocks.

TIP

Getting your stock portfolio to yield more income is easier than you think. Many investors increase income using proven techniques such as covered call writing. Covered call writing is beyond the scope of this book, but we encourage you to find out more about it and whether it applies to your situation. Talk to your financial advisor or read up on it — it's covered more fully in *Trading Options For Dummies*, 3rd Edition, by Joe Duarte (Wiley, 2017). You can also find great educational material on this option strategy (and many others) at the Chicago Board Options Exchange (www.cboe.com).

Understanding Income Stocks Basics

We certainly think that dividend-paying stocks are a great consideration for those investors seeking more income in their portfolios. We especially like stocks with higher-than-average dividends that are known as income stocks. Income stocks take on a dual role in that they can not only appreciate but also provide regular income.

Getting a grip on dividends

When people talk about gaining income from stocks, they're usually talking about dividends. A dividend is nothing more than money paid out to the owner of stock. You purchase dividend stocks primarily for income — not for spectacular growth potential.

Dividends are sometimes confused with interest. However, dividends are payouts to owners, whereas interest is a payment to a creditor. A stock investor is considered a part owner of the company she invests in and is entitled to dividends when they're issued. A chartered bank, on the other hand, considers you a creditor when you open an account. The bank borrows your money and pays you interest on it. Unlike interest payments, a company may choose to cease paying common dividends at any time, without being in default. Although investors would be disappointed if dividends were halted, they are nevertheless a discretionary payment by the company.

A dividend is quoted as an annual number but is usually paid on a quarterly basis. For example, if a stock pays a dividend of $4, you're probably paid $1 every quarter. If, in this example, you have 200 shares, you're paid $800 every year (if the dividend doesn't change during that period), or $200 per quarter. Getting that regular dividend cheque every three months (for as long as you hold the stock) can be a nice perk. It's sort of like a short-term mini-pension!

A good income stock has a higher-than-average dividend (typically 4 percent or higher).

Dividend rates aren't guaranteed — they can go up or down, or in some cases when a company is in financial distress, the dividend can be discontinued. Fortunately, most companies that issue dividends continue them indefinitely and actually increase dividend payments from time to time. Historically, dividend increases have equalled (or exceeded) the rate of inflation.

Recognizing who's well-suited for income

Who is best suited to income stocks? They can be appropriate for many investors, but they're especially well-suited for the following individuals:

>> **Conservative and novice investors:** Conservative investors like to see a slow-but-steady approach to growing their money while getting regular dividend cheques. Novice investors who start slowly also benefit.

>> **Retirees:** Growth investing (which we describe in Chapter 8) is best suited for long-term needs, whereas income investing is best suited to current needs. Retirees may want growth in their portfolios, but they're more concerned with regular income that can keep pace with inflation.

>> **Dividend reinvestment plan (DRP) investors:** For those investors who like to compound their money with DRPs, income stocks are perfect. DRPs are exactly what they sound like — they are preset administrative plans that reinvest dividends to buy more stock. They represent a very small portion of stock investing, but it's worthwhile for you to know they exist. Check out www.dripprimer.ca/canadiandriplist for a primer on DRIPs and a list of Canadian companies offering these plans. Some people call this the "get rich eventually" approach.

Advantages of income stocks

Income stocks tend to be among the least volatile of all stocks, and many investors view them as defensive stocks. Defensive stocks are stocks of companies that sell goods and services that are generally needed no matter what shape the economy is in. (Don't confuse defensive stocks with defence stocks, which specialize in goods and equipment for the military.) Food, beverage, and utility companies are great examples of defensive stocks. Many of these utilities are in industries where the firm is a monopoly (sole supplier) or oligopoly (one of a few firms) that control supply in the region, with little competition. Even when the economy is experiencing tough times, people still need to eat, drink, and turn on the lights. Companies that offer relatively high dividends also tend to be large firms in established, stable industries.

TIP

Some industries in particular are known for high-dividend stocks. Utilities (such as electric, gas, and water), real estate investment trusts (REITs), and the energy sector (oil and gas royalty trusts) are places where you definitely find income stocks. You'll have no trouble at all finding a large assortment of high-dividend stocks on the Toronto Stock Exchange, because many of the stocks listed on the TSX, and included in its indexes, fall into one of these industry sectors. Yes, you can find high-dividend stocks in other industries and on foreign stock markets, but you find a higher concentration of them in these industries, especially in Canada. For more details, see the sections highlighting these industries later in this chapter.

Disadvantages of income stocks

Before you say, "Income stocks are great! I'll get my chequebook and buy a batch right now," take a look at the following potential disadvantages (ugh!). Income stocks do come with some fine print.

What goes up . . .

Income stocks can go down as well as up, just as any stock can. The factors that affect stocks in general — politics (Chapter 15), industry and sector changes (Chapter 13), and so on — affect income stocks, too. Fortunately, income stocks don't get hit as hard as other stocks when the market is declining, because high dividends tend to act as a support to the stock price. Therefore, income stocks' prices usually fall less dramatically than other stocks' prices in a declining market.

Interest-rate sensitivity

Income stocks can be sensitive to rising interest rates. When interest rates go up, other investments (such as corporate bonds, newly issued Canadian Treasury securities, and bank guaranteed investment certificates) are more attractive. When your income stock yields 4 percent and interest rates go up to 5 percent, 6 percent, or higher, you may think, "Hmm. Why settle for a 4 percent yield when I can get 5 percent or better elsewhere?" As more and more investors sell their low-yield stocks, the prices for those stocks fall.

Another point to note is that rising interest rates may hurt the company's financial strength. If the company is highly leveraged with debt and has to pay a lot of interest, that may affect the company's earnings, which in turn may affect the company's ability to continue paying dividends.

REMEMBER

Dividend-paying companies that experience consistent falling revenues tend to cut dividends. In this case, consistent means two or more years.

The effect of inflation

Although many companies raise their dividends on a regular basis, some don't. Or if they do raise their dividends, the increases may be small. Some utilities that are monopolies or oligopolies are heavily regulated by government agencies, which may limit their ability to raise revenues and dividends. If income is your primary consideration, you want to be aware of these facts. If you're getting the same dividend year after year and this income is important to you, rising inflation becomes a problem.

Say that you have XYZ stock at $10 per share with an annual dividend of 30 cents (the yield is 30 cents divided by $10, or 3 percent). If you have a yield of 3 percent two years in a row, how do you feel when inflation rises 6 percent one year and 7 percent the next year? Because inflation means costs are rising, inflation shrinks the value of the dividend income you receive. In other words, your dividend income alone can't keep up with your inflated cost of living. Fortunately, studies show that in general, dividends do better in inflationary environments than bonds and other fixed-rate investments. Usually, the dividends of companies that provide consumer staples (food, energy, and so on) meet or exceed the rate of inflation.

PLAYING IT SAFE WITH INCOME-GENERATING ALTERNATIVES

If you're an investor seeking income but you're nervous about the potential risks associated with income stocks, here are some non-stock alternatives:

- **Treasury securities:** Issued by the federal government and considered the safest investments in the world. Canadian Treasury securities are sold to the public to pay off maturing debt and raise money to operate the government. Three general types of treasury securities are sold in Canada and the U.S. Treasury bills (T-bills) mature in three months, six months, or one year. Treasury notes (Canada notes) are intermediate-term securities and mature in two to ten years. Treasury bonds (Canada bonds) are long-term securities that have maturities ranging from 10 to 30 years. U.S. T-bills have much larger minimum purchase requirements than Canadian T-bills, which require minimums from $5,000 (for terms of 6 to 12 months) up to $25,000 (for 30- to 60-day terms). A U.S.-denominated Canadian Treasury bill (guaranteed by the Canadian government) has a minimum requirement of US$100,000.

- **Bank certificates of deposit (CDs):** These investments are backed up (to a limit of $100,000) by the Canada Deposit Insurance Corporation (CDIC) and are very safe.

- **Guaranteed Investment Certificates (GICs):** Like CDs, GICs are safe and also guaranteed (again, up to a limit of $100,000) by the CDIC.

- **Income-generating exchange traded funds (ETFs) and mutual funds:** Income ETFs are dividend and diversified income funds that in many cases make periodic payouts of cash. The iShares Dow Jones Canada Select Dividend Index Fund (XDV-T) is one of many ETFs that generate income. (We discuss ETFs in more detail in Chapter 5.) Also, many mutual funds, such as Canadian Treasury–bond mutual funds and corporate bond funds, are designed for income investors. They offer diversification and professional management, and you can usually invest small amounts.

Canada Revenue Agency's cut

The Canadian government taxes stock dividends on a more favourable basis than, say, income from employment or interest income. Find out from your tax advisor the extent to which this is (or will be) an issue for you. See Chapter 21 for essential information on Canadian taxes for Canadian stock investors. In that chapter, we discuss dividend tax credits, capital gains and capital losses, and other special tax treatments related to stock investing.

Analyzing Income Stocks

As we explain in the preceding section, even conservative income investors can be confronted with different types of risk. (Chapter 4 covers risk and volatility in greater detail.) Fortunately, this section helps you carefully choose income stocks so that you can minimize unwanted outcomes.

TIP

Look at income stocks in the same way you do growth stocks when assessing the financial strength of a company. Getting nice dividends comes to a screeching halt if the company can't afford to pay them. If your budget depends on dividend income, then monitoring the company's financial strength is that much more important. You can apply the same techniques we list in Chapters 8 and 11 for assessing the financial strength of growth stocks to your assessment of income stocks.

Pinpointing your needs first

You choose income stocks primarily because you want or need income now. As a secondary point, income stocks have the potential for steady, long-term appreciation. So if you're investing for retirement needs that won't occur for another 20 years, maybe income stocks aren't suitable for you — a better choice may be to invest in growth stocks because they're more likely to grow your money faster over a lengthier investment term. (We explain who's best suited to income stocks earlier in this chapter and in Chapter 2.)

If you're certain you want income stocks, do a rough calculation to figure out how big a portion of your portfolio you want income stocks to occupy. Suppose that you need $25,000 in investment income to satisfy your current financial needs. If you have bonds that give you $20,000 in interest income and you want the rest to come from dividends from income stocks, you need to choose stocks that pay you $5,000 in annual dividends. If you have $80,000 left to invest, you need a portfolio of income stocks that yields 6.25 percent ($5,000 divided by $80,000 equals a yield of 6.25 percent; we explain yield in more detail in the following section).

You may ask, "Why not just buy $80,000 of bonds (for instance) that yield at least 6.25 percent?" Well, if you're satisfied with that $5,000 and inflation for the foreseeable future is 0 or considerably less than 6.25 percent, then you have a point. Unfortunately, notable inflation and higher taxation on bonds will probably be with us for a long time. Fortunately, the steady growth that income stocks provide is a benefit to you.

REMEMBER

Every investor is different. If you're not sure about your current or future needs, your best choice is to consult with a financial planner. Flip to Chapter 7 for more on robo-advisors and Appendix A for a list of helpful resources.

Checking out yield

REMEMBER

Because income stocks pay out dividends — income — you need to assess which stocks can give you the highest income. How do you do that? The main thing to look for is yield, which is the percentage rate of return paid on a stock in the form of dividends. Looking at a stock's dividend yield is the quickest way to find out how much money you'll earn versus other dividend-paying stocks (or even other investments, such as a bank account). Table 9-1 illustrates this point. Dividend yield is calculated in the following way:

Dividend yield = Dividend income ÷ Stock investment

The next two sections use the information in Table 9-1 to compare the yields from different investments and to show how evaluating yield helps you choose the stock that earns you the most money.

TABLE 9-1 **Comparing Yields**

Investment	Type	Investment Amount	Annual Investment Income (Dividend)	Yield (Annual Investment Income ÷ Investment Amount)
Smith Co.	Common stock	$20 per share	$1.00 per share	5%
Jones Co.	Common stock	$30 per share	$1.50 per share	5%
Wilson Bank	Savings account	$1,000 deposit	$10.00 (interest)	1%

REMEMBER

Don't stop scrutinizing stocks after you acquire them. You may make a great choice that gives you a great dividend, but that doesn't mean the stock will stay that way indefinitely. Monitor the company's progress for as long as it's in your port-folio by using resources such as www.bloomberg.com and www.stockhouse.com (see Appendix A for more resources).

Examining changes in yield

Most people have no problem understanding yield when it comes to bank accounts. If we say a bank Guaranteed Investment Certificate (GIC) from the Bank of Montreal has an annual yield of 2.5 percent, you can figure out that if $1,000 is deposited in it, a year later it will generate $1,025 (slightly more if you include compounding). The GIC's market value in this example is the same as the deposit amount: $1,000. That makes it easy to calculate.

REMEMBER

How about stocks? When you see a stock listed in the financial pages, the dividend yield is provided, along with the stock's price and annual dividend. The dividend yield in the financial pages is always calculated as if you bought the stock on that given day. Just keep in mind that based on supply and demand, stock prices change every business day (virtually every minute!) that the market's open, so the yield changes daily as well. So keep the following two things in mind when examining yield:

>> **The yield listed in the financial pages may not represent the yield you're receiving.** What if you bought stock in Smith Co. (see Table 9-1) a month ago at $20 per share? With an annual dividend of $1, you know your yield is 5 percent. But what if today Smith Co. is selling for $40 per share? If you look in the financial pages, the yield quoted is 2.5 percent. Gasp! Did the dividend get cut in half? No, not really. You're still getting 5 percent because you bought the stock at $20 rather than the current $40 price; the quoted yield is for investors who purchase Smith Co. *today*. They pay $40 and get the $1 dividend, and they're locked into the current yield of 2.5 percent. Although Smith Co. may have been a good income investment for you a month ago, it's not such a hot pick today (from a yield lens) because the price of the stock has doubled, cutting the yield in half. Even though the dividend hasn't changed, the yield has changed dramatically because of the stock price change.

>> **Stock price affects how good of an investment the stock may be.** Another way to look at yield is by looking at the investment amount. Using Smith Co. in Table 9-1 as the example, the investor who bought, say, 100 shares of Smith Co. when they were $20 per share only paid $2,000 (100 shares x $20 — leave out commissions to make the example simple). If the same stock is purchased later at $40 per share, the total investment amount is $4,000 (100 shares x $40). In either case, the investor gets a total dividend income of $100 (100 shares x $1 dividend per share). Which investment is yielding more — the $2,000 investment

or the $4,000 investment? Of course, it's better to get the income ($100 in this case) with the smaller investment amount of $2,000 (a 5 percent yield is better than a 2.5 percent yield).

Comparing yield between different stocks

All things being equal, choosing Smith Co. or Jones Co. is a coin toss. It's looking at your situation and each company's fundamentals and prospects that will sway you. What if Smith Co. is an auto stock (like General Motors during the last recession) and Jones Co. is a Canadian utility serving the Vancouver metro area? Now what? During any of the past few recessions, the North American automotive industry struggled tremendously, but utilities in both Canada and the U.S. were generally in much better shape. In that scenario, Smith Co.'s dividend is in jeopardy, whereas Jones Co.'s dividend is more secure. Another issue is the payout ratio (see the next section). Therefore, companies whose dividends have the same yield may still have different risks.

Looking at a stock's payout ratio

REMEMBER

You can use the payout ratio to figure out what percentage of a company's earnings is being paid out in the form of dividends (earnings = sales – expenses). Keep in mind that companies pay dividends from their net earnings. Therefore, the company's earnings should always be higher than the dividends the company pays out. Here's how to figure a payout ratio:

Dividend (per share) ÷ Earnings (per share) = Payout ratio

Say that the company CashFlow Now, Inc. (CFN), has annual earnings (or net income) of $1 million. Total dividends are to be paid out of $500,000, and the company has 1 million outstanding shares. Using those numbers, you know that CFN's earnings per share (EPS) is $1 ($1 million in earnings ÷ 1 million shares) and that it pays an annual dividend of 50 cents per share ($500,000 ÷ 1 million shares). The dividend payout ratio is 50 percent (the 50-cent dividend is 50 percent of the $1 EPS). This number is a healthy dividend payout ratio because even if CFN's earnings fall by 10 percent or 20 percent, plenty of room still exists to pay dividends.

TIP

If you're concerned about your dividend income's safety, watch the payout ratio. The maximum acceptable payout ratio should be 80 percent, and a good range is 50 to 70 percent. A payout ratio of 60 percent or lower is considered very safe (the lower the percentage, the safer the dividend). Examples of Canadian stocks that in 2018 yielded a payout ratio in the 50 to 60 percent "safe zone" include Toronto Dominion Bank (50 percent), Intact Financial Corporation (53 percent), Emera Inc. (55percent), and Agrium (56 percent).

REMEMBER

When a company suffers significant financial difficulties, its ability to pay dividends is compromised. (Good examples of stocks that have had their dividends cut in recent years due to financial difficulties are Canadian oil industry companies, although the price of oil has begun to rebound, and the fortunes of oil and other resource extraction companies may soon improve. (We discuss resource sector opportunities in Chapter 13.) So if you need dividend income to help you pay your bills, be aware of the dividend payout ratio.

Studying a company's bond rating

Bond rating? Huh? What's that got to do with dividend-paying stocks? Actually, a company's bond rating is very important to income stock investors. The bond rating offers insight into the company's financial strength. Bonds get rated for quality for the same reasons that consumer agencies rate products like cars or toasters. Standard & Poor's (S&P) is the world's major independent rating agency that looks into bond issuers. S&P looks at the bond issuer and asks, "Does this bond issuer have the financial strength to pay back the bond and the interest as stipulated in the bond indenture?" Standard & Poor's (www.standardandpoors.com) and similar bond rating agencies like the Canadian-rooted DBRS (http://dbrs.com) are there to help.

To understand why this rating is important, consider the following:

>> **A good bond rating means that the company is strong enough to pay its obligations.** These obligations include expenses, payments on debts, and declared dividends. If a bond rating agency gives the company a high rating (or if it raises the rating), that's a great sign for anyone holding the company's debt or receiving dividends.

WARNING

>> **If a bond rating agency lowers the rating, that means the company's financial strength is deteriorating.** This is a red flag for anyone who owns the company's bonds or stock. A lower bond rating today may mean trouble for the dividend later on.

>> **A poor bond rating means that the company is having difficulty paying its obligations.** If the company can't pay all its obligations, it has to choose which ones to pay. More often, a financially troubled company chooses to cut dividends or (worst-case scenario) not pay dividends at all.

TIP

The highest rating issued by S&P is AAA. The grades AAA, AA, and A are considered investment grade, or of high quality. Bs and Cs indicate a poor grade, and anything lower than that is considered very risky (the bonds are referred to as junk bonds). So if you see a XXX rating, then . . . gee . . . you'd better stay away! (You may even get an infection.)

WARNING

Just because a bond rating company issues a rating does not mean that the rating is accurate. It is strictly an estimate. Look no further than all of those banks and other public companies that went under during the financial crisis a decade or so ago. Very few had a rating worse than BB! Right.

WARNING

Why do bond rating agencies get it wrong from time to time? Sometimes, it's because the company that an agency evaluates doesn't give the agency complete, relevant, and accurate information from which it can formulate a fair rating. Also, external influences such as the state of the Canadian housing, or oil and gas markets, weigh heavily on a bond rating but are difficult for the agency to fully assess. In the worst-case scenario, a company may try to unduly influence a bond rating agency in order to get a better rating. Because a company can select and pay a rating agency, you can see how opinion shopping for a favourable rating may become a very real risk.

Diversifying your stocks

REMEMBER

If most of your dividend income is from stock in a single company or single industry, consider reallocating your investment to avoid having all your eggs in one basket. Concerns about diversification apply to income stocks as well as growth stocks. If all your income stocks are in the Canadian electric utility industry, then any problems in that industry are potential problems for your portfolio as well. Refer to Chapter 4 for more on risk.

Exploring Some Typical Income Stocks

Although virtually every industry has stocks that pay dividends, some industries have more dividend-paying stocks than others. You won't find too many dividend-paying income stocks in the computer or biotech industries, for instance. The reason is that these types of companies need a lot of money to finance expensive research and development (R&D) projects to create new products. Without R&D, the company can't create new products to fuel sales, growth, and future earnings. Computer, biotech, and other innovative industries are better for growth investors. Keep reading for the scoop on stocks that work well for income investors.

Utilities

Utilities generate a large cash flow. (If you don't believe us, look at your gas, water, and electric bills!) Cash flow includes money from income (sales of products and/or services) and other items (such as the selling of assets, for example). This cash flow is needed to cover expenses, loan payments, and dividends. Utilities are considered the most common type of income stocks, and many investors have at least one utility company in their portfolio. Investing in your own local utility isn't a bad idea — at least it makes paying the utility bill less painful. Examples of Canadian utility companies are TransAlta (TA) and Fortis (FTS), which both trade on the TSX and pay dividends.

REMEMBER

Before you invest in a public utility, consider the following:

>> **The utility company's financial condition:** Is the company making money, and are its sales and earnings growing from year to year? Make sure the utility's bonds are rated A or higher (we cover bond ratings in the earlier section "Studying a company's bond rating").

>> **The company's dividend payout ratio:** Because utilities tend to have a good cash flow, don't be too concerned if the ratio reaches 70 percent. From a stability and safety point of view, however, the lower the rate, the better. See the earlier section "Looking at a stock's payout ratio" for more on payout ratios.

>> **The company's geographic location:** If the utility covers an area that's doing well and offers an increasing population base and business expansion, that bodes well for your stock. Good resources for researching population and business data are Statistics Canada (www.statcan.gc.ca) and the U.S. Census Bureau (www.census.gov).

TIP

The utility sector is not alone in having many dividend-paying stocks. Also check out the stocks of large companies participating in sectors such as finance (like banks and insurance companies), pipelines, basic materials (for example, chemicals, aluminum, gold, and steel); services (airlines, media, entertainment, travel, and accommodation) consumer goods (food, automobile, and healthcare products); and industrial goods.

Real estate investment trusts (REITs)

Real estate investment trusts (REITs) are a special breed of stock. A REIT is an investment that has elements of both a stock and a mutual fund (a pool of money received from investors that's managed by an investment company).

>> A REIT resembles a stock in that it's a company whose stock is publicly traded on the major stock exchanges, and it has the usual features that you expect from a stock — it can be bought and sold easily through a Canadian broker, income is given to investors as a dividend distribution, and so on.

>> A REIT resembles an exchange traded or mutual fund in that it doesn't make its money selling goods and services; it makes its money by buying, selling, and managing an investment portfolio of real estate investments. It generates

revenue from rents and property leases, as any landlord does. Also, some REITs own mortgages and gain income from the interest.

A Canadian unitholder of a Canadian REIT typically receives a distribution on a quarterly or monthly basis, depending on the REIT. The Canadian Income Tax Act allows the distribution to represent some combination of income, capital gain, or return of capital. (We discuss tax implications in Chapter 21).

As a REIT unitholder, you are subject to the appropriate tax on the income and capital gain parts of the distribution, unless you hold the REIT in a tax-exempt vehicle such as an RRSP. You will get a T3 slip for Canada Revenue Agency tax filing purposes either from your broker or directly from the REIT. The slip shows how much is income, how much is a capital gain, and so on. You may also be interested to know that the taxable income that flows to unitholders reduces the taxable income of the REIT. In other words, REITs are typically exempt from tax at the trust (company) level as long they distribute at least 90 percent of their income to their Canadian unitholders. But even REITs that stick to this tax law are still exposed to corporate taxation on retained income.

If you invest in U.S. REITs, you should consult a tax advisor to figure out the exact tax implications of investing in a foreign REIT, because the tax rules and trust rules are different in each country. In general, however, U.S. and Canadian REITs are themselves exempt from corporate taxes as long as they meet certain criteria, such as dispensing almost all of their net income to unitholders. This provision is the reason why REITs generally issue generous dividends or distributions. Beyond this status, REITs are, in a practical sense, like any other publicly traded company. You can find REITs listed on the Toronto Stock Exchange.

The main advantages to investing in REITs include the following:

>> Unlike other types of real estate investing, REITs are easy to buy and sell. In other words, they are liquid. You can buy a REIT through your online broker, just as you can to purchase any stock.

>> REITs have higher-than-average yields. Because they must distribute a very high percentage of their income to unitholders, their dividends usually yield a return of 4 to 13 percent.

>> REITs involve a lower risk than the direct purchase of real estate because they use a portfolio approach diversified among many properties. Because you're investing in a company that buys the real estate, you don't have to worry about managing the properties — the company's management does that on a full-time basis. Usually, the REIT doesn't just manage one property; it's diversified in a portfolio of different properties.

>> Investing in a REIT is affordable for small Canadian investors. REIT shares usually trade in the $10 to $40 range, meaning that you can invest with very little money.

WARNING

REITs do have disadvantages. Although they tend to be diversified with various properties, they're still susceptible to risks tied to the general real estate sector. Real estate investing in the U.S. and Canada has again reached lofty and in many cases record-high levels recently, which means that a downturn may be imminent. In Canada, especially in Vancouver and Toronto, real estate prices are near record highs. Whenever you invest in an asset (like real estate or REITs in recent years) that has already skyrocketed due to artificial stimulants (in the case of real estate, very low interest rates and too much credit and debt), the potential losses can offset any potential (unrealized) income. Also, if interest rates rise, watch for REITs to be pressured downward because real estate companies are often leveraged with debt.

TIP

When looking for a REIT, analyze it the way you'd analyze a property. Look at the location and type of property. If shopping malls are thriving in Edmonton, Toronto, and Winnipeg and your REIT buys and sells shopping malls in those areas, then you'll probably do well. On the other hand, the ongoing rise of online shopping may also threaten these types of REITs. Also, if your REIT invests in office buildings across the country and the office building market is overbuilt and having tough times, you'll have a tough time, too.

TIP

Choosing REITs with a view toward quality and strong fundamentals (location, potential rents, trends, and so forth) is still a good idea.

Royalty trusts

In recent years, the oil and gas sector has generated much interest as the whole sector boomed, then crashed, and is now recovering. Some income investors have capitalized on this price increase by investing in energy stocks called royalty trusts. Royalty trusts are companies that hold assets such as oil-rich and/or natural gas–rich land and generate high fees from companies that seek access to these properties for exploration. The fees paid to the royalty trusts are then disbursed as high dividends to their shareholders. During the early part of this decade, royalty trusts sported yields in the 7 to 12 percent range. More recently, the yields were much lower. However, with oil prices recovering, this is an equity investment worth, um, exploring. See Appendix A for resources on royalty trusts and other income investments.

WARNING

Although energy has been a hot field in recent years and royalty trusts have done well, keep in mind that their payout ratios are very high (often in the 90 to 100 percent range), so dividends will suffer if their cash flow shrinks. (We discuss payout ratios in detail earlier in this chapter.)

IN THIS CHAPTER

» **Defining technical analysis**

» **Talking about trends**

» **Checking out charts**

» **Using technical indicators for investing decisions**

Chapter **10**

Understanding Technical Analysis

I n our early days as stock investors, we rarely used technical analysis, but in our later years, we came to see it as a useful part of our overall investing approach. Yes, technical analysis is . . . well . . . technical, but it can help you time your decision about when you want to buy, sell, or hold a particular stock. In short, fundamental analysis (what the bulk of this book discusses) tells you what to buy, and technical analysis tells you when to buy. We won't make this chapter an exhaustive treatment of this topic (we bet you just said, "Whew!"), but we do want to alert you to powerful techniques and accessible resources that will give you a leg up in today's volatile and uncertain markets, an environment where being nimble and quick with stock trades may pay off.

TIP

We'd like to mention some resources right out of the gate. Use the following resources to discover more information about technical analysis and how it can be applied to stocks that trade in Canada, the U.S., and around the world:

» Big Charts (www.bigcharts.com)

» Canadian Society of Technical Analysts (www.csta.org)

» Incredible Charts (www.incrediblecharts.com)

» International Federation of Technical Analysts (www.ifta.org)

- >> Online Trading Concepts (www.onlinetradingconcepts.com)

- >> StockCharts.com (www.stockcharts.com)

- >> Stocks & Commodities magazine (www.traders.com)

- >> StockTA.com (www.stockta.com)

- >> *Technical Analysis For Dummies,* 3rd Edition, by Barbara Rockefeller (Wiley) (www.dummies.com)

- >> TraderPlanet (www.traderplanet.com)

Comparing Technical Analysis and Fundamental Analysis

When figuring out what to do in the investment world, most professionals use one of two basic approaches: fundamental analysis and technical analysis (many use some combination of the two). Both approaches are used in a number of markets ranging from the stock market to commodities, but we limit this chapter to stock investing. The main differences between fundamental analysis and technical analysis are pretty easy to understand:

- >> **Fundamental analysis** goes into the economics of the company itself, such as sales and profit data, as well as external factors affecting it, such as politics, regulations, and industry trends.

- >> **Technical analysis** tries to understand where a stock's price is going based on market behaviour as evidenced in its market statistics (presented in charts, price, and trading volume data). Technical analysis doesn't try to figure out the worth of an investment; it's used to figure out where the price of that stock or investment is trending.

In the following sections, we talk about the main principles of technical analysis, and we note its pros and cons as compared to fundamental analysis. We also explain how to combine technical analysis with fundamental analysis, and we list some tools of the trade.

Under the hood of technical analysis

To get the most benefit from using technical analysis, you need to understand how it operates and what it is that you're looking at. Technical analysis, for the purposes of this book, is based on the following assumptions.

The price is the be-all and end-all

The premise of technical analysis is that the stock's market price provides enough information to render a trading decision. Those who criticize technical analysis point out that it considers the price and its movement without paying adequate attention to the fundamental factors of the company. The argument made favouring technical analysis is that the price is a snapshot that, in fact, does reflect the basic factors affecting the company, including the company's (or investment's) fundamentals.

REMEMBER

Technical analysts (also called technicians or chartists) believe that the company's fundamentals, along with broader economic factors and market psychology, are all priced into the stock, removing the need to actually consider these factors separately. The bottom line is that technicians look at the price and its movement to extract a forecast for where the stock is going.

The trend is your friend

The price of a stock tends to move in trends. In the world of technical analysis, the phrase "the trend is your friend" is as ubiquitous as the phrase "you spoiled the broth, now you lie in it!" is in the restaurant industry. Maybe even more so. Following the trend is a bedrock principle in technical analysis, and the data either supports the trend or it doesn't. When a trend in the stock's price is established, its tendency is to continue. The three types of trends are up, down, and sideways (but you knew that). (See the later section "Staying on Top of Trends" for more information.)

If it happened before, it will happen again

Another foundational idea in technical analysis is that history tends to repeat itself, mainly in terms of price movement. The repetitive nature of price movements is attributed to market psychology; in other words, market participants tend to provide a consistent reaction to similar market stimuli over time. If enough investors use these technical trading strategies, they can affect the stock market. Whether these strategies are predictive or self-fulfilling prophecies remains to be seen. Regardless of your beliefs, however, understanding how various members of the investing community actually think is useful.

Technical analysis uses chart patterns to analyze market movements and understand trends. Although many of these charts have been used for more than 100 years, they're still believed to be relevant because they illustrate patterns in price movements that often repeat themselves. (We talk about chart patterns in more detail later in this chapter.)

The good and bad of technical analysis

Although technical analysis is the "star" of this chapter, it does have its shortcomings. The major drawback of technical analysis is that it's a human approach that tracks human behaviour in a particular market. In other words, just because it's called technical analysis doesn't mean that it's technical à la the laws of physics. It's called technical analysis because the data you look at is technical. But the movement of the price of the underlying stock or investment is due to the cumulative decisions of many buyers and sellers who are human — and therefore fallible.

Why mention this? Everyone is looking to make money, and many trading systems and approaches are based on technical analysis. Unfortunately, making profitable investments isn't a matter of 2 + 2 = 4. If technical analysis made things so easy that mere computer models or trading systems could give you a voilà-moneymaking decision, everyone could — and would — do it. Yet, that's not the case.

Here's our take on it. We favour fundamental analysis for longer-term investing. We also view technical analysis as a supplementary add-on lens to fundamental analysis. We shun technical analysis for choosing individual stocks because we don't see the long-term value in it. Long-term investors don't have to bother with things such as triangles, pennants, cup-and-handles, or other paraphernalia. Long-term investors just ask fundamental questions like "Is the company making money?" or "Are financial and economic conditions still favourable for my investment?" When the fundamentals are in your favour, any short-term move against you is a buying opportunity (provided that you choose wisely from the start). But unfortunately, too many investors aren't patient, and they get too busy with the short-term trees to be bothered by the long-term forest. Yet that long-term forest has a lot more green, if you know what we mean (we hope we're not meandering here).

TECHNICAL STUFF

If you were to do a nose count of successful investors in stock market history and what approaches they used, you'd find that those long-term investors who used some variation of fundamental analysis (such as those who used a value-investing approach) overwhelmingly comprise the larger category. Legendary investors like Warren Buffett and Peter Lynch rarely looked at a chart. Think about it: Warren Buffett is obviously one of history's greatest success stories in the world of stock investing. His track record and multibillion-dollar net worth attest to this. Yet, he rarely (if ever) looks at any technical analysis. He isn't concerned with short-term squiggles and fluctuations. He is indeed a long-term investor, and one of his greatest assets is patience. He has held some stocks for decades. The point makes for an interesting observation into human nature. Everyone wants to succeed like Warren Buffett, but few are willing to go the distance and mirror his patience.

The short term is a different animal. It requires more attention and discipline. You need to monitor all the indicators to see whether you're on track or whether the signals are warning of a change in course. The technicals can be bearish one month and bullish the next. And the month after that, the signals can be mixed and give no clear warnings at all. Being a proficient technician ultimately requires more monitoring, more trading, and more hedging. This, of course, also leads to higher broker transaction costs.

Note that all this activity also means more taxes to the Canada Revenue Agency (CRA), more transaction costs (commissions and the like), and more administrative work (tax reporting and so on). After all, who do you think will pay more taxes to the CRA: someone who buys and holds for a year or longer or someone who makes the same profit by jumping in and out based on which way the technical winds are blowing? Short-term gains generally have less favourable trading costs and related taxes than long-term gains. Sometimes the issue isn't what you make but what you keep (Canadian tax rules and implications are covered in Chapter 21).

REMEMBER

But before you throw out technical analysis with the bath water, read on. Those who use technical analysis in short-term trading or speculating in larger-scope investments tend to do better than those who don't use it. That means that if you apply technical analysis to something larger than a company, such as an index or a commodity, you'll tend to do better. If you're getting into trading stocks and/or stock-related exchange-traded funds (ETFs; refer to Chapter 5), then understanding the basics of technical analysis will make you, overall, a better (and hence more profitable) trader. Because short-term market behaviour and psychology can be very mercurial and irrational (human), technical analysis has its usefulness. It's most useful for those folks who are trading and/or speculating during a relatively short time frame measured in days, weeks, or months. It isn't that useful when you're trying to forecast where a stock's price will be a year or more down the road.

Combining the best of both worlds

We think that a useful way to combine both fundamental analysis and technical analysis is to take advantage of the strength of each. Fundamental analysis helps you understand what to invest (or trade or speculate) in, whereas technical analysis guides you as to when to do it. Because markets ebb and flow, zig and zag, technical analysis can help you spot low-risk points to either enter or exit a trade. Technical analysis, therefore, helps you stack the deck in your favour. Considering how markets have been going lately, every little bit helps.

Blending the two approaches has been done with some success. Obviously, if the fundamental and the technical factors support your decision, then the chance for a profitable trade has more going for it. How does this blend occur?

For an example, look at the concepts of oversold and overbought (see the section "The Relative Strength Index," later in this chapter). If you're looking at buying a stock (or other investment) because you think it's a strong investment (based on your fundamental analysis) but you're not sure about when to buy, you want to look at the technical data. If the data tells you that it has been oversold, it's a good time to buy. Oversold just means that the market was a little too extreme in selling that particular investment during a particular period of time. This happened in 2015 when the stocks of many Canadian and international oil companies sold off, in many cases to a share price below a company's liquidation value (meaning, roughly, cash on hand plus net marketable assets). Technical analysis revealed and confirmed an oversold state for many oil companies at that time. So being a contrarian, because of good technical insight, can add value.

TIP

By the way, we like to think that the technical terms oversold and overbought have a parallel to fundamental terms such as undervalued and overvalued. Because fundamental analysis is a major part of a school of thought referred to as value investing, the concepts make sense (yes, we're into value investing). Just as investing in an undervalued stock is usually a good idea, so is buying a stock that has been oversold. It's logical to presume that an oversold stock is undervalued (all things being equal). Of course, the other terms (overbought and overvalued) can also run in tandem. We may as well finish here before you're overwhelmed and underinterested.

On the other hand, the fundamentals can help a technical analyst make a better trading decision. Say that a technical analyst has a profitable position in a particular stock called Getting Near a Cliff Corp. (GNAC). If the technical indicators are turning bearish and the new quarterly earnings report for GNAC indicates a significantly lower profit, then selling GNAC's stock is probably a good idea. (Of course, because you're reading this book, you're doing something better like immediately putting on a trailing stop, right? See Chapter 17 for details on trailing stops.)

Using the technician's tools

When you roll up your sleeves and get into technical analysis, what will you be dealing with? It depends on what type of technical analyst you are. In technical analysis, there are two subcategories: those who predominantly use charts (these technicians are called . . . chartists!) and those who predominantly use data (such as price and volume data). Of course, many technicians use a combination of both (and we discuss both later in this chapter):

>> **Charts:** Charts are the neat pictures that graph price movements (such as chart patterns).

>> **Data:** Data includes price and volume information (along with technical and behavioural indicators derived from it).

Technical analysts don't look at the fundamentals because they believe that the marketplace (as depicted in the charts, price, and volume data) already takes into account the fundamentals.

Staying on Top of Trends

Identifying trends is a crucial part of technical analysis. A trend is just the overall direction of a stock (or another security or a commodity); you can see trends in technical charts (we provide details about charts later in this chapter). Which way is the price headed? In the following sections, we describe different types of trends, talk about trend length, and discuss trend lines and channel lines.

Distinguishing different trends

REMEMBER

Three basic trends exist:

>> **An uptrend or bullish trend** is when each successive high is higher than the previous high and each successive low is higher than the previous low.

>> **A downtrend or bearish trend** is when each successive high is lower than the previous high and each successive low is lower than the previous low.

>> **A sideways trend or horizontal trend** shows that the highs and the lows are both in a generally sideways pattern with no clear indication of trending up or down (at least not yet).

It's easy to see which way the stock is headed in Figure 10-1. Unless you're a skier, that's not a pretty picture. The bearish trend is obvious.

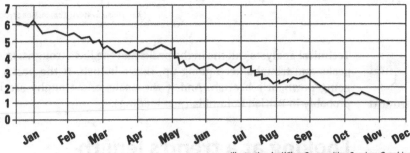

FIGURE 10-1: Generic chart sloping in a definite downward direction.

Illustration by Wiley, Composition Services Graphics

What do you do with a chart like Figure 10-2? Yup . . . looks like somebody's heart monitor while he's watching a horror movie. A sideways or horizontal trend just shows a consolidation pattern that means that the stock will break out into an up or down trend.

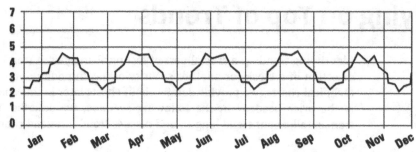

FIGURE 10-2:
Generic chart showing a sideways pattern.

Illustration by Wiley, Composition Services Graphics

Regardless of whether a trend is up, down, or sideways, you'll notice that it's rarely (closer to never) in a straight line. The line is usually jagged and bumpy because it's really a summary of all the buyers and sellers making their trades. Some days the buyers have more impact, and some days it's the sellers' turn. Figure 10-3 shows all three trends.

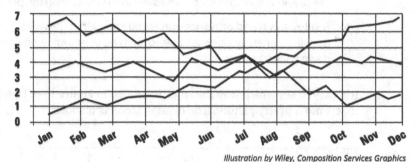

FIGURE 10-3:
Chart that simultaneously shows an up, down, and sideways trend.

Illustration by Wiley, Composition Services Graphics

REMEMBER

Technical analysts call the highs peaks and the lows troughs. In other words, if the peaks and troughs keep going up, that's bullish. If the peaks and troughs keep going down, it's bearish. And if the peaks and troughs are horizontal, you're probably in British Columbia (just kidding).

Looking at a trend's length

With trends, you're not just looking at the direction; you're also looking at the trend's duration, or the length of time that it goes along. Trend durations can be (you guessed it) short-term, intermediate-term, or long-term.

>> **A short-term (or near-term) trend** is generally less than a month.

>> **An intermediate-term trend** is up to a quarter (three months) long.

>> **A long-term trend** can last up to a year. And to muddy the water a bit, the long-term trend may have several trends inside it (don't worry; the quiz has been cancelled).

Using trendlines

A trendline is a simple feature added to a chart: a straight line designating a clear path for a particular trend. Trendlines simply follow the peaks and troughs to show a distinctive direction. They can also be used to identify a trend reversal, or a change in the opposite direction. Figure 10-4 shows two trendlines: the two straight lines that follow the tops and bottoms of the jagged line (which shows the actual price movement of the asset in question).

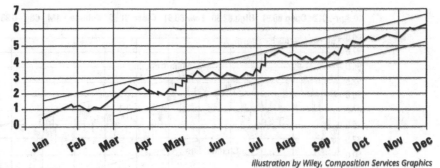

Illustration by Wiley, Composition Services Graphics

FIGURE 10-4: Chart that shows the jagged edge going upward along with the trendlines.

Watching for resistance and support

REMEMBER

The concepts of resistance and support are critical to technical analysis the way tires are to cars. When the rubber meets the road, you want to know where the price is going.

>> *Resistance* is like the proverbial glass ceiling in the market's world of price movement. As a price keeps moving up, how high can or will it go? That's the $64,000 question, and technical analysts watch this closely. Breaking through resistance is considered a positive sign for the price, and the expectation is definitely bullish.

>> **Support** is the lowest point or level that a price is trading at. When the price goes down and hits this level, it's expected to bounce back, but what happens when it goes below the support level? It's then considered a bearish sign, and technical analysts watch closely for a potential reversal even though they expect the price to head down.

Channel lines are lines that are added to show both the peaks and troughs of the primary trend. The top line indicates resistance (of the price movement), and the lower line indicates support. Resistance and support form the trading range for the stock's price. The channel can slope or point upward or downward, or go sideways. Technical traders view the channel with interest because the assumption is that that the price will continue in the direction of the channel (between resistance and support) until technical indicators signal a change. (To us, this tells us to change to a different Netflix Canada channel, but that's just us. Please continue reading. . . .) Check out the channel in Figure 10-5; it shows you how the price is range-bound. The emphasis on trends is to help you make more profitable decisions because you're better off trading with the trend than not.

10-Apr-2012 **Open** 80.91 **High** 82.80 **Low** 80.61 **Close** 81.50 **Volume** 1.3M **Chg** –0.36 (–0.43%)

FIGURE 10-5:
Chart showing
a channel.

Illustration by Wiley, Composition Services Graphics

In Figure 10-5, you see a good example of a channel for a particular fictitious stock. In this case, the stock is zigzagging downward, and toward the end of the channel, it indicates that the stock is getting more volatile as the stock's price movement is outside the original channel lines. This tells the trader/investor to be cautious and on the lookout for opportunities or pitfalls (depending on your outlook for the stock).

Getting the Scoop on Technical Charts

Charts are to technical analysis what pictures are to photography. You can't avoid them 'cause you're not supposed to. If you're serious about trading stocks (or ETFs, commodities, or whatever), charts and the related technical data come in handy. In the following sections, we describe different types of charts and chart patterns.

Checking out types of charts

Technical analysts use charts to "diagnose" an investment's situation the same way any analyst uses different tools and approaches. Different charts provide fresh angles for viewing the data. In terms of visualization and utility, the following are the four most common charts used in technical analysis.

Line charts

A chart simply shows a series of prices plotted in a graph that displays how the price has moved over a period of time. The period of time can be a day, week, month, year, or longer. The prices that are usually chosen for a line chart are the closing prices for those market days.

With a year-long line chart (like those that appear earlier in this chapter), you can see how the stock has progressed during the 12-month period, and you can do some simple analysis. When were the peaks? How about the troughs? What were the strongest seasons for this stock's price movement?

TIP

We prefer to use five-year charts; we like to encourage our clients, students, and readers to focus on the longer term because positive results can be easier to predict and achieve.

Bar charts

Bar charts are a little fancier. Whereas the line chart gives you only the closing prices for each market day, the bar chart gives you the range of trading prices for each day during the chosen time period. Each trading day is a vertical line that represents the price movements, and you see the stock's high, low, and closing prices.

In a bar chart, the vertical line has two notches. The notch on the left indicates the opening price, and the notch on the right indicates the closing price. If the opening price notch is higher than the closing price notch, the line is in red to indicate that the closing price of the stock declined versus the opening price. An up day is in black, and the closing price notch is higher than the opening price notch.

Candlestick charts

Candlestick charts have been all the rage in recent years. They're basically bar charts, but they're a little more complex. A candlestick chart provides a more complete picture by adding a unique visualization of other data that simple charts don't contain, such as the high, low, and closing price of the security the chart is tracking, and bullish or bearish trends by using colours. It stands to reason that because candlestick charts provide a bit more information in a visual form than bar charts, they can provide more guidance in trading. Candlestick charting is too involved to adequately describe in this space, so please continue your research with the resources provided at the start of this chapter.

TECHNICAL STUFF

The full name for these charts is Japanese candlestick charts because they originated as a form of technical analysis in the 17th century, when the Japanese were trading in rice markets. You know, they do look like candlesticks (but we're waxing eloquent here).

Point-and-figure charts

A more obscure chart that chartists use is the point-and-figure chart. When you look at it, you'll notice a series of X's and O's. The X's represent upward price trends, and the O's represent downward price trends. This type of chart enables the stock trader to easily determine which prices are "support levels" and which are "resistance levels" to better judge buy and sell prices. X's and O's are also used by Canadian Football League coaches to depict offensive and defensive alignments and plays. Sorry, we couldn't resist that one!

Picking out chart patterns

Chart patterns are the graphical language of technical analysis, and a very interesting language at that. Chart patterns come in all shapes, sizes, and colours. Some look like the jagged lines of a saw. Some look like a simple bar chart. Still others look like multi-coloured candlesticks. Anything goes, as long as it fits into a web page!

For technical analysts, the pattern is important because it provides a potential harbinger for what is to come. It's not 100 percent accurate, but it's usually accurate better than 50 percent of the time as odds go. In the world of trading, being right more than 50 percent of the time can be enough. Usually a proficient technician is better than that. The following sections cover common chart patterns.

REMEMBER

Technical analysts don't say that the next step after a particular pattern is a certainty; it's a *probability*. Probable outcomes tend to materialize. Increasing the probability of success for more-profitable decision making (entering or exiting a trade) is the bottom-line mission of technical analysis.

Above the rest: The head and shoulders

The head and shoulders pattern is essentially bearish. It's usually a signal that an uptrend has ended and the pattern is set to reverse and head downward. Technical analysts consider this to be one of the most reliable patterns.

The pattern shows three peaks and two troughs. The three peaks break down into the tall centre peak (the head) and the shorter peaks (the shoulders) that are on either side of the centre peak. The two troughs form the neckline.

The head and shoulders pattern tells technical analysts that the preceding trend basically ran out of gas. The selling pressures build up and overpower the buyers. Hence, the price starts to come down. The shoulder on the right is like a last effort for the bullish trend to regain its traction, but to no avail. Keep in mind that the neckline in this pattern is the support (which we discuss in the earlier section "Watching the channel for resistance and support"). As support is broken, the tendency is a bearish expectation.

In reverse: The reverse head and shoulders

As you can infer, this pattern is the opposite of the prior chart pattern, and it's essentially bullish. This pattern signals that a downtrend has ended and is set to reverse and head upward. In this pattern, you have three troughs and two peaks. The middle trough is usually the deepest one. The small trough on the right is an interim low, which is higher than the middle trough low and typically indicates the trend is moving upward.

In this pattern, buying pressures build up and form a base from which to spring upward. Note that a bullish pattern is a series of higher highs and higher lows. In the reverse head and shoulders pattern, the neckline is resistance (which we discuss earlier in this chapter). When resistance is broken, the expectation is for an upward move.

Wake up and smell the coffee: The cup and handle

This pattern is generally bullish. In the pattern, the price first peaks and then craters into a bowl-shaped trough (the cup). It peaks again at the end with a small downward move (the handle) before it moves up. This pattern basically tells the technician that the stock's price took a breather to build support and then continued its bullish pattern.

Twice as nice: The double top and the double bottom

Both the double top and double bottom chart patterns indicate a trend reversal:

>> **The double top** is essentially a bearish pattern wherein the price makes two attempts (the double top) to break through resistance but fails to do so. The bottom of the trough between the two peaks indicates support. However, the two failed attempts at the resistance level are more significant than the support at the trough, so this pattern signals a potential downturn for that stock's price.

>> **The double bottom** is the opposite reversal pattern. It's a bullish pattern because the support level indicators are stronger than the resistance. This pattern signals a potential upturn in the stock's price. Because this indicates a support level, bullish traders tend to look at it as a generally safe entry point to get positioned for the next potential up-move in the stock.

TECHNICAL STUFF

Triple tops and triple bottoms are variations of double tops and double bottoms. These are sideways or horizontal patterns that do portend a trend reversal. Don't even ask about quadruple tops and bottoms! Those are moves that only snowboarders in Banff and fans of Cirque du Soleil talk about.

Triangles (And we don't mean Bermuda!)

A triangle is formed when the resistance line and the support line converge to form the triangle point that shows a general direction in the stock's price movement. Remember that the trend is your friend, so this is an important technical indicator. There are three types of triangles:

>> **Symmetrical:** The symmetrical triangle points sideways, telling you it's a horizontal pattern that becomes a setup for a move upward or downward when more price movement provides a bullish or bearish indicator.

>> **Ascending:** The ascending triangle is a bullish pattern.

>> **Descending:** The descending triangle is bearish.

Of course, if you see a divergent trapezoidal and octagonal candlestick formation supported in a bowl-shaped isosceles triangle, do nothing! Just take two aspirin and try again tomorrow.

Time to cheer: Flags and pennants

Flags and pennants are familiar chart patterns that are short-term in nature (usually not longer than a few weeks). They're continuation patterns that are formed immediately after a sharp price movement, which is usually followed by a sideways price movement. Both the flag and the pennant are similar except that the flag is triangular whereas the pennant is in a channel formation (we talk about channels earlier in this chapter).

Cut it up: Wedges

The wedge pattern can be either a continuation or reversal pattern. It seems to be much like a symmetrical triangle, but it slants (up or down), whereas the symmetrical triangle generally shows a sideways movement. In addition, the wedge forms over a longer period of time (typically three to six months).

Watch your step: Gaps

A gap in a chart is an empty space between two trading periods. This pattern occurs when the difference in the price between those two periods is substantial. Say that in the first period, the trading range is $10 to $15. The next trading session opens at $20. That $5 discrepancy will appear as a large gap between those two periods on the chart. These gaps are typically found on bar and candlestick charts. Gaps may happen when positive (or negative) news comes out about the company, and initial buying pressure causes the price to jump in the subsequent period as soon as trading commences.

Three types of gaps exist: breakaway, runaway, and exhaustion. The breakaway gap forms at the start of a trend, and the runaway gap forms during the middle. So what obviously happens when the trend gets tired at the end? Why, the exhaustion gap, of course! See, this stuff isn't that hard to grasp.

Surveying Technical Indicators

An indicator is a mathematical calculation that can be used with the stock's price and/or volume. The end result is a value that's used to anticipate future changes in price. There are two types of indicators: leading and lagging.

>> **Leading** indicators are forward-looking and help you profit by attempting to forecast what prices will do next. They provide greater rewards at the expense of increased risk. They perform best in sideways or trading markets. They work by measuring how overbought or oversold a stock is.

>> **Lagging** (or trend-following) indicators are best suited to price movements in relatively long trends. They don't warn you of any potential changes in price. Lagging indicators have you buy and sell in a mature trend, when the risk is reduced.

The following sections describe a variety of leading and lagging indicators.

The Relative Strength Index

As noted in the earlier section "Combining the best of both worlds," the technical conditions of overbought and oversold are important to be aware of. They're good warning flags to help you time a trade, whether that means getting in or getting out of a position. The Relative Strength Index (RSI) is a convenient metric for measuring the overbought/oversold condition. Generally, the RSI quantifies the condition and gives you a number that acts like a barometer. On a reading of 0 to 100, the RSI becomes oversold at about the 30 level and overbought at about the 70 level.

The RSI is a metric usually calculated and quoted by most charting sources and technical analysis websites. It's generally considered a leading indicator because it forewarns potential price movements.

TIP

For Canadian stock investors, we think the RSI is particularly useful for timing the purchase or sale of a particular stock. We know when we're looking at a favourite stock that we like and notice that its RSI is below 30, we check to see whether anything is wrong with the stock (did the fundamentals change?). If nothing is wrong and it's merely a temporary, market-driven event, we consider buying more of the stock. After all, if we loved a great stock at $40 and it's now cheaper at $30, all things being equal, we have a great buying opportunity. Conversely, if we're not crazy about a stock and we see that it's overbought, we consider either selling it outright or at least putting a stop-loss order on the stock (see Chapter 17).

Moving averages

In terms of price data, a favourite tool of the technical analyst is the moving average. A moving average is the average price of a stock over a set period of time (which can range from five days to six months — or sometimes longer). It's considered a lagging indicator. Frequently a chart shows price movements as too jumpy and haphazard, so the moving average smoothes out the price movements to show a clearer path. This important data stabilizing technique helps to decipher the stock's trend and plot out the support and resistance levels. Moving averages are also very helpful in identifying all the various peaks and troughs necessary to analyze the trend's direction. Three types of moving averages exist: simple, linear, and exponential.

A snapshot: Simple moving averages (SMA)

The first (and most common) type of average is referred to as a simple moving average (SMA). You calculate it by simply taking the sum of all the past closing prices over the chosen time period and dividing the result by the number of prices used in the calculation. For example, in a ten-day simple moving average, the last ten closing prices are added together and then divided by ten.

Say that the prices for the last ten trading days (in order) are $20, $21, $22, $20, $21, $23, $24, $22, $22, and $24. It's hard to derive a trend from that data, but a moving average can help. First you add up all the prices; in this case, the total is $219. Then you take the total of $219 and divide it by ten (the total number of trading days). You get an average price of $21.90. As you do this with more and more price data (in ten-day chronological sets), you can see a trend unfolding.

Say that on the 11th day, the closing price is $26. At this point, the next ten-day trading period starts with $21 (the closing price from the second day in the example from the preceding paragraph) and ends with a new closing price for the tenth day, $26. Now when you add up this new ten-day range, you get a total of $225. When you divide that number by ten, you get the average of $22.50 ($225 total divided by ten days). In this brief and simple example, the ten-day moving average tells you that the price trend is up (from $21.90 to $22.50).

Of course, you need to see a much longer string of ten-day sets to ascertain a useful ten-day moving average, but you get the point. These averages can also be plotted on a graph to depict the trend and help render a trading decision. The more time periods you graph, the easier it is to see how strong (or weak) the trend is.

Technical analysts most frequently use 10-day, 20-day, and 50-day averages for short-term trading. To confirm longer-term trends, they also watch the 100-day and 200-day moving averages. Of course, other time frames are used as well, but these are the most common.

The longer-period moving averages help to put the short terms in perspective so that the trader can still view the big picture. In other words, you may have a stock "correct" or pull back and see its price fall significantly, but does it mean that a trend has reversed? If the stock is in a long-term bull market, it's common for it to violate (or go below) its short-term (such as 10-, 20- or 50-day) moving averages temporarily. The more serious red flags start to appear when it violates the longer-term averages, such as the 200-day moving average. And if it violates the ten-year moving average . . . hey . . . watch out!

More complex tactics: Linear and exponential averages

Some critics believe that the SMA is too limited in its scope and therefore not as useful as it should be. Therefore, they use more involved variants of the SMA such as the linear weighted average (LWA) and the exponential moving average (EMA).

These averages are too involved to adequately cover in this book. You can get more details on them through the resources at the start of this chapter. For beginners, though, the SMA is definitely sufficient.

Moving average convergence/divergence

The moving average convergence/divergence (MACD) is a lagging indicator that shows the relationship between two moving averages of prices. The MACD is calculated by subtracting the 26-day exponential moving average (EMA) from the 12-day EMA. A nine-day EMA of the MACD, called the signal line, is then plotted on top of the MACD, which acts as a trend-based trigger for making buy and sell orders.

TIP

That's the technical definition of the MACD, but don't worry if you didn't understand it on the first go-round. Fortunately, it's not something that you have to calculate on your own; the MACD indicator is usually provided by the technical analysis software or trading service that you may use. Its purpose is to simply create more precision in what is otherwise only a guess at where a stock price may go next.

Crossovers and divergence

A crossover is the point when the stock's price and an indicator intersect (or cross over). It's used as a signal to make a buy or sell order. Say that a stock, for example, falls past $20 per share to $19, and the 20-day moving average is $19.50. That would be a bearish crossover, and it would indicate a good time to sell or risk further downward movement. The opposite is true as well; some crossovers indicate a good time to buy.

Divergence occurs when the price of a stock and an indicator (or index or other related security) part company and head off in opposite directions. Divergence is considered either positive or negative, both of which are signals of changes in the price trend.

>> **Positive divergence** occurs when the price of a stock makes a new low while a bullish indicator starts to climb upward.

>> **Negative divergence** happens when the price of a stock makes a new high, but bearish indicators signal the opposite, and instead the closing price at the end of the trading day is lower than the previous high.

Crossovers and divergence are usually leading indicators.

Oscillators

Oscillators are indicators that are used when you're analyzing charts that have no clear trend. Moving averages and other indicators are certainly important when the trend is clear, but oscillators are more beneficial under either of the following circumstances:

>> When the stock is in a horizontal or sideways trading pattern

>> When a definite trend can't be established because the market is volatile and the price action is uneven

Oscillators may be either leading or lagging indicators, depending on what type they are. Momentum oscillators, for example, are considered leading indicators because they're used to track the momentum of price and volume. Use the resources mentioned earlier to do your homework on oscillators.

Bollinger bands

Bollinger bands have nothing to do with musical groups. A band is plotted two standard deviations away from a simple moving average. The bollinger band (a lagging indicator) works like a channel and moves along with the simple moving average.

Bollinger bands help the technical analyst watch out for overbought and oversold conditions. Basically, if the price moves closer to the upper band, it indicates an overbought condition. If the price moves closer to the lower band, it indicates an oversold condition.

3 Picking Winners

IN THIS PART . . .

Use basic accounting principles to figure out a company's value and financial health.

Read and understand what companies say about themselves and what others say about them.

Find out about sectors and small caps and the emerging marijuana industry.

Diversify your portfolio by investing in Asian stocks.

Understand how government and politics relate to stock investing.

Chapter 11

Using Accounting Basics to Choose Winning Stocks

oo often, the only number investors look at when they look at a stock is the stock price quote. Yet what really drives the stock price is the company behind that single number. To make a truly good choice in the world of stocks, you have to consider the company's essential financial information. What does it take to see these important numbers?

This book in your hands and a little work on your part are all you need to succeed. This chapter takes the mystery out of the numbers behind the stock. The most tried-and-true method for picking a good stock starts with picking a good company. Picking a company means looking at its products, services, industry, and financial strength. Considering the problems that the market has witnessed in recent years — such as corporate debt problems and derivative meltdowns wreaking havoc on public companies and financial firms around the world — this chapter is more important than ever. Don't underestimate it. Because accounting is the language of business, understanding the basics behind the numbers can save your portfolio.

Recognizing Value When You See It

If you pick a stock based on the value of the underlying company that issues it, you're a value investor — an investor who looks at a company's value to judge whether you can purchase the stock at a good price. Companies have value the same way many things have value, such as eggs or elephant-foot umbrella stands. And there's a fair price to buy them at, too. Take eggs, for example. You can eat them and have a tasty treat while getting nutrition as well. But would you buy an egg for $1,000 (and no, you're not a starving millionaire on a deserted island)? Of course not. But what if you could buy an egg for 5 cents? At that point, it has value and a good price. This kind of deal is a value investor's dream.

Value investors analyze a company's fundamentals (earnings, assets, and so on) to see whether the information justifies purchasing the stock. They see whether the stock price is low relative to these verifiable, quantifiable factors. Therefore, value investors use fundamental analysis, whereas other investors may use technical analysis. Technical analysis looks at stock charts and statistical data, such as trading volume and historical stock prices (We take a closer look at technical analysis for investors in Chapter 10.) Some investors use a combination of both strategies.

History has shown that the most successful long-term investors have typically been value investors using fundamental analysis as their primary investing approach. The most consistently successful long-term investors were — and are — predominately value investors (yes, we count ourselves in this crowd as well). Here, we describe different kinds of value and explain how to spot a company's value in several places.

Understanding different types of value

Value may seem like a murky or subjective term, but it's the essence of good stockpicking. You can measure value in different ways (as you discover in the following sections), so you need to know the differences and understand the impact that value has on your investment decisions.

Market value

REMEMBER

When you hear someone quoting a stock at $47 per share, that price reflects the stock's market value. The total market valuation of a company's stock is also referred to as its market cap or market capitalization. How do you determine a company's market cap? With the following simple formula:

Market capitalization = Share price × Number of shares outstanding

If Canuck Corp.'s stock is $35 per share and it has 10 million shares outstanding (or shares available for purchase), its market cap is $350 million. Granted, $350 million may sound like a lot of money, but Canuck Corp. is considered a small cap stock. (For more on small cap stocks, see Chapter 1.)

Who sets the market value of stock? The market, of course! Millions of investors buying and selling directly and through intermediaries such as mutual funds determine the market value of any particular stock. If the market perceives that the company is desirable, investor demand for the company's stock pushes up the share price.

WARNING

The problem with market valuation is that it's not always a good indicator of a good investment. In recent years, plenty of companies have had astronomical market values, yet they've proven to be very risky investments. For example, think about Valeant Pharmaceuticals of Montreal, which for a brief period was the largest company on the TSX in terms of market capitalization. Shares of Valeant reached a peak of $335 in July 2015. Then things went south. A catastrophic combination of controversial drug price hikes and an alleged multimillion-dollar kickback scheme caused those shares to tumble to as low as $12.75. It has since recovered a bit, but the damage to the company's reputation still places pressure on the stock price today. In fact, the company has since changed its name to Bausch Health Companies to cosmetically distance itself from its troubled past. Because market value is a direct result of the buying and selling of stock investors, it can be a fleeting thing. This precariousness is why investors must understand the company behind the stock price.

Book value and intrinsic value

Book value (also referred to as accounting value) looks at a company from a balance sheet perspective (assets – liabilities = net worth, or stockholders' equity). It's a way of judging a firm by its net worth to see whether the stock's market value is reasonable compared to the company's intrinsic value. *Intrinsic* value is tied to what the market price of a company's assets — both tangible (such as equipment) and intangible (such as patents) — would be if sold.

Generally, market value tends to be higher than book value. If market value is substantially higher, the value investor becomes more reluctant to buy that particular stock — it's overvalued. The closer the stock's market capitalization is to the book value, the safer the investment, if the company is well-run.

WARNING

We like to be cautious with a stock whose market value is more than twice its book value. If the market value is $1 billion or more and the book value is $500 million or less, that's a good indicator that the business may be overvalued, or valued at a higher price than its book value and ability to generate a profit. Just understand that the farther the market value is from the company's book value, the more you'll pay for the company's real potential value. And the more you pay, the greater the risk that the company's market value (the stock price, that is) can decrease.

Sales value and earnings value

A company's intrinsic value is directly tied to its ability to make money. For this reason, many analysts like to value stocks from the perspective of the company's income statement. Two common and very important barometers of value are expressed in ratios: the price-to-sales ratio (P/S) and the price-to-earnings (P/E) ratio. In both instances, the price is a reference to the company's market value (as reflected in its share price). Sales and earnings are references to the firm's ability to make money. These two ratios are covered more fully in the later section "Tooling around with ratios."

REMEMBER

For investors, the general approach is clear. The closer the market value is to the company's intrinsic value, the better. And, of course, if the market value is lower than the company's intrinsic value, you have a potential bargain worthy of a closer look. Part of looking closer means examining the company's income statement (which we discuss later in this chapter), also called the profit and loss statement, income statement, or simply the P&L. A low price-to-sales ratio is 1 or below (say, for example, 0.7), a medium P/S is between 1 and 2, and a high P/S is 3 or higher.

Putting the pieces together

When you look at a company from a value-oriented perspective, here are some of the most important items to consider (see the later section "Accounting for Value" for more information):

>> **The balance sheet, to figure out the company's net worth:** A value investor doesn't buy a company's stock because it's cheap, but because it's undervalued (the company is worth more than the price its stock reflects — its market value is as close as possible to its book value).

>> **The income statement, to figure out the company's profitability:** A company may be undervalued from a simple comparison of the book value and the market value, but that doesn't mean it's a screaming buy. For example, what if you find out that a company is in trouble and losing money this year? Do you buy its stock then? No, you don't. Why invest in the stock of a losing company? (If you do, you aren't investing — you're gambling or speculating.) The heart of a firm's value, besides its net worth, is its ability to generate profit and cash.

>> **Ratios that let you analyze just how well (or not so well) the company is doing:** Value investors basically look for a bargain. That being the case, they generally don't look at companies that everyone is talking about, because by that point, the stock of those companies ceases to be a bargain. The value investor searches for a stock that will eventually be discovered by the market and then watches as the stock price goes up. But before you bother digging into the fundamentals to find that bargain stock, first make sure that the company is making money.

The more ways that you can look at a company and see value, the better:

>> **Examine the P/E ratio.** One of the first things we look at is the P/E ratio. Does the company have one? (This question may sound dumb, but if the company's losing money, it may not have one.) Does the P/E ratio look reasonable, or is it in triple-digit, nosebleed territory?

>> **Check out the debt load.** Next, look at the company's debt load (the total amount of liabilities). Is it less than the company's equity? Are sales healthy and increasing from the prior year? Does the firm compare favourably in these categories versus other companies in the same industry? This is a critical piece of information because in today's unforgiving economy, high debt loads can quickly destroy a company.

TIP

>> **Think in terms of tens.** To us, there's beauty in simplicity. You'll notice that the number ten comes up frequently as we measure a company's performance, juxtaposing all the numbers you need to be aware of. If net income is rising by 10 percent or more, that's fine. If the company is in the top 10 percent of its industry, that's great. If the industry is growing by 10 percent or better (sales and so on), that's terrific. If sales are up 10 percent or more this year, that's wonderful. A great company doesn't have to have all these things going for it, but it should have as many of these things happening as possible to ensure greater potential success.

Does every company/industry have to neatly fit these criteria? No, of course not. But it doesn't hurt you to be as picky as possible. You need to find only a handful of stocks from thousands of choices. (Hey, this approach has worked for us, our clients, and our students for decades — 'nuff said.)

TIP

Value investors can find thousands of companies that have value, but they can probably buy only a handful at a truly good price. The number of stocks that can be bought at a good price is relative to the market. In mature bull markets (ones in a prolonged period of rising prices), a good price is hard to find; most stocks have probably seen significant price increases, but in bear markets (markets in a prolonged period of falling prices), good companies at bargain prices are easier to come by and represent great stock investing opportunities.

Accounting for Value

Profit is to a company what oxygen is to a human. Without profit, a company can't survive, much less thrive. Without profit, it can't provide jobs, pay taxes, or invest in new products, equipment, or innovation. Without profit, it eventually goes bankrupt, and the price of its stock plummets toward zero.

In the heady days leading up to both of the last two bear markets, many investors lost a lot of money simply because they invested in stocks of companies that weren't making a profit. Lots of public companies ended up like bugs that just didn't see the windshield coming their way. Companies such as Nortel and Lehman Brothers entered the graveyard of rather-be-forgotten stocks. Research In Motion, now called Blackberry, escaped the graveyard but still superficially changed its name in a move designed to escape its mistake-ridden past. Stock investors as a group lost trillions of dollars investing in glitzy or derivative-fuelled companies that sounded good but weren't making money. When their brokers were saying, "buy, buy, buy," their hard-earned money was saying, "bye, bye, bye!" What were they thinking?

Stock investors need to pick up some rudimentary knowledge of accounting to round out their stock-picking prowess and to be sure that they're getting a good value for their investment dollars. As we mentioned earlier, accounting is the language of business. If you don't understand basic accounting, you'll have difficulty being a successful investor. Investing without accounting knowledge is like travelling without a map. However, if you can run a household budget, using accounting analysis to evaluate stocks is easier than you think, as you find out in the following sections.

TIP

Finding the relevant financial data on a company isn't difficult in the age of information and 24-hour Internet access. Websites such as www.nasdaq.com and www.sedar.com can give you the most recent balance sheets and income statements of most public companies. You can find out more about public information and company research in Chapter 6.

Breaking down the balance sheet

REMEMBER

A company's balance sheet gives you a financial snapshot of what the company looks like in terms of the following equation:

Assets – liabilities = Net worth (or net equity)

In the following sections, we list questions that a balance sheet can answer and explain how to use it judge a company's strength over time.

Answering a few balance sheet questions

Analyze the following items that you find on the balance sheet:

>> **Total assets:** Have they increased from the prior year? If not, was it because of the sale of an asset or a write-off (uncollectable accounts receivable, for example)?

>> **Financial assets:** In recent years, many companies (especially U.S. banks and some Canadian resource companies) had questionable financial assets (such as subprime mortgages and heavy debt loads) that went bad, and they had to write them off as unrecoverable losses or sell large assets to meet debt repayment obligations. Does the company you're analyzing have a large exposure to financial assets that are low-quality (and hence, risky) debt?

>> **Inventory:** Is inventory higher or lower than last year? If sales are flat but inventory is growing, that may be a problem, perhaps caused by obsolete inventory.

>> **Debt:** Debt may be the biggest weakness on the corporate balance sheet. Make sure that debt isn't a growing item and that it's under control. In recent years, debt has become a huge problem.

>> **Derivatives:** A *derivative* is a speculative and complex financial instrument that doesn't constitute ownership of an asset (such as a stock, bond, or commodity) but is a promise to convey ownership. Some derivatives are quite acceptable because they're used as protective or hedging vehicles (this use isn't our primary concern). But they're frequently used to generate income and can then carry risks that can increase liabilities. Standard options and futures are examples of derivatives on a regulated exchange, but the derivatives we're talking about are a different animal and in an unregulated part of the financial world. Some economists estimate that the worldwide derivatives market is more than ten times total world gross domestic product. The number or value often mentioned is one *quadrillion,* or 1,000 times one trillion dollars. These stratospheric numbers can easily devastate a company, sector, or market (as the credit crisis and Great Recession of over a decade ago showed).

Find out whether the company dabbles in these complicated, dicey, leveraged financial instruments. Find out (from the company's regulatory filings in SEDAR or EDGAR; see Chapter 12) whether it has derivatives and, if so, the total amount. Having derivatives that are valued higher than the company's net equity may cause tremendous problems. Derivatives problems sank many, ranging from stodgy banks (Barings Bank of England) to affluent counties (Orange County, California) to once-respected hedge funds (LTCM) to corporations (Lehman Brothers).

>> **Equity:** Equity is the company's net worth (what's left in the event that all the assets are used to pay off all the company debts). The stockholders' equity should be increasing steadily by at least 10 percent per year. If not, find out why.

Table 11-1 shows you a brief example of a balance sheet.

TABLE 11-1

XYZ Balance Sheet — December 31, 2013

Assets (What the Company Owns)	Amount
1. Cash and inventory	$5,000
2. Equipment and other assets	$7,000
3. TOTAL ASSETS (Item 1 + Item 2)	$12,000
Liabilities (What the Company Owes)	
4. Short-term debt	$1,500
5. Other debt	$2,500
6. TOTAL LIABILITIES (Item 4 + Item 5)	$4,000
7. NET EQUITY (Item 3 – Item 6)	$8,000

By looking at a company's balance sheet, you can address the following questions:

>> **What does the company own (assets)?** The company can own assets, which can be financial, tangible, and/or intangible. An asset is anything that has value or that can be converted to or sold for cash. Financial assets can be cash, investments (such as stocks or bonds of other companies), or accounts receivable. Assets can be tangible items such as inventory, equipment, or buildings. They can also be intangible things such as licences, patents, trademarks, or copyrights. For example, companies like Facebook and Alphabet (which is better known as Google and includes its other subsidiaries) are not just enormous "cash asset" generators — they also have tremendously valuable patent, licence, and other intangible or intellectual property "assets."

>> **What does the company owe (liabilities)?** A liability is anything of value that the company must ultimately pay someone else for. Liabilities can be invoices (accounts payable) or short-term or long-term debt. Watch liabilities carefully when you study financial statements. If they are growing quickly when other parts of the business, such as sales, are not doing well or keeping pace, this may spell trouble.

» **What is the company's net equity (net worth)?** After you subtract the liabilities from the assets, the remainder is called net worth, net equity, or net stockholders' equity. This number is critical when calculating a company's book value.

Assessing a company's financial strength over time

The logic behind the assets/liabilities relationship of a company is the same as that of your own household. When you look at a snapshot of your own finances (your personal balance sheet), how can you tell whether you're doing well? Odds are that you start by comparing some numbers. If your net worth is $5,000, you may say, "That's great!" But a more appropriate remark is something like, "That's great compared to, say, a year ago."

TIP

Compare a company's balance sheet at a recent point in time to a past time. You should do this comparative analysis with all the key items on the balance sheet, which we list in the preceding section, to see the company's progress (or lack thereof). Is it growing its assets and/or shrinking its debt? Most important, is the company's net worth growing? Has it grown by at least 10 percent since a year ago? All too often, Canadian investors stop doing their homework after they make an initial investment. You should continue to look at the firm's numbers regularly so that you can be ahead of the curve. If the business starts having problems, you can get out before the rest of the market starts getting out (which causes the stock price to fall).

REMEMBER

To judge the financial strength of a company, ask the following questions:

» **Are the company's assets greater in value than they were three months ago, a year ago, or two years ago?** Compare today's asset size to the most recent two years to make sure that the company is growing in size and financial strength.

» **How do the individual items compare with prior periods?** Some particular assets that you want to take note of are cash, inventory, and accounts receivable.

» **Are liabilities such as accounts payable and debt about the same, lower, or higher compared to prior periods? Are they growing at a similar, faster, or slower rate than the company's assets?** Debt that rises faster and higher than items on the other side of the balance sheet is a key warning sign of potential financial problems.

>> **Is the company's net worth or equity greater than the preceding year? And is that year's equity greater than the year before?** In a healthy company, the net worth is constantly rising. As a general rule, in good economic times, net worth should be at least 10 percent higher than the preceding year. In tough economic times (such as a recession), 5 percent is acceptable. Seeing the net worth grow at a rate of 15 percent or higher is great. Don't lose sight of this important financial indicator.

TIP

When evaluating a stock, look under the management discussion and analysis (MD&A) section of the annual report for discussion about commitments, contingencies, and pledged assets. Determine roughly how big the potential impact can be if some of these commitments turn into reality.

WARNING

Whenever the economy goes into a period of recession, many Canadian and U.S. companies will suffer losses. This typically qualifies them for tax credits to be received in a future tax period. Many companies will recognize this as a special item (revenue) on the income statement in the current year to boost the bottom line. A tax asset is also booked on the balance sheet. Invariably, after a year or so, window dressers make the tax asset (tax credit receivable) disappear — the company reevaluates the likelihood of actually qualifying for the credit and determines that it stands no chance of collecting from the CRA or Uncle Sam. The tax asset gets written off, a special charge is created (in the year a company would prefer to see a charge), and the investor is left with even more distorted financial statements.

WARNING

Many, if not most, public companies have pension plans for employees, and corresponding obligations to adequately fund those plans. If there's any deficiency in the amount that's contributed to the plan, the company ultimately has to fund the shortfall. Cash infusions dig into the company's cash balances and can potentially impair its ability to do the things it wants to. During any challenging economic period, this becomes an important issue. Many companies will fail to adjust downward the assumptions underpinning their pension plans, such as the returns the plan's investments will generate in upcoming years. Some pension plans are still based on assumptions that their investment funds will grow at 7 percent or more, when in fact future forecasted returns are expected to be lower.

Looking at the income statement

REMEMBER

Where do you look if you want to find out what a company's profit is? Check out the firm's income statement. It reports, in detail, a simple accounting equation that you probably already know:

Sales – expenses = Net profit (or net earnings, or net income)

Look at the following figures found on the income statement:

>> **Sales:** Are they increasing? If not, why not? By what percentage are sales increasing? Preferably, they should be 10 percent higher than the year before. Sales are, after all, where the money comes from to pay for all the company's activities (such as expenses) and create subsequent profits.

>> **Expenses:** Do you see any unusual items? Are total expenses reported higher than the prior year, and if so, by how much? If the total is significantly higher, why? A company with large, rising expenses will see profits suffer, which isn't good for the stock price.

>> **Research and development (R&D):** How much is the company spending on R&D? Companies that rely on new product development (such as pharmaceuticals or biotech firms) should spend at least as much as they did the year before (preferably more) because new products mean future earnings and growth.

>> **Earnings:** This figure reflects the bottom line. Are total earnings higher than the year before? How about earnings from operations (leaving out expenses such as taxes and interest)? The earnings section is the heart and soul of the income statement and of the company itself. Out of all the numbers in the financial statements, earnings have the greatest single impact on the company's stock price.

Table 11-2 shows you a brief example of an income statement.

TABLE 11-2

XYZ Income Statement for Year Ending 12/31/2013

Total Sales (Or Revenue)	Amount
1. Sales of products	$11,000
2. Sales of services	$3,000
3. TOTAL SALES (Item 1 + Item 2)	$14,000
Expenses	
4. Marketing and promotion	$2,000
5. Payroll costs	$9,000
6. Other costs	$1,500
7. TOTAL EXPENSES (Item 4 + Item 5 + Item 6)	$12,500
8. NET INCOME (Item 3 − Item 7) (In this case, it's a net profit)	$1,500

Looking at the income statement, investors can try to answer these questions:

>> **What sales did the company make?** Businesses sell products and services that generate revenue (known as sales or gross sales). Sales also are referred to as the *top line*.

>> **What expenses did the company incur?** In generating sales, companies pay expenses, like payroll, utilities, advertising, and administration.

>> **What is the net profit?** Also called net earnings or net income, net profit is the bottom line. After paying for all expenses, what profit did the company make?

The information you glean should give you a strong idea about a firm's current financial strength and whether it's successfully increasing sales, holding down expenses, and ultimately maintaining profitability. You can find out more about sales, expenses, and profits in the sections that follow.

Sales

Sales refers to the money that a company receives as customers buy its goods or services. It's a simple item on the income statement and a useful number to look at. Analyzing a business by looking at its sales is called top line analysis.

REMEMBER

Investors should take into consideration the following points about sales:

>> **Sales should be increasing.** A healthy, growing company has growing sales. They should grow at least 10 percent from the prior year, and you should look at the most recent three years. The extent to which sales increase from quarter to quarter greatly influences a stock's price movement, one way or another.

>> **Core sales (sales of those goods or services that the company specializes in) should be increasing.** Frequently, the sales figure has a lot of stuff lumped into it. Maybe the company sells widgets (what the heck is a widget, anyway?), but the core sales shouldn't include other things, such as the sale of a building or other one-time or unusual items. Take a close look. Isolate the firm's primary and regular offerings and ask whether these sales are growing at a reasonable rate (such as 10 percent).

>> **Does the company have odd items or odd ways of calculating sales?** To this day and in the context of our still-low-interest-rate environment, many companies boost their sales by aggressively offering affordable financing with easy repayment terms. Say you find out that Suspicious Sales Inc. (SSI) had annual sales of $50 million, reflecting a 25 percent increase from the year before. Looks great! But what if you find out that $20 million of that sales

number comes from sales made on credit that the company extended to non-creditworthy buyers? Some companies that use this approach later have to write off losses as uncollectable debt because the customers ultimately can't pay for the goods.

TIP

If you want to get a good clue as to whether a company is artificially boosting sales, check its accounts receivable (listed in the asset section of its balance sheet). Accounts receivable refers to money that is owed to the company for goods that customers have purchased on credit. If you find out that sales went up by $10 million (great!) but accounts receivable went up by $20 million (uh-oh), something just isn't right. That may be a sign that the financing terms were too easy, and the company may have a problem collecting payment (especially in a recession).

Expenses

How much a company spends has a direct relationship to its profitability. If spending isn't controlled or held at a sustainable level, it may spell trouble for the business.

REMEMBER

When you look at a company's expense items, consider the following:

>> **Compare expense items to the prior period.** Are expenses higher than, lower than, or about the same as those from the prior period? If the difference is significant, you should see commensurate benefits elsewhere. In other words, if overall expenses are 10 percent higher compared to the prior period, are sales at least 10 percent more during the same period? If advertising expenses are up, did sales rise in a meaningful and predictable way?

>> **Are some expenses too high?** Look at the individual expense items. Are they significantly higher than the year before and as compared to industry peers? If so, why?

>> **Have any unusual items been expensed?** An unusual expense isn't necessarily a negative. Expenses may be higher than usual if a company writes off uncollectable accounts receivable as a bad debt expense. Doing so inflates the total expenses and subsequently results in lower earnings. Pay attention to nonrecurring charges that show up on the income statement, and determine whether they make sense.

Profit

Earnings, or profit, is the single most important item on the income statement. It's also the one that receives the most attention in the financial media. When a company makes a profit, it's usually reported as earnings per share (EPS). So if you hear that XYZ Corporation (yes, the infamous XYZ Corp.!) beat last quarter's earnings by a penny, here's how to translate that news. Suppose that the company made $1 per share this quarter and 99 cents per share last quarter. If that company had 100 million shares of stock outstanding, its profit this quarter is $100 million (the EPS times the number of shares outstanding), which is $1 million more than it made in the prior quarter ($1 million is 1 cent per share times 100 million shares).

TIP

Don't simply look at current earnings as an isolated figure. Always compare current earnings to earnings in past periods (usually a year). For example, if you're looking at a retailer's fourth-quarter results, don't compare them with the retailer's third-quarter outcome. Doing so is like comparing apples to oranges. What if the company usually does well during the December holidays but poorly in the fall? In that case, you don't get a fair comparison.

A strong company should show consistent earnings growth from the period before (the prior year or the same quarter from the prior year), and you should check the period before that, too, so that you can determine whether earnings are consistently rising over time. Earnings growth is an important barometer of the company's potential growth and bodes well for the stock price.

REMEMBER

When you look at earnings, here are some things to consider:

>> **Total earnings:** This item is the most watched. Total earnings should grow year to year by about 10 percent and more.

>> **Operational earnings:** Break down the total earnings and look at a key subset — that portion of earnings derived from the company's core and regular activity. Is the company continuing to make money from its primary goods and services?

>> **Nonrecurring items:** Are earnings higher (or lower) than usual or than expected, and if so, why? Frequently, the difference results from irregularly occurring and atypical items such as the sale of an asset or a large depreciation write-off.

TIP

We like to keep percentages as simple as possible. Ten percent is a good number because it's easy to calculate and it's a good benchmark. However, 5 percent isn't unacceptable if you're talking about tough times, such as a recession. Obviously, if sales, earnings, and/or net worth are hitting or surpassing 15 percent, that's great.

WARNING

Some retailers, and especially Internet e-tailers, use coupon promotions to promote higher sales volumes. That's fine. What is not fine is when companies engage in window dressing where they exclude the value (cost) of promotional giveaways when booking revenue. They have found a more dubious approach. Assume for a moment that someone buys a music CD for $30 and uses a $10 coupon to make the purchase. Under generally accepted accounting rules, just $20 of revenue ought to be booked. But some retailers would book $30 in revenue and charge the $10 in promotional costs to marketing expenses. The auditors should catch this, but tell that to Sino-Forest or Lehman Brothers investors who also relied on auditors. Such accounting voodoo may result in artificially higher sales and gross margin, better top-line comments from financial analysts, and inflated share price. Can you spell "distortion"?

WARNING

A company can turn a variety of what should be expenses into assets by depreciating capital assets (resources that last more than one year) more slowly than otherwise required under the principle of reasonableness (in other words, by easing it slowly into expenses). With certain types of costs incurred, management can judgmentally overestimate a period of useful benefit to longer than one year. That would let management justify recording part of it on the balance sheet (as an asset) instead of on the income statement (as an expense). This serves to artificially boost profits.

Tooling around with ratios

A ratio is a helpful numerical tool that you can use to find out the relationship between two or more figures found in a company's financial data. A ratio can add meaning to a number or put it in perspective. Ratios sound complicated, but they're easier to understand than you may think.

Say that you're considering a stock investment and the company you're looking at has earnings of $1 million this year. You may think that's a nice profit, but in order for this amount to be meaningful, you have to compare it to something. What if you find out that the other companies in the industry (of similar size and scope) had earnings of $500 million? Does that change your thinking? Or what if the same company had earnings of $75 million in the prior period? Does that change your mind?

Two key ratios to be aware of are

>> Price-to-earnings (P/E) ratio

>> Price-to-sales (P/S) ratio

TIP

Every investor wants to find stocks that have a 20 percent average growth rate over the past five years and have a low P/E ratio (sounds like a dream). Use stock screening tools available for free on the Internet to do your research. A stock screening tool lets you plug in numbers, such as sales or earnings, and ratios, such as the P/E ratio or the debt to equity ratio, and then click! — up come stocks that fit your criteria. These tools are a good starting point for serious investors. Most Canadian brokers have them at their websites (such as TD Waterhouse at www.tdwaterhouse.ca and BMO InvestorLine www.bmo.com/investorline/). Some excellent stock screening tools can also be found at TMX (www.tmxmoney.com), Bloomberg (www.bloomberg.com), Nasdaq (www.nasdaq.com), and Market-Watch (www.marketwatch.com). Check out Appendix B for even more on ratios.

The P/E ratio

The price-to-earnings (P/E) ratio is very important in analyzing a potential stock investment because it's one of the most widely regarded barometers of a company's value, and it's usually reported along with the company's stock price in the financial page listing. The major significance of the P/E ratio is that it establishes a direct relationship between the bottom line of a company's operations — the earnings (or net profit) — and the stock price.

The P in P/E stands for the stock's current price. The E is for earnings per share (typically the most recent 12 months of earnings). The P/E ratio is also referred to as the earnings multiple or just multiple.

REMEMBER

You calculate the P/E ratio by dividing the price of the stock by the earnings per share. If the price of a single share of stock is $10 and the earnings (on a per-share basis) are $1, then the P/E is 10. If the stock price goes to $35 per share and the earnings are unchanged, then the P/E is 35. Basically, the higher the P/E, the more you pay for the company's earnings.

Why would you buy stock in one company with a relatively high P/E ratio instead of investing in another company with a lower P/E ratio? Investors buy stocks based on expectations. They may bid up the price of the stock (subsequently raising the stock's P/E ratio) because they feel that the company will have increased earnings in the near future. Perhaps they feel that the company has great potential (a pending new invention or lucrative business deal) that will eventually make it more profitable. More profitability in turn has a beneficial impact on the firm's stock price. The danger with a high P/E is that if the company doesn't achieve the hoped-for results, the stock price can fall.

Look at two P/E ratios to get a balanced picture of the company's value:

>> **Trailing P/E:** This P/E is the most frequently quoted because it deals with existing data. The trailing P/E uses the most recent 12 months of earnings in its calculation.

>> **Forward P/E:** This P/E is based on projections or expectations of earnings in the coming 12-month period. Although this P/E may seem preferable because it looks into the near future, it's still considered an estimate that may or may not prove to be accurate.

The following example illustrates the importance of the P/E ratio. Say that you want to buy a business and we're selling a business. You come to us and say, "What do you have to offer?" We say, "Have we got a deal for you! We operate a retail business downtown that sells spatulas. The business nets a cool $2,000 profit per year." You say, "Uh, okay, what's the asking price for the business?" We reply, "You can have it for only $1 million! What do you say?"

If you're sane, odds are that you politely turn down that offer. Even though the business is profitable (a cool $2,000 a year), you'd be crazy to pay a million bucks for it. In other words, the business is way overvalued (too expensive for what you're getting in return for your investment dollars). The million dollars would generate a better rate of return elsewhere and probably with less risk. As for the business, the P/E ratio of 500 ($1 million divided by $2,000) is outrageous — definitely an overvalued company, and a lousy investment.

What if we offered the business for $12,000? Does that price make more sense? Yes. The P/E ratio is a more reasonable 6 ($12,000 divided by $2,000). In other words, the business pays for itself in about 6 years (versus 500 years in the prior example).

Looking at the P/E ratio offers a shortcut for investors asking the question, "Is this stock overvalued?" As a general rule, the lower the P/E, the safer (or more conservative) the stock is. The reverse is more noteworthy: The higher the P/E, the greater the risk.

When someone refers to a P/E as high or low, you have to ask the question, "Compared to what?" A P/E of 30 is considered very high for a large cap electric utility but quite reasonable for a small cap, high-technology firm. Keep in mind that phrases such as large cap and small cap are just a reference to the company's market value or size (refer to Chapter 1 for details on these terms). Cap is short for capitalization (the total number of shares of stock outstanding × the share price).

The following basic points can help you evaluate P/E ratios:

>> **Compare a company's P/E ratio with its industry.** Electric utility industry stocks, for example, generally have a P/E that hovers in the 9–14 range. So, an electric utility with a P/E of 45 indicates something is wrong with that utility. (We touch on analyzing industries in Chapter 13.)

>> **Compare a company's P/E with the general market.** If you're looking at a small cap stock on the Nasdaq that has a P/E of 100 but the average P/E for established companies on the Nasdaq is 40, find out why. You should also compare the stock's P/E ratio with the P/E ratio for major indexes such as the Dow Jones Industrial Average (DJIA), the Standard & Poor's 500 (S&P 500), the S&P/TSX Composite, and the Nasdaq Composite. Stock indexes are useful for getting the big picture, and we include them in Chapter 6 and Appendix A.

>> **Compare a company's current P/E with recent periods** (such as this year versus last year). If it currently has a P/E ratio of 20 and it previously had a P/E ratio of 30, you know that either the stock price has declined or earnings have risen. In this case, the stock is less likely to fall. That bodes well for the stock.

>> **Low P/E ratios aren't necessarily a sign of a bargain,** but if you're looking at a stock for many other reasons that seem positive (solid sales, strong industry, and so on) and it also has a low P/E, that's a good sign.

>> **High P/E ratios aren't necessarily bad,** but they do mean that you should investigate further. If a company is weak and the industry is shaky, heed the high P/E as a warning sign. Often, a high P/E ratio means that investors have bid up a stock price, anticipating future income.

WARNING

>> **Watch out for a stock that doesn't have a P/E ratio.** In other words, it may have a price (the P), but it doesn't have earnings (the E). No earnings means no P/E, meaning that you're better off avoiding the stock. Can you still make money buying a stock with no earnings? You can, but you aren't investing; you're speculating.

The P/S ratio

The price-to-sales (P/S) ratio is a company's stock price divided by its sales. Because the sales number is rarely expressed as a per-share figure, it's easier to divide a company's total market value (we explain market value earlier in this chapter) by its total sales for the last 12 months.

TIP

As a general rule, a stock trading at a P/S ratio of 1 or less is a reasonably priced stock worthy of your attention. For example, say that a company has sales of $1 billion and the stock has a total market value of $950 million. In that case, the P/S is 0.95. In other words, you can buy $1 of the company's sales for only 95 cents. All things being equal, that stock may be a bargain.

Analysts use the P/S ratio as an evaluation tool in these circumstances:

>> In tandem with other ratios to get a more well-rounded picture of the company and the stock.

>> When they want an alternate way to value a business that doesn't have earnings.

>> When they want a true picture of the company's financial health, because sales are tougher for companies to manipulate than earnings.

>> When they're considering a company offering products (versus services). The P/S ratio is more suitable for companies that sell items that are easily counted (such as products). Firms that make their money through loans, such as banks, aren't usually valued with a P/S ratio because deriving a usable P/S ratio for them is more difficult.

REMEMBER

Compare the company's P/S ratio with other companies in the same industry, with the industry average, to get a better idea of the company's relative value.

Chapter **12**

Decoding Company Documents

F inancial documents — good grief! Some Canadians would rather suck a hospital mop than read some dry corporate or government report. Yet if you're serious about choosing stocks, you should be serious about your research. Fortunately, it's not as bad as you think (put away that disgusting mop). When you see that some basic research helps you build wealth, it gets easier.

In this chapter, we discuss the basic electronic and traditional paper documents that you come across (or should come across) most often in your investing life. These documents include essential information that all investors need to know, not only at the time of the initial investment decision but also for as long as that stock remains in their portfolio.

TIP

If you plan to hold a stock for the long haul, reading the reports covered in this chapter is helpful. If you intend to get rid of the stock soon or hold it only for the short term, reading these reports diligently isn't quite as important.

Reading Annual Reports

When you're a regular stockholder, the company sends you its annual report. If you're not already a stockholder, contact the company's shareholder service department for a hard copy or to get a copy e-mailed to you, or look for an Investor Relations link to it on the company's website.

TIP

You can often view a company's annual report on its website. Any search engine can help you find it. Downloading or printing the annual report is easy.

The following resources also provide access to annual reports:

>> **The Public Register's annual report service:** Go to www.prars.com to order a hard copy or to www.annualreportservice.com to view Canadian (such as Barrick Gold or Bank of Montreal) and U.S. company reports online. This organization maintains a big collection of annual reports.

>> **AnnualReports.com:** Search for reports at www.annualreports.com, with links to the TSX, NYSE, and European exchanges.

>> **The free annual report service of *The Wall Street Journal*:** If you read this newspaper's financial pages and see a company with the club symbol (like the one you see on a playing card), then you can order that company's annual report by visiting www.wsj.com.

You need to carefully analyze an annual report to find out the following:

>> **How well the company is doing:** Are earnings higher, lower, or the same as the year before? How are sales doing? You can find these numbers clearly presented in the annual report's financial section.

>> **Whether the company is making more money than it's spending:** How does the balance sheet look? Are assets higher or lower than the year before? Is debt growing, shrinking, or about the same as the year before? For more details on balance sheets, see Chapter 11.

>> **What management's strategic plan is for the coming year:** How will management build success? This plan is usually covered in the beginning of the annual report — often in the letter from the chairman of the board.

REMEMBER

Your task boils down to figuring out where the company has been, where it is now, and where it's going. As an investor, you don't need to read the annual report like a novel — from cover to cover. Instead, approach it like a newspaper and jump around to the relevant sections to get the answers you need to decide whether you should buy or hold on to the stock. We describe the makeup of the annual report and proxy materials in the following sections.

Analyzing the annual report's anatomy

Not every company puts its annual report together in exactly the same way — the style of presentation varies. Some annual reports have gorgeous graphics or coupons for the company's products, whereas others are in a standard black-and-white typeface with no cosmetic frills at all. But every annual report does include common basic content, such as the income statement and the balance sheet. The following sections present typical components of an average annual report. (Keep in mind that not every annual report presents the sections in the same order.)

The letter from the chairman of the board

The first thing you see is usually the letter from the chairman of the board — the "Dear Stockholder" letter that communicates views from the head muckety-muck. The chairman's letter is designed to put the best possible perspective on the company's operations during the past year. Be aware of this bias; no one in upper management wants to panic stockholders. If the company is doing well, the letter will certainly point it out. If the company is having hard times, the letter will put a positive spin on the company's difficulties. If the *Titanic* had had an annual report, odds are that the last letter would have reported: "Great news! A record number of our customers participated in our spontaneous moonlight swimming program. In addition, we confidently project no operating expenses whatsoever for the subsequent fiscal quarter."

REMEMBER

To get an idea of what issues the company's management team feels are important and what goals it wants to accomplish, keep these questions in mind:

>> What does the letter say about changing conditions in the company's business? How about in the industry?

>> If any difficulties exist, does the letter communicate a clear and logical action plan (cutting costs, closing money-losing plants, and so on) to get the company back on a positive track?

>> What's being highlighted and why? Is the firm focusing on research and development for new products, or on a new deal with China or India?

>> Does the letter offer apologies for anything? If, for example, it fell short of sales expectations, does the letter offer a reason for the shortcoming?

>> Did the company make (or will it make) new acquisitions or major developments (say, selling products to China, or a new marketing agreement with a Financial Post 500 or Fortune 500 company)?

Read an annual report (or any messages from upper management) in the same way you read or hear anything from a politician — be more concerned with means than ends. In other words, executives, don't tell us what the goal is (greater profitability, or peace on earth); tell us how you're going to get there. Executives may say "we will increase sales and profits," but saying "we will increase sales and profits by doing X, Y, and Z" is a better message because you can then decide for yourself whether the road map makes sense.

The company's offerings

This section of an annual report can have various titles (such as "Sales and Marketing"), but it generally covers what the company sells. You should understand the products or services (or both) that the business sells and why customers purchase them. If you don't understand what the company offers, then understanding how it earns money, the driving force behind its stock, is more difficult.

REMEMBER

Are the company's core or primary offerings selling well? If, for example, the earnings of Tim Hortons are holding steady but earnings strictly from coffee and donuts are slowly fizzling, that's a cause for concern. If a business ceases making money from its specialty, be cautious. Here are more questions to ask:

>> How does the company distribute its offerings? Through a website, malls, representatives, or some other means? Does it sell only to the Canadian market, or is its distribution international? Generally, the greater the scope of distribution, the greater the potential sales and, ultimately, the higher the stock price.

>> Are most of the company's sales to a definable marketplace? For example, if most of the sales are to war-torn or politically unstable countries, like Liberia, Eritrea, or Venezuela, you should worry. If the company's customers aren't doing well, that has a direct impact on the company and, eventually, its stock.

>> How are sales doing versus market standards? In other words, is the company doing better than the industry average? Is it a market leader in what it offers? The firm should be doing better than (or as well as) its peers in the industry. If the company is falling behind its competitors, that doesn't bode well for the stock in the long run.

>> Does the report include information on the company's competitors and related matters? You should know who the company's competitors are because they have a direct effect on the company's success. If customers are choosing the competitor over your firm, the slumping sales and earnings will ultimately hurt the stock's price.

Financial statements

Look over the various financial statements and find the relevant numbers. Every annual report should have (at the very least) a balance sheet and an income statement. Catching the important numbers on a financial statement isn't that difficult to do. However, it certainly helps when you pick up some basic accounting knowledge. Chapter 11 can give you more details on evaluating financial statements.

First, review the income statement (also known as the profit and loss statement, or simply P&L). It gives you the company's sales, expenses, and the result (net income or net loss). Next, look at the balance sheet. It provides a snapshot of a point in time (annual reports usually provide a year-end balance sheet that commonly falls on December 31st but it could be any date) that tells you what the company owns (assets), what it owes (liabilities), and the end result (net worth). For a company to be healthy, assets should always be greater than liabilities, without exception.

WARNING

Carefully read the footnotes to the financial statements. Sometimes big changes are communicated in small print. In current times, especially be wary of small print pointing out other debt or derivatives. Derivatives are complicated and (lately) very risky vehicles. Problems with derivatives were one of the major causes of the market turmoil that destroyed financial firms on Wall Street during late 2008. AIG, for example, is a major insurer that had to be bailed out by the Federal Reserve before it went bankrupt (shareholders suffered huge losses). Canadian financial firms like banks are generally not as exposed to derivative losses because Canadian financial institutions are better regulated with more conservative lending and investing regulations.

WARNING

Derivatives are a huge land mine, and large U.S. money centre banks still carry them. According to the Bank for International Settlements (www.bis.org) and as mentioned in Chapter 11, major money centre banks are carrying trillions of dollars' worth of derivatives, in some cases more than the gross domestic product of small countries! (Whew! Now we see why banks give away so many Starbucks coupons.) Derivatives are especially worth being aware of if you're considering bank or other financial stocks for your portfolio.

Summary of past financial figures

The summary of past financial figures gives you a snapshot of the company's overall long-term progress. How many years does the annual report summarize? Some reports summarize three years, but most go back two years.

Management issues

The annual report's management issues section includes a reporting of current trends and issues, such as new developments happening in the industry that affect the company. See if you agree with management's assessment of economic and market conditions that affect the firm's prospects. What significant developments in society does management perceive as affecting company operations? Does the report include information on current or pending lawsuits?

External auditor's opinion letter

Annual reports typically include comments from the company's independent accounting firm. It may be an opinion letter or a simple paragraph with the accounting firm's views regarding the financial statements.

TIP

The external auditor's opinion letter offers an opinion about the accuracy of the financial data presented and information on how the statements were prepared. This is important. Check to see whether the letter includes any footnotes regarding changes in certain numbers or how they were reported. For example, a company that wants to report higher earnings may use a conservative method of measuring depreciation rather than a more aggressive approach. In any case, you should verify the numbers by looking at the company's financial documents filed with Canadian and U.S. securities regulators (we describe these documents in more detail later in this chapter).

Company identity data

The company identity data section informs you about the company's subsidiaries (or lesser businesses that it owns), brands, and addresses. It also contains standard data such as the headquarters location and names of directors and officers. Many reports also include data on the directors' and officers' positions in stock ownership at year's end.

Stock data

The stock data section may include a history of the stock price, along with information such as what exchange the stock is listed on, stock symbol, company dividend reinvestment plan (if any), and so on. It also includes information on stockholder services and whom to contact for more information.

Going through the proxy materials

As a shareholder (or stockholder — same thing), you're entitled to vote at the annual shareholders meeting. If you ever get the opportunity to attend one, do so.

You get to meet other shareholders and ask questions of management and other company representatives. Usually, the shareholder services department provides you with complete details. At the meetings, shareholders vote on company matters, such as approving a new audit firm or deciding whether a proposed merger with another company will go forward.

If you can't attend (usually true for the majority of shareholders), you can vote by proxy. Voting by proxy essentially means that you vote by mail. You indicate your votes on the proxy statement (or card) and authorize a representative to vote at the meeting on your behalf. The proxy statement is usually sent to all shareholders, along with the annual report, just before the meeting.

Dig Deeper: Getting a Second Opinion

A wealth of valuable information is available for your investing pursuits. The resources in this section are just a representative few — a good representation, though. To get a more balanced view of the company and its prospects (instead of relying only on the annual report), take a look at several different sources of information for the stocks you're researching.

TIP

The information and research certain sources provide can be expensive if you buy or subscribe on your own. But fortunately, most of the resources we mention are usually available in the business reference section of a well-stocked public library, and some can be found for free online.

SEDAR, SEDI, and the SEC

In Canada, publicly traded companies (and investment funds) are required to file business and financial information with provincial securities regulators. These reports are entered into a government-sponsored database called SEDAR — the System for Electronic Document Analysis and Retrieval (www.sedar.com). The rules of who files what were established at the federal level by the Canadian Securities Administrators (CSA) regulatory body and are overseen by each provincial securities regulatory body.

SEDAR lets enterprises file securities documents electronically. And it gives you, the Canadian investor, fast and free access to important information about companies, such as financial statements, annual reports, and transparent disclosures of any major changes that recently occurred in a company.

In the U.S., the comparable online resource can be found at the Securities and Exchange Commission (SEC) website's "Filings and Forms" section at (`www.sec.gov/edgar.shtml`). This online tool is even more advanced than SEDAR. In addition to letting you search and access SEC statutory filings, it also provides registered users with an e-mail alert every time a certain reporting firm files a document and then links you to that document.

Individual Canadian investors can access downloadable data from both websites. This means that you can download SEDAR and SEC reports to read them later. The content available at these websites is critical to investors because it contains all financial, legal, and other types of statutory (mandatory) declarations that are important in the investment decision making process. For example, financial statements tell you whether a company is fiscally fit. And information about legal matters (like big lawsuits) that are important enough to influence your decision to buy or sell a stock can also be found on these sites. Any material changes, like a new senior executive appointment, or a major shift in operations to China, will also be described in both websites. Both websites are updated in near real time.

WARNING

Be aware of the fact that annual reports may include more than 50 pages, and they often exceed 100 pages. For example, Canadian and U.S. annual reports include financial statements with notes; supplementary data; wordy management discussions of financial conditions and operations results; business descriptions; legal proceedings; shareholder voting matters; insider transactions; executive compensation; and leasing agreements. Fun stuff! So be selective about how much information you want — and need — to download.

Company document filings

The serious investor doesn't overlook the wealth of information that can be culled from documents filed on SEDAR and with the SEC. Take the time and effort to review the following documents, because they offer great insight regarding a company's activities. When you search the SEDAR and SEC databases, you're asked (via a drop-down menu or report number) which type of document you want. These are the documents that investors typically look at:

>> **Annual reports and filings:** These include shareholder information covering the firm's fiscal year. It works like the annual report you get from the company, except with more detailed financial information.

>> **Quarterly financial statements:** Quarterly reports that include shareholder information for the company's last quarter. This statement gives you the same basic information as the annual report, but it details only three months' worth of activity. Don't wait 12 months to see how your company is progressing.

Make a habit of seeing how the company is doing by comparing its recent quarterly report with one that covers the same quarter last year. Is the profit higher or lower? How about sales? Debt?

>> **Material change reports:** Special reports that are the result of a significant contract, lawsuit, or other material event.

>> **Notices of annual or special meetings:** Information about annual general meetings (AGMs) and voting matters such as candidates seeking election to the board of directors, approving an increase in authorized capital stock, or approving a merger or acquisition.

The preceding items can all be found at both the SEDAR and SEC websites.

REMEMBER

Not every company has the same fiscal year. A company with a calendar year fiscal year (ending December 31) files quarterly statements for each of the first three quarters and then an annual report for the final quarter, where it reports its fourth quarter data along with the results for the full year.

Insider reports

TIP

The System for Electronic Disclosure by Insiders (SEDI) is linked to SEDAR and is a searchable free Canadian online service for the viewing of insider report filings, as required by various provincial securities regulations. If you wish to view the ownership levels or stock buying and selling activity of insiders who have filed insider reports in SEDI, go to www.sedi.ca and use its precise search tool to help you find this key information. For the comparable U.S.-listed company information, go to www.sec.gov/edgar.shtml.

Two types of insiders exist: those who work within a company (senior executives, officers, directors) and those outside the company who have a significant (10 percent or more) ownership of company stock. Tracking insider activity is very profitable for investors who want to follow in the footsteps of the people in the know. See Chapter 20 for more on insider activity.

REMEMBER

Every time an insider (such as the CEO or controller) buys or sells stock, the transaction has to be submitted to SEDI or reported to the SEC. The insider actually reports the trade prior to transacting it. These reports are publicly available documents that allow you to see what the insiders are actually doing. Hearing what they say in public is one thing, but seeing what they're actually doing with their stock transactions is more important.

Value Line

The Value Line Investment Survey, one of many information products provided by Value Line Publishing, Inc., is considered a long-time favourite by many stock investing professionals. You can look it over at any library that has a good business reference department. In the survey, Value Line covers the largest public companies and ranks them by financial strength and other key business factors. To get more information about Value Line, including subscription costs, either head to the library or visit www.valueline.com.

Standard & Poor's

Another ubiquitous and venerable publisher is Standard & Poor's (S&P). It issues credit ratings that are forward-looking opinions about credit risk. Standard & Poor's credit ratings represent the agency's opinion about the ability and willingness of an issuer, such as a corporation or government, to meet its credit obligations in full and on time. Credit ratings are also about the credit quality of things like corporate bonds, municipal bonds, or mortgage-backed securities, and the likelihood of default. Although Standard & Poor's has a number of quality information products and services for individual and institutional investors, here are three you should take a look at:

>> **S&P Stock Reports:** Available at many libraries and typically included within your existing discount broker service, this report comes out periodically and reports on stocks on the NYSE and the largest firms listed on Nasdaq and S&P/TSX. It gives a succinct, two-page summary of each stock, offering a snapshot of the company's current finances, along with a brief history and commentary on the company's activities. This guide also rates companies based on their financial strength.

>> **The S&P Industry Survey:** S&P gives detailed reports on the top industries, cramming a lot of information about a given industry in four to seven pages. This annual publication provides a nice summary of what's happened in each industry in the past 12 months, what the industry looks like today, and what the prospects are for the coming year. It also provides the important numbers (earnings, sales, and industry ranking) for the top 50 to 100 firms in each industry.

>> **S&P Bond Reports:** Yes, this book is about stocks. But a company's bond rating is invaluable for stock investors. S&P analyzes the strength of the bond issuer and ranks the bond for creditworthiness. If S&P gives a company a high rating, you have added assurance that it's financially strong. You want the company to have a bond rating of AAA, AA, or A, because these ratings tell you that the company is "investment-grade."

Check out www.standardandpoors.com for more on its publications.

Moody's Investment Service

Another stalwart publisher, Moody's, offers vital research on stocks and bonds. Moody's has served Canada's investors since 1901, and rates more than 300 Canadian corporate and public finance (government) issuers. Moody's Canada-based analysts cover a variety of industry sectors, including financial institutions, media and telecommunications, oil and gas, power and gas utilities and pipelines, paper and forest products, and project and infrastructure finance. Check out www.moodys.ca for more information.

TIP

A stock rated highly by both Moody's and S&P is a great choice for investors wanting value investments. Moody's *Handbook of Common Stocks* is worth checking out and is often available in library reference sections. It offers stock and bond guides similar to S&P with an independent bond-rating service.

Brokerage reports

Traditionally, brokerage reports have been a good source of information for investors seeking informed opinions about stocks. And they still are, but in recent years some brokers have been penalized for biased reports. Brokers should never be your sole source of information.

The good

Research departments at brokerage firms provide stock reports and make them available for their clients and investment publications. The firms' analysts and market strategists generally prepare these reports. Good research is critical, and brokerage reports can be very valuable. What better source of guidance than full-time experts backed up by million-dollar research departments? Brokerage reports have some strong points:

>> The analysts are pros who should understand the value of a company and its stock. They analyze and compare company data every day.

>> Analysts have at their disposal tremendous information and historical data that they can sift through to make informed decisions.

>> If you have an account with the firm's discount or full- service brokerage arm, you can usually access the information at no cost.

The bad

WARNING

At their worst, brokerage reports are quite bad. Brokers make their money from commissions and investment banking fees (nothing bad here). However, they can find themselves in the awkward position of issuing brokerage reports on companies that are (or could be) customers of the brokerage firm that employs them (hmmm — could be bad). Frequently, this relationship results in a brokerage report that paints an overly positive picture of a company that can be a bad investment (yup, that's bad).

The ugly

During the past few recessions and nasty market meltdowns, all too many brokerage reports issued glowing praise of companies that were either mediocre or dubious. The reports conveniently ignored the economic context that the companies they reported on operated in. Investors bought up stocks such as biotech stocks with no revenue and real estate stocks in an overheated residential real estate market. The sheer demand pushed up stock prices, which gave the appearance of genius to analysts' forecasts, yet the stock prices rose essentially as a self-fulfilling prophecy. The stocks were way overvalued and were cruisin' for a bruisin'. Analysts and investors were feeling lucky.

Investors, however, lost a ton of money (ooh, ugly). Money that people painstakingly accumulated over many years of work vanished in a matter of months as the inevitable bear market would hit (ooh, ugly). The bear market that hit during the Great Recession over a decade ago was especially brutal. Canadian retirees who had trusted the analysts saw nest eggs lose 40 to 70 percent in value (yikes, very ugly). Investors lost trillions during these major downturns, much of it needlessly. We're sure that lots of those folks thought that they should have put that money in things that had enduring value instead . . . such as cookies and cases of merlot.

REMEMBER

During the recent bear market, a large number of lawsuits and complaints were filed against brokerage firms. Wall Street, Bay Street, and Main Street learned some tough lessons. Regarding research reports from brokerage firms, the following points can help you avoid getting a bad case of the uglies:

>> Ask, "Is the provider of the report a biased source?" That is, is the broker getting business in any way from the company he's recommending?

>> Never, never, *never* rely on just one source of information, especially if it's the same source that's selling you the stock or other investment.

>> Do your research first before you rely on a brokerage report. Check out annual reports and the other documents recommended earlier.

>> Do your due diligence before you buy stocks anyway. Look at Parts 1 and 2 to understand your need for diversification, risk tolerance, and so on.

>> Verify the information at the library or online (see Appendix A).

Although we generally don't rely on Bay Street brokerage analysts, we do track some independent investment analysts or their businesses. We mention some of our favourites in Appendix A.

Doing Your Own Research

You don't need to spend an excessive amount of time or money, but you should maintain your own library of resources. You may need only one shelf (or a small amount of memory on your computer's hard drive), but why not have a few investment facts and resources at your fingertips? We maintain our own libraries loaded with books, magazines, newsletters, and tons of great stuff downloaded on our computers for easy search and reference. When you start your own collection, follow these tips:

>> **Keep some select newspapers.** *Barron's, The Wall Street Journal, National Post, The Globe and Mail,* and *Investor's Business Daily* regularly have editions worth keeping. For example, *The Globe and Mail* and *The Wall Street Journal* usually publish a year-in-review issue in January. *Barron's* has special issues reviewing brokers and financial websites.

>> **Subscribe to financial magazines.** Publications such as Canadian MoneySaver magazine and *MoneySense* offer great research and advice, and regularly review stocks and provide resources for investors.

>> **Keep annual reports.** Regarding the stocks that are the core holdings in your portfolio, keep all the annual reports (or at the very least, the most recent three).

>> **Go to the library's business reference section periodically to stay updated.** Hey, you pay the taxes that maintain the public library — you may as well use it to stay informed.

>> **Use the Internet for research.** The web offers plenty of great sites to peruse; we list some of the best in Appendix A.

Chapter **13**

Sectors, Small Caps, and the Marijuana Space

Suppose you have to bet your entire nest egg on a one-kilometre race. All you need to do is select a winning group. Your choices are the following:

Group A: Thoroughbred race horses

Group B: Overweight Elvis impersonators

Group C: Lethargic snails

This isn't a trick question, and you have one minute to answer. Notice that we didn't ask you to pick a single winner out of a giant mush of horses, Elvii, and snails; we only asked you to pick the winning group in the race. The obvious answer is the thoroughbred race horses (and no, they weren't ridden by the overweight Elvis impersonators, because that would take away from the eloquent point being made). In this example, even the slowest member of Group A easily outdistances the fastest member of either Group B or C.

Industries, like groups A, B, and C in our example, aren't equal, and life isn't fair. After all, if life were fair, Elvis would be alive and the impersonators wouldn't exist. Fortunately, picking stocks doesn't have to be as difficult as picking a winning racehorse. The basic point is that it's easier to pick a successful stock from a group of winners (a growing, vibrant industry). Understanding industries only enhances your stock-picking strategy.

A successful, long-term investor looks at the industry (or the basic sector) just as carefully as she looks at the individual stock. Luckily, choosing a winning industry to invest in is easier than choosing individual stocks, as you find out in this chapter. We know some investors who can pick a winning stock in a losing industry, and we also know investors who've chosen a losing stock in a winning industry (the former is far outnumbered by the latter). Just think how well you can do when you choose a great stock in a great industry! Of course, if you repeatedly choose bad stocks in bad industries, you may as well get out of the stock market altogether (maybe your calling is to be a celebrity impersonator instead!).

Note: This chapter and Chapter 19 go into megatrends such as the medical marijuana and cryptocurrency industries, which are different animals from sectors and industries. Megatrends are major developments that have or may have a monumental effect on various parts of our economy. Those parts are the various sectors that are the benefactors (or victims) of these effects.

Telling the Difference between a Sector and an Industry

Very often, investors confuse an industry with a sector. Even though it may not be a consequential confusion, some clarity is needed here.

A sector is simply a group of interrelated industries. An industry is typically a category of business that performs a more precise activity; you can call an industry a subsector. Investing in a sector and investing in an industry can mean different things for the investor. The result of your investment performance can also be very different.

Healthcare is a good example of a sector that has different industries. Within the sector of healthcare, there are a variety of industries: pharmaceuticals, drug retailers, health insurance, hospitals, medical equipment manufacturers, and so on. And within the individual healthcare industries are public companies like Shoppers Drug Mart, Sun Life Financial, and others that trade on Canadian and other stock exchanges.

REMEMBER

Healthcare is actually a good (great!) example of why you should know the distinction between a sector and an industry. Within a given sector (like healthcare), you have industries that behave differently during the same economic conditions. Some of the industries are cyclical (like medical equipment manufacturers), whereas some are defensive (like drug retailers). In a bad economy, cyclicals tend to go down while defensive stocks generally hold their value. In a good or booming economy, cyclicals do very well while defensive stocks tend to lag behind. (We talk more about cyclical and defensive industries later in this chapter.)

Given that fact, an exchange-traded fund (ETF) that reflects the general health-care sector would be generally flat because some of the industries that went up would be offset by those that went down. Flip to Chapter 5 for more about ETFs.

Interrogating the Sectors and Industries

Your common sense is an important tool in choosing sectors and industries with winning stocks. This section explores some of the most important questions to ask yourself when you're choosing a sector or industry.

Which category is the industry fall in?

Most industries can be placed neatly in one of two categories: cyclical and defensive. In a rough way, these categories generally translate into what society wants and what it needs. Society buys what it wants when times are good and holds off when times are bad. It buys what it needs in both good and bad times. A want is a "like to have," whereas a need is a "must have." *Capisce?*

Cyclical industries

REMEMBER

Cyclical industries are industries whose fortunes rise and fall with the Canadian economy's rise and fall. In other words, if the economy and the stock market are doing well, Canadian consumers and investors are confident and tend to spend and invest more money than usual, so cyclical industries tend to do well. Real estate and automobiles are great examples of cyclical industries.

Your own situation offers you some common-sense insight into the concept of cyclical industries. Think about your behaviour as a consumer, and you get a revealing clue into the thinking of millions of consumers. When you (and millions of others) feel good about your career, your finances, and your future, you have a greater tendency to buy more (or more expensive) stuff. When people feel financially strong, they're more apt to buy a new house or car, or make some other large financial commitment. Also, Canadians take on more debt because they feel confident that they can pay it back. In light of this behaviour, what industries do you think would do well?

The same point holds for business spending. When businesses think that economic times are good and foresee continuing good times, they tend to spend more money on large purchases such as new equipment or technology. They think that when they're doing well and are flush with financial success, reinvesting that money in the business to increase future success is a good idea.

Defensive industries

Defensive industries are industries that produce goods and services that are needed no matter what's happening in the economy. Your common sense kicks in here, too. What do you buy even when times are tough? Think about what millions of Canadians buy no matter how bad the economy gets. A good example is food — people still need to eat regardless of good or bad times. Other examples of defensive industries are utilities and healthcare.

REMEMBER

In bad economic times, defensive stocks tend to do better than cyclical stocks. However, when times are good, cyclical stocks tend to do better than defensive stocks. Defensive stocks don't do as well in good times because Canadians don't necessarily eat twice as much or use up more electricity.

How do defensive stocks grow? Their growth generally relies on two factors:

>> **Population growth:** As more and more Canadian consumers are born, more people become available to buy things.

>> **New markets:** A company can grow by seeking out new groups of consumers to buy its products and services. Coca-Cola and Maple Leaf Foods, for example, were both early movers that found brand new markets in Asia. As pure communist regimes fell from power and more societies embraced a free market and consumer goods, the companies sold more beverages and food items, and their stocks soared.

TIP

One way to invest in a particular industry is to take advantage of exchange-traded funds (ETFs), which have become very popular in recent years. ETFs are structured much like mutual funds but are fixed portfolios that trade like a stock. If you find a winning industry but you can't find a winning stock (or don't want to bother with the necessary research), then ETFs are a great consideration. You can find out more about ETFs at websites such as www.etfdb.com or by turning to Chapter 5.

Is the sector growing?

The question may seem obvious, but you still need to ask it before you purchase stock. The saying "the trend is your friend" applies when choosing a sector in which to invest, as long as the trend is an upward one. If you look at three different stocks that are equal in every significant way but you find that one stock is in a sector growing 15 percent per year while the other two stocks are in sectors that have either little growth or are shrinking, which stock would you choose?

Sometimes the stock of a financially unsound or poorly run company goes up dramatically because the sector it's in is very exciting to the public. The most obvious example is Internet stocks from two decades ago. Stocks such as Nortel shot up to incredible heights because investors thought the Internet was the place to be. Sooner or later, however, the measure of a successful company is its ability to be profitable (Nortel eventually went bankrupt). Serious investors look at the company's fundamentals (refer to Chapter 11 to find out how to do this) and the prospects for the industry's growth before settling on a particular stock.

TIP

To judge how well a sector or industry is doing, various information sources monitor all the sectors and industries and measure their progress. Some reliable and well-known sources include the following:

>> Canoe Money (www.canoe.ca/Money)

>> *The Globe and Mail* (www.theglobeandmail.com)

>> MarketWatch (www.marketwatch.com)

>> *National Post* (www.nationalpost.com)

>> Standard & Poor's (www.standardandpoors.com)

>> *The Wall Street Journal* (www.wsj.com)

>> Yahoo! Finance (http://finance.yahoo.com)

>> Yahoo! Finance Canada (http://ca.finance.yahoo.com)

The preceding sources generally give you in-depth information about the major sectors and industries. Visit their websites to read their current research and articles along with links to relevant sites for more details. For example, *The Globe and Mail* and *The Wall Street Journal* both publish current indexes for all the major sectors (like commodities) and industries (like oil and gas, copper, corn, and gold) so that you can get a useful snapshot of how well each one is doing.

TIP

Standard and Poor's (S&P) Industry Survey is an excellent source of information on U.S. and Canadian industries. Besides ranking and comparing industries and informing you about their current prospects, the survey also lists the top companies by size, sales, earnings, and other key information. What we like is that each industry is covered in a few pages, so you get the critical information you need without reading a novel. The survey and other S&P publications are available on the S&P website or in the business reference section of most libraries (your best bet is to head for the library because the survey is rather expensive).

Are the sector's products or services in demand?

Look at the products and services that are provided by a sector or an industry. Do they look like things that society will continue to want? Are there products and services on the horizon that could replace them? What does the foreseeable future look like for the sector?

REMEMBER

When evaluating future demand, look for a sunrise industry — one that's new or emerging or has promising appeal for the future. Good examples of sunrise industries in recent years are biotech and Internet social media, which includes companies like Groupon, Facebook, and Canada's Shopify. In contrast, a sunset industry is one that's either declining or has little potential for growth. For example, you probably shouldn't invest in the DVD manufacturing industry because demand is shifting toward digital content delivery instead. Owning stock in a strong, profitable company in a sunrise industry is obviously the most desirable choice.

Current research unveils the following megatrends:

>> The aging of Canada: More senior citizens than ever are living in North America. Because of this fact, financial and healthcare services that touch on eldercare or the financial concerns of the elderly will prosper.

>> Advances in high technology: Internet, fintech, artificial intelligence, blockchain (more on this in Chapter 19), telecom, social media, autonomous and electric cars, medical, and biotechnology innovations will continue.

>> Security concerns: Terrorism, international tensions, and security issues on a personal level mean more attention for national defence, homeland security, cyber security, and related matters.

>> Energy challenges: Traditional and nontraditional sources of energy (such as solar, fuel cells, and so on) will demand society's attention as it faces shrinking supplies of the world's available crude oil.

What does the industry's growth rely on?

An industry doesn't exist in a vacuum. External factors weigh heavily on its ability to survive and thrive. Does the industry rely on an established megatrend? Then it will probably be strong for a while. Does it rely on factors that are losing relevance? Then it may begin to decline soon. Technological and demographic changes are other factors that may contribute to an industry's growth or fall.

REMEMBER

Keep in mind that a sector will continue to grow, shrink, or be level, but individual industries can grow, shrink, or even be on a track to disappear. If a sector is expanding, you may see new industries emerge. For example, the greying of the U.S. and Canada is an established megatrend. As millions of North Americans climb into their later years, profitable opportunities await companies that are prepared to cater to them. Perhaps an industry (subsector) offers great new medical products for senior citizens. Maybe autonomous electric car manufacturers like Tesla may allow senior citizens to safely stay in their cars a lot longer. We already see these types of trends emerging as Shoppers Home Health Care stores and Tesla dealerships open across Canada. What are the prospects for growth?

Is the industry dependent on another industry?

REMEMBER

This twist on the prior question is a reminder that industries frequently are intertwined and can become codependent. When one industry suffers, you may find it helpful to understand which industries will subsequently suffer. The reverse can also be true — when one industry is doing well, other industries may reap the benefits.

In either case, if the stock you choose is in an industry that's highly dependent on other industries, you should know about it. If you're considering stocks of resort companies and you see the headlines blaring, "Airlines losing money as public stops flying," what do you do? This type of question forces you to think logically and consider cause and effect. Logic and common sense are powerful tools that frequently trump all the number-crunching activity performed by analysts.

Who are the leading companies in the industry?

After you've chosen the industry, what types of companies do you want to invest in? You can choose from two basic types:

>> **Established leaders:** These companies are considered industry leaders or have a large share of the market. Investing in these companies is the safer way to go; what better choice for novice investors than companies that have already proven themselves?

>> **Innovators:** If the industry is hot and you want to be more aggressive in your approach, investigate companies that offer new products, patents, or technologies. These companies are probably smaller but have a greater potential for growth in a proven industry.

Is the industry a target of government action?

You need to know if Parliament is targeting an industry, because intervention by politicians and bureaucrats (rightly or wrongly) can have an impact on an industry's economic situation. Find out about any political issues that face a company, industry, or sector (see Chapter 15 for political considerations).

WARNING

Investors need to take heed when political "noise" starts coming out about a particular industry. An industry can be hurt either by direct government intervention or by the threat of it. Intervention can take the form of lawsuits, investigations, taxes, regulations, or sometimes an outright ban. In any case, being on the wrong end of government intervention is one of the greatest external threats to a company's survival.

REMEMBER

Sometimes, government action helps an industry. Generally, beneficial action takes two forms:

>> **Deregulation or tax decreases:** Government sometimes reduces burdens on an industry. A great example is the gradual removal of certain barriers in the medical and recreational marijuana industry in Canada. (We discuss this sector later in this chapter.) Another example is progressive government deregulation that led the way to more innovation in the telecommunications industry. This trend, in turn, laid the groundwork for more innovation and growth in the Internet and the expansion and improvement of cellphone services.

>> **Direct funding:** Government has the power to steer taxpayer money toward business as well. In recent years, federal and provincial governments have provided tax credits and other incentives for alternative energy such as solar power, as well as for an array of individual companies that are leaders in innovation. For example, in 2018 the Government of Canada rolled out an intellectual property (IP) strategy, through which the government intends to increase IP funding and foster an ecosystem that supports business growth, innovation, and competition. Certain public companies listed on the Toronto Stock Exchange will definitely benefit as well.

Outlining Traditional and Key Canadian Sectors and Industries

This section highlights some sectors and industries that Canadian stock investors should take note of. Consider investing some of your stock portfolio in those that look promising (and, of course, avoid those that look problematic).

REMEMBER

Many investors can benefit from a practice referred to as sector rotation (not quite like crop rotation, but close enough). The idea is that you shift money from one sector to another based on current or expectant economic conditions. A number of variations of this concept exist, but in most cases, they follow some essential ideas. If the economy is doing poorly or if the outlook appears bearish, you shift to defensive sectors such as consumer staples and utilities. If the economy is doing well, you shift money to cyclicals such as technology and base materials, which is something that Canada is especially rich in. Given today's fickle economic conditions, sector rotation makes sense and is worth a look by long-term investors. Find out more using the resources we mention in the earlier section "Is the sector growing?" and in Appendix A.

Resources and commodities

The Canadian economy is highly concentrated in commodities, as well as other sectors such as bank and consumer goods and services, especially those offerings driven by the real estate sector. The TSX reflects this unique and integrated ecosystem. Canadian stocks trading on the TSX and other Canadian exchanges are decidedly concentrated in commodities companies like Barrick, a world-leading gold-mining company, and Suncor Energy, which produces oil. In fact, commodities comprise over 30 percent of the TSX Index. Add to this the fact that the majority of Canadians' portfolios are held in domestic stocks, almost 60 percent, and you can see that this special sector is very important to Canadians.

We also added extra content on commodities in this fifth edition. That's because commodities have recently been in a bear market for several years at the time of this writing, so they represent compelling value investing opportunities to consider. However, the purpose of this section is not to identify specific names of winning stocks. Rather, our objective as always is to show you how to pick the winners by focusing on what drives the prices of commodity and other stocks.

What exactly is a commodity?

We know you know what the word *commodity* means. But in the lingo and subculture of the stock market, analysts and investors like to break things into subcategories. We offer some insights about this in this "sub" section.

A *commodity* for stock-investing purposes is a financial instrument, asset, or resource that trades in the *primary* economic sector rather than in the manufactured and value-added products sector. In other words, it's pretty well the stuff you get or grow right from the ground up. Here come the subsets. *Soft* commodities are a category of commodities that includes agricultural products like coffee, wheat, canola, corn, fruit, and sugar. *Hard* commodities are also physical resources that are mined, such as gold, copper, diamonds, silver, and oil. That wasn't hard, was it? Drilling these down even further, hard commodities are often subcategorized as *base* metals and *precious* metals.

What drives commodity prices?

At their root, commodities are driven by strong fundamental trends — namely those of supply and demand. It doesn't get more fundamental than that. Other non-commodity asset classes can be driven by the psychology of greed, hype, or fear. Commodities are purer in this regard. These two fundamentals almost always prevail over the longer term, so commodity price movements are somewhat predictable to those who are patient.

REMEMBER

World growth remains the main driver of commodity prices. In other words, people will always want and need energy, food, and stuff to build and trade with in order to be able to move around and just survive!

Moving toward some more specific macro drivers, did you know that on an overall basis, Canadian commodity prices are more heavily influenced by China than by the U.S.? That's because China is physical goods-driven and the U.S. is now more services-driven. Commodities fulfill the more physical economic needs of other countries. Another interesting fact that cannot be ignored is that the Canadian stock market, in the context of its global trade nature and heavy commodity profile, is 80 percent (very highly) correlated to the Chinese economy. The moral of this story is that successful Canadian commodity stock investors also keep an eye on the Chinese economy.

Oil, gas, and mining

It has been a rough five years for both oil exploration and development companies and miners. Only now have those that survived the commodities bear market begun to emerge with cleaner balance sheets and good business plans. The mining industry, for example, is slowly emerging from the doldrums. Stories of growth and discovery of new oil and base metal reserves are now more frequently found in Canadian business news stories. Indicators of the beginning of a recovery in overall commodity production and prices include a resurgence in the number of Canadian initial public offerings in 2018. Also, prices for precious metals like gold and silver are stable if not growing, always a good signal.

TIP

Gold ETFs are based on "electronic gold" that doesn't involve the ownership of physical bullion or the picking of individual stocks. These financial instruments, discussed in Chapter 5, allow Canadians to be exposed to the gold market without the risk of price volatility due to a bad stock pick or pure speculation.

DRIVERS OF OIL PRICES

As we've said, we're not here to pick individual stocks for you. Instead we teach you what to look for. When it comes to oil prices, keep an eye on the essential drivers of demand. In the case of oil, the first elementary driver is demand itself. Okay, that was easy. Other drivers of demand and price include OPEC supply and non-OPEC supply decisions you often hear about in the news. Production cuts obviously mean oil will rise in price. Weather, war, and conflict also drive up oil prices as fears increase that supplies will be curtailed through damage or sanctions. Raw and meaningless speculation in the financial markets also drives oil prices up or down. Finally, national and international strategic petroleum reserves and inventories are reported regularly, so watch out for that news as well. Don't just pick one driver in isolation but rather try to paint a bigger picture trend and invest accordingly. Once you have first diagnosed the big picture using these criteria, then proceed to analyze individual stocks in the manner we teach throughout this book.

DRIVERS OF GOLD PRICES

The last of the big three Canadian commodity sectors we mention after mining and oil is gold. Gold has multiple drivers you need to watch for as well. The U.S. dollar and U.S. monetary policy go hand in hand, and the strength of the U.S.US dollar needs to be watched when investing in gold. The stronger the dollar, typically the weaker the gold price. International demand for jewelry, especially in countries like India and China, need to be watched as well. At the simple and basic level, gold generates demand from its inherent quality as a store of value. When fiat paper currencies are weak, gold is a strong alternate store of value. Also note that although gold only has about 10 percent use within industrial applications, it is still significant as a driver of price. Finally, other drivers of demand to consider include speculative investment demand, geopolitics, and gold mining activity.

Moving in: Real estate

It's worldwide news that Canada's housing market, especially in Vancouver and Toronto, has reached stratospheric levels. The real estate market actually fueled a significant part (about 1 to 1.5 percent) of the gross domestic product growth of Canada over the last few years. This means that lots of companies associated with real estate — everything from the banks to Home Depot — benefitted from the boom. But how long will this sector growth continue? Will it stabilize or fall? Which companies are impacted most by real estate?

The answer to that question depends on your investment time frame. It also depends whether you're referring to residential or commercial real estate, two sub-sectors that are different animals and have different drivers of demand.

Some analysts believe that Canada's hot residential real estate market is getting a big lift from house-hungry Millennials and migration into Canada. They expect these two population cohorts to bolster other less heated markets like Montreal and Ottawa as they consider more affordable options beyond Toronto and Vancouver. Yet all this frothy behavior may end in the longer term, again because supply tends to catch up to or exceed demand over the long term.

The reason we highlight Canada's lofty real estate market is because it's a classic example of a cyclical bellwether industry — one that has a great effect on many other industries that may be dependent on it. However, even we didn't imagine it would be this cyclical or powerful. Nevertheless, real estate is always looked at as a key component of economic health because as we already mentioned, so many other industries — including building materials, mortgages, household appliances, and contract labour services — are tied to it. A booming real estate industry bodes well for much of the Canadian economy.

Housing starts are one way to measure real estate activity. This data is an important leading indicator of health in the industry. Housing starts indicate new construction, which means more business for related industries.

Keep an eye on both the Canadian and U.S. real estate industry for negative news that may be bearish for the domestic economy and the stock market. Because real estate is purchased with mortgage money, investors and analysts watch the mortgage market for trouble signs such as rising delinquencies and foreclosures. These statistics are a warning for general economic weakness.

Learn to recognize a bubble. In a *bubble*, or *mania*, the prices of the assets such as real estate experience a bull market and skyrocket to extreme levels, which excites more and more investors to jump in, causing prices to rise even further. It gets to the point where seemingly everyone thinks it's easy to get rich by buying this particular asset, and almost no one notices that the market has become unsustainable. After prices are exhausted and start to level off, investor excitement dies down, and then investors try to exit by selling their holdings to realize some profit. As more and more sell off their holdings, demand decreases while supply increases. The mania dissipates, and the bear market appears. If this happens to residential real estate, many stocks of companies that rely on this real estate subsector will also enter a bear market.

Banking on it: Financials

Banking and financial services are intrinsic parts of any economy, and Canada's economy is no different. Debt is the most important sign of this industry for investors. If a company's debt is growing faster than the economy, you need to watch how that debt impacts stocks. If debt gets out of control, it can be disastrous for the economy.

220   PART 3 Picking Winners

The amount of debt and debt-related securities recently reached historic and troublesome levels. This was enabled by the still-low interest-rate environment that makes corporate borrowing cheap and easy. This trend means that many financial stocks of companies like banks that are owed money are at risk if a recession hits anytime soon.

WARNING

Investors in U.S. and some Canadian financial stocks should be selective in this industry and should embrace only those lenders that are conservative in their balance sheet and are generally avoiding overexposure in areas such as international finance and derivatives.

Exploring Small Caps and Speculative Stocks in Any Sector

This chapter is about seizing stock investing opportunities, and most opportunities start on the ground floor. A good example is the marijuana sector, which we discuss to close out this chapter. Before doing so, we recognize the marijuana sector as speculative in nature so we want to first arm you with some additional and more specific information about new and small capitalization companies before getting into actual marijuana stock-investing principles.

Many of the previously discussed commodity stocks on the S&P/TSX and other Canadian exchanges are also smaller in size and new to the stock market. The very nature of that sector is speculative. Will resource companies find something in the ground or not? That's the daily question they face. Other resource stocks are giants that are established and face a bit less uncertainty. The key point to remember is that the stocks of emerging companies generally start out as micro or small cap stocks. This chapter is a good place to explore what small cap stock investing is all about if you're considering these stocks.

The attractive potential of small cap stocks

Everyone wants to get in early on a hot new stock. Why not? You buy Shlobotky, Inc., at $1 per share and hope it zooms to $98 before lunchtime. Who doesn't want to buy a cheap stock today that could become the next Apple or Walmart? This possibility is why investors are attracted to small cap stocks.

Small cap (or *small capitalization*) refers to the company's market size, as we explain in Chapter 1. Small cap stocks have a market value under $1 billion. Investors may face more risk with small caps, but they also have a chance for greater gains. Canada's stock market is replete with small cap stocks.

Out of all the types of stocks, small cap stocks continue to exhibit the greatest amount of growth, but also the greatest volatility. In the same way that a tree planted last year has more opportunity for growth than a mature 100-year-old redwood, small caps have greater growth potential than established large cap stocks. Of course, a small cap doesn't exhibit spectacular growth just because it's small. It grows when it does the right things, such as increasing sales and earnings by producing goods and services that customers want.

REMEMBER

For every small company that becomes a Financial Post FP500 firm, hundreds of companies don't grow at all or go out of business. When you try to guess the next great stock before any evidence of growth, you're not investing — you're speculating. Have you heard that one before? Of course you have, and you'll hear it again. Don't get us wrong — there's nothing wrong with speculating. But it's important to know when you're speculating. If you're going to speculate in small stocks hoping for the next Alphabet (Google), use the info in the following sections to increase your chances of success.

Knowing when to avoid IPOs

Initial public offerings (IPOs) are the birthplaces of public stocks, or the proverbial ground floor. The IPO is the first offering to the public of a company's stock. The IPO is also referred to as "going public." Because a company going public is frequently an unproven enterprise, investing in an IPO can be risky. Here are the two types of IPOs:

>> **Start-up IPO:** This is a company that didn't exist before the IPO. In other words, the entrepreneurs get together and create a business plan. To get the financing they need for the company, they decide to go public immediately by approaching an investment banker. If the investment banker thinks it's a good concept, the banker will seek funding (selling the stock to investors) via the IPO.

>> **A private company that decides to go public:** In many cases, the IPO is done for a company that already exists and is seeking expansion capital. The company may have been around for a long time as a smaller private concern, but now decides to seek funding through an IPO to grow even larger (or to fund a new product, promotional expenses, and so on). Facebook, Shopify, and Groupon are examples of such IPOs.

Which of the two IPOs do you think is less risky? That's right — the private company going public. Why? Because it's already a proven business, which is a safer bet than a brand-new start-up.

Great stocks started as small companies going public. You may be able to recount the stories of Federal Express, Dell, Home Depot, Shopify, and hundreds of other great successes. But do you remember an IPO by the company Lipschitz & Farquar? No? We didn't think so. It's among the majority of IPOs that don't succeed.

WARNING

IPOs have a dubious track record of success in their first year. Studies periodically done by the brokerage industry have revealed that IPOs actually decline in price 60 percent of the time (more often than not) during the first 12 months. In other words, an IPO has a better-than-even chance of dropping in price. For Canadian stock investors, the lesson is clear: Wait until a track record appears before you invest in a company this way. If you don't, you're simply rolling the dice (in other words, you're speculating, not investing!). Don't worry about missing that great opportunity; if it's a bona fide opportunity, you'll still do well after the IPO.

Making sure a small cap stock is making money

REMEMBER

We emphasize two points when investing in stocks:

>> **Make sure a company is established.** Being in business for at least three years is a good minimum.

>> **Make sure a company is profitable.** It should show net profits of 10 percent or more over two years or longer.

These points are especially important for investors in small stocks. Plenty of start-up ventures lose money but hope to make a fortune down the road. A good example is a company in the biotechnology industry. Biotech is an exciting area, but it's esoteric, and at this early stage companies are finding it difficult to use the technology in profitable ways. You may say, "But shouldn't I jump in now in anticipation of future profits?" You may get lucky, but when you invest in unproven, small cap stocks, you're speculating.

Analyzing small cap stocks before you invest

The only difference between a small cap stock and a large cap stock is a few zeros in their numbers and the fact that you need to do more research with small caps. By sheer dint of size, small caps are riskier than large caps, so you offset the risk by accruing more information on yourself and the stock in question. Plenty of information is available on large cap stocks because they're widely followed. Small cap stocks don't get as much press, and fewer analysts issue reports on them. Here are a few points to keep in mind:

WARNING

>> **Understand your investment style.** Small cap stocks may have more potential rewards, but they also carry more risk. No investors should devote a large portion of their capital to small cap stocks. If you're considering retirement money, you're better off investing in large cap stocks, exchange-traded

funds (ETFs; refer to Chapter 5), investment-grade bonds, and/or mutual funds. For example, retirement money should be in investments that are either very safe or have proven track records of steady growth over an extended period of time (five years or longer).

>> **Check with the SEC and SEDAR.** Get the financial reports that the company must file with the SEC and SEDAR (such as its quarterly reports — see Chapter 12 for more details).

>> **Check other sources.** See whether brokers and independent research services, such as Value Line, follow the stock. If two or more different sources like the stock, it's worth further investigation. Check the resources in Appendix A for more information before you invest.

Marijuana Stock Investing in Canada

Canada's leadership in the marijuana sector has made the world stand up and take notice. We hear an endless stream of news about the issues surrounding this sector. As we know, where there is change there is also opportunity, and Canadian stock investors are stepping up to the plate to consider adding marijuana stocks in their portfolios.

Whether you use marijuana or simply invest in this budding (sorry, we couldn't resist) industry, you can get into real legal or financial trouble. But that trouble only comes if you don't know and follow the rules, be they rules about *using* it or just *investing* in it through stocks. A good starting point to avoiding trouble is knowing the specific rules and regulations in place about marijuana today — and, of course, reading this book to learn about stock investing and risk principles that also apply to marijuana stock investing.

Rules of the game

Canada was a pioneer in the legalized use of marijuana for medical purposes as far back as two decades ago. Today, it is also legally permitted to purchase, grow, and possess limited, regulated, and tested amounts of cannabis in Canada. Let's now take a very brief history tour to see how we got here.

Way back in 2014, it became legal for Canadian medical patients to possess medical marijuana from a licensed distributor but only with a prescription provided by a still-practicing Canadian physician. That was a mouthful! Then, in 2016, new additional legislation allowed patients possessing a prescription from a doctor to grow their own medical marijuana plant and use the bud. They could even designate a third party grower to grow it for them. In case you were wondering, as we were, the maximum limit is still five outdoor plants or two indoor plants.

Canada now possesses a draft but rigid legal framework to oversee the production, distribution, sale and possession of cannabis across Canada. In fact, the free world is watching how Canada's industry framework has allowed for the legal, efficient, and effective production and cultivation of cannabis. The good news is that the new legislation is aimed at restricting access to cannabis by underaged Canadian youth, deterring and reducing crime around it, and protecting the users of the drug through strict safety requirements and quality control measures. Also, the legacy program for accessing cannabis for medical purposes will continue under the new Act. As you can see, it is important for investors to understand the ever-changing legalities surrounding the medical marijuana industry.

REMEMBER

Regulations in Canada and the U.S. differ from the municipal, provincial, and state levels all the way to the federal level.

WARNING

If you are like most news-watching Canadians, you have undoubtedly heard about occasional raids on pot dispensaries on Queen Street in Toronto, West Hastings Street in Vancouver, and elsewhere all across Canada. That's because even under the new law, some dispensaries may be operating illegally. Canadians who buy medical marijuana from an unproven dispensary are also placing themselves at risk of possible exposure to pesticides, heavy toxic metals, and nasty pathogens.

A plant by any other name . . .

In addition to knowing the risk and regulations faced by the actual business behind any stock, successful stock investors also have to possess a sound grasp and knowledge of the business. Warren Buffet never invests in businesses he doesn't understand.

Will that be marijuana or cannabis?

You may have heard of the terms *marijuana* and *cannabis* and wondered about the difference. We did, and our fogginess was not even because we smoked any of the above. We promise. *Marijuana* refers to the plant scientifically known as cannabis — more specifically, to three recognized species that include *Cannabis sativa*, *Cannabis indica*, and *Cannabis ruderalis*.

The cannabis plant is a source of hundreds of compounds. Two in particular, called delta-9-tetrahydrocannabinol (THC) and cannabidiol, are the most widely tested elements for medicinal uses. *Hemp*, another term you hear lots about, is a variety of the *Cannabis sativa* plant species that is grown specifically for the industrial uses of its derived products.

So next time you hear news stories about marijuana, you'll likely hear about these terms. You'll also realize that marijuana and cannabis refer to the same plant, so from here on, we use the terms *cannabis* and *marijuana* interchangeably.

Learning the lingo

You can't have a discussion of marijuana or cannabis without the slang. It just wouldn't be cool. You may as well know it —it's a distinctly Canadian thing! The shredded flowers, buds, and leaves of a marijuana plant come in a green, brown, or gray mix. It's smelly.

Marijuana that is rolled up like a cigarette is called a *joint,* and if you roll it like a cigar it's a *blunt.* Marijuana can also be smoked in a pipe. That's just called a *pipe.* Some Canadians incorporate it into cookies, common food, or brew it as a flavoured tea. Canadians who smoke oils from the marijuana plant practice what is referred to as *dabbing.* Other slang names for marijuana include *pot, weed, grass, herb,* or *boom.*

It's also interesting to note that smoking weed isn't the main trend. Actually, quite a few pot users are turning away from the smoking variety of marijuana. The smoke has a problem: people's lungs get coated and choked with tar under long-term use. More and more users are tending toward new ways to consume pot. These alternative ways to consume include vaporizing, eating cannabis-infused food like crackers and drinks like lemonade, ingesting oils taken in capsules or added to food or drink, applying tinctures directly under the tongue, and using topical lotions and balms. Do you see the brand new industries cropping up like we do?

WARNING

This is not a stock-investing warning, but do know that cannabis can make you feel relaxed, silly, sleepy, and happy. It can also make you nervous and scared. Your senses of hearing, sight, and touch may be altered. Your judgment may also be significantly impaired. Okay, back to stock investing.

Why invest in marijuana stocks?

As with any new industry, there are good opportunities for investors in Canadian cannabis stocks willing to do their research. The fact that Canada has provided other countries with a legal and operational template for politicians and producers to mimic and the fact that Canada has first mover advantage in a politically friendly context make the opportunity to invest in this industry undeniable. But, of course, the risks are many.

In the U.S., about 40 states have already legalized medicinal or recreational pot. Pot is already entrenched in the healthcare industry, so it already has a small but important base market. What better endorsement is there than a hospital or doctor sanctioning its careful — and we emphasize the word *careful* — use? As all this slow but steady acceptance is happening, the investment community has swooped in for a piece of the action. The flow of capital is vital, and something you need to watch, for any emerging sector to grow and flourish.

REMEMBER

Companies involved in the cultivation, production, and distribution of weed have many opportunities to access a Canadian stock listing. Many continue to seize this opportunity. In Canada, cannabis company listings can be found on the Toronto Stock Exchange (TSX), the TSX Venture, and the Canadian Securities Exchange (CSE). (We discuss these and other exchanges in Chapter 6.)

Looking at what the past and present is telling us

Let's take a look at where we've been so far, with numbers, which always tell part of a story. Arcview Market Research, a prominent marijuana market research company, reported that legal pot sales in 2017 were $10 billion in North America. The company recently estimated that by the end of 2021, sales could reach $25 billion. That's a big enchilada of a number. There are now at the time of this writing 100 Canadian publicly listed companies supporting this ecosystem with a market capitalization value of $30 billion.

Pictures also tell a story, in this case graphical ones based on numbers. One of our favorite indexes is the Canadian Marijuana Index (www.marijuanaindex.com), which provides a great snapshot of marijuana stock performance. It has useful charts and other indicators and metrics helpful in gauging future stock and sector performance. As with any emerging industry, this leading index has been volatile. Investors still trying to find their way within the weed sector are on pins and needles when it comes to bad news, and inversely become euphoric when good news surfaces about the industry or a specific company. This index hit a high of over 1,000 in early 2018, then experienced a pullback and has settled at a more stable level.

TIP

Go to marijuanaindex.com to access indexes for the North American, U.S., and Canadian marijuana markets. From there, you can see the universe of constituent stocks you may consider investing in. It's a great site to visit for basic weed stock information.

WARNING

The marijuana stock market currently consists of several micro cap players with very small market share. Most of these small fish are pretenders that are not large enough to trade on the main Canadian and U.S. exchanges and instead trade on over-the-counter exchanges or are backed by lesser-known venture capital funds. Be careful here. You can be taken for a ride. Pump-and-dump stock schemes abound in any emerging industry as owners and managers of unscrupulous companies get a listing, pump up the stock with fake news, and sell off their own insider shares. Vile weeds!

Looking at future indicators

The basic infrastructure — access to financial markets, the ability to produce marijuana, and lots of smart visionaries with sound business plans — is now in place, and the ecosystem is thriving. Now that cannabis is legal, other indicators of growth to watch for include new listings of Canadian cannabis companies on major U.S. exchanges like the NYSE or Nasdaq. Canopy, one of Canada's biggest marijuana companies, applied to be listed on the NYSE and is expected to be approved. This was huge news in Canada because the NYSE has a certain cache that will lend credibility to the sector.

Watch for merger and acquisition activity as well. Recently, Aurora Cannabis made a $3 billion all-stock offer to buy its rival and licensed producer MedReleaf to create an 800-pound gorilla in the cannabis sector. Together, the combined company is poised to produce 580,000 kilograms of cannabis annually, representing over 50 percent of expected Canadian demand in 2020.

What other countries do is critical. Look for developments in Italy, Sweden, and of course the U.S. to see if their own markets will further open up domestic as well as foreign supply of medical and legal marijuana. And see how many U.S. companies are seeking listings on Canadian exchanges. If banks like BMO support the industry, that's another great sign that the sector will continue to thrive.

Although U.S. laws and Food and Drug Administration regulations are still in a state of flux, one has to ask if our neighbors to the south represent the next big opportunity and super-catalyst. If so, then Canadian suppliers are uniquely poised to capitalize. That's because Canada is one of only two countries — the other is the Netherlands — that currently exports cannabis, to well over 20 countries. It also helps the future of this sector that the number of companies that have been authorized by Health Canada to produce medicinal marijuana across the country has been steadily increasing.

Legal and regulatory risk factors

We've pointed out the legal and regulatory context of not just the marijuana issue, but also stock investing in this sector. So it stands to reason that the top risks will be legal, regulatory, competitive, and political in nature. There are some things you really need to watch for as you invest in cannabis stocks.

You'll have no trouble finding companies with sound business strategies to legally grow and distribute cannabis and then, based on those plans, find financing and a stock listing. The operators often know the business and what they're doing. Although those operating and financial areas represent risks you need to monitor, they're not primary risks. The big risks are as follows:

>> Cannabis companies sell to a limited and highly regulated market, making product demand and business expansion to meet demand uncertain.

>> The Canadian government's legalization of recreational cannabis is definitely and obviously a huge opportunity for this sector as a whole. However, the easing of laws works the other way in the eyes of individual licensed producers, who will expect to lose market share because some actually benefit from a more regulated market.

>> There are low barriers to entry for new medical marijuana producers and other companies servicing the pot ecosystem, although getting a licence to produce is still a big initial hurdle. Even so, there are many publicly traded cannabis companies, and that number is growing by the month.

>> Big Tobacco and Big Pharma are poised to steal away customers from pioneering pot firms, siphoning market share that would have otherwise gone to the true innovators and risk takers.

>> Cannabis stocks sport lofty market capitalizations in the context of existing sales and sometimes unwarranted speculative appeal. They'll need revenue growth to justify current stock prices, let alone move higher.

WARNING

Government can definitely get in the way of recreational marijuana production, sale, and use. Political interference on hot button issues like this can and ought to be expected. The issue is the nature and extent of the meddling. Although unlikely to happen soon in Canada given the recent legalization, there is still some residual risk. This risk particularly exposes companies with U.S. assets in that those very assets may be seized at any time by U.S. authorities.

WARNING

The Toronto Stock Exchange is keeping a watchful eye on listed Canadian cannabis companies holding U.S. marijuana assets and wants to ensure that the firms are complying with U.S. regulations. That exposes both the listing status of companies listed on the TSX as well as the underlying assets themselves. Marijuana companies with 100 percent of their operations and assets in Canada are likely a much safer investment.

Evaluating micro cap marijuana stocks

When evaluating a marijuana stock, micro cap or otherwise, consider the extent to which the company can lay claim to the following favorable factors:

>> Market valuation is reasonable

>> Sales and marketing is broad and effective

- » Top consumer retail channels like pharmacies and liquor stores back the product

- » Cultivation facilities are state-of-the-art

- » Low growing costs and high efficiencies

- » High quality core and ancillary products

- » Competitive pricing for similar products

- » Hedging strategy via permits to sell cannabis to foreign markets exists

- » Profitability and cash generation evident

- » Minimal exposure to changes in U.S. legislation

- » Strong base in high-quality medicinal marijuana

- » Sells extracts and cannabis oils that yield high profit margins

Highly speculative pot-related stocks

Some biotech firms are developing cannabinoid drugs which, if they pass clinical trials, could be strong sellers in treating neurological and other disorders. The risk here is that the shares of these firms may have already been hyped to the skies on the dicey prospect that their products under development will pan out. Tread carefully here.

Low-risk pot-related stocks

Consider investing indirectly in this sector. Scotts Miracle-Gro is a $3.2 billion (sales) market leader in the North American lawn-care and garden business. A significant upside for the firm is the specialized soil and plant nutrients it sells to a burgeoning marijuana industry.

Constellation Brands, another blue chip, anchored by its popular Corona beer and Robert Mondavi wines, is a safe play on marijuana with its approximately 10 percent stake in industry leader Canopy Growth.

And by way of subsidiary, Shoppers Drug Mart, Loblaw Cos. Ltd., is angling to be a major pot retailer with its 2,400 or so stores across Canada. Pending federal approval of Shoppers' pot-retailing applications, the company has already signed up both Aphria and MedReleaf as marijuana suppliers.

In addition to investing in stocks of companies such as these, consider ETFs. Horizons ETF Management inaugurated the Horizons Medical Marijuana Life Sciences (TSX:HMMJ) on the Toronto Stock Exchange, with 14 marijuana stocks included in the fund as of now.

Chapter **14**

Investing in Asian Stock Markets

I n our early days of investing, we noticed that stock investors were most comfortable investing in domestic stocks. Soon after, the Internet exploded with tremendous functionality, empowering Canadian stock investors with online tools that virtually placed us on par with old-guard brokers. Through these tools and information resources, investors noticed that the world of global investing was within their personal grasp.

Then, in 2005, the Canadian Income Tax Act underwent a profound and long overdue change. The Tax Act no longer imposed a limit on foreign content within Registered Retirement Savings Accounts (RRSPs) or Tax-Free Savings Accounts (TFSAs). (We discuss taxes in Chapter 21.) Canadians investors were soon off to the races, trading even more U.S. stocks. Today, momentum is taking them well outside of North America and Europe. One such notable trend over the last decade has been the steady influx of stock investment capital into the Asian markets.

Asian stock markets have been around for over a century. They sport robust national stock markets representing trillions of dollars, meaning investment opportunities abound. It all started with Japan. Hong Kong, Singapore, South

Korea, Taiwan, Thailand, Vietnam, India, and China all followed. But it is China that became a mega-stock market in a very short period of time, despite its later entry into the world financial markets.

Asia is typically viewed through lens of developed or developing economies. The Asian Tigers, as they are called, are developed nations and include, along with Japan, the autonomous territories or countries of Hong Kong, Singapore, South Korea, and Taiwan. China, though still undeveloped in terms of financial market maturity and political certainty, has enormous opportunity due to its massive economic size.

The rapid growth of all Asian markets, something which occurred during a long period of robust industrialization that started half a century ago, came to a crashing halt in 1997 when Asia was struck with its very own home-grown financial crisis. It weathered that terrible storm, and to this day Asian economies in general are still thriving, with bumps along the way. China, South Korea, Thailand, Indonesia, and Malaysia are now additional exporting powerhouses. Double-digit stock market returns have left Western stock investors green with envy, even as the North American bull market had its own strong results over the last few years.

Why Invest in Asia?

Your decision to invest in Asia, however small or large in amount, is all about that market's past positive results and future compelling opportunities. To be sure, Asian financial and stock markets are nowhere near as mature and well-governed as the U.S. market. It's not even close. (We show you what risks to watch for later in this chapter, so don't worry.) However, Asia opens up access to a significant portion of the world economy and stock markets, and if you invest carefully, you stand to benefit by way of good returns and broader diversification.

The numbers tell a story

According to statistics, stock market returns in Asia have sometimes outperformed those closer to home. This has been most pronounced in higher growth and more modern emerging markets. The short-term track record is good. More importantly — and as crazy as it sounds — there *is* a track record to speak of.

Asian stock markets are big and have further to run in terms of growth. For example, Canadian equities only comprise about 3percent of the developed world's total market capitalization, and over the last few years have been underperforming most other developed countries, as well as some underdeveloped ones. This means many of the world's most attractive stock-investment gems reside outside Canadian borders. Even if we use a wide-angle lens, North American exchanges open up "only" 45 percent of the world's capital markets.

Not only is China the world's second-largest economy, it also accounts for a mammoth *one-third* of global economic growth. According to some economic metrics, its output is bigger than the U.S., Canada, and Europe combined. Add in other Asian countries, and the numbers become even more impressive.

Yes, but . . .

If your "Spidey" sense is tingling, you're not alone. We don't take investing in Asian — and Chinese stock markets in particular — lightly. Risks abound. All-too-frequent news about permanent presidencies, suppression of individual rights, curbed free speech, restriction of Internet access, and questionable financial transactions abound.

Yet we recognize the opportunity behind the fact that the Chinese government is walking on a tightrope. On the one hand, you have its instinct to suppress freedoms and increase its meddling and control. On the other hand, the Chinese government realizes that if it suppresses too much and breaks the trust of financial markets, it will choke off the very finances that fuel the nation's incredible economic growth. In our view, the Communist Party president and his apparatus have a vested interest in promoting economic growth in order to keep potential social unrest at bay. With social stability, the stage is set for greater market stability and opportunity. Remember that many of the new middle class of China, having now tasted the better things in life like entertainment, better healthcare, good education, and proper housing, are not going to allow the government to give that economic growth up. That means that the markets, even under a Communist regime, will be allowed to do what markets do — behave capitalistically. In China, the two coexist. The Asian stock markets are indeed open for business.

Investing in Chinese Stocks Directly

Canadian stock investors have no reason not to consider including at least some measure of foreign stocks in their investment portfolios, and Asian stocks can be part of that. It doesn't have to be much, and as you will see in this chapter there are also super easy ways to accomplish this. In this section, though, we begin with the harder and trickier stuff, including trading Asian stocks that reside directly on foreign exchanges in Asia, including China.

We've found that trading on foreign exchanges can be quite a rewarding experience. To reach that reward takes a bit of patience, planning, and research — in other words, time and effort. Yuck. You have to put up with the vast time difference between your Canadian residence and the foreign Asian exchanges. Finding accurate, complete, relevant, and reliable company information in a language you understand can be frustrating at first. But if you're diligent, you eventually get the hang of it. Also, dealing with foreign rules on accounting and financial disclosure and executing reasonably priced foreign exchange transactions in order to trade stocks in Hong Kong dollars or Chinese yuan require patience and tenacity.

To invest in Chinese stocks directly, you need to take three general steps:

1. Open a brokerage account.

2. Select the foreign stock exchange you want to trade in.

3. Select appropriate Asian stocks.

The next section takes you through those processes.

Open a brokerage account and buy Hong Kong dollars or yuan

Many, though not most, of Canada's top brokerage houses allow trading in Chinese stocks on Chinese and Asian stock exchanges. The extent to which you can do so varies. At a minimum, though, all Canadian brokers will allow you to trade in Chinese stocks listed on U.S. exchanges as well as ETFs, something we discuss later in this chapter. However, some brokerage houses operating in Canada, like HSBC and a handful of others are market leaders and first movers and give you access to foreign exchanges outside North America.

For the purposes of this chapter, don't worry about how to place an order. That process is virtually universal in nature. Chapter 17 discusses all manner of brokerage accounts and online or phone orders. We won't repeat that here. One key point to remember for now is that there are *different* ways to invest in Chinese and other Asian stocks, all depending on your risk appetite, brokerage house offerings, and personal preferences. Another point to keep in mind is that there are different foreign stock exchanges all across Asia for you to choose from.

TIP

When you're ready to invest in Asian shares, contact your existing Canadian brokerage house, if you have an account, and they will guide you through the foreign stock trading process and answer your questions. Each broker deals with these types of transactions in a different way and to different extents. With some online stock trading platforms (which are still evolving in Canada), you may also be able to trade stocks on your own. Check out your online investment service to get a sense of what your options are.

Ticks and fees

Here is the first real unwelcome surprise. Trading in Asia costs more than trading domestically. That's because your broker has to undertake many more administrative tasks in order to execute your stock trade. Fair enough.

In a typical brokerage house fee structure, you have a choice of flat-fee commission, percentage-of-trade commissions, tiered, or a blend of these. Flat fees can start at $30 or more, and percentage-of-trade commissions are often higher than flat rates due to their variable nature. A fairly straightforward trade on the stock exchange in Sydney will cost you about $95. But the real cost run-up occurs with the layers of additional and annoying market-specific fees that are often levied. For instance, there are stamp duties, extra trading fees, and withholding taxes in Hong Kong. Stamp duty is a tax that is levied on documents regarding the sale or transfer of properties, including stocks and shares. You guessed it. If you pay a stamp duty, you get a stamp on your documents.

WARNING

The Korea Stock Exchange (KSE) and other Asian exchanges may impose larger mandatory *tick* sizes on higher-priced stocks. *Tick size* is the minimum price movement of a stock. A tick size of 0.10 means the stock has a tick value and increment of ten cents. With large tick spreads, you may end up paying much more for a stock than you otherwise would with a lower tick size.

HSBC InvestDirect

HSBC InvestDirect is one of Canada's first movers in the area of Asian stock trading from Canada. HSBC allows you to trade in about 25 major global stock markets, including Australia (Australian Securities Exchange), China (Hong Kong Exchange, Shanghai Stock Exchange, and the Shenzhen Stock Exchange), Japan (Tokyo Stock Exchange), and Singapore (Jardine Strategic).

HSBC InvestDirect (http://hsbc.ca/investdirectdemo) is a division of HSBC Securities (Canada) Inc., a wholly owned subsidiary of, but separate entity from, HSBC Bank Canada. As we explain shortly, you'll need to fund your brokerage account with foreign currency. HSBC InvestDirect lets you execute stock trades in more than ten different currencies, including Hong Kong dollars, euros, Japanese yen, Australian dollars, New Zealand dollars, Singapore dollars, and Canadian and U.S. dollars.

TD Waterhouse

TD Waterhouse (www.td.ca) is also a leader in this space. Its global platform requires phone service to access Chinese and most other Asian markets. You can execute online trades for shares listed on the Sydney, Hong Kong, and Singapore stock exchanges. Trades can settle in seven currencies.

Interactive Brokers Canada

Interactive Brokers Canada (www.interactivebrokers.ca) provides online and phone access to Asia/Pacific exchanges, including the Australian Stock Exchange (ASX), Hong Kong Stock Exchange (SEHK), Shanghai-Hong Kong Stock Connect (SEHKNTL), Shenzhen-Hong Kong Stock Connect (SEHKSZSE), Tokyo Stock Exchange (TSEJ), Singapore Exchange (SGX), and the Korea Stock Exchange (KSE).

Shanghai-Hong Kong Stock Connect, for example, is a cross-border investment channel that connects the Shanghai Stock Exchange with the Hong Kong Stock Exchange. Under this arrangement, investors in each market are able to trade shares on the other market. So if you can access the Hong Kong exchange, you are also able to access the Chinese mainland markets of Shanghai and Shenzhen. (We revisit these exchanges shortly.)

Buy yuan and Hong Kong dollars

The legal tender in Hong Kong is called the *Hong Kong dollar*, or HKD in short. It is legally pegged to the U.S. dollar at a rate of about 8 HKD to 1 U.S. dollar (USD). As you know, exchange rates fluctuate on an ongoing basis.

REMEMBER

The *yuan* is the name of a unit of the *renminbi* currency of China. Don't get confused. Something may cost 2 yuan or 20 yuan. It wouldn't be correct to say that it costs "two renminbi." It's similar to how we say a half a pint costs two British pounds, not "two Sterlings."

Once you've opened up an account with HSBC, TD Waterhouse, Interactive Brokers Canada, or any other broker in Canada, determine how much you want to invest and where — Hong Kong or mainland China exchanges — and convert your Canadian or U.S. funds into the target and germane currency used in the respective foreign stock exchange.

Access the Hong Kong Stock Exchange and other exchanges

You just opened a brokerage account and are ready to trade Asian stocks directly. Congratulations. You're an early adopter of this form of international stock investing. Now comes the next part: figuring out which stock exchange playing field to participate in. Your choices are many, and we highlight the distinctive features of each in this section.

Your decision may be based on chicken and egg thinking. Has a certain stock come to your attention, and you're wondering how to access it? Or are you more comfortable starting with the big picture first — beginning with the country and index you're most familiar with? There's no right answer, and it really doesn't matter. Either way, you have to analyze your stocks the way we teach you throughout this book. That's the common denominator.

Next, we introduce you to some of the key Chinese and other Asian exchanges — those in Hong Kong, Shanghai, Shenzhen, Tokyo, and beyond.

HK Exchange

The Stock Exchange of Hong Kong Limited, commonly abbreviated in your newspaper's financial section as SEHK, is Asia's third-largest stock exchange by *market capitalization* (shares outstanding multiplied by share price). It ranks in size just behind the Tokyo Stock Exchange and Shanghai Stock Exchange. It's the sixth largest exchange in the world with a market capitalization of $3 trillion USD.

ALPHABET SOUP

Companies incorporated and listed in China can issue different classes of shares depending on where they're listed and who's allowed to own them. These classes are called A, B, and H, which are all renminbi-denominated shares though traded in different currencies, depending on where they're listed. Chinese companies incorporated and listed outside of mainland China are typically referred to as Red Chips, P Chips, S Chips, or N Shares, depending on their ownership structure, place of business operations, and listing location.

A and B Shares are listed in China. A Shares trade in yuan. B Shares trade in USD on the Shanghai Exchange and in HKD on the Shenzhen Exchange. A Shares are the hardest to access by foreigners, including Canadians; B Shares are easier to trade by Canadians.

Shares that are H, Red Chip, or P Chip are listed in Hong Kong, and the trading currency is the HKD. Many companies with H Share listings also have A Share listings, effectively offering a gateway to purchasing hard-to-access A Shares. H Shares represent companies that are incorporated in China but trade on the Hong Kong Stock Exchange. Companies offering Red Chip stocks are owned by the state, provinces, or municipalities of China and are typically not pure business plays so they are risky. S Chips are listed in Singapore, and N Shares are listed in the U.S. Both trade in their respective currencies. They're available to Canadian investors, typically under Stock Connect programs.

The SEHK has more than 2,000 listed companies, about 1,000 originating from mainland China. The rest originate from Hong Kong (about 850) and other countries and regions such as Macau, Taiwan, Malaysia, the United States, and Singapore (the other 150 or so).

China and its own separatist movement

Hong Kong and mainland Chinese people have a bit of a thing going. It's like sibling rivalry. To an outsider, you would think nothing is wrong. Although you may think Hong Kong is a province of China, it's not that straightforward. The relationship between the two territories is described in the media as "one country, two systems." The key point here to keep in mind is that Hong Kong is far more democratic, which means less government interference in the markets. Keep that in mind as you explore exchanges to trade on.

The Chinese exchanges: Shanghai and Shenzhen

There are two primary mainland China stock exchanges: the Shanghai Stock Exchange and the Shenzhen Stock Exchange. The Shanghai Stock Exchange (SSE) is, naturally, based in Shanghai, China. This exchange is the world's fourth largest stock market by market capitalization at about $4.3 trillion USD. The Shanghai Exchange is still not easily accessible to Canadian investors and is often interfered with by policy decisions made by the Chinese Government. These types of sudden policy pronouncements can make life miserable if your stock is at the wrong end of a government decision.

The Shenzhen Stock Exchange (SZSE) is located in the city of Shenzhen and operates in mainland China. It boasts a market capitalization of over $3 trillion USD and is one of the world's top ten largest stock exchanges. A decade ago, it was barely on the map.

TIP

The S&P China A Composite Index provides a comprehensive equity market benchmark for investors in China. It's a great way to get a big-picture sense of market performance. The index is composed of all A Share stocks listed on the SSE and SZSE stock exchanges. Through this index you can drill down and see sector breakdowns. Another index is the The S&P China 500. It includes the 500 largest Chinese companies. All Chinese share classes including A Shares and offshore listings can be found in this index.

THE OPPORTUNITIES

The Shanghai exchange is quite a different animal compared to the Hong Kong exchange. In the former, two-thirds of the market is represented by small capitalization stocks; in the latter, small capitalization stocks make up one-fifth.

However, one area that makes Shanghai stand out is that it's more reflective of the Chinese economy. That's because it has a relatively higher concentration in financial, transportation, healthcare, and industrial stocks. This fact makes it a compelling stock market to invest in because it unlocks an entire nation and its habits to the global investor. Another advantage of the SSE (and even the SZSE) is that it is generally not as correlated to other major global markets. That's because it's still a new market. However, this attribute makes it a great diversification vehicle.

THE RISKS

Now that we've shown you the good, let's take a peak at the bad and ugly. The Shanghai and Shenzhen stock exchanges are volatile, trendy, and therefore risky. Regional and global investors alike are not placing enough attention on the types of investing fundamentals described in this book. In other words, don't bet the farm on any stock in this market, and don't place too much of your investing capital into any one of these markets even if you buy a basket of stocks. There's no point in diversifying in a stock market that at times behaves like the Titanic. To add to your risks, many companies lack the types of reporting standards that Canadian and U.S. investors are used to. Not only are the standards and minimum information requirements weak, some only report in Cantonese or Mandarin, and many don't even publish annual reports! This is especially the case with the small cap stocks on the SSE and SZSE. Even the professional fund managers that invest in Asian stocks find it difficult to find out what's going on in smaller companies.

Tokyo Stock Exchange

The Tokyo Stock Exchange, or TSE/TYO for short, has been around for ages. It's a big one, in fact it's the third-largest stock exchange in the world by market capitalization, clocking in at $5 trillion. It is the largest exchange in Asia, with about 2,400 listed companies. The main index tracking Tokyo Stock Exchange constituents is the Nikkei 225 index of companies that you often read about in the papers or hear on the radio.

TIP

Follow this index if you're interested in Asian stock investing because it's a bell-wether indicator of overall market health in Asia.

Asia Pacific Exchanges: Australia and Singapore

The Australian Securities Exchange, or ASX, is Australia's main stock exchange. The ASX has a market capitalisation of around $1.6 trillion USD, making it one of the world's top 15 exchanges by market capitalization. An interesting factoid is that the ASX is the first major financial market to open every business day. One major advantage is that it strives to meet the highest global regulatory standards. The ASX is among the most secure in the world, and this helps keep its financial markets stable and trustworthy. In fact, the ASX has more than 150 years of experience. It has over 7 million share owners holding one or more of almost 2,200 listed companies. You may want to dip your toes in this Asia Pacific market first.

The Singapore Exchange (SGX) boasts Asia's leading and most trusted market infrastructure. It deals with equities, fixed income financial instruments, and derivatives in compliance with high regulatory standards. It is Asia's most international, multi-asset exchange. About 40 percent of listed companies and 75 percent of listed corporate bonds originate outside of Singapore. SGX is globally recognised for its risk-management and clearing-house capabilities. That means it's an efficient and resilient exchange, with few successful cyber attacks or business interruptions. The stock exchange has 800 listings, and like Canada many of the listings are in the resources and financial services sectors. It's a great way to diversify into things Canadians already know about: resources.

Look up and buy stock using local stock tickers

Now that you know the bigger picture of stock investing in Asian markets, you just need to identify the Chinese and other Asian stocks you want to buy. Without an up close and personal knowledge of China, for instance, picking individual stocks is a challenge at best. A good approach is to apply all the lessons you learn in this book, because stock investing principles are pretty much universal in nature. To do that with some measure of success, the very minimum requirement is to make sure you have the best available information. That information is best found in annual and quarterly reports that are complete, understandable, relevant, reliable, current, and in accordance with CPA financial reporting standards.

WARNING

As mentioned earlier, it can be a challenge, but unless the preceding criteria can be met *do not* invest under any circumstances. Doing so would be gambling, not investing. That's the minimum, but it may be sufficient if you are investing with risk capital (money you can to a certain extent afford to lose).

One final word on listed Asian stocks. The stock tickers may be numeric. The companies in Table 14-1 represent the largest Chinese companies that are also listed on more easily accessible North American and Hong Kong exchanges.

TABLE 14-1: ## Ten Largest Chinese Companies

Company	Ticker	Capitalization ($B)
Tencent Holdings	HKG:0700	488
Alibaba Group	NYSE:BABA	474
Industrial & Commercial Bank of China	HKG:1398	316
China Construction Bank	HKG:0939	238
Petrochina	NYSE:PTR	213
China Mobile	NYSE:CHL	205
Ping An Insurance Group	HKG:2318	194
Bank of China	HKG:3988	178
Agricultural Bank of China	HKG:1288	175
China Life Insurance	HKG:2628	129
China Petroleum & Chemical	NYSE:SNP	104

Investing in American Depository Receipts (ADRs) of Chinese Companies

If your only objective is to invest in the largest Chinese stocks, then you don't need to worry, as you can see from the preceding table. Investing in these large cap stocks is totally feasible. But there are hundreds of other Chinese and Asian stocks available to invest in.

The next and easier way to access these stocks is through North American exchanges like the NYSE and Nasdaq, and even through the U.S. over-the-counter market. Within these U.S. exchanges are stocks of Asian and other countries (like the U.K. and South Africa), called American Depository Receipts, or ADRs for short. ADRs are shares of blue-chip Chinese (or other) companies that are *interlisted* as ADRs on the New York Stock Exchange. If you've already opened a discount brokerage account, then you're already adept at trading foreign stocks— that is, if our neighbour to the south counts as "foreign." Because American companies represent about half the foreign stock universe as measured by market capitalization, you can access part of the other half through ADRs trading on exchanges you already know.

An ADR is a legal certificate that represents ownership of a non-U.S. and non-Canadian foreign company. The Chinese shares, for example, underpinning an exchange-listed ADR are purchased on the company's Chinese exchange and held by a custodian bank in China. ADRs are then issued by a U.S. depositary bank like BNY Mellon or Citibank.

Foreign companies utilize depositary banks to set up an ADR for a number of reasons. The obvious one is to open up access to the large pool of North American capital. Other reasons include a desire to build corporate brand and recognition, diversify shareholder base, and improve trading liquidity.

Now that we know why companies become listed as ADRs, let's figure out why Canadian stock investors would want to buy U.S.-traded ADRs to access Asian stocks. Although it seems like a very circuitous approach, there are several benefits, including the following:

>> **Canadian brokers:** ADRs may be acquired and sold through all Canadian discount and full-service brokers with exactly the same trading processes you experience when you buy other shares on a U.S. exchange.

>> **Reporting in English:** Annual and quarterly reports exist by regulation and are also written in English.

>> **Full disclosure:** ADRs meet U.S. regulatory listing requirements, so you get the same level of disclosure you do with other U.S.-listed securities.

>> **Compliance with accounting standards:** Companies are required to follow International Financial Reporting Standards (IFRS).

>> **Mature companies:** Companies that issue ADRs tend to be established and financially stable multinational companies.

>> **Good exchange rates and familiar currencies:** Stock trades and dividends are denominated in U.S. currency, minimizing currency foreign exchange costs because rate spreads are usually favorable.

Check out a complete list of Chinese ADRs trading on the US Exchanges at http://topforeignstocks.com/foreign-adrs-list/the-full-list-of-chinese-adrs/. A similar list, this one containing both ADR and non-ADR Chinese stocks trading on the Nasdaq exchange, can be found at www.nasdaq.com/screening/companies-by-region.aspx?region=Asia&country=China.

Other Ways to Invest in China

In addition to the Asian stock investing channels and strategies described in preceding sections, there are other ways as well. The good news is that we end this chapter with what we consider more straightforward and potentially less risky ways to access some great Asian stocks.

Investing in Chinese companies on U.S. non-ADR exchanges

Not all Chinese companies list in Asia. Many list directly on the Nasdaq or NYSE without ADR status. Sina Corporation, Sohu.com, and Alibaba Group Holding, Ltd. are a few of the giants that trade in this manner. Japanese companies like Sony Corporation and Toyota Motor Corporation are non-ADR listings. Some stocks, like Samsung of South Korea, trade over the counter. Disclosure and reporting by these types of companies are just as robust and stringent as ADR companies that trade on the New York Stock Exchange or Nasdaq.

North American multinationals in China

Many U.S. and international companies actually operate in China, beyond doing business in China from afar. Check out the following homemade but relevant site showing a large list of American companies with boots on the ground in China: www.jiesworld.com/international_corporations_in_china.htm. You will recognize many of the names. The companies either own full-blown factories or have factories producing components of products or the products themselves in China and on their behalf. These companies sell to both Chinese and non-Chinese markets.

Although it may be effective and feel safe to target shares of multinational companies whose products are "must haves" for the growing Chinese middle class, risks remain. Names like Apple, Starbucks, Boeing, General Motors, Ford, Walmart, and Hollywood studios like Universal all stand to benefit from growth. But what happens if a trade war erupts? In 2018 it did erupt and where this is all going to end up is still unclear. The risk of tariff wars remains. These are the types of considerations to be aware of.

Investing in ETFs

Exchange-traded funds are another way to invest in China and the rest of Asia. (Chapter 5 covers ETFs.) BMO has a China Equity Index ETF that invests in ADRs listed in New York and traded in U.S. dollars. A similar ETF is the Global X China Consumer ETF. Yet another is the BLDRS Asia 50 ADR Index Fund, built to track the performance of 50 Asian market-based depository receipts.

TIP

Check out the assets under management within an ETF. Doing so gives you a glimpse into where institutional investors, who hopefully did the hard research, are putting their money. After all, they have the financial and human resources to analyze which stocks and financial instruments provide the best opportunity.

Investing in country or regional funds

By now, you know we are not fans of mutual funds. However, they represent yet another way you can invest in Asian stock markets. These funds will mostly be organized as *country* or *regional* funds. The brokerage arms of most Canadian banks as well as discount brokers offer mutual funds that consist of Chinese shares. Many Asian-themed mutual funds have performed well recently. However, country funds can be risky because all it takes is one international crisis of a financial or political nature, and your funds will rapidly decline in value.

Chapter **15**

The Big Economic and Political Picture

Politics can be infuriating, disruptive, meddlesome, corrupting, and harmful. Don't let that fool you — it has its bad side, too! Even if politics doesn't amuse or interest you, you can't ignore it. If you aren't careful, it can wreak great havoc on your stock portfolio. Politics wields great influence on the economic and social environments, which in turn affects how companies succeed or fail. This success or failure in turn either helps or hurts your stock's price. Politics (manifested in taxes, regulations, tariffs, price controls, capital controls, and other government actions) can make or break a company, industry, or sector quicker than any other external force.

REMEMBER

What people must understand (especially government policymakers) is that a new tax, law, regulation, or government action has a macro effect on a stock, an industry, a sector, or even an entire economic system, whereas a company has a micro effect on an economy. The following gives you a simple snapshot of these domino effects:

Politics → policy → economy → sector → industry → company → stock → stock investor

Now, this chapter doesn't moralize about politics or advocate a political point of view; after all, this book is about stock investing. In general, policies can be good or bad regardless of their effect on the economy — some policies are enacted to achieve greater purposes even if they kick you in the wallet. In the context of this chapter, politics is covered from a cause-and-effect perspective: How does politics affect prosperity and stock investing in particular?

REMEMBER

A proficient stock investor can't — must not — look at stocks as though they exist in a vacuum. Our favourite example of this rule is the idea of fish in a lake. You can have a great fish (your stock) among a whole school of fish (the stock market) in a wonderful lake (the economy). But what if the lake gets polluted (bad acid rain policy)? What happens to the fish? Politics controls the lake and can make it hospitable — or dangerous — for the participants. You get the point. The example may sound too simple, yet it isn't. So many people — political committees, corporate managers, bureaucrats, and politicians — still get this picture so wrong time and time again, to the detriment of the economy and stock investors. Heck, we don't mind if they get it wrong with their money, but their actions make it tough for your money.

Although the two inexorably get intertwined, we do what we can to treat politics and economics as separate issues.

Tying Together Politics and Stocks

The campaigns heat up. Conservatives, liberals, socialists, environmentalists, separatists, and libertarians joust in the battlefield of ideas and vie for your attention and subsequent votes. But after all is said and done, voters make their decisions. Election day brings a new slate of politicians into office, and they in turn joust and debate on new rules and programs in the legislative halls of power. Before and after election time, investors must keep a watchful eye on the proceedings. In the following sections, we explain some basic political concepts that relate to stock investing.

REMEMBER

Our discussion here isn't restricted to Canadian politics. In fact, in this highly interconnected world economy, the discussion about the political landscape's effect on Canadian stock investing can't even be restricted to North American politics. As long as a company operates in another country, it will be affected by the politics of that country. Ultimately, the effect of this interconnectedness trickles down to the company, stock, and individual investor level.

The effects of politics on stock investing

For stock investors, politics manifests itself as a major factor in investment-making decisions in the ways shown in Table 15-1.

TABLE 15-1   **Politics and Investing**

Possible Legislation	Effect on Investing
Taxes	Will a new tax affect a particular stock (industry, sector, or economy)? Generally, more or higher taxes ultimately have a negative impact on stock investing. Income taxes, carbon taxes, and capital gains taxes are good examples.
Laws	Will the federal government (or, in some instances, provincial legislatures) pass a law that will have a negative impact on a stock, the industry, the sector, or the economy? Price controls — laws that unilaterally set the price of a product, service, or commodity — are examples of negative laws. We discuss price controls later in this chapter.
Regulations	Will a new (or existing) regulation have a negative (or positive) effect on the stock of your choice? Generally, more or tougher regulations, like those geared to safety or the environment, may have a negative impact on stocks.
Government spending and debt	If government agencies spend too much or misallocate resources, they may create greater burdens on society, which will be bearish for the economy and stock market.
Money supply	The money supply of a nation — the dollars you use — is influenced by the Bank of Canada. In the U.S., it's influenced by the Federal Reserve. The Bank of Canada doesn't directly control money supply; the U.S. Federal Reserve exerts more direct control. Either way, both bodies exert some measure of influence. How can money supply affect stocks? Big time! Increasing or decreasing the money supply can result in either an inflationary or a deflationary environment, which can help or hurt the economy, specific sectors and industries, and your stock picks.
Interest rates	The Bank of Canada and the Federal Reserve have crucial and significant influence. They can raise or lower key interest rates that in turn can have an effect on the entire economy and the stock market. When interest rates go up, it makes credit more expensive for companies. When interest rates go down, companies can get cheaper credit, which can be better for profits.
Government bailouts or subsidies	A bailout is when the government intervenes directly in the marketplace and uses either tax money or borrowed money to bail out a troubled enterprise. This is generally a negative because funds are diverted by force from the healthier private economy to an ailing enterprise. Subsidies are similar but are usually associated with companies or industries under a lesser level of distress.

REMEMBER

When many of the factors in Table 15-1 work in tandem, they can have a magnified effect that can have tremendous consequences for your stock portfolio. Alert Canadian investors keep a constant vigil when the legislature is open for business, and they adjust their portfolios accordingly.

POLITICS, STOCKS, AND "TAXMAGEDDON"

As we write this fifth edition, both Canada and the United States are in the throes of political change. Stock investors (both individuals and portfolio managers) will make decisions based on the outcomes — especially any changes in the Canadian political leadership landscape, or with NAFTA, the North American Free Trade Agreement. By the time you read this, either the stock market was happy with the decisions or it wasn't. However, we will take a leap of faith and say that if the leaders don't reverse the pending effects of "national debt overload," then the effect on both economies (hence the stock market) will be very negative. Whether this reversal will actually happen remains to be seen as this book goes to press, but it's safe to write that increased taxes (especially if they're too onerous) will have a negative impact on stocks (regardless of which political party dominates the House of Commons or Congress). We must remember (and we must remind Canadian politicians . . . constantly) that increasing taxes means taking money out of the private sector (where goods and services are produced) and shifting these funds to venues (good or bad) that aren't productive for the growth of the economy.

Ascertaining the political climate

REMEMBER

The bottom line is that you ignore political realities at your own (economic) risk. To be and stay risk-aware, ask yourself the following questions about the stock of each company in which you invest:

>> What laws will directly affect my stock investment adversely?

>> Will any laws affect the company's industry or sector?

>> Will any laws affect the company's sources of revenue?

>> Will any laws affect the company's expenses or supplies?

>> Am I staying informed about political and economic issues that may possibly have a negative impact on my investment?

>> Will such things as excessive regulations, price controls, or new taxes have a negative impact on my stock's industry?

Here are some examples: Canadian oil and gas service and exploration companies benefited from the global need for more energy supplies. But investment opportunities didn't stop there. As oil and gas supplies became costly and problematic, alternative energy sources gained national attention. The debate about wind power, solar power, and other exciting new technologies, such as fuel cells, was rekindled. As traditional sources of energy, like crude oil, became more expensive, alternative sources, such as Alberta's tar sands, became more economically viable, at least when the price of crude remained high. Investors who anticipated the new interest in alternative energy sources sought companies that would logically benefit. The federal government for decades had restrictions on offshore drilling growth near Newfoundland, but the energy industry ultimately received Canadian tax credits as offshore expansion restrictions were eventually removed.

Today's even bigger issue in Canada is the pending approval of very controversial pipelines to the east, west, and south of Canada. Politicians have to appease either the environmentalists or businesses. When those decisions ultimately turn into new regulations, there will be an immediate impact on the stock prices of oil sector companies.

Regardless of the merits (or demerits) of the situation, investors must view it through the lens of economic causes and effects, which in turn leads to their decisions on which companies (stocks) are impacted positively or negatively.

Nonsystemic and systemic effects

Politics can affect investments in two basic ways: nonsystemic and systemic:

>> Nonsystemic means that the system isn't affected but a particular participant is affected.

>> Systemic means that all the players in the system are affected. Laws typically affect more than just one company or group of companies; rather, they affect an entire industry, sector, or the entire economy — more "players" in the economic system.

In this case, the largest system is the economy at large: To a lesser extent, an entire industry or sector can be the system that's affected. Politics imposes itself (through taxes, laws, regulations, and so on) and can have an undue influence on all (or most) of the members of that system.

Nonsystemic effects

Say you decide to buy stock in a company called Hockey Sticks Unlimited, Inc. (HSU). You believe that the market for hockey sticks has great potential and that HSU stands to grow substantially. How can politics affect HSU? What if Canadian politicians believe that HSU is too big and that it controls too much of the hockey stick industry? Maybe they view HSU as a monopoly and want the federal government to step in to shrink HSU's reach and influence for the benefit of competition and Canadian consumers. Maybe the government believes that HSU engages in unfair or predatory business practices and is in violation of antitrust (or antimonopoly) laws. If the government acts against HSU, it's a nonsystemic issue — the action is directed toward the participant (in this case, HSU), and not the hockey stick industry in general.

What happens if you're an investor in HSU? Does your stock investment suffer as a result of government action directed against the company? Let's just say that the stock price will be tipped and end up lost in the stands.

Systemic effects

Say politicians want to target the golf industry for intervention because they maintain that golf should be free or close to it for all to participate in and that a law must be passed to make it accessible to all, especially those who can't afford to play. The following law is enacted: "Canadian law #67590305598002 declares that from this day forward, all golf courses must charge only one dollar for any golfer who chooses to participate."

That law sounds great to any golfer. But what are the unintended effects when such a law becomes reality? Many people may agree with the sentiment of the law, but what about the actual cause-and-effect aspects of it? Obviously, all things being equal, golf courses will be forced to close. Staying in business is uneconomical if their costs are higher than their income. If they can't charge any more than a dollar, how can they possibly stay open? Ultimately (and ironically), no one can play golf. The law would be a "triple bogey" for sure!

What happens to investors of a golf-related company that operates in Canada? If the world of golf shrinks, demand for that company's product or service shrinks as well. The stock's value will certainly be stuck in a sand trap.

REMEMBER

Examples of politics creating systemic problems are endless, and no systemic issue is bigger than Canada's renegotiation of NAFTA with the U.S. and Mexico. In this case, the ultimate impacts, however difficult to predict, will be expansive for all parties. But you get the point. Companies are ultimately part of a system, and those that control or maintain the rules overseeing that system can have far-reaching effects. All Canadian investors are advised to be vigilant about systemic effects on their stocks.

Understanding price controls

Stock investors should be very wary of price controls, which are a great example of regulation. A price control is a fixed price on a particular product, commodity, or service mandated by the government. The Canadian dairy industry, for example, is protected with price controls. Because of this complex array of dairy quotas and controls, the OECD estimates that dairy prices in Canada are more than double the world market price. However, these controls are directly in the crosshairs of U.S. NAFTA negotiators and legislators who argue that this practice represents an unfair subsidy.

WARNING

Price controls can keep prices artificially high or low as well, and have been tried continually throughout history (Canadians experienced them in the late '70s, under former prime minister Pierre Trudeau). They've continually been removed over time, especially the controls that kept prices low, because they ultimately do more harm than good to businesses. That's because although the artificially lower price encourages consumption, production is discouraged and the industry suffers. After all, what company wants to make a product if it can't sell it for a decent profit?

Central banks

Central banks are the government entities that are charged with the responsibility of managing the supply of currency that's used in the economy. The problem with this is the obvious tendency of central banks to overproduce the supply of currency. This pronounced overproduction leads to the condition of having too much currency, which leads to the problematic condition of inflation. If too many units of currency (such as dollars or yen, for example) are chasing a limited supply of goods and services, consumers end up paying more money for goods and services (ugh!), but this is the reality that occurs when central banks create too much of the currency.

WARNING

Many economists warn that as the U.S. and the European Economic Community continue to print money to finance its stimulus packages and huge debt levels, the risk of inflation will soar. If inflation does occur, vote-hungry politicians will be tempted to implement price controls in certain industry segments, especially those most prone to inflationary pressures, such as oil and food. Keep a sharp eye on this potential storyline to see if it actually unfolds.

Poking into Political Resources

Ignoring what's going on in the world of politics is like sleepwalking in the Canadian Rockies on a cold winter day — a bad idea! You have to be aware of what's going on. Governmental data, reports, and political rumblings are important clues to the kind of environment that's unfolding for the economy and financial markets. Do your research with the following resources so you can stay a step ahead in your stock-picking strategies.

Government reports to watch out for

The best analysts look at economic reports from private and government sources. For private reports and commentaries on the economy, investors can turn to sources such as the American Institute for Economic Research (www.aier.org), the Mises Institute (www.mises.org), and Moody's (www.economy.com). Sources like MarketWatch (www.marketwatch.com) and Bloomberg (www.bloomberg.com) are good too.

In Canada, the National Post and The Globe and Mail routinely list the release dates of key domestic economic reports in their business pages. Also check out major Canadian chartered banks' publications and economic websites. For example, see the data release calendars on the RBC Economics Research website (www.rbc.com/economics). The C.D. Howe Institute's website (www.cdhowe.org) is also a great source of information.

GDP

Gross domestic product (GDP), which measures a nation's total output of goods and services for the quarter, is considered the broadest measure of economic activity. Although GDP is measured in dollars, it's usually quoted as a percentage. You typically hear a news report that says something like, "The economy grew by 2.5 percent on an annualized basis last quarter." Because the GDP is an important overall barometer of the Canadian economy, the key thing to remember is that it should be a positive number. Reports on the Canadian and U.S. GDP are released quarterly by Statistics Canada (www.statcan.gc.ca) and by the U.S. Department of Commerce (www.commerce.gov), respectively. Type "Canadian Economic Observer" in the search bar on Statistics Canada's home page to take you to its flagship publication for Canadian economic statistics, including the GDP.

REMEMBER

You should regularly monitor the GDP along with economic data that relates directly to your stock portfolio. The following list gives some general guidelines for evaluating the GDP of developed countries whose economies are quite mature, like Canada, the United Kingdom, and the United States:

>> More than 3 percent: This number indicates strong growth and bodes well for stocks. At 5 percent or higher, the economy is sizzling!

>> 1 to 3 percent: Indicates moderate growth; can occur either as the economy is rebounding from recession or slowing from a strong period.

>> 0 percent or negative (as low as –3 percent): This number indicates that the economy either isn't growing or is actually shrinking a bit. A negative GDP is considered recessionary (growth is receding).

>> Less than –3 percent: A GDP this low indicates a very difficult period for the economy. A GDP less than –3 percent, especially for two or more quarters, indicates a serious recession or possibly a depression.

Some developing countries, or emerging markets, can record significantly higher GDP growth than developed countries. For example, in the last decade China regularly recorded an annual GDP of 10 percent or more.

TIP

Looking at a single quarter isn't that useful. Track the GDP over many consecutive quarters to see which way the general economy is trending. When you look at the GDP for a particular quarter of a year, ask yourself whether it's better (or worse) than the quarter before. If it's better (or worse), then ask yourself to what extent it has changed. Is it dramatically better (or worse) than the quarter before? Is the economy showing steady growth, or is it slowing? If several quarters show solid growth, the overall economy is generally bullish. Because GDP is a lagging indicator, you should also be aware of how the actual numbers compare to what the forecasters predicted.

Higher economic growth typically translates into better sales and profits for companies, which in turn bodes well for their stocks (and, of course, the investors who hold these stocks). Traditionally, if two or more consecutive quarters show negative growth (an indication that economic output is shrinking), the economy is considered to be in a recession. A recession can be a painful necessity; it usually occurs when the economy can't absorb the total amount of goods being produced, because of either a lack of demand or excess production. A bear market in stocks usually accompanies a recession.

REMEMBER

The GDP is a rough estimate at best. It can't calculate all the factors that go into economic growth. For example, crime has a negative effect on economic growth, but it's not reflected in the GDP. Still, most economists agree that the GDP provides an adequate snapshot of the overall economy's progress.

Unemployment

In Canada, unemployment statistics are provided by Statistics Canada (www. statcan.gc.ca) and Human Resources Development Canada (www.hrsdc.gc.ca). In the U.S., they are provided by the Bureau of Labor Statistics (www.bls. gov). This information gives investors a snapshot of the health and productivity of the economy.

The Consumer Price Index

The CPI is a statistic that tracks the prices of a representative basket of goods and services monthly. This statistic, which is also computed by Statistics Canada and the U.S. Bureau of Labor Statistics, is meant to track price *inflation*, the expansion of the money supply. This monetary inflation usually leads to price inflation, which means that the price of goods and services rises. Inflation, therefore, isn't the price of goods and services going up; it's actually the price or value of money going down. Canadian investors should pay attention to the CPI because a low-inflation environment is generally good for stocks (and bonds, too), whereas high inflation is generally more favourable for sectors such as commodities and precious metals.

Websites to surf

To find out about new laws being passed or proposed in Canada, go to the Department of Justice's website (www.justice.gc.ca). For the States, see Congress's primary legislative websites: the U.S. House of Representatives (www.house.gov) and the U.S. Senate (www.senate.gov). For presidential information, check the White House's website at www.whitehouse.gov.

TIP

You also may want to check out THOMAS, the service provided by the Library of Congress, at thomas.loc.gov or www.congress.gov. THOMAS is a search engine that helps you find any piece of U.S. legislation, either by bill number or keyword. This search engine is an excellent way to find out whether an industry is being targeted for increased regulation or deregulation. When the telecom industry was deregulated in the mid-1990s, the industry grew dramatically (related stocks went up).

Turn to the following sources for economic data:

>> Canadian Taxpayers Federation, www.taxpayer.com

>> Conference Board, www.conferenceboard.org

>> Conference Board of Canada, www.conferenceboard.ca

>> U.S. Department of Commerce, www.doc.gov

>> The Federal Reserve, www.federalreserve.gov

>> Moody's Analytics, www.economy.com/indicators

>> Grandfather Economic report, www.grandfathereconomicreport.com

TIP

You can find more resources in Appendix A. The more knowledge you pick up about how politics and government actions can help (or harm) an investment, the better you'll be at growing (and protecting) your wealth.

4

Investment Strategies and Tactics

Chapter **16**

Discovering Screening Tools

When you're spanning the stock-investing world, it can be daunting to see literally thousands of stocks to choose from — and that's just the U.S. and Canadian stock markets. Many thousands more are there to be discovered across global stock markets (Chapter 14, for example, introduces investing in the vast realm Asian stock markets.) Where would a stock investor (especially a novice investor) even begin to look?

Well, reading a book like this is a good start. It gives you some parameters and guidelines to help you make a sound choice among the companies that are available as publicly traded stocks. As we often emphasize, you may be purchasing a stock, but you're really investing in a company. That company has financial data and other information that you can review and narrow your search by keeping to some definable (and searchable) standards.

This is why we appreciate and embrace stock screening tools. A *stock screening tool* is an online program found on many financial websites and brokerage sites that sifts through tons of stocks and their relevant data (profits, sales, and so on) with parameters that you set. It works like a search engine but within a huge closed database that is regularly updated with public company data. You'll find one or more stocks that fit the parameters you set.

In this chapter we provide the most common parameters for tools that screen stocks and exchange-traded funds (ETFs). But first, we give you some basics about these tools. Keep in mind that with these tools, you're looking for companies primarily based on your very own search criteria. You can find stocks and ETFs based on a variety of critical standards and metrics that you define and set.

TIP

For some great sites that have stock, ETF, and/or index screening tools (especially for fundamental analysis) and capture most of the universe of stocks, check out the following:

>> **Yahoo! Finance** (http://finance.yahoo.com/screener)

>> **Yahoo! Finance Canada** (http://ca.finance.yahoo.com/screener)

>> **MarketWatch** (www.marketwatch.com/tools/stockresearch/screener)

>> **Nasdaq** (www.nasdaq.com)

Understanding Screening Tool Basics

After you familiarize yourself with the components and practicality of stock screening tools, you'll be hooked and you'll wish that you had used them sooner. In the following sections, we break down the essentials.

Choosing the category

The first thing you typically see with a stock screening tool is the category. Actually, this means the industry (see Chapter 13 for an introduction to industries). Many screeners (such as the one at Yahoo! Finance, http://finance.yahoo.com) go into subcategories. If you're looking for a transportation company, for example, you may get "transportation-trucking," "transportation-rail," and "transportation-shipping."

Distinguishing min vs. max

Min and *max* are the yin and yang of the stock screening world. When you set your parameters for stocks, you need to set a minimum and a maximum. If, for example, you're looking for a "profitable stock," that means you need to set a parameter of minimum profit and maximum profit. The stock investor takes the long view and stays patient and focused for successful stock investing.

REMEMBER

Some stock screeners use a different approach, such as "less than" and "greater than," but it essentially serves the same purpose for your searches.

Setting value ranges

In some cases, you may need to choose a range. Perhaps you're looking for stocks in a particular price range. A stock screening tool may provide choices such as 0–10, 10–20, 20–30, 30–40, 40–50, and over 50. Another typical range you may see is market capitalization (the total market value of the company's stock) or dividend yields (the dividend amount divided by the stock price).

Searching regardless of your entry

Most screening tools allow you to do a search whether you enter one value or parameter or many. If you choose to search for a stock in all categories and enter only, say, a dividend yield with a minimum value of 2 and a maximum value of 999 and no other entries, then you'll get hundreds of stocks.

However, if you input plenty of parameters, then you'll get very few stocks (or none at all). If you ask for stocks with features A, B, C, D, and E, then you won't get as many results. Be selective — that's the whole point of using stock screeners — but don't go overboard trying to find the perfect stock because it may not exist. Such "analysis paralysis" screening approaches rarely represent a good use of your time.

REMEMBER

Getting close to perfection is probably good enough, but the more important point is to avoid the bad choices such as companies that have too little income, have net losses, or carry too much debt. Don't lose site of other investing fundamentals like doing your homework, not panicking when the market dives, not timing the market, and ignoring valuation.

Touring a Stock Screening Tool

Most stock screening tools have some basic elements that are very useful in helping you narrow your search for the right stocks in your portfolio. Figures 16-1 and 16-2 show a typical stock screener from Yahoo! Finance (http://finance. yahoo.com/screener).

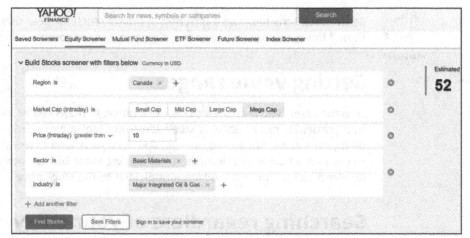

FIGURE 16-1:
A typical stock
screening tool.

Source: Yahoo! Finance

Symbol	Name	Price (Intraday)	Change	% Change	Volume	Avg Vol (3 month)	Market Cap ∨	PE Ratio (TTM)	52 Week Range
RDSB.L	Royal Dutch Shell plc	2,562.50	-8.00	-0.31%	3.549M	5.628M	224.604B	13.91	
RDSA.L	Royal Dutch Shell plc	2,523.50	-7.50	-0.30%	3.744M	5.819M	224.727B	1,369.98	
ECN.MX	Ecopetrol S.A.	303.70	0.00	0.00%	0	200	16.188T	266.01	
BP-B.L	BP p.l.c.	163.00	0.00	0.00%	4.256k	3,300	111.036B	7.38	
BP-A.L	BP p.l.c.	145.50	0.00	0.00%	1.438k	3,518	111.036B	6.58	
BP.L	BP p.l.c.	558.30	+2.30	+0.41%	22.398M	39.511M	111.495B	25.26	
XOM.BA	Exxon Mobil Corporation	449.50	0.00	0.00%	110	71	8.371T	91.80	

FIGURE 16-2:
Results of
screening.

Source: Yahoo! Finance

REMEMBER With the minimums and maximums in the following sections, there will be variations. Some tools allow lower minimums and higher maximums than the Yahoo! tool. Also, some market analysts and financial advisors are more or less lenient than we are with these numbers. Don't sweat it. Do your research and come up with similar numbers that you're comfortable with.

Sector and industry categories

In this opening choice in your stock screener, and even if this is near the bottom of the screener parameters, first choose the sector and industry in which you're looking for a stock. This is important because the sector and industry are part of what makes the stock successful. Even if you choose a mediocre stock but it's in a strong or growing industry, you can still do well. This screen alone can yield an interesting if overwhelming number of results.

REMEMBER A *sector* is a group of interrelated industries. For example, the healthcare sector has varied industries in its ecosystem such as hospitals, medical device manufacturers, pharmaceuticals, drug retailers, and so on. Choosing an industry instead of a sector narrows your choices.

Region

Pick a part of the world that interests you. You'll not only find China, discussed in Chapter 14, but other world stock markets as well. You can easily get lost in exploration of this tab.

Market cap

As Chapter 1 mentions, *market capitalization* (or *market cap*) is a reference to a company's market value (calculated as share price times total shares outstanding). A *small cap* stock has a market cap of under $1 billion, so if you're interested in such a stock, you'd enter a minimum capitalization of $0 and a maximum of $1 billion. If you're more risk averse, then you'd set the criteria for a large cap stock and put in a minimum of, say, $10 billion.

Share price

Are you looking for an inexpensive stock that's under $10 per share? If so, you'd enter $0 as the minimum share price and $10 as the maximum share price. At this level, you may end up with a small cap stock that may be too risky for you, so make sure you check out the next section.

TIP

If the share price isn't a material concern, enter $0 as the minimum share price and put a large number, such as $999, in the maximum share price field so you'd essentially be searching all stocks without concern to share price.

Dividend yield

Clicking the "Add another filter" tab reveals a vast world of other criteria. Choose the Dividend Yield criteria for a walkthrough. This field is perfect for those looking for dividend income (Chapter 9). In general, dividend-paying stocks called *income stocks* tend to have a dividend yield that exceeds 3.5 percent (some say that the range is 3 to 4 percent). For the maximum entry, you'd put in an inordinately high number such as 999 percent.

TIP

If the dividend yield isn't an issue for you (because you're looking for growth stocks, for example), then you'd leave this blank.

Beta (volatility)

To continue our walkthrough, click the Beta screener tab in the same manner as you did for the Dividend Yield criteria. Are you looking for stocks that are very volatile, or do you prefer stable, boring stocks? No matter which, it's good to know the beta of a stock. *Beta* (which we discuss in Chapter 4) measures the volatility of a stock against a standard of the general stock market, such as the S&P 500. The market is assigned a beta of 1.0. If a stock is twice as volatile as the general stock market, it will have a beta of 2.0. If it's 2.5 times as volatile as the stock market, it will have a beta of 2.5, and so on. If the stock has a beta of .80 (under the market's 1.0), then it's 20 percent less volatile than the general stock market (you get the picture). So, if you want a feature of low volatility in your search parameters, you'd enter a minimum beta of 0 and a maximum beta of either 1.0 or a lower beta as you see fit.

If you were a speculator and you were trading options, then a high volatility feature would be important to you. You might choose a minimum beta of 2.0 and put in the maximum beta of, say, 999. Imagine if you did find the option of a stock with a beta that high — you'd be in volatility heaven!

Now that you've entered these criteria, click the Find Stocks tab to see a list of results. From this list, you can then apply the principles described in this book to select a stock you want to invest in. The other screening criteria we discuss shortly are just a few of the many other criteria you can choose from. You're wise to consider these in your screening process. Also note that most of the other online screening tool providers work in much the same way, but perhaps with more or fewer criteria.

Sales and profitability

After choosing the industry (covered earlier in this chapter), the most important aspect is the sales and profitability. The net profit is a critical metric when analyzing a company.

Sales revenue

For sales revenue, there may be absolute numbers or percentages. In some stock screeners, there may be ranges such as "under $1 million in sales" up to "over $1 billion in sales." On a percentage basis, some stock screeners may have a minimum and a maximum. An example of this would be if you wanted companies that increased their sales by at least 10 percent. You'd enter 10 in the minimum percentage and either leave the maximum blank or plug in a high number such as 999. Another twist is you may find a stock screener that shows sales revenue with an average percentage over three or five years so you can see more consistency over an extended period.

Profit margin

Profit margin is basically what percent of sales is the company's net profit. If a company has $1 million in sales and $200,000 in net profit, then the profit margin is 20 percent ($200,000 divided by $1,000,000). For this metric, you'd enter a minimum of 20 percent and a maximum of 100 percent because that's the highest possible (but improbable) profit margin you can reach.

REMEMBER

The data you can sift through isn't just for the most recent year; some stock screeners give you a summary of three years or longer, such as what that company's profit margin has been over a three-year period, so you can get a better view of the company's consistent profitability. The only thing better than a solid profit in the current year is a solid profit year after year.

Valuation ratios

For value investors (who embrace fundamental analysis), the following parameters are important to help home in on the right values. (Check out Appendix B for more details on this and many other ratios.)

Price-to-earnings ratio

The P/E ratio (price-to-earnings ratio) is one of the most widely followed ratios, and we consider it the most important valuation ratio (and it can be considered a profitability ratio as well). It ties the current stock price to the company's net earnings. The net earnings are the heart and soul of the company, so always check this ratio.

All things being considered, we generally prefer low ratios (under 15 is good, under 25 is acceptable). If we are considering a growth stock, we definitely want a ratio under 40 (unless there are extenuating circumstances that we like and that aren't reflected in the P/E ratio).

WARNING

Generally, beginning investors should stay away from stocks that have P/Es higher than 40, and definitely stay away if the P/E is in triple digits (or higher), because that's too pricey. Pricey P/Es can be hazardous, as those stocks have high expectations and are very vulnerable to a sharp correction. In addition, definitely stay away from stocks that either have no P/E ratio or that show a negative P/E. In these instances, it's a stock where the company is losing money (net losses). A company that's losing money means that buying the stock is *not* investing — it's speculating.

REMEMBER

Make sure your search parameters have a minimum P/E of, say, 1 and a maximum of between 15 (for large cap, stable, dividend-paying stocks) and 40 (for growth stocks) so that you have some measure of safety (or sanity!).

If you want to speculate and find stocks to go short on (or buy puts on), two approaches apply:

>> You can put in a minimum P/E of, say, 100 and an unlimited maximum (or 9,999 if a number is needed) to get very pricey stocks that are vulnerable to a correction.

>> A second approach is putting in a maximum P/E of 0, which indicates you're searching for companies with losses (earnings under zero).

WARNING

Shorting is risky speculation. The safer and more assured route is investing in stocks tied to quality, profitable companies for the long term.

Price/book ratio

A major valuation is the *price-to-book* (P/B) ratio. This compares the price of the stock (market capitalization) to the net asset value (or "book" value) of the underlying company. Ideally, the ratio should be 1-to-1, where the market value and the book value are at parity, but you won't usually find that. Just know that the closer the market value is to the book value, the better the value. A P/B ratio of under 4 is optimal; if it's higher, it's getting too pricey.

WARNING

A market value that's much higher than the book value may indicate an overvalued stock, so tread carefully here. In the stock screener's P/B ratio field, consider entering a minimum of 0 but making the maximum 4, because buying a stock whose market capitalization is four times greater than the company's book value is getting pricey.

Price/sales ratio

In terms of calculation, this ratio is similar to the P/B ratio in the preceding section, but just substitute the book value with the total annual sales. Again, a price-to-sales (P/S) ratio close to 1 is positive. When market capitalization greatly exceeds the sales number, then the stock leans to the pricey side. In the stock screener's P/S field, consider entering a minimum of 0 or leave it blank. A good maximum value would be 3.

PEG ratio

You obtain the PEG (price-to-earnings growth) ratio when you divide the stock's P/E ratio by its year-over-year earnings growth rate. Typically, the lower the PEG, the better the value of the stock. A PEG ratio over 1.00 suggests that the stock is overvalued, and a ratio under 1.00 is considered undervalued. Therefore, when you use the PEG ratio in a stock screening tool, leave the minimum blank (or 0), and use a maximum of 1.00.

SCREENING STOCKS WITH TECHNICAL ANALYSIS

Earlier in this chapter, we use criteria and financial data (the "fundamentals"), but many stock screeners have the ability to use technical analysis (see Chapter 10 for details) by using technical indicators. Technical analysis is more important for those with a short-term focus, such as stock traders and short-term speculators. Here are some common technical indicators:

- **Moving averages:** Looking for stocks that are trading above their 50-day moving average or have fallen below it? How about the 200-day moving average, which can be a more reliable indicator of the stock's near-term strength (or weakness)?

- **Relative Strength Indicator:** The RSI is one of our favorite technical indicators. It basically tracks a stock in terms of being overbought or oversold in the near term. If a stock has an RSI of over 70, then it's overbought, and the stock is vulnerable to declining in the near future. A stock with an RSI under 30 is considered oversold, and that's potentially an opportunity for the stock to rally in the near term.

  Don't use the RSI to determine what to buy, but certainly consider it as a way to time a purchase (or sale). In other words, if you're attracted to a stock and want to buy, consider getting it in the event that it's oversold. That gives you the chance to get a stock you want at a favorable price.

  When you do your search and you're using the RSI as one of your criteria, consider using a maximum RSI of 50, which is essentially in the middle of the range, with a minimum RSI of 0. If you're looking to speculate by going short, make sure your minimum RSI is 70 and the maximum is unlimited.

Here are some popular screening tools online for technical analysis:

- **StockCharts** (www.stockcharts.com)

- **TMX Stock Screener** (http://web.tmxmoney.com/screener)

- **Globe Investor** (www.globeinvestor.com)

- **StockFetcher** (www.stockfetcher.com)

- **Market In & Out** (www.marketinout.com)

Other valuation ratios

Some stock screeners may include other ratios. One good one is the average five-year ROI (return on investment), which gives you a good idea of the stock's long-term financial strength. Others may have an average three-year ROI. Because this is an average (percentage terms) over five years, do a search for a minimum of 10 percent and an unlimited maximum (or just plug in 999 percent). If you do get one that's anywhere near 999 percent, by the way, call us and let us know.

Analyst estimates

The Yahoo! stock screener has a category called "Analyst Estimates" just in case you want to screen stocks based on the "buy, sell, or hold" views of widely followed analysts. This can add another helpful filter to your searches, but we wouldn't bet the farm on it. However, it may serve to validate what you found on your own.

You can check out what analysts expect in terms of earnings per share (EPS) growth for either one or five years. If you're looking for strong earnings growth for potential investing, use a minimum of, say, 15 percent so you find companies that have strong earnings growth (put "up more than 15 percent" in the entry field). If you're bearish and looking to go short companies with falling earnings, put in a negative such as "down more than 10 percent."

For average analyst recommendations, you can put in a range of 1 to 5, where 1 is a strong buy rating and 5 is a strong sell rating. This way, you can use analyst views to further filter the results you're looking for in order to make more confident buy or sell decisions.

Checking Out an ETF Screening Tool

In addition to stock screeners, there are also screeners for bonds, mutual funds, and now exchange-traded funds (ETFs; see Chapter 5). Figure 16-3 is a typical ETF screener like many online.

With ETF screeners, you won't find minimum and maximum as much as with stock screeners. There are more varied categories to filter through and different performance criteria. Here we cover the main categories.

TIP

Keep in mind that most of the popular financial sites (such as Yahoo! Finance and MarketWatch) have good ETF (as well as stock) screeners; most of the stock brokerage sites have search and screening tools as well. Some other popular sites that have ETF screening tools include ETF Database (www.etfdb.com/screener) and ETF Screen (www.etfscreen.com).

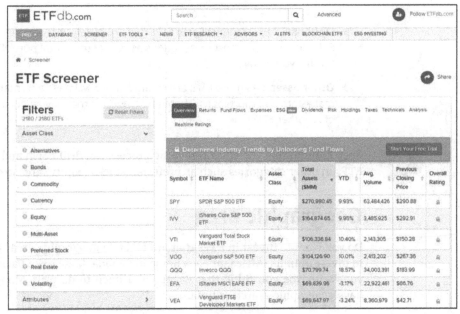

Courtesy of ETFdb.com

FIGURE 16-3:
A typical ETF
screening tool.

Asset class

An ETF is a conduit. When you buy an ETF, you're really buying what's in the
ETF's portfolio. The portfolio has assets, and you need to choose what assets you
want to find with the ETF screener. Here are the major choices:

>> **Stocks:** Within the stocks category are subcategories ranging from small caps
to large caps to preferred stocks. Yet another filter in the mix is whether the
stocks pay dividends.

>> **Bonds:** Bonds are a form of debt, and there are different classes of debt, so
there are different bond ETFs to choose from. There are bond ETFs that have
investment grade bonds (with A or better bond ratings, although some
consider BBB the minimum investment grade), and there are high-yield bonds
(translation: lower-rated or low-quality "junk" bonds).

>> **Commodities:** Typically, these ETFs have futures contracts covering the range
of commodity choices. There are ETFs in grains, base metals, energy, and
so on.

>> **Currencies:** These ETFs have futures contracts covering currencies ranging
from the U.S. dollar to virtually any major currency that trades on global
markets.

>> **Options:** There are few (if any) ETFs that are purely into options, but some ETFs do have an exposure to options as part of their total portfolio, so see if this fits your goals.

>> **Other assets:** As more ETFs are created, more will have alternatives such as real estate and mortgages. There are even ETFs that have a portfolio of . . . other ETFs!

TIP

Keep in mind that the stock screening process can drill down and help you peruse ETFs in other categories such as preferred stocks, equity, and so on.

Geographic area

Do you want to invest in ETFs that are tied to a geographic area? Maybe you want to invest in India, Africa, or back home in Canada. Maybe the Pacific Rim interests you, or maybe you think that Europe is primed to do well. Many ETF screeners have geographic search criteria.

Inverse and leveraged ETFs

ETFs can make money when stocks or other assets go up, but there are also *inverse ETFs* that are designed to go up when the underlying assets go down. If, for example, you feel that Nasdaq stocks will crash, then consider getting an inverse ETF that will gain if and when that event occurs.

WARNING

There are inverse ETFs for stocks, commodities, currencies, and other assets. Inverse ETFs are a form of speculating, so tread carefully here.

Leveraged ETFs are basically designed to double or triple the move of the underlying asset. Say that you're really, and we mean really, bullish on the S&P 500. In that case, consider a "2x" or "3x" leveraged ETF that will essentially attempt to double or triple the underlying asset's move.

Other considerations

The preceding categories are the basics, but many investors that use ETF screeners find other criteria for finding appropriate ETFs for their portfolios. Some screeners help you find the best ETFs for income or for tax advantages. Still others have criteria to filter for ETFs that have active management (most ETFs have a passive portfolio) or for total returns year-to-date.

Chapter 17

Understanding Brokerage Orders and Trading Techniques

I nvestment success isn't just about which stocks to choose; it's also about how you choose those stocks. Frequently, investors think that good stockpicking means doing your homework and then making that buy (or sell). However, you can take it a step further to maximize profits (or minimize losses).

A while back, during the last major market correction, a multitude of Canadian investors were slammed mercilessly by a tumultuous market; many could have used some simple techniques and orders that could have saved them some grief. Investors who used stop-loss orders avoided some of the trillion-dollar carnage that hit the stock market during that scary time. As a stock investor, you can take advantage of this technique and others available through your standard brokerage account (refer to Chapter 7 for details). This chapter presents some of the best ways you can use these powerful techniques, which are useful whether you're buying or selling stock.

Checking Out Brokerage Orders

Orders you place with your stockbroker fit neatly into three categories:

» Time-related orders

» Condition-related orders

» Advanced orders (such as "trade triggers"; more about these in Chapter 18)

At the very least, get familiar with the first two types of orders because they're easy to implement, and they're invaluable tools for wealth-building and (more important) wealth-saving! Advanced orders usually are combinations of the first two types.

TIP

Using a combination of orders helps you fine-tune your strategy so that you can maintain greater control over your investments. Speak with your discount or full-service broker about the different types of orders you can use to maximize the gains (or minimize the losses) from your stock-investing activities. You also can read the broker's policies on stock orders at the brokerage website. In the case of robo-advisors (discussed) in Chapter 7, most use a similar but not identical approach to brokers in that they tend to automatically rebalance your portfolio from time to time to make sure your target mix of growth equities, dividend equities, and bonds, for example, remain consistent in good times or bad.

On the clock: Time-related orders

A time-related order is just that — the order has a time limit. Typically, investors use these orders in conjunction with condition-related orders, which we describe later in this chapter. The two most common time-related orders are day orders and good-til-cancelled (GTC) orders.

Day orders

A day order is an order to buy or sell a stock that expires at the end of that particular trading day. If you tell your broker, "Buy BYOB, Inc., at $37.50 and make it a day order," you mean that you want to purchase the stock at $37.50. But if the stock doesn't hit that price, your order expires, unfilled, at the end of the trading day. Why would you place such an order? Maybe BYOB is trading at $39, but you don't want to buy it at that price because you don't believe the stock is worth it. Consequently, you have no problem not getting the stock that day.

When would you use day orders? It depends on your preferences and personal circumstances. We rarely use day orders because few events cause us to say, "Gee,

I'll just try to buy or sell between now and the end of today's trading action." However, you may feel that you don't want a specified order to linger beyond today's market action. Perhaps you want to test a price. ("I want to sell stock A at $39 to make a quick profit, but it's currently trading at $37.50.) A day order is the perfect strategy to use in this case.

REMEMBER

If you make a trade and don't specify a time limit with the order, most (if not all) Canadian brokers will automatically treat it as a day order.

Good-til-cancelled orders

A good-til-cancelled (GTC) order is the most commonly requested order by investors, and it's one that we use and recommend often. The GTC order means just what it says: The order stays in effect until it's successfully transacted or until the investor cancels it. Although GTC orders are inherently time-related, they're always tied to a condition, such as the stock achieving a certain price.

TIP

Although the order implies that it can run indefinitely, most brokers have a limit of 30 or 60 days (or more). We've seen the limit as high as 90 days. By that time, either the broker cancels the order or contacts you (usually by e-mail) to see whether you want to extend it. Ask the broker's customer service personnel about the particular policy.

GTC orders are always coupled with condition-related orders (see the next section for the lowdown on conditional orders). For example, say that you think ASAP Corp. stock would make a good addition to your portfolio, but you don't want to buy it at the current price of $48 per share. You've done your homework on the stock, including looking at the stock's price-to-earnings ratio, price-to-book ratio, and so on (see Appendix B for more on ratios), and you say, "Hey, this stock isn't worth $48 a share. I'd only buy it at $36 per share." (It's overpriced or overvalued according to your analysis.) How should you proceed? Your best bet is to ask your broker to do a GTC order at $36. This request means that your broker will buy the shares if and when the stock price drops to the $36 mark (unless you cancel the order). Just make sure that your account has the funds available to complete the transaction.

REMEMBER

To be successful with GTC orders, you need to know the following:

>> **When you want to buy:** In recent years, people have had a tendency to rush into buying a stock without giving some thought to what they could do to get more for their money. Some investors don't realize that the stock market can be a place for bargain-hunting consumers. If you're ready to buy a quality pair of socks for $16 in a department store but the sales clerk says that those

same socks are going on sale tomorrow for only $8, what do you do —
assuming that you're a cost-conscious consumer? Unless you're barefoot,
you probably decide to wait. The same point holds true with stocks.

Say that you want to buy SOX, Inc., at $26, but it's currently trading at $30. You
think that $30 is too expensive, but you'd be happy to buy the stock at $26 or
lower. However, you have no idea whether the stock will move to your desired
price today, tomorrow, next week, or even next month (or maybe never). In
this case, a GTC order is appropriate.

>> **When you want to sell:** What if you buy some socks at a department store and
you discover that they have holes (darn it!)? Wouldn't you want to get rid of
them? Of course you would. If a stock's price starts to unravel, you want to be
able to get rid of it as well.

Perhaps you already own SOX at $25 but are concerned that market condi-
tions may drive the price lower. You're not certain which way the stock will
move in the coming days and weeks. In this case, a GTC order to sell the stock
at a specified price is a suitable strategy. Because the stock price is $25, you
may want to place a GTC order to sell it if it falls to $22.50, to prevent further
losses. This strategy is also called a *stop loss* which we discuss in greater detail
in the next section. Again, in this example, GTC is the time frame, and it
accompanies a condition (sell when the stock hits $22.50).

At your command: Condition-related orders

A condition-related order (also known as a conditional order) is an order that's
executed only when a certain condition is met. Conditional orders enhance your
ability to buy stocks at a lower price, to sell at a better price, or to minimize potential losses. When stock markets become bearish or uncertain, conditional orders
are highly recommended.

A good example of a conditional order is a limit order. A limit order may say, "Buy
Mojeski Corp. at $45." But if Mojeski Corp. isn't at $45 (this price is the condition), then the order isn't executed. We discuss limit orders, as well as market
orders and stop-loss orders, in the following sections.

Market orders

When you buy stock, the simplest type of order is a market order — an order to
buy or sell a stock at the market's current best available price. Orders don't get
any more basic than that. Here's an example: Kowalski, Inc., is available at the
market price of $10. When you call your broker and instruct her to buy 100 shares
"at the market," the broker implements the order for your account, and you pay
$1,000 plus commission.

We say "current best available price" because the stock's price is constantly moving, and catching the best price can be a function of the broker's ability to process the stock purchase. For very active stocks, the price change can happen within seconds. It's not unheard of to have three brokers simultaneously place orders for the same stock and get three different prices because of differences in the brokers' capabilities. The difference may be pennies, but it's a difference nonetheless. (Some computers are faster than others.)

The advantage of a market order is that the transaction is processed immediately, and you get your stock without worrying about whether it hits a particular price. For example, if you buy Kowalski, Inc., with a market order, you know that by the end of that phone call (or website visit) you're assured of getting the stock. The disadvantage of a market order is that you can't control the price at which you purchase the stock. Whether you're buying or selling your shares, you may not realize the exact price you expect (especially if you're dealing with a volatile stock).

Market orders get finalized in the chronological order in which they're placed. Your price may change because the orders ahead of you in line cause the stock price to rise or fall based on the latest news.

Stop-loss orders

A stop-loss order (also called a stop order) is a condition-related order that instructs the broker to sell a particular stock in your portfolio only when the stock reaches a particular price. It acts like a trigger, and the stop order converts to a market order to sell the stock immediately.

The stop-loss order isn't designed to take advantage of small, short-term moves in the stock's price. It's meant to help you protect the bulk of your money when the market turns against your stock investment in a sudden manner.

Say that your Kowalski, Inc., stock rises to $20 per share and you seek to protect your investment against a possible future market decline. A stop-loss order at $18 triggers your broker to sell the stock immediately if it falls to the $18 mark. In this example, if the stock suddenly drops to $17, it still triggers the stop-loss order, but the finalized sale price is $17. In a volatile market, you may not be able to sell at your precise stop-loss price. However, because the order automatically gets converted into a market order, the sale will be done, and you'll be spared further declines in the stock.

The main benefit of a stop-loss order is that it prevents a major loss in a stock that you own. It's a form of discipline that's important in investing in order to minimize potential losses. Investors can find it agonizing to sell a stock that has fallen. If they don't sell, however, the stock often continues to plummet as investors continue to hold on while hoping for a rebound in the price.

TIP

Most investors set a stop-loss amount at about 10 to 15 percent below the current market value of the stock. This percentage gives the stock some room to fluctuate, which most stocks tend to do from day to day. If you're extra nervous, consider a tighter stop-loss, such as 5 percent or less.

Please keep in mind that this order is a trigger and a particular price is not guaranteed to be captured because the actual buy or sell occurs immediately after the trigger is activated. If the market at the time of the actual transaction is particularly volatile, then the price realized may be significantly different.

In the following sections, we describe a certain type of stop-loss order (called a trailing stop), and we talk about the use of beta measurement of volatility with stop-loss orders.

TRAILING STOPS

Trailing stops are an important technique in wealth preservation for seasoned stock investors and can be one of your key strategies in using stop-loss orders. A trailing stop is a stop-loss order that an investor actively manages by moving it up along with the stock's market price. The stop-loss order "trails" the stock price upward. As the stop-loss goes upward, it protects more and more of the stock's value from declining.

Imagine that you bought stock in Peach Inc. (PI) for $30 a share. A trailing stop is in place at, say, 10 percent, and the order is GTC (presume that this broker places a time limit of 90 days for GTC orders). At $30 per share, the trailing stop is $27. If PI goes to $40, your trailing stop automatically rises to $36. If PI continues to rise to $50, your trailing continues along with it to $45. Now say that PI reverses course (for whatever reason) and starts to plummet. The trailing stop stays put at $45 and triggers a sell order if PI reaches the $45 level.

In the preceding example, we use a trailing stop percentage, but trailing stops are always available in dollar amounts as well. For example, say that PI is at $30, and we put in a trailing stop of $3. If PI rises to $50, our trailing stop will reach $47. If PI then drops from this peak of $50, the trailing stop stays put at $47 and triggers a sell order if PI actually hits $47. You get the picture. Trailing stops can help you sleep at night . . . especially in these turbulent times.

REMEMBER

William O'Neill, founder and publisher of Investor's Business Daily, advocates setting a trailing stop of 8 percent below your purchase price. That's his preference. Some investors who invest in volatile stocks may put in trailing stops of 20 or 25 percent. Is a stop-loss order desirable or advisable in every situation? No. It depends on your level of experience, your investment goals, and the market environment. Still, stop-loss orders (trailing or otherwise) are appropriate in many cases, especially if the market seems uncertain (or you are!).

REMEMBER

A trailing stop is a stop-loss order that you actively manage. The stop-loss order is good-til-cancelled (GTC), and it constantly trails the stock's price as it moves up. To successfully implement stop-loss orders (including trailing stops), you should

>> Realize that Canadian brokers usually don't place trailing stops for you automatically. In fact, they won't (or shouldn't) place any type of order without your consent. Deciding on the type of order to place is your responsibility. You can raise, lower, or cancel a trailing stop order at will, but you need to monitor your investment when substantial moves do occur to respond to the movement appropriately.

>> Change the stop-loss order when the stock price moves significantly. Hopefully, you won't call your broker every time the stock moves 50 cents. Change the stop-loss order when the stock price moves around 10 percent. For example, if you initially purchase a stock at $90 per share, ask the broker to place the stop-loss order at $81. When the stock moves to $100, cancel the $81 stop-loss order and replace it at $90. When the stock's price moves to $110, change the stop-loss order to $99, and so on.

>> Understand your broker's policy on GTC orders. If your broker usually considers a GTC order expired after 30 or 60 days, you should be aware of it. You don't want to risk a sudden drop in your stock's price without the stop-loss order protection. Make a note of your broker's time limit in your electronic calendar so that you remember to renew the order for additional time.

>> Monitor your stock. A trailing stop isn't a "set it and forget it" technique. Monitoring your investment is critical. Of course, if the investment falls, the stop-loss order prevents further loss. Should the stock price rise substantially, remember to adjust your trailing stop accordingly. Keep raising the safety net as the stock continues to rise. Part of monitoring the stock is knowing the beta, which you can read more about in the next section.

USING BETA MEASUREMENT

To be a successful investor, you need to understand the volatility of the particular stock you invest in. In stock market parlance, this volatility is also called the beta of a stock. Beta is a quantitative measure of the volatility of a given stock (mutual funds and portfolios, too) relative to the overall market, usually the S&P 500 index. (For more information on the S&P 500 and indexes in general, refer to Chapter 5.) Beta specifically measures the performance movement of the stock as the S&P moves 1 percent up or down. A beta measurement above 1 is more volatile than the overall market, whereas a beta below 1 is less volatile. Some stocks are relatively stable in terms of price movements; others jump around.

Because beta measures how volatile or unstable the stock's price is, it tends to be uttered in the same breath as "risk" — more volatility indicates more risk. Similarly, less volatility tends to mean less risk. (Chapter 4 offers more details on the topics of risk and volatility.)

TIP

You can find a company's beta at websites that provide a lot of financial information about companies, such as Nasdaq (www.nasdaq.com) or Yahoo! Finance Canada (http://ca.finance.yahoo.com).

The beta is useful to know when it comes to stop-loss orders because it gives you a general idea of the stock's trading range. If a stock is currently priced at $50 and it typically trades in the $48 to $52 range, then a trailing stop at $49 doesn't make sense. Your stock would probably be sold the same day you initiated the stop-loss order. If your stock is a volatile growth stock (like a technology stock) that may swing up and down by 10 percent, you should more logically set your stop-loss at 15 percent below that day's price.

REMEMBER

The stock of a large cap company in a mature industry like the Canadian banking industry tends to have a low beta — one close to the overall market. Small and mid cap stocks in new or emerging industries tend to have greater volatility in their day-to-day price fluctuations; hence, they tend to have a high beta. (You can find out more about large, small, and mid cap stocks in Chapter 1; Chapter 4 has more about beta.)

Limit orders

A limit order is a very precise condition-related order implying that a limit exists either on the buy or the sell side of the transaction. You want to buy (or sell) only at a specified price. Period. Limit orders work well if you're buying the stock, but they may not be good for you if you're selling the stock. Here's how they work in both instances:

>> **When you're buying:** Just because you like a particular company and you want its stock doesn't mean that you're willing to pay the current market price. Maybe you want to buy Kowalski, Inc., but the current market price of $20 per share isn't acceptable to you. You prefer to buy it at $16 because you think that price reflects its true market value. What do you do? You tell your broker, "Buy Kowalski with a limit order at $16" (or you can enter a limit order at the broker's website). You have to specify whether it's a day order or a GTC order, both of which we discuss earlier in this chapter.

What happens if the stock experiences great volatility? What if it drops to $16.01 and then suddenly drops to $15.95 on the next move? Nothing happens, actually, which you may be dismayed to hear. Because your order was limited to $16, it can be transacted only at $16 — no more and no less. The only way for this particular trade to occur is if the stock rises back to $16. However, if the price keeps dropping, then your limit order isn't transacted and may expire or be cancelled.

>> **When you're selling:** Limit orders are activated only when a stock hits a specific price. If you buy Kowalski, Inc., at $20 and you worry about a decline in the share price, you may decide to put in a limit order at $18. If you watch the news and hear that Kowalski's price is dropping, you may sigh and say, "I sure am glad I put in that limit order at $18!" However, in a volatile market, the share price may leapfrog over your specified price. It could go from $18.01 to $17.99 and then continue its descent. Because the stock price never hit $18 on the mark, your stock isn't sold. You may be sitting at home satisfied (mistakenly) that you played it smart, while your stock plummets to $15, $10, or worse! Having a stop-loss order in place is best.

Investors who aren't in a hurry can use a limit order to try to get a better price when they decide to sell. For example, maybe you own a stock whose price is at $50 and you want to sell, but you think that a short-term rally in the stock is imminent. In that case, you can use a limit order such as, "Sell the stock at the sell limit order of $55 and keep the order on for 30 days."

TIP

When you're buying (or selling) a stock, most if not all Canadian brokers interpret the limit order as "buy (or sell) at this specific price or better." For example, presumably, if your limit order is to buy a stock at $10, you'll be just as happy if your broker buys that stock at $9.95. That way, if you don't get exactly $10 because the stock's price was volatile, you'll still get the stock at a lower price. Talk to your broker to be clear on the meaning of the limit order.

The joys of technology: Advanced orders

Canadian brokers have added sophisticated capabilities to the existing repertoire of orders that are available for stock investors. One example is advanced orders, which provide investors with a way to use a combination of orders for more sophisticated trades. An example of an advanced order is something like, "Only sell stock B, and if it sells, use the proceeds to buy stock D." You get the idea. Our brokerage firms have the following on their websites, and we're sure that more firms will do the same. Inquire with yours and see the benefit of using advanced orders such as the following:

>> "One order cancels another order": In this scenario, you enter two orders simultaneously with the condition that if one order is executed, the second order is automatically cancelled.

>> "One order triggers another order": Here, you submit an order, and if that order is filled, another order is automatically submitted. Many Canadian brokers have different names for these types of orders, so ask them if they can provide such an order.

Other types of advanced orders and order strategies are available (and covered in Chapter 18), but you get the picture. Talk to your brokerage firm and find out what's available in your particular account. Canadian investors need to know that today's technology allows them to have more power and control over the implementation of buying and selling transactions. We love it!

Buying on Margin

Buying on margin means buying securities, such as stocks, with funds you borrow from your broker. Buying stock on margin is similar to buying a house with a mortgage. If you buy a house at a purchase price of $100,000 and put 10 percent down, your equity (the part you own) is $10,000, and you borrow the remaining $90,000 with a mortgage. If the value of the house rises to $120,000 and you sell (for the sake of simplicity, we don't include closing costs in this example), you make a profit of 200 percent. How is that? The $20,000 gain on the property represents a gain of 20 percent on the purchase price of $100,000, but because your real investment is $10,000 (the down payment), your gain works out to 200 percent (a gain of $20,000 on your initial investment of $10,000).

WARNING

Buying on margin is an example of using leverage to maximize your gain when prices rise. Leverage is simply using borrowed money when you make an asset purchase in order to increase your potential profit. This type of leverage is great in a favourable (bull) market, but it works against you in an unfavourable (bear) market. Say that a $100,000 house you purchase with a $90,000 mortgage falls in value to $80,000 (and property values can decrease during economic hard times). Your outstanding debt of $90,000 exceeds the value of the property. Because you owe more than you own, you're left with a negative net worth.

REMEMBER

Leverage is a double-edged sword. Don't forget that you need approval from your brokerage firm before you can buy on margin. To buy on margin, you typically fill out the form provided by that brokerage firm to be approved. Check with the broker because each firm has different requirements.

In the following sections, we describe the potential outcomes of buying on margin, we explain how to maintain a balance, and we provide some pointers for successfully buying on margin.

Examining marginal outcomes

Suppose you think that the stock for the company Mergatroid, Inc., currently at $40 per share, will go up in value. You want to buy 100 shares, but you have only $2,000. What can you do? If you're intent on buying 100 shares (versus simply buying the 50 shares that you have cash for), you can borrow the additional $2,000 from your broker on margin. If you do that, what are the potential outcomes?

If the stock price goes up

This outcome is the best for you. If Mergatroid goes to $50 per share, your investment is worth $5,000 and your outstanding margin loan is $2,000. If you sell, the total proceeds will pay off the loan and leave you with $3,000. Because your initial investment was $2,000, your profit is a solid 50 percent because your $2,000 principal amount generated a $1,000 profit. (For the sake of this example, we leave out any charges, such as commissions and interest paid on the margin loan.) However, if you pay the entire $4,000 upfront without the margin loan, your $4,000 investment generates a profit of $1,000, or 25 percent. Using margin, in this example, you double the return on your money.

Leverage, when used properly, is very profitable. However, it's still debt, so understand that you must pay it off eventually, regardless of the stock's performance.

If the stock price fails to rise

If the stock goes nowhere, you still have to pay interest on that margin loan. If the stock pays dividends, this money can defray some of the margin loan's cost. In other words, dividends can help you pay off what you borrow from the broker. (Flip to Chapter 3 for an introduction to dividends.)

Having the stock neither rise nor fall may seem like a neutral situation, but you pay interest on your margin loan with each passing day. For this reason, margin trading can be a good consideration for conservative investors if the stock pays a high dividend. Many times, a high dividend from 4,000 dollars' worth of stock can sometimes exceed the margin interest you have to pay on the $2,000 (50 percent) you borrow from the broker to buy that stock.

If the stock price goes down, buying on margin can work against you. What if Mergatroid goes to $38 per share? The market value of 100 shares is then $3,800, but your equity shrinks to only $1,800 because you have to pay your $2,000 margin loan. You're not exactly looking at a disaster at this point, but you'd better be careful, because the margin loan exceeds 50 percent of your stock investment. If it goes any lower, you may get the dreaded margin call, which happens when the broker actually contacts you to ask you to restore the ratio between the margin loan and the value of the securities. See the following section for information about appropriate debt-to-equity ratios.

Maintaining your balance

REMEMBER

When you purchase stock on margin, you must maintain a balanced ratio of margin debt to equity of at least 50 percent. If the debt portion exceeds this limit, you're required to restore that ratio by depositing either more stock or more cash into your brokerage account. The additional stock you deposit can be stock that's transferred from another account.

To continue the example from the preceding section: If Mergatroid goes to $28 per share, the margin loan portion exceeds 50 percent of the equity value in that stock — in this case, because the market value of your stock is $2,800 but the margin loan is still at $2,000, the margin loan is a worrisome 71 percent of the market value ($2,000 divided by $2,800 = 71 percent). Expect to get a call from your broker to put more securities or cash into the account to restore the 50 percent balance. You can run, but you can't hide. The broker knows where you live!

If you can't come up with more stock, other securities, or cash, the next step is to sell stock from the account and use the proceeds to pay off the margin loan. For you, that means realizing a capital loss — you lose money on your investment.

TIP

The Investment Industry Regulatory Organization of Canada (IIROC) and the U.S. Federal Reserve Board govern margin requirements for their respective Canadian and U.S. brokers. Both regulatory bodies dictate margin requirements set by brokers for their customers. For most listed stocks, it's 50 percent, but the ratio can vary upwards or downwards. Discuss this rule with your broker to fully understand your (and your broker's) risks and obligations.

Striving for success on margin

Margin, as you can see from the previous sections, can escalate your profits on the upside but magnify your losses on the downside. If your stock plummets drastically, you can end up with a margin loan that exceeds the market value of the stock you used the loan to purchase. In past bear markets, stock losses hurt many people, and a large number of those losses were made worse because people didn't manage the responsibilities involved with margin trading. In the most recent bear market, margin debt again hit very high levels, and that subsequently contributed to tumbling stock prices.

WARNING

If you buy stock on margin, use a disciplined approach. Be extra careful when using leverage, such as a margin loan, because it can backfire. Keep the following points in mind:

>> Have ample reserves of cash or marginable securities in your account. Try to keep the margin ratio at 40 percent or less to minimize the chance of a margin call.

>> If you're a beginner, consider using margin to buy stocks in large companies that have relatively stable prices and pay good dividends. Some people buy income stocks that have dividend yields that exceed the margin interest rate, meaning that the stock ends up paying for its own margin loan. Just remember those stop-loss orders, which we discuss earlier in this chapter.

>> Constantly monitor your stocks. If the market turns against you, the result will be especially painful if you use margin.

>> Have a payback plan for your margin debt. Taking margin loans against your investments means that you're paying interest. Your ultimate goal is to make money, and paying interest eats into your profits.

Going Short and Coming Out Ahead

The vast majority of stock investors are familiar with buying stock, holding onto it for a while, and hoping its value goes up. This kind of thinking is called going long, and investors who go long are considered to be long on stocks. (These people are also called longs.) Going long essentially means that you're bullish and seeking your profits from rising prices. However, astute investors also profit in the market when stock prices fall. Going short (also called shorting a stock, selling short, or doing a short sale) on a stock is a common technique for profiting from a stock price decline. Some investors (often simply called shorts) have made big profits during bear markets by going short. A short sale is a bet that a particular stock is going down.

Most people easily understand making money by going long. It boils down to "buy low and sell high." Piece of cake. Going short means making money by selling high and then buying low. Huh? Thinking in reverse isn't a piece of cake. Although thinking of this stock adage in reverse may be challenging, the mechanics of going short are really simple. Consider an example that uses a fictitious company called DOA, Inc. As a stock, DOA ($50 per share) is looking pretty sickly. It has lots of debt and plummeting sales and earnings, and the news is out that DOA's industry will face hard times for the foreseeable future. This situation describes a stock that's an ideal candidate for shorting. The future may be bleak for DOA, but it's promising for savvy investors. The following sections provide the full scoop on going short.

TIP First things first. To go short, you have to be deemed (by your broker) creditworthy — your account needs to be approved for short selling. When you're approved for margin trading, you're probably set to sell short, too. Talk to your broker (or check on the broker's website for information) about limitations in your account regarding going short.

REMEMBER

You must understand brokerage rules before you conduct short selling. The broker must approve you for it (refer to Chapter 7 for information on working with brokers), and you must meet the minimum collateral requirement, which is commonly $2,000 or 50 percent (whichever is higher) of the shorted stock's market value. If the stock generates dividends, those dividends are paid to the stock's owner, not to the person who borrows to go short. Check with your broker for complete details.

WARNING

Because going short on stocks has greater risks than going long, we strongly advise beginning investors not to try shorting stocks until they become much more seasoned.

Setting up a short sale

This section explains how to go short. Say that you believe DOA is the right stock to short — you're pretty sure its price is going to fall. With DOA at $50, you instruct your broker to "go short 100 shares on DOA." (It doesn't have to be 100 shares; we're just using that as an example.) Here's what happens next:

1. Your broker borrows 100 shares of DOA stock, either from his own inventory or from another client or broker.

That's right. The stock can be borrowed from a client, no permission necessary. The broker guarantees the transaction, and the client/stock owner never has to be informed about it because she never loses legal and beneficial right to the stock. You borrow 100 shares, and you'll return 100 shares when it's time to complete the transaction.

2. Your broker then sells the stock and puts the money in your account.

Your account is credited with $5,000 (100 shares × $50) in cash — the money gained from selling the borrowed stock. This cash acts like a loan on which you're going to have to pay interest.

3. You buy the stock back and return it to its rightful owner.

When it's time to close the transaction (because either you want to close it or the owner of the shares wants to sell them, so you have to give them back), you must return the number of shares you borrowed (in this case, 100 shares). If you buy back the 100 shares at $40 per share (remember that you shorted this particular stock because you were sure its price was going to fall) and those 100 shares are returned to their owner, you make a $1,000 profit. (To keep the example tidy, we don't include brokerage commissions and interest.)

Oops! Going short when prices grow taller

WARNING

We bet you guessed that the wonderful profitability of selling short has a flip side. Say that you were wrong about DOA and that the stock price rises from the ashes as it goes from $50 to $87. Now what? You still have to return the 100 shares you borrowed. With the stock's price at $87, that means you have to buy the stock for $8,700 (100 shares at the new, higher price of $87). Ouch! How do you pay for it? Well, you have that original $5,000 in your account from when you initially went short on the stock. But where do you get the other $3,700 ($8,700 less the original $5,000)? You guessed it — your pocket! You have to cough up the difference. If the stock continues to rise, that's a lot of coughing. Again, you can run, but you can't hide!

How much money do you lose if the stock goes to $100 or more? A heck of a lot. As a matter of fact, there's absolutely no limit to how much you can lose. Did we forget to say "no limit"? That's why going short can be way riskier than going long. When going long, the most you can lose is 100 percent of your money. When you go short, however, you can lose more than 100 percent of the money you invest. Yikes!

TIP

Because the potential for loss is unlimited when you short a stock, we suggest that you use a stop order (also called a buy-stop order) to minimize the damage. Better yet, make it a GTC order (discussed earlier in this chapter). You can set the stop order at a given price, and if the stock hits that price, you buy the stock back so that you can return it to its owner before the price rises even higher. You still lose money, but you limit your losses. Like a stop-loss order, a buy-stop order effectively works to limit your loss. This is a very important tip to keep in mind to mitigate your potential loss.

Feeling the squeeze

If you go short on a stock, you have to buy that stock back sooner or later so that you can return it to its owner. What happens when a lot of people are short on a particular stock and its price starts to rise? All those short sellers are scrambling to buy the stock back en masse so that they can close their transactions before they lose too much money. This mass buying quickens the pace of the stock's ascent and puts a squeeze (called a short squeeze) on the investors who've been shorting the stock.

REMEMBER

Going short can be a great manoeuvre in a declining (bear) market, but it can be brutal if the stock price goes up. If you're a beginner, stay away from short selling until you have enough experience (and money) to risk it.

Chapter **18**

Using Trade Triggers and Advanced Conditional Orders

I n the age of knowledge, grasshopper, we must be one with the technology. Especially, locust, when technology can help you make more profit. In that spirit, uh . . . cricket, we take the topic of brokerage orders from Chapter 17 to another level.

Brokerage orders that you can automate on a website is (in our humble opinion) one of the greatest uses of investing technology. Chapter 17 is about placing single transaction orders, such as a stop-loss order or a trailing stop. In this chapter, we introduce you to more advanced brokerage orders, whereby it's possible to enter a combination order containing two or more orders that may be triggered by market events (this stuff is cool . . .).

REMEMBER

No one says that you need to use a trade trigger or an advanced conditional order. For most folks (even us), the basic orders that we describe in Chapter 17 suffice most of the time. However, it's good to know that if you encounter a challenging situation due to market conditions or your changing preferences and circumstances, you can structure an order or a set of orders to satisfy your investing/trading/speculating needs.

Trying Trade Triggers

A *trade trigger* is any event that sets a trade in motion (stock or otherwise). The trade trigger can be a singular event (such as the movement of an individual stock) or a market-wide event (such as a major index reaching a certain level). Trade triggers are used to make something automatically occur, such as the selling or buying of stocks when a particular price level is reached. Essentially, trade triggers carry out the function of "if this happens, then do that." If a trigger is, well, triggered, the trade is deployed, and the stock trader receives an email notice as soon as the transaction is done.

Those who trade (versus invest in) stocks use trade triggers regularly to keep from having to constantly monitor the daily swings in market movements. Most Canadian brokerage firms offer this technology to everyone, including frequent traders.

In the following sections, we explain the different types of trade triggers and provide pointers on how to set one up.

Surveying different types of trade triggers

We think that trade triggers can be extremely useful to stock investors (and those who do options or track indexes). The following sections cover the three different types of trade triggers.

Using a stock

Chapter 17 gives you the scoop on basic triggers such as limit orders. A buy limit order, for example, says that "if and when XYZ stock hits the price of $50, then buy 100 shares." And usually a time is attached, such as "this order is good for the day" or "this order is good-til-cancelled."

However, a more sophisticated trade trigger can be set in motion by a separate event that's not directly associated with the movement of a particular stock. The trade trigger may be the movement of an entirely different stock. It may be one you own, or one you don't.

With trade triggers, the activity or attributes of any stock can trigger an order for another stock. If you feel there's a correlation between the prices of two different stocks, you can set up a trade trigger similar to the one in the following example.

Say that you want to buy 100 shares of Apple (APPL) stock, but only when Alphabet Inc.'s (GOOG) stock price falls to $1,000 per share within the next 30 days. The trade trigger would be set to "buy 100 shares of APPL when GOOG is equal to (or less than) $1,000, and this order will be GTC (good-til-cancelled) but will expire 30 days from when the order is entered." (Google is the biggest segment of the larger Alphabet digital conglomerate that possesses the actual stock exchange listing — in essence it's still the Google we know today.)

As you can see, your creativity can take you to new levels of investing nirvana (whatever that may be!). Use triggers such as these when you come across opportunities in your favourite stocks. Do your research on stocks that you would like to buy; start with Chapter 6 and also the resources in Appendix A.

Using an index

The investor can make a buy or sell trade using a major market index (rather than a stock) as the trigger. If you feel that certain movements of indexes may influence or correlate to the movement of individual stocks (or options), you can set up a trigger to place an order if the conditions you specify are met. (Indexes include the Dow Jones Industrial Average and the S&P 500; refer to Chapter 5 for details.)

You can execute a sell order on a particular stock, for example, which is triggered when the Dow rises to a certain level. Or if, say, the S&P 500 index is reflecting a strong rally and you think it will be overbought when it reaches, say, 1700, you can set your order to sell a stock when this index reaches that level. The S&P/TSX Composite Index can likewise be used as a trigger, as can other major world indexes, depending on the broker you use.

TIP

Frequently, major market movements set up buying or selling opportunities in the stocks that you're following. The idea that you can automate the process with trade triggers is very appealing. The timing is entirely up to you, but Chapter 17 (on brokerage orders) can come in handy for setting up your scenarios, leading indicators, and related trade triggers.

Using an option

Call and put options can also be part of your trade trigger strategy. Options are speculative vehicles that have an expiration date, where you're betting on the direction of an underlying asset. You buy a call option if you're "betting" that the underlying asset will go up, and you buy a put option if you're "betting" that the underlying option will go down. (For more information on options and how to use them, go to the educational sections of websites such as www.cboe.com, www.888options.com, and www.m-x.ca/accueil_en.php.)

For instance, say you're bullish on XYZ stock (the world's most famous noncompany!); you'd like to buy a call option but only on a day when XYZ is down so that you get a favourable price for the call option. Say that XYZ is at $70, and you'd like to buy a call option when the price dips to $65.

Perhaps the particular call option you're eyeing (say it's "XYZ call option $67.50") is priced at a premium of $175. (This would be quoted as a premium of $1.75 because a single option is based on 100 shares; therefore, a multiplier of 100 is in the price.) But you may want to buy the stock at this cheaper price and the option at the lower cost of $150 (quoted as $1.50) or better. You would set your trigger as follows: When XYZ stock goes to $65 or better (meaning that the stock price hits the price of $65 or lower — that $65 price acts as the "trigger"), buy "XYZ call option $67.50" at the specific price of $1.50 or better (meaning that you would be glad to purchase at a price lower than $1.50).

If XYZ stock does indeed fall to $65, your broker would enter an order at $1.50 (this would specifically be called a "buy limit order"). When (and if) the particular call option falls to the price of $1.50, a purchase would be made, and you would end up buying that call option for $150 (plus commissions).

Entering trade triggers

REMEMBER

So you're excited to use a trade trigger, but how, exactly, do you enter one? Every Canadian brokerage firm has the glossary and tutorials necessary to guide you through the process of placing an order. The main components of the trade trigger order are

>> The order action: Is it a buy or sell order?

>> The order type: Is it a market order, a stop-loss order, or a limit order? Refer to Chapter 17 for more information.

>> The quantity to be bought or sold: 100 shares? More? Less?

>> The symbol of the security to be bought or sold: This one's self-explanatory.

>> The limit price and/or activation price for the order: This may or may not be applicable based on the type of order selected.

>> The expiration for the order: Is it a day order or good-til-cancelled? Refer to Chapter 17 for details.

WARNING

Keep in mind that not every broker performs these transactions the same way or labels these orders as we do. Speak to your broker's customer service representative and discuss this list with him.

Here are a few more handy hints for establishing a trade trigger:

>> A trigger alert can be "activated" by a variety of sources. For example, you can have a trigger alert occur when a major market index, such as the DJIA or

S&P/TSX Composite, hits a certain level. Or, these alerts can be based on a particular stock that's on the New York Stock Exchange, Nasdaq, the Over the Counter Bulletin Board (OTCBB), or even "The Pink Sheets" (where you find small cap and micro cap stocks).

>> Some brokers can get very sophisticated with trade triggers, while other brokers may not do them at all (yet). Talk with your brokerage firm's customer service department to see what triggers are available for traders and investors to use.

>> Triggers on stocks and options are normally activated during regular market hours (9:30 a.m. to 4:00 p.m. EST).

>> Talk with your broker about how long the triggers will stay on (until the triggers are activated or until they expire). Some brokers may have different time frames from the usual good-til-cancelled time frame. The broker will usually send you an e-mail if the trigger is activated or if it expires.

>> If the trigger involves the purchase of a security, make sure that you have either enough cash for the order amount or enough margin to cover the purchase (refer to Chapter 17 for details on buying on margin). Do a tally of the total amount you need — a combination of triggers or conditional orders may involve more than one purchase.

Considering Advanced Conditional Orders

Advanced conditional orders let you combine two or three orders that, if filled, will either cancel or trigger additional orders. Conditional orders are available for both stocks and call or put option orders (make sure that you're approved for options trading by your brokerage firm). In the following sections, we list different kinds of advanced conditional orders and explain how to place them.

Checking out different types of advanced conditional orders

Imagine saying to yourself, "Gee, I'm committed to my current stock, Stock A, and I hope it continues to go up. I'd love to get Stock B, but the only way I'd buy Stock B is if Stock A were crashing and I sold it because I lost hope in its future."

It's kinda like being at the supermarket and saying, "I'll buy the veal only if the beef isn't on sale, but if the beef is on sale, I'll get that (unless it's Tuesday, which is chicken day, of course)." You get the point. Sometimes the situation (whether in the stock market or just real life) is a combination "what-if/then-that" scenario.

The following are three of the most common advanced conditional orders that you'll encounter:

- ➤➤ **One cancels another (OCA) order:** In this case, you actually submit two simultaneous orders. If one is filled, the other is automatically cancelled. Say you want to buy one of two stocks but not both. With the OCA order, you can do that because filling the order to buy Stock A will automatically cancel the order to buy Stock B.

- ➤➤ **One triggers another (OTA) order:** If this order is filled, another order is automatically and subsequently submitted. Say you own a stock (Stock A) and would like to buy another stock (Stock B) but only if you can use the purchase money from the proceeds from the sale of Stock A. The OTA order says that if Stock A hits a certain price, sell Stock A and then subsequently buy Stock B.

- ➤➤ **One triggers two (OTT) order:** If this order is filled, it automatically submits two subsequent orders. Say you own a stock (Stock A) at $50 a share and you're worried that it may fall below $48. You would like to buy Stock B at $45 and then enter a stop-loss order for Stock B at $40. The OTT order would sell Stock A when it hits $48 and then enter two subsequent orders: buy Stock B at $45 and put on a stop-loss order for Stock B at $40.

As you get more knowledgeable and confident in your investing pursuits, you may want to try the following advanced conditional orders, which build on those in the preceding list.

- ➤➤ **OT/OCA:** One order triggers an OCA order. When you submit an order and it's filled, two orders are simultaneously submitted. If one of the second set of orders is filled, the other one is cancelled.

- ➤➤ **OT/OTA:** One order triggers an OTA order. When you submit an order and it's filled, another order is subsequently submitted, and if that second order is filled, a third order is subsequently submitted.

- ➤➤ **OT/OTT:** If one order is filled, it automatically submits two subsequent orders simultaneously. Oh yeah . . . you can get crazy with this stuff. (Keep in mind that every broker treats these orders a bit differently, so check with your broker to get the specifics.)

We guess the only order left is the OT/DOA (don't ask — just kidding).

Placing advanced conditional orders

Although advanced conditional orders may seem complicated, like anything else, they become easy as you break down the process.

TIP

Before we get to the actual process, remember that you need to set clearly in your mind what you actually want to occur and what possibilities you want to take into account long before you talk to your broker or head to your broker's website to create the orders. You may want to write down your thoughts as clearly as possible.

Some of these steps will vary because every Canadian brokerage firm runs things a little differently, but the essential steps should be the same.

1. Choose the security.

   In this order, are you trading a stock, exchange-traded fund (ETF), or option?

2. Search out the symbol.

   What is the symbol of the stock or ETF (or option)?

3. Choose the quantity.

   How many shares of the stock or ETF do you want? Or how many option contracts?

4. Figure out the basic order type.

   Is it a market order, limit order, or other type of order? (Refer to Chapter 17 for details.)

5. Check the condition.

   Indicate that this order is conditional.

6. Check the "What if" operator in your order.

   Did you mean "greater than or equal to" or "less than or equal to"? Check with your broker to be sure your order does exactly what you intend for it to do.

7. Choose the second security.

   Repeat Steps 2–6 for this security.

8. Choose the third security.

   Repeat Steps 2–6 for this security.

9. Set the cancellation condition.

   Under what circumstance should the order be cancelled? Say you want to buy XYZ stock when it hits $50 but not above that price. In that case, you set the cancellation condition at $50.

10. Set the time factor.

Specify that the order(s) is good for a day or provide an expiration date.

11. Review and confirm your order.

Lastly, review that the order is structured to your specifications. Not sure? Cancel and try again!

Your success with trade triggers doesn't mean you need to master all the different types that we mention in this chapter. However, it's good to master at least one or two to make your trading and investing more successful.

Chapter **19**

Bitcoin and Alternative Digital Currencies

I f you haven't heard of Bitcoin yet, you probably don't have an Internet connection. Alternately, you've been hearing so much of it lately that your head is ready to explode. Even among high tech experts, it's difficult to wrap one's head around the concept. Lucky for you, a plain language *For Dummies* book, courtesy of us, is just what the doctor ordered to at least partially relieve your digital currency-induced migraine.

Here, we take you through the high level as well as through a little of the gory detail. This journey involves just the right mix of content to give you a basic but pretty complete understanding of how you can successfully invest in digital currency. We begin the chapter with a discussion of the nature of digital currency. Fasten your seatbelt. This is going to be a ride like no other!

The Look and Feel of a Freshly Minted Cryptocurrency

A good way to explore digital currency or cryptocurrency — we will use these terms interchangeably — is to first ask what "regular" currency is. In the good old days (the really old ones, like the 1700s), currency in North America included commodities. The commodity could be anything. Beaver pelts were a commodity commonly used in Canada as a currency. One pelt got you one kilogram of sugar, 15 fish hooks, and a litre of whisky. In the mid-18th century, to be more practical, coins and later paper money were used. But the coins and paper were always backed by commodities, usually gold or silver.

About 50 years ago, *fiat* (not the car — Latin for "it shall be") became the normal form of currency almost everywhere. Fiat represents currency that is not backed by a physical commodity. Fiat currency derives value from scarcity driven by the fundamentals of supply and demand. It is also backed by the strength of the related government. Fiat currency like the Loonie is declared by a central authority such as the Bank of Canada or the Federal Reserve in order to be legal tender. If Canadians or Americans lose faith in the fiat currency, the money might be worthless. Scary, right?

What is digital or "crypto" currency?

Cryptocurrency (or *digital* or *alternative* currency) is a digital and potentially investable asset that is global in scope. It knows no borders. It was designed to function primarily as a medium of exchange. But is that its true and only role? Before we delve into that question shortly, let's open the hood of digital currency and examine its features and unique attributes.

Cryptocurrency as its name suggests uses the mathematical field of cryptography to secure financial transactions across the Internet, validate transactions to create trust, and keep the whole digital currency ecosystem running. Money can be transmitted in anonymity. We know, we're getting technical and will revisit these rather technical bits later in this chapter.

A defining attribute and global allure of cryptocurrency is its organic and autonomous nature — is not issued, controlled, interfered with, or manipulated by any central bank or other government authority. Digital currencies instead rely on decentralized control. This is made possible by the architecture of something called the blockchain. Bitcoin, a cryptocurrency first released in 2009, is considered to be the first digital currency. We explain the blockchain, and its star attraction — Bitcoin — shortly.

REMEMBER

Digital currency = cryptocurrency = alternative currency. We use these terms interchangeably. Later on, we may also refer to these as coins and tokens. Welcome to the wild lexicon of the crypto ecosystem.

Is cryptocurrency really currency?

To answer this question, let's apply cryptocurrency to the traditional and logical definition of money:

>> **Medium of exchange:** Cryptocurrencies can definitely serve as a medium of exchange, and many are designed to do just that. Digital currencies (or coins) like Bitcoin, Etherium, Dash, Ripple, and Stellar are examples of this functionality. Today, you and anyone else may choose to transact in cryptocurrency, fiat currency, or beaver pelts if you want.

>> **Store of value:** Using Bitcoin as an example of a well-known and reasonably accepted digital currency, you can argue that it acts as a store of value. That may be a stretch, as digital currency is highly speculative in nature. Bitcoin is only as valuable as the market says it is, and the volatility in price (about $20,000 USD in early 2018 to $7,000 at the time of writing) hardly seems like a stable "store" of value. In fact, the difficulty in unlocking (*crystallizing*) its value by redeeming it back into fiat money was partly responsible for its price crash. The "store" of value for Bitcoin is compromised by the fact the currency is decentralized (therefore not backed), is digital (thus vulnerable to hackers), and is one of thousands of competitors (impairing its ability to store predictable and undiluted value).

>> **Unit of account:** Cryptocurrencies are all over the map when viewed through the lens of price stability. They exhibit very high volatility and trade at different prices within different exchanges (we discuss exchanges later on in this chapter). Regular fiat currency, on the other hand, has a centralized price aggregation process that promotes price stability. This volatility and unpredictability of the price of Bitcoin and its cryptocurrency cousins impairs their usefulness as units of account.

And the verdict is . . .

Sadly for some, and applying the criteria just given, cryptocurrencies don't serve the traditional role of a currency. Happily for us, and the main reason we've included this chapter in a book about stock investing, cryptocurrencies are an investable asset class (like stocks) that trade on exotic exchanges (like stock market stock exchanges). We emphasize that although the scope of this book is about classic stock investing, this is a highly speculative and new form of investing, but one you should know about.

The cryptocurrency ecosystem in Canada and the U.S. is monitored by the same regulatory and oversight bodies (U.S. Securities and Exchange Commission and Ontario Securities Commission) as stocks. The SEC and OSC do this because they reached the same conclusion we just did. The term *cryptocurrency* is a flat-out misnomer, with Bitcoin (discussed later) perhaps being the only exception.

Cryptocurrency is an investment asset with a speculative streak. It can be a security or a commodity, each with different oversight and regulatory implications. Either way it is an investment asset. In addition, no credible law firm would ever give an opinion in writing that cryptocurrency is not a security to invest in, because it absolutely can be. Other descriptors include *crypto-assets*, but this too represents an investable security rather than a form of money.

REMEMBER

In a nutshell, digital currency is like money but isn't truly money, yet it has value as an asset and you can invest in it. The nature of digital currency and who regulates what and how will be the subject of endless debate over the next few years. Keep your eye out for new and changing regulations as they are announced.

The Blockchain: Recording Your Cryptocurrency on a Public Ledger

A *blockchain* is a distributed (shared) database. This database is a *ledger*, which is essentially a record book, and this record book is shared. Each line item entry in this shared record book can be thought of as a *block*. Using a simple lens, let's think of the blockchain as a *shared record book*.

Now is where things get different in a very cool way. This is not your granddad's record book — you know, that single copy that stays in a corner of one room but can be viewed by all family members. The one with the coffee stains. No, no, and no. There are hundreds and thousands and tens of thousands of copies of this record book. The copies are stored on business servers, PCs, and laptops all around the world. That's why the million-dollar word in the world of blockchain technology is *decentralized*. In other words, the blockchain is disparate, democratic, and not controlled by any centralized entity other than the true singular owner of the record. This is one of its amazing appeals.

Another appeal (and unique feature) of the blockchain is that it is built on a foundation of trust and validation. This is a paradigm shift that is poised to change business processes around the world. That's because the record book — or blockchain, or database, or any way you want to describe it — can be used to record many kinds of things and transactions. It's particularly suited to transactions where *trust* is critical. For the purposes of this book, we'll use the transmission of cryptocurrency as the main example and most-used current application of the blockchain.

When Peter sends digital currency to Sam, a new line item is created in the record book (blockchain) that details the particulars of that transaction, including the amount, type of digital currency (Bitcoin, Ethereum, or other digital currency), recipient, and more. This information-rich line item then gets transmitted to hundreds of other computers, so they have a carbon digital copy of the record. Those computers validate that this transaction is authorised and bona fide. We won't take you too deeply into the nuts and bolts of how this validation is technically done because it's beyond the scope of this book. We only touch on it in the section called "Mining for Bitcoin gold." The thing that matters here is that trust is established by having hundreds of watchers or validators work to endorse and approve the transaction and get it recorded in the blockchain. The ultimately authorized transaction is replicated accurately and completely on every copy of the record.

There is no one bank or other central broker or single entity that has sole control or ownership of the shared record book containing the transaction between Peter and Sam. You no longer need to rely on a middleman. The record book is owned by everyone who possesses a copy accessible on their computer. But having a copy does not equate to having control. In this way, the blockchain builds trust, is efficient, and is less costly to everyone in its ecosysytem.

TECHNICAL STUFF

A blockchain is immutable, meaning it's *irreversible*. Every line item entry lives forever. That means tampering with this shared record book for fraudulent or questionable purposes is practically impossible.

Going back to the example of Peter sending currency to Sam, let's assume that the founding "genesis" entry in the record book was by someone called Satoshi. Satoshi founded the new digital currency that Peter is transferring to Sam. Satoshi says 30 million digital coins now exist. He's a nice guy, and sends 50 to Peter and 100 to Sam. To receive those coins, Peter and Sam would have provided Satoshi with their *digital wallet addresses*. This is like when you provide your new employer your bank account details to receive a direct payroll deposit. In the blockchain world, instead of a transparent bank transit and account numbers, Peter and Sam instead possess very lengthy and secret codes (or jumbled letters and numbers) that assign to them ownership of certain line items. The line items in this part of the blockchain (or record book) now actually relate to their wallet coordinates.

The key point here is this: Only Peter and Sam can create new line items with the digital coins they receive from Satoshi. They control the line items. Once Peter has the coins, he is now poised to send all 50 of his coins to Sam. As Peter proceeds to create his new line item that asserts that he has placed 50 coins in Sam's wallet, he can no longer control where those 50 coins go from there — only Sam the recipient can exert control. In this way, thousands of people can possess a copy of the record, without being able to tamper with, collude, or otherwise add or delete new line items relating to any of the other 30 million digital coins documented in the blockchain.

To sum this up, and in the context of digital currency, the blockchain is a digital record book of all transactions that have taken place in the exchange of cryptocurrency. The most famous blockchain architecture as it is called, is the Bitcoin network. We cover Bitcoin a bit later in this chapter. The Bitcoin and similar networks keep track of new digital currency "coins" or "tokens" as they are generated. (We introduce you to networks, coins, and tokens in this chapter as well.) In the end, the blockchain functions like the legendary Library of Alexandria, but like that great library to this day, has no physical centralized presence.

At any point in time, the blockchain tracks who has how much of a given type of digital currency. The blockchain grows minute by minute in increments called, of course, *blocks*. The blocks are gated and secured by strong cryptography — the digital equivalent of keys and iron gates (see the next section for more on cryptography). The blockchain starts with raw, meaningless data that, when put together, transforms into a valuable, trusted, time-stamped, and very meaningful collection of information. This amazing construct, managed by a peer-to-peer network that sticks to a standardized protocol, cannot be changed retroactively. It is a foundation and pillar of trust.

Encryption: The Key to Anonymity and Security on the Blockchain

It's pretty obvious that when you willingly leave important personal and valuable information out in the "digital open" to a bunch of computers, you're going to want a few assurances. The number one and two priorities will be data security and privacy protection. In other words, you want to protect yourself against piracy and preserve your privacy. These priorities are achieved through encryption.

A great irony between using cryptocurrency and using regular online money transfers with BMO, TD Bank, and other Canadian banks is that with digital currency you can actually record your holdings on a piece of paper with the encrypted code showing what you own is actually 100 percent secure, at least from online hacking. (We discuss wallets and other places to store your cryptos later in this chapter.) With cryptocurrencies, as long as you don't associate your name or other identifier to a digital currency's address, you will remain anonymous, and others cannot hack into and steal your cryptocurrency. The cryptocurrency ecosystem does not keep track of users and names. Rather, it keeps track of addresses where the money digitally resides.

The technicalities of all this are beyond the scope of this book, but the underlying architecture and principle are straightforward. Each currency's address has two essential pieces of cryptographic information: a *public key* and a *private key*. The public key, which in the case of Bitcoin is what the "Bitcoin address" is created from, is like an email *address*. Anyone can appropriately access the public address and send Bitcoins to it. The private key, or address, is similar to an email *password*. Only with the private key can the owner send Bitcoins from it. It is very important to keep this private key secure and confidential. To transmit Bitcoins and other digital currencies from an address, you need to prove to the blockchain ecosystem that you actually own the private key that matches the public address, all without revealing the private key. This "proving" is achieved through a cool area of mathematics known as cryptography.

Your public key

Let's look at this a little closer. A public key is like an identification number associated with, say, your gym or professional association membership. If someone wanted to send you Ethereum, all you have to do is supply that person with your "Ether" address — essentially, your easier-to-read public key. For example, if Barb has 10 Ether at an address called UVW321, and Bert has no Ether in his generated Ether address XYZ654, then Barb can send 5 Ether coins to XYZ654. After the transaction is executed on the blockchain, Barb and Bert both possess 5 Ethereum coins. Anyone using the Ethereum blockchain can actually see how much money "UVW321" and "XYZ654" have — but no one has a clue who owns the addresses because the private keys are not disclosed.

Your private key

Barb and Bert each have a second and closely-guarded private key which only they themselves know — the other half of their digital currency addresses. It is this private key that confers to the owner of each coin total control over it. Unlike a bank, which can theoretically seize assets, no one else has control except the one who has the private key. That means if you lose your private key, anyone who simply finds it can take control and anonymously steal your digital currency.

REMEMBER

Coin owners are not identifiable to the public, but many cryptocurrency exchanges are now required by law to collect the personal information of their registered users.

Mining for Bitcoin Gold

As mentioned, private keys need to be secured, but even assuming they are, you may still wonder how the blockchain is itself kept secure. How do you know some transaction isn't bogus? How do you know that a scammer didn't simply record false ownership in Bitcoin or an altcoin he or she never owned in the blockchain record? The answer is with a process called *mining*.

With cryptocurrency blockchain networks, *mining* refers to a validation of transactions. For this validation effort, miners who succeed in calculating the solution to complex math problems typically get new cryptocurrency as a reward. Calculations are executed with very powerful and specialized computer processors. People or companies that engage in this process are called *miners*. Miners compete with one another or work collaboratively to obtain a solution to the mathematical puzzle. The first individual miner or group or company to solve the particular puzzle is rewarded with new digital coins, like Bitcoin, or tokens or even other assets.

REMEMBER

Entire technical manuals have been written to describe how mining works. We just have room to give you a sense of what's involved. The key point about mining is that it's the incentive, glue, oil, and gas that keep the blockchain running.

HOW CANADIANS VIEW AND USE CRYPTOCURRENCY

The Ontario Securities Commission (OSC) may not have the strongest enforcement statistics of its own to brag about, but it sure can do useful surveys that generate cool statistics of others. A 2018 OSC survey report found that in Ontario alone, 5 percent of the Ontario population, or 500,000 Ontarians, owned digital currency. A further 4 percent had held crypto assets prior to the survey. This would translate to roughly 3 million Canadians having had some direct exposure to cryptocurrency.

The survey also delved into the nature and extent of the uses of digital currency. Canadians are using digital currency to pay for flights, hotels, movies, furniture, games, apps, movies, and much more. Canadians are cautious and wise. Of the survey respondents who possessed digital currency, one half of Ontarians spent less than $1,000; and about 10 percent spent more than $10,000. That may not sound like much, but the whole digital currency space really only exploded into public consciousness in 2015. Those mild numbers also suggest a cautious and risk-aware approach reflective of sound diversification principles. We are proud of you.

The drivers of enthusiasm were also probed by the OSC's survey. Almost 50 percenty obtained their digital currency out of interest in the underlying technology, whereas another 18 percent liked the potential of the trust-powered blockchain architecture underpinning digital currency to prevent fraud-related losses. Forty-two percent acquired digital currency for investment purposes to make a profit. One quarter of Ontarians who had cryptocurrency used it to make payments in Canada or the U.S. Fourteen percent wanted to make international remittances to family and others. Interestingly, only about 12 percent of respondents cited lack of trust in the stability of Canadian banks or government as a reason for owning cryptocurrency, and this is not surprising given the great Canadian track record in this area. (Asking Venezuelans the same question would yield vastly different survey results. We are truly sad at their state of affairs.)

Bitcoin: The 500-Pound Digital Currency Gorilla

Bitcoin was the creation of a person (or group) called Satoshi Nakamoto. It launched in 2009. The purpose of Bitcoin was to create a new electronic cash system that was completely decentralized with no primary server or central authority. In 2011, Satoshi Nakamoto made transparent the source code and logic to peers in the Bitcoin community — and has more or less disappeared from public view.

Bitcoin is *the* cryptocurrency. The big enchilada. It's likely the first digital currency you obtain in exchange for your fiat (Canadian dollar) currency. With Bitcoin, there are no actual minted coins. Recall at the outset of this chapter that we concluded that digital currency is *not* currency. That's true in the strictest sense. But if there is one coin that almost transcends into the realm of "traditional" currency, it's Bitcoin. For now, Bitcoin is considered by the public to be a digital asset built to work as a currency. The question about whether Bitcoin is a currency, security, or commodity continues to be disputed at the regulator level. However, recently in the eyes of regulators, Bitcoin was deemed not to be a security, although a vast sea of other cryptocurrencies, especially those offered in an Initial Coin Offering, are considered to be securities falling under the watchful eye of the same regulators that regulate stocks.

Bitcoin, like virtually all digital currencies (except Ripple), is totally decentralized, and that is its point. The idea that that a government, a bank, or any other authority controls it would be like garlic to a Bitcoin vampire. Bitcoin and all cryptocurrency owners are anonymous by design. There are no names, social insurance security numbers, or other transparent identifiers. Rather, the Bitcoin platform (the blockchain) connects buyers and sellers through encryption keys.

Bitcoin is not issued by any national mint. Rather, it is "mined" using powerful online computers by people and companies. Mining (discussed earlier) involves performing a combination of complex math and robust recordkeeping. Computers running special mining software inscribe Bitcoin transactions in the openly available digital record book called the blockchain. Miners compete simultaneously to solve mathematical puzzles and be the first to record the transaction in a standards-based and bona fide way. Only the first miner to solve equations gets paid in Bitcoin.

Fundamentally, the value of one Bitcoin is determined by what people will pay for it, in much the same way as stocks. Also driving value is the fact that Satoshi Nakamoto stated that only 21 million Bitcoins can ever be mined, and about 13 million have been mined so far. This limited supply is like gold, but unlike gold possesses no real intrinsic value. This also separates Bitcoin from stocks, which are driven by factors such as a company's revenues, earnings, and other factors. Yet, companies are also valued based on intangibles like their innovation and brand, so there still is some commonality between how a Bitcoin is valued and how a stock is valued. Perhaps reality lies somewhere in between. Perhaps Bitcoin is in a class all of its own.

New Kids on The Blockchain: Altcoins

There are other and different types of cryptocurrencies. If you are even vaguely exposed to the world of Bitcoin, cryptocurrency, and the blockchain, you've probably come across the terms *coins* or *altcoins* (which are somewhat intuitive terms in the context of cryptocurrency) as well as *tokens* (which may leave you scratching your head). The first thing to note is that all coins and tokens are forms of cryptocurrency. The builders of the world of digital currency love to pitch curveballs, and the next curveball is a dandy: most of the coins or altcoins don't even function as currency.

Coins or altcoins

Altcoins include all coins that are an alternative to Bitcoin, but of these altcoins, most are variations (called *forks* or *spawn*) of Bitcoin, as they are built using Bitcoin's open source original protocol with tweaks to its protocol codes. Some names of altcoins that you may recognize and that are variants of Bitcoin's codes include Litecoin, Namecoin, Peercoin, and Auroracoin. The remainder of altcoins, not generated from Bitcoin's protocol, have created their own native blockchains and protocols that support their own distinct cryptocurrencies. Examples of these coins include Ethereum, Ripple, Omni, Nxt, and Counterparty. The one thing all altcoins have in common is that they each essentially run their own blockchain, the record book where transactions concerning their own coins occur in.

Tokens

Tokens are a cryptocurrency as well. What sets tokens apart from other digital currencies is that they represent a particular asset (such as ownership equity in a stock or bond) or utility (where tokens provide holders with future access to a product or service they can purchase later on). Think subway token here.

Most tokens hitch a ride on another cryptocurrency's blockchain. For example, the Ethereum blockchain is used by over 60 tokens. Tokens are therefore easier to create. Issuers of tokens don't need to build a native and proprietary blockchain from the ground up. They just have to follow a standard platform like the Ethereum or other blockchain.

Tokens can represent any assets that are fungible and tradable. An item is *fungible* if it is able to replace or be replaced by another identical item. Money is fungible since it can be raised from employment and used to buy a car, for example. Notice how tokens are starting to look like the currency of the old days that was backed by commodities like gold and silver? Digital currency created for one purpose can easily be used for another use, and those other uses are boundless.

Tokens are created and distributed to the public through a process called an Initial Coin Offering (ICO). We warn you about ICOs in a section later in this chapter called "Regulatory Oversight and Fraud: Caveat, Emptor!" You have likely read about such offerings in the paper, next to discussion about stocks. The ICO process is similar to an Initial Public Offering (IPO) for stocks.

TECHNICAL STUFF

Altcoins building their own blockchain include Ethereum, Ripple, and NXT. Altcoins renting space in the Bitcoin blockchain include litecoin, peercoin, and dogecoin. There are dozens of other coins either residing on their own native blockchains or using the Bitcoin protocol. You can search these names on your favourite search engine to learn more about what others are saying about them, or go to Coinmarketcap.com to access all you need to know about every coin at the technical and investing levels.

TIP

Tokens that need to catch a bus on whole other blockchains are few and far between. But you can find them by going to Coinmarketcap.com and using the filter to isolate only tokens. The search result will include a column showing the platform used by the token.

Buying and Selling Cryptocurrencies on Digital Currency Exchanges

As described in Chapter 6, there are several stock exchanges where you can buy and sell stocks, exchange-traded funds, and related equities. *Cryptocurrency exchanges* (also known as *digital currency exchanges* or *DCEs*) operate in much the same way, allowing you to trade digital currencies for other financial assets, such as fiat currency like the Canadian Loonie, or for different digital currencies. DCEs are the gateway to the digital currency ecosystem. These exchanges can make money, like stock exchanges do, by keeping the spreads between buying and selling prices as transaction fees or by simply charging transaction fees in return for matching buyers with sellers.

DCEs come in different forms. Some are bricks-and-mortar businesses that are happy to deal with paper currencies in exchange for digital currencies. Other DCEs are purely online businesses that only exchange money and digital currencies that are transmitted electronically. You will likely notice that many if not most DCEs operate outside of Canada and the U.S., where regulatory oversight — actually a good thing for the integrity of the cryptocurrency ecosystem — is perceived by DCEs to be a roadblock to their own rapid growth. Nevertheless, foreign DCEs often handle Canadian or at least U.S. fiat currencies. Many give you an assorted and impressive menu of asset withdrawal options. For example, DCEs can send cryptocurrency to your personal cryptocurrency wallet, which is common with all DCEs. Others can do cool things like convert your digital currency balances into anonymous prepaid cards that you can use to withdraw funds from ATMs worldwide! The bottom line is you have many options and many available services.

The four types of digital currency exchanges you need to know about are broker exchanges, trading exchanges, decentralized exchanges, and P2P exchanges. We next explore the nature, advantages, and disadvantages (or warnings) regarding each of them.

Broker exchanges

A *broker exchange* is simply one that allows you to buy digital currency, much as you would expect. By *buying* we mean you exchange your fiat Canadian currency for digital currency (cryptocurrency) or you cash out (sell) your digital currency for fiat. This is the digital currency exchange we recommend you begin with. Coinsquare.com and Quadrigacx.com are Canadian examples of such exchanges. Coinbase.com, CoinMama.com, Kraken.com, and CEX.io are some U.S. and international versions of broker exchanges.

Broker exchanges are fairly established, well-funded, and well-known exchanges. They were often the first movers in the digital currency ecosystem. They place a premium on speedy and good customer service and offer you an intuitive and useful trading interface. They're ideal for Canadians new to the crypto world because most allow you to connect your bank debit or credit cards and buy and sell your digital currency using Canadian or U.S. dollars.

WARNING

Broker exchanges offer only a limited number of the most used and accepted digital currencies (like Bitcoin, Ethereum, Litecoin, and Bitcoin Cash) on their platforms, and transaction fees tend to be higher in exchange for the enhanced conveniences we've mentioned. If you plan on keeping your digital currency at the exchange (and not in wallets, as we discuss and recommend later in this chapter), then DCEs are not your most secure option. If your broker exchange gets hacked, you *could* lose all your digital currency.

REMEMBER

With broker exchanges, digital currencies can't be accessed until you provide your personal identification and it goes through a rigorous verification process, which takes time and effort.

Trading exchanges

In the cryptocurrency ecosystem, *trading exchanges* are considered to be the traditional exchange. In other words, Bitcoin veterans don't need any business like a broker exchange to hold their hand. In fact, they resent outside help from "Big Brother." It's a subculture thing. These veterans already have digital currencies in hand and are ready to trade them for other cryptocurrencies. This type of digital-to-digital trading is done most often on trading exchanges. For example, if you own Bitcoin and would like to own some Ripple, you could use a trading exchange. Examples of trading exchanges are many and include Binance, Kucoin, Bittrex, Changelly, and Poloniex.

Trading exchanges provide a large selection of different and exotic digital coins and tokens in their marketplace, in addition to the most popular coins like Bitcoin and Ethereum. They also offer a gateway to some coins that are just emerging from their ICO. On a classic trading exchange, user interfaces tend to also be intuitive and user-friendly. Transaction fees are cheaper than more full-service exchanges, like broker exchanges, which is always a good thing. The most reputable trading exchanges will insist on verifying your identity. That's not a bad thing, but it does take some time.

WARNING

A large selection of coins and tokens is available on trading exchanges, and this can spell confusion, which can lead to mistakes. Lesser-known tokens will struggle to become as well known as the first movers like Bitcoin, Ripple, and Ethereum.

REMEMBER

Much like you can't fund your trading exchange with fiat Canadian currency, you can't sell your cryptocurrency for fiat currency on a trading exchange.

WARNING

The level of security on the better known exchanges is decent but not foolproof, as evidenced by recent news of hacking. If the trading exchange is compromised by thieves, your digital currency, to the extent that you didn't transfer them to a safer digital or paper wallet (see later in this chapter) could be stolen.

Decentralized trading exchanges

A decentralized trading exchange (DEX) lets you trade digital currency with other digital currency investors directly through the blockchain channel. There is no intermediary to guide you. In addition, there is no centralized server or business involved in a trade execution transaction, so you don't register the same way you would with a broker or trading exchange. You simply create an account by literally clicking one button and securely recording the generated unique account number. Examples of DEXes include IDEX (http://idex.market), EtherDelta (http://etherdelta.com), and WavesDEX (http://wavesplatform.com).

With a DEX (because there's no middleman company), you maintain complete control of your digital currency and private keys. Because it's not a company, a DEX can't be targeted (it simply does not exist as an identifiable single physical entity) and therefore can't be hacked to rob you of your digital currency — so long as you never reveal your private key. A DEX is ideal for connecting to your cold storage wallets (discussed later). You always maintain your anonymity with a DEX.

WARNING

These types of exchanges are still in their infancy, so they offer lower trading volumes. This translates into price volatility as well as longer trade execution times because there are fewer buyers, sellers, and market makers (traders who provide liquidity for a premium). Trading times are also longer because it takes longer to validate a transaction on the blockchain.

REMEMBER

With a DEX, there are fewer types of coins and tokens on offer at any given time, fees are higher than on broker or trading exchanges, and customer service is almost nonexistent. They're not for the faint of heart.

Peer-to-peer exchanges

A *peer-to-peer (P2P) exchange* lets you buy or sell digital currency with a simple signup and no verification of your identification. P2P exchanges are particularly strong at allowing you to purchase coins and tokens with fiat currency, and cash out with fiat cash. Buyers connect with sellers via such P2P platforms, all on their own. Examples of P2P exchanges include LocalEthereum (`http://localethereum.com`) and LocalBitcoins (`www.localbitcoins.com`).

Direct peer-to-peer buying and selling is an efficient method of trading digital currencies. You can stay completely anonymous and can purchase coins and tokens with cash, PayPal, and debit cards.

WARNING

Buyers typically pay a premium over market prices, and P2P fees are the highest of all the options discussed in this section. Large transaction amounts and volumes are few and far between because these transactions are largely between individuals and not large companies. P2P exchanges are also vulnerable to scams because you're never certain about who, you're trading with. The selection of digital currencies tends to be limited.

Canadian cryptocurrency exchanges

There are a number of Canadian exchanges as well, and we mentioned some of them in the previous section. In this section, we dive a little deeper. Knowing about these exchanges is important because the step of converting Canadian fiat currency into cryptocurrency should be the easiest and most seamless. In other words, once you find an exchange that makes this essential step easy for you, the process of hopping from one exchange to another is fairly universal. By that we mean that regardless of the exchange used, when you're exchanging one crypto for another digital coin or token, you're essentially cutting, pasting, and matching one transferor address with another recipient address.

Coinsquare

This is the preeminent Canadian digital currency exchange in terms of visibility, branding, marketing, and number of registered users. Coinsquare (www. coinsquare.com) is a broker exchange, and this means your Canadian fiat currency doesn't have to be exchanged into U.S. dollars or other fiat currency before you execute a trade for Bitcoin or any other digital currency on offer at Coinsquare. It also boasts enhanced security for the period of time that your digital currency is held within the broker, and not in a wallet. It does this with a stated 95 percent *cold storage* policy (meaning assets may not be accessed with a computer), which makes access by hackers to your digital coins virtually impossible. Acceptable currencies in Coinsquare accounts include Canadian and U.S. dollars, British pounds, Euros, and Australian dollars.

QuadrigaCX

QuadrigaCX (www.quadrigacx.com) has a very clean and simple platform that is easy to understand and use. This broker exchange supports a small number of coins, but that's fine if your preliminary objective is to get started in trading with as many funding options as possible. Despite a wide array of options, some are a bit atypical. Other options, such as debit cards, are only accepted if they meet certain criteria mentioned on the QuadrigaCX website.

Canadian Bitcoins

This Bitcoin exchange (www.canadianbitcoins.com) also offers a wide array of payment methods, so funding your account is straightforward. Funding options include Interac Online, direct debit from your bank account, and cash. However, administrative process problems have caused a few users to complain about service time and trade execution accuracy. Always look at the reviews of exchanges before signing on. This is a broker exchange, so you have to provide identification.

ezBtc

This Canadian digital currency exchange (www.ezbtc.ca) boasts a broad portfolio of popular as well as lesser-known cryptocurrencies. It also provides trading in Canadian dollars. Because it too is a broker exchange, you have to first go through an identification verification process.

Morrex

Morrex (www.morrex.com) is one of the oldest Bitcoin broker exchanges in Canada. It offers trading in Bitcoin, Feathercoin, and Litecoin.

Selecting the right exchange for you

One recurring theme we stress throughout this book is doing your homework before making important investment decisions. This includes deciding which platform you'll use to buy and sell securities — in this case, trading digital currency. The following is a brief checklist of considerations to think about as you prepare to trade cryptocurrency:

>> **Cost:** All modern digital currency exchanges should have transparent disclosure of transaction fee information on their websites. Before joining any DCE, make sure you fully understand deposit, transaction, and withdrawal fees. In the cryptocurrency ecosystem, fees can vary by wide margins depending on the exchange. Also take into account foreign exchange transaction fees. If you use foreign crypto exchanges like Kraken, which is based in Japan, you'll find yourself needing to pay additional fees to take into account the foreign exchange costs of converting Canadian dollars into the exchange's home currency — in this case, the yen.

>> **Funding and withdrawal options:** Each exchange offers different funding and withdrawal methods, and the selection can be confusing. In Canada, it's hard to find a bank that will let you make significant transfers to an exchange via debit or credit card. However, larger transfers are often available through bank wire or bank draft transfers, although it may take over a week to actually see the funds deposited into your cryptocurrency exchange. Quadrigacx.com is a Canadian exchange described in the preceding section that lets you fund in many different, though confusing, ways. It offers funding and withdrawal channels with names like Flexepin Voucher, INTERAC Online, Crypto Capital, and QCX Voucher. Others allow PayPal. Even though many options can be confusing, it's not a bad thing. Each option has different costs.

>> **Identity verification:** Don't trade on any exchange that doesn't require at least some measure of identity verification. If you set up an account just to receive digital currency from another person, the identity requirement may be limited to name and address. That's okay. Once you get into deposits and withdrawals, you'll understandably have to provide a lot more, likely including your passport, drivers licence, and/or recent copy of a utility bill to verify that you are actually you. Verification can take a few days, but it protects the exchange against fraud, and that's also good for you.

>> **Reputation:** The best way to find out about an exchange is to search the web using the name of the exchange followed by the word "review." You will likely come up with sites like www.cryptocompare.com, www.coincentral.com, and of course a site aptly named www.bestbitcoinexchange.net. Other industry websites and online forums like BitcoinTalk (www.bitcointalk.org) or Reddit.com (www.reddit.com) let you ask questions.

>> **Security:** The ability of the exchange to thwart hacking goes hand in hand with reputation. Look for exchanges offering cold storage as well as two-factor authentication (an option of two passwords to access your account). Stay away from any exchange that was ever hacked.

>> **Customer support and ease of use:** We may be asking for too much here. The whole point of digital currency is to avoid a centralized Big Brother. To that end, it's reasonable to expect a bit less service than you would, say, at a five star restaurant. A lot less. Check out the message forums like Reddit to see what people are saying. If ease of use is good, something that's a big plus, then your need for customer support will be less.

>> **Geography:** Some specific functions and apps offered by exchanges are only available from certain countries. Just be sure to read the fine print to ensure the exchange you want to use provides you with full access to all of its functions in Canada.

>> **Coin pairs:** Pairs are good for you. Whenever you trade one cryptocurrency with another cryptocurrency, or with a fiat currency, a menu at the exchange will offer what's known as a *pair* — the coin on the left is what you buy, and the one on the right is the coin or token you pay with. For example, if you want to buy Bitcoin with Canadian fiat currency, the pair will show as XBT/CAD. These are the standardized codes of the currency. If you want to sell Bitcoin to buy Ripple, the pairing will be XRP/XBT, with XRP being the code for Ripple. Favour the exchange offering the greatest selection of pairs and the ability to trade Canadian fiat if you're starting out.

>> **Liquidity:** As with the stock market, the best exchanges are those that are well utilized with lots of digital currency offerings and loads of volume, just like with a stock exchange.

Setting up your first digital exchange accounts

Every exchange does things a bit differently, and for different reasons. Some are broker exchanges, and others are P2P exchanges. If you're starting out, some variation of the following steps and overall digital currency trading process is required:

1. Open up a broker exchange account, preferably a Canadian one to begin with. Submit the requested identification to verify your identity. This improves the integrity of the whole ecosystem.

2. Deposit Canadian or U.S. fiat currency into the broker exchange account to set the stage for buying Bitcoin or Ethereum. You don't have to settle for just these two coins, but doing so gives you maximum flexibility to buy all sorts of other exotic cryptocurrencies available on other types of exchanges that you'll eventually want to use.

3. Proceed to open up and use one or two more accounts at trading, DEX, or P2P exchanges.

4. Once you've verified all your accounts, transfer the Bitcoin or Ethereum from your Canadian exchange to some of these other exchanges. Your enrolment in other exchanges will be driven by the factors we already mentioned you should look at when evaluating exchanges, as well as the digital currencies you want to transact.

TIP

For a comprehensive list of international digital currency exchanges, check out http://list.wiki/Cryptocurrency_Exchanges. It's a bit overwhelming at first but does have a description of each exchange and the currencies and fees each charges in a one-stop repository.

Regulatory Oversight and Fraud: Caveat, Emptor!

There are significant risks in the digital currency ecosystem. In fact, we discuss many types of different risks throughout this chapter.

The entire digital currency ecosystem has grown so fast that U.S. and Canadian regulators have had a very hard time keeping up. The Ontario Securities Commission is barely able to keep up and enforce the occasional foibles on Canadian exchanges that deal with stocks, let alone cryptocurrencies.

The much more powerful U.S. Securities and Exchange Commission (SEC) has at least indicated that every initial coin offering (ICO) it has seen has the attributes of a security. This means that the SEC is now an oversight body for the cryptocurrency space, especially as it relates to ICOs. It will now hold ICOs to the same tough standards that it does with stock sales.

As for coins already issued, the SEC is of the opinion that many are more like commodities than securities. This just means that another body will regulate them, not that they will *not* be regulated. The real story here is that this added credibility will be a big positive driver of growth of and trust in cryptocurrencies.

WARNING

An ICO is a fundraising channel similar to crowdfunding. Through ICOs, new blockchains and similar initiatives sell their underpinning crypto tokens in exchange for Bitcoin or other digital or fiat currency. As we've said, it's analogous to an Initial Public Offering (IPO) of shares of a company. ICOs exist in order to incentivise blockchain protocol development. $12 billion has been raised this way since 2014.

WARNING

Most ICOs raise money pre-product and that opens the door wide open to fraudsters. Participating in an ICO is one of the most speculative and risky things you can do in the crypto space, which is itself very speculative. We advise you stay away from this dark and dangerous corner of the Wild West.

The Canadian Securities Administrators (CSA) made a conclusion similar to the SEC's about ICOs and digital token offerings, deeming them be to securities. It also said exchanges that allow users to trade tokens or coins are formally considered to be marketplaces, just like the TSX. This means Canadian cryptos need to comply with Canadian government regulations and also fall within the scope of CSA oversight.

TMX GETS A PIECE OF THE CRYPTO ACTION

TMX Group operates stock exchanges including the Toronto Stock Exchange (TSX), TSX Venture Exchange, Montréal Exchange, and a handful of other specialty exchanges, depositories, and clearing houses. The Group's wholly owned subsidiary, Shorcan Digital Currency Network, or Shorcan DCN for short, launched a new cryptocurrency brokerage service (an exchange within an exchange) focused on Bitcoin and other more widely accepted and recognized digital currencies. BMO, already actively involved in Ripple, a growing and very popular cryptocurrency, is adding credibility to this ecosystem, and more specifically will provide Shorcan DCN with banking services to support the exchange's payment and settlement process. Shorcan DCN will also create new benchmarks for cryptocurrency (much like the S&P/TSX Composite Index is a benchmark for stocks).

This move represents institutionalization of the Canadian cryptocurrency ecosystem and digital coins as an asset class. It's yet another important driver of the continued growth of digital currencies. This development also represents a new revenue source for the TMX, and it is not alone. In the U.S., the Chicago Board Options Exchange and Chicago Mercantile Exchange launched derivatives that predicted the future price of digital currencies. It was likely these very derivatives that popped the cryptocurrency bubble that peaked at the beginning of 2018. This rapid over and under-correction in prices will eventually stabilize as the ecosystem continues to grow and cull blockchain firm winners from losers.

To get around some of these new, tougher rules, and to still be able to legitimately build great and innovative blockchain models, some blockchain firms are raising money under the SEC's crowdfunding rules. This lets these startups access a broader stakeholder group, as long as they stick to the SEC's $50 million cap and full disclosure and transparency exists. This is the trend at the time of this writing.

Yet another way to get around the rules without killing off the digital currency ecosystem is by focusing on where investors reside rather that where the company is based. In other words, some European and Asian startups are barring U.S. and Canadian investors from accessing their digital currencies through ICOs or even through crowdsourcing. Again, if this promotes the growth of the ecosystem, we say so be it.

Picking Winners: First Determine Value

This section is all about how to value cryptocurrency, and we have the answer for you: There *is* no valuation formula. It's just too early in the history of digital currency to create new and proven types of valuation formulas and approaches. Those currently used by business valuation and equity analysts for businesses and stocks, such as discounted cash flow or net asset value models, simply don't apply to digital currency. (Appendix B is all about ratios, and Chapter 16 has lots to say about screening for value, but it's all geared to the financial statements behind stocks and the companies that issue those stocks.)

The best we can offer is a key fundamental truth, and one that holds true for stocks as well as for Bitcoin and its digital currency brethren:

> The *value* is the meeting point of what a buyer is willing to pay and a seller is willing to let go.

Okay, you can throw the tomatoes at us now, but we still stand by this truth. It's a simple one, based on the fundamental law of supply and demand and driven by the dissemination of useful information.

The good news is that there is a second principle. This principle has less to do with *valuation* and more to do with *evaluation*. It deals less with the question of "how much do I pay?" and more with the question "should I buy?" Value is about more than dollar value. That would be shallow. In short, there are certain *drivers*, or root causes of changes in value. We're happy to discuss and explore these drivers. These factors are the pillars by which practical, understandable, and universally applicable formulas can be built and tested in the future as the cryptocurrency track record evolves. These drivers and factors are the basis of your evaluation of individual digital currencies.

Evaluating the factors that move digital currency prices

You've seen this in the movies. The artist is about to begin painting. The canvas is either blank or still in early stages of progress. She raises her hand with her thumb sticking up and squints. Why? For the same reason we ask you to kind of do the same thing as you read this section.

The artist first sizes up the landscape. Is the crypto market too volatile at the moment? What type of digital currency is the crypto investor interested in — a token or a coin? The artist also uses her thumb to block out distractions. Is the recent volatility due to hype, fear, or greed? Good digital currency investors block that nonsense out to a large extent. She also uses her thumb to line up images and objects that she is about to paint. Is the digital currency one of several like items so that a reasonable investment decision can be made among choices? Lastly, she uses her thumb to size up the object. Is the digital coin investor sizing up the coin's place and relative market cap position in the cryptocurrency market? Are the coin's uses more compelling than other competitors, even outside of the digital currency space?

This section presents you with some drivers of value that will help you evaluate digital currency. Then you'll be in a position to speculate and, dare we say, invest with some measure of risk management having been applied.

What moves Bitcoin's value, the crypto leader?

We'll use Bitcoin as the key example representative of the entire cryptocurrency space, even though that's not at all the case. The inherent value of Bitcoin is influenced by things like transaction execution speeds, number of transactions, the cost of mining a coin over time, the robustness of the open source code, and the support activity within the Bitcoin development community. Recall how much value Apple gets from its ecosystem of cheaply acquired but immensely popular and voluminous app providers.

Bitcoin's value is also powerfully driven by its *utility*, or in layperson's terms, what its platform can do for you. Add in a mix of scarcity and current and potential supply (much like a company can authorize and issue more stock any time it wishes, or reduce it), and demand and you start to build a recipe for value. For the really inventive valuators, the factors just mentioned can also be considered in a technical, marketing, and investor psychology context that includes historic price and volume trends, potential updates (like when Apple rolls out new iPhones), and even the extent to which pure and shameless speculation comes to bear.

What moves all individual cryptocurrencies?

Our objective is to build a foundation for deeper and more proven valuation models in the future. For now, we focus on applying common sense — something no one has a monopoly on.

Comparing any cryptocurrency with related corporations and their stocks

One way to conceptualize digital assets is to find analogies to companies. For example, Rich Uncle Pennybags from the board game Monopoly is definitely not sitting on a desk in a company headquarters with the name Bitcoin on it. In fact, Pennybags is running, just like many CEOs of companies whose businesses are about to be disrupted by the blockchain. But we digress.

Bitcoin, for example, is best compared to an online payment system like PayPal, except that this "company" or Bitcoin entity is decentralized (has no head office) and distributed (has many stakeholders of all economic statures and locations). Bitcoin also functions like an online bank (it's entirely digital and currency oriented), like a central bank (it's the 800-pound gorilla of cryptos), and like a government (it's overseen by an open source community with agreed-upon rules and protocols). Its board of directors is everyone contributing a copy of the blockchain. Bitcoin's imaginary finance department is represented by miners, and its investors are you and everyone else who holds even a tiny fraction of one Bitcoin. Bitcoin's imaginary dividends are called *forks*. Like a stock, when more people want it, it rises in value (market cap), and its brand affects its worldwide value. As Bitcoin innovates like Apple and becomes user-friendly like Google, its value increases.

If you view Bitcoin like a technology "company," then Bitcoin, Ethereum, and Ripple would probably be the FANG (Facebook, Amazon, Netflix, and Google) of the digital currency world today. Interestingly enough, Ripple actually *is* a company (with an associated coin) and is is seriously backed by Canada's Bank of Montreal (BMO). The more you're able to see the parallels between a cryptocurrency and a company, the more it is arguable that Bitcoin and its cousins are fit to create, store, and increase in value. But value is not a one-trick pony. Other factors need to be considered.

Utility

At the beginning of this chapter, we discuss the history of traditional currency and how it became more useful than trading, say, gold or beaver pelts. Bitcoin, like the

Loonie (which we think is a crazier name than Bitcoin and many other cryptocurrencies, by the way) is valuable because it's useful as a currency (has utility), even though it doesn't exactly fit that definition in the strictest sense. The digital record book (the blockchain) lets us account for transactions and balances, and therefore Bitcoin has added utility here as well. Worldwide acceptance and recognition of Bitcoin as a global payment system saves time and high foreign exchange fees, further enhancing its utility.

Bitcoin's platform may not be the fastest, but the attributes we just mentioned as well as first-mover advantage help it preserve value. The widely accepted protocols and software that underpin Bitcoin make it the Microsoft-ish operating system of the digital currency world. Utility begets value, and if digital currencies were only valued through utility, then Ripple would be the leader for its fast payment processing times; Bitcoin for its currency flavour and universal acceptance; and Ethereum for overall operating system power and robustness of design.

Companies have lots of assets that have tremendous *value in use*, in much the same way that dirty but working heavy machinery used in extracting minerals in gravel pits creates value if you find minerals. Those rusty assets beget sales of minerals and receipt of cash inflows, and those cash flows in turn get discounted by bean counters in a valuation model for companies called *discounted cash flow*. In the same way, Bitcoin has a value in use, so there is a value driven by utility. It's just that we don't yet know how to best attribute a specific value to Bitcoin solely based on its use.

Business case or White Paper

A *White Paper* in the digital currency ecosystem is synonymous with a prospectus for companies about to issue stock in an IPO. A *prospectus* is essentially a business case outlining the five Ws of the stock offering. The White Paper answers the same questions but for digital coins and tokens, often just prior to a launch of a new currency via an ICO. A White Paper outlines and describes everything you need to know about the currency before investing in an ICO, trading it on an exchange post-IPO, or using it to purchase something else (like bartering).

Specifically, a White Paper includes the commercial potential and intended use, as well as technical and financial details, hopefully in a language that can be easily understood by everyone. A White Paper answers questions like "what does the project or coin do?" As Warren Buffet says, if you don't understand the company, don't buy its stock. A strong White Paper explains what the best use of the token or coin will be. The original Bitcoin White Paper represents a leading practice to refer to on how a succinct, understandable, and user-friendly business case should be written. Other matters addressed by a White Paper include why the whole world needs this in the first place, and why it's implemented on the blockchain.

WARNING

Many of the ICOs we're witnessing are either just plain old web applications that can easily be hosted on a server, or they're unscrupulous, failing businesses that are trying to cash in on the blockchain trend to obtain hype-based access to capital. Use your judgement when evaluating a White Paper and an ICO.

Demand and supply

In our discussion about tokens and coins in this chapter, we mention how some digital currencies operate on different blockchains. For instance, some currencies use Bitcoin, others use Ethereum, and still others use their own. As time passes, one blockchain will emerge as the superhighway, leaving the others as dusty side roads. To the extent that the coin you invest in is part of the superhighway, it will be expected to enjoy greater demand by default. Of course, the other factors we mention in this section still count.

Lest we forget the golden rule of economics, the price or value of anything is largely driven by supply. That's why diamonds are forever. Cryptos for the most part (Ripple is one of a few exceptions) have limited supply, and that's a key driver of value. Just keep in mind that market capitalization is really what you need to look at when you attribute value to digital currency. Coinmarketcap.com shows the maximum supply for all digital currencies.

Coin mining costs

Keeping the blockchain running costs money. Though that cost is distributed and spread across many computers and their owners, it can begin to add up. Electricity alone is one of the biggest expense items, especially where it's used to run powerful mining farms (businesses like Hashchain Technology) that are dedicated to mining a certain type of digital currency, such as Bitcoin and Dash. In addition, solving complex encrypted problems and securing and recording transactions on the blockchain (record book) take time and drive up cost. Seek out lower-cost endeavours.

Effort to develop, implement, and maintain

Getting a specific coin to market takes a lot of up-front software research and development cost and time. Once the coin is released into the market through an ICO, it takes effort and money to secure the record book and validate transactions. Maintaining the coin's architecture and functionality also takes time and costs money. If you assume that work creates value, then that's a factor in attributing some value to the currency. Ripple, a payments processor geared to businesses, and Stellar, doing the same thing but focusing on individuals, operate in a manner that takes less work to secure than Bitcoin does. Using a company as an example, that's like saying that those two cryptocurrencies have higher *contribution margins* (less costs eating away at revenues).

Scalability

Cryptocurrency is essentially software that can be updated and made more useful, more powerful, faster, and easier to access and use. A given digital coin's *architecture* (the software program and design) can be upgraded and, along with faster computers and a faster Internet, can make the coin's or token's functionality more efficient, effective, and economical to use. To the extent that the coin is scalable in this way, value is added.

Community discussion boards

As mentioned, Coinmarketcap.com (Figure 19-1) is the preeminent cryptocurrency dashboard that will provide you with frequently updated price, chart, volume, market cap and other information, all at a glance. Although we are not fans of discussion boards, other than for entertainment value, the issues discussed are often relevant. Sometimes you even find useful and perhaps even very important information in these chat rooms. The forums have the benefit of different perspectives, but it's the Wild West in there, and it's up to you to separate the trolls from the knowledgeable contributors.

FIGURE 19-1:
Coinmarketcap.
com.

Courtesy of Coinmarketcap.com

To access the message boards at www.coinmarketcap.com, click any of the listed currencies. You'll see a menu of items including icons for Message Board and/or Chat (see Figure 19-2).

FIGURE 19-2: Ethereum charts and links on Coinmarketcap. com.

You can also check out Cointelegraph.com, a news site focusing on Bitcoin. Cryptocoinsnews.com boasts decent news blogs about Bitcoin and other digital currencies. Coindesk.com is another behemoth of digital currency news. All these other sites will often have special news and deep technical discussion about the specific coins you're looking at, in addition to their bigger picture reporting of crypto news.

Speculation

Today, *speculation* can be considered to be the primary factor that gives cryptocurrency value. Canadians stock investors are familiar with this, especially in the speculative extractive industries of precious metals and oil and gas exploration. Speculation begets price movement. Is the coin mentioned in mainstream news? Is it about to be listed on yet another digital exchange? Is it supported by or associated with a blue chip company? Is it accepted more widely each week?

During the dot-com age decades ago, speculation was king. Today, billion-dollar contracts are transacted digitally, and companies like Amazon, Facebook, and Alphabet have higher market caps than many small countries. Of course, there will be bubbles, but those are just growing pains and a separation of pretenders from the real thing.

Compare market capitalizations

Coinmarketcap.com also lets you compare raw market caps from coin to coin, or token to token. You can even compare the price movement between coins on its chart tool. You can be really creative and compare the coins to the market caps of companies on the stock market that do similar things and operate in similar industries. For instance, you can compare Ripple to Paypal, and Stellar to Western Union. From this, like the painter raising her thumb, you can get perspective and a sense of potential for wider adoption and ultimately a larger market cap and price.

TIP

While you're at Coinmarketcap.com, pull up a chart and analyze the price trends. Analyzing price movements can help you make decisions, much like we discuss in Chapter 10 about technical analysis.

First-mover advantage

Bitcoin, Ethereum, and Ripple are first movers, much like Amazon was a first mover in the dot-com era. First movers enjoy tremendous advantage. This is a significant value driver.

What will enhance digital currency adoption and move crypto markets?

In the stock market, it's always best to invest in an individual stock when the entire market generally moves up as well. It's no different with cryptocurrency. Not long ago, we witnessed a massive but short-lived bull market in digital currency prices, where Bitcoin hovered around $20,000 U.S.! Early adopters of digital currency definitely benefitted. What drove this? Will a bull market return? Here are a number of big picture trends to watch for:

>> **Nasdaq exchange and crypto listings:** At the time of this writing Nasdaq formally announced that it is "open to launching a cryptocurrency exchange in the future as the regulatory environment evolves." When this happens, or even if individual high-profile companies behind digital currencies like Ripple list on mainstream exchanges, the digital currency ecosystem will move higher in total market capitalization.

- » **Faster transaction times for key digital currencies:** Bitcoin will only be able to call itself a "full on" digital currency as opposed to a store of value once it sports a faster transaction time. Currently, it behaves more like a cheque you take to and cash at a bank. Ethereum and Ripple are positioning themselves as having vastly faster transaction times — measured in seconds. In our world of instant information access and gratification, this is a key success factor. If in the future you can pay for your Starbucks coffee in Ripple, you won't want to see your hot coffee turn cold because of long transaction clearance times. No company like Starbucks or even Joe's Corner Store would tolerate losing customers due to long processing times.

- » **Increased acceptance of alternative coins:** By now, many people know about the top ten coins by market capitalization. They also hear about Bitcoin and the blockchain on a daily basis in the news. Unfortunately, the news is mostly negative or skeptical. This was also the case in the mid-1990s when the Internet broke out into the mainstream. It was largely mocked. But as with the Internet, expect public and corporate acceptance of digital currency to grow. When this happens, prices will stabilize and grow.

- » **Ease of conversion to fiat currency:** As we explained earlier, not all exchanges allow you to transact with Canadian dollar fiat currency. This is a problem as it creates complexity and inconvenience. Just like banks are making it easier each year to transact online with bill payments and enquiries, the crypto ecosystem must find ways to be more intuitive and convenient to use. The best place to start is by making it easy to deposit and withdraw fiat currency to and from digital exchanges.

- » **Positive news:** In the news world, slow news days tend to be filled with disaster stories about cryptocurrency fraud and poor oversight. The extent of this type of news topic pales in comparison to the number of white collar crimes perpetrated on a daily basis. Positive news will come in both higher frequency and with positive stories about creative and innovative ways that digital currency and the blockchain are being used.

- » **Negative news about banks and fiat currencies:** The next time you see a bank failure or bailout, or news about a fiat currency crashing, you can almost be certain that the digital currency market will behave a bit like a safe haven. In fact, it's beginning to behave like "digital" gold, since gold (in ingots or as certificates) has always been considered to be a safe store of value during market turbulence.

- » **More regulatory clarity:** There are over four regulators in the U.S. alone trying to figure out who has lead oversight. If cryptocurrencies are a security, then the Securities and Exchange Commission (SEC) has oversight authority. If digital currencies are deemed to be a commodity, as Bitcoin and Ethereum have recently been declared by the SEC, then there is less SEC regulation, which is considered a positive (less interference) by individual digital currencies. We believe that oversight, by whatever regulatory body, is a positive for the entire market. As for the SEC, it is currently focusing less on individual coins and more on how they receive funding and are marketed.

>> **Investor psychology:** No one wants to miss out on a bull stock market. It's no different with digital currency, and we witnessed this herd mentality in late 2017 and early 2018. Investor psychology cannot be underestimated in influence, and it's an indicator you need to be sensitive to.

Final thoughts on value and picking the right digital currency

Cryptos don't just have value because we agree on a price today. They have the potential to possess fundamental value. This section laid out the building blocks by which value can be attributed in an accretive and reasoned way. To be sure, there is still no formula, but there is an approach. There is no value, but there is evaluation. Is the coin accepted and popular? Is it well-understood? Does it have a solid development history backed by good people and an understandable White Paper? Is the currency trusted? Does it boast an active community of followers on Reddit or a specialized bulletin or message board? Is the coin truly a store of value and medium of exchange that is scarce? If so, it will enjoy a higher value than any digital currency that does not have enough of these attributes.

Holding Your Crypto Assets in a Wallet

With broker and trading exchanges, as mentioned, once you execute a trade for a digital currency, you can simply leave it at the exchange. That's what most of the clients of Mt. Gox, a Tokyo-based Bitcoin exchange did a few years ago. That was one of the world's largest exchanges at the time, and you guessed it — it was hacked. The era of digital wallets was born.

REMEMBER

A digital cryptocurrency *wallet* stores the public and private keys or addresses (discussed earlier in this chapter) that enable digital currencies to be spent or received. A public key, for example, makes it easy for others to send digital currency into your digital wallet. (In fact, the wallet doesn't even have to be digital — more on that in a moment.)

Wallets provide a one-stop, one-spot repository for you to keep track of all your public and private addresses, and therefore your digital currency. Because these addresses are essentially anonymous, you can utilize as many addresses as you want. Although that's a good way to spread your risk of losing your wallet forever, managing multiple wallets (think accounts) can get quite tedious. This is all exacerbated by the fact that some currencies demand their own wallets and won't let other coins into that wallet. It's like the Microsoft–Apple compatibility wars of the 1990s. Wallets can be quite proprietary in nature. On the brighter side, a backup of a wallet is possible, and it helps you prevent losing your assets.

There are several types of wallets to consider. They differ in the ways they let you store and access your digital currency. Wallets can be broken down into three categories: software, hardware, and paper. We'll look at software wallets first, which can be further split into desktop, online, and mobile wallets.

Software wallets: Desktop, online, and mobile

To store digital currencies, you have the following three software wallets to choose from (or combine):

>> **Desktop:** These wallets are downloaded and installed on your desktop computer or laptop. They are only accessible from that device. These wallets provide one of the highest levels of security from hackers, although they're not *fully* hack-proof. If you leave your computer passwords unattended and visible, or if your computing device downloads a virus, your funds may be stolen or lost.

>> **Online:** If you have an online Gmail or Yahoo! email account, your emails are stored in the cloud, meaning on some server somewhere. Online wallets also operate and reside in a similar cloud environment. The convenience is that the account and wallet can be accessed from any computing device in any location — you can trade cryptocurrency while you're on vacation. The downside is that your private keys are vulnerable to online third-party breaches because they're held by a third party, which if it's not careful with its security controls, can cause you to lose your currency through denial of access attacks and theft.

>> **Mobile:** Mobile wallets operate as phone apps. They're useful because they're portable. These wallets are simpler to use than desktop or online wallets because of their limited size. Just make sure you don't lose your phone, especially if the personal data in it isn't backed up.

Hardware and paper wallets

Hardware wallets store your private keys on a hardware device like a USB. Although hardware wallets are digital in nature, just like software wallets, a distinguishing feature is that with a hardware wallet, transactions you made online are stored offline. That in itself adds a measure of extra security. Also, like software wallets, hardware wallets can support multiple (though not all) digital currencies. When you're ready to transact, you just plug in your hardware wallet device to a computer, enter your PIN code, send or receive currency, and confirm the transaction.

Paper wallets are easy to use and provide a tremendous level of security. By *paper wallet*, we mean a physical, handwritten copy or computer printout of your public and private keys. This can also refer to an app that securely and anonymously generates a pair of keys, which are then printed out. The transfer of Bitcoin or any other digital currency into your paper wallet is done through the transfer of digital funds from your software wallet (described in the preceding section) to the public address shown on your paper wallet. To withdraw digital currency, you transfer funds from your paper wallet to your software wallet, a process called *sweeping*, which prevents swiping. Sweeping is either performed manually by keying in your private keys or by scanning the QR code on the paper wallet. A QR code, or Quick Response code, is the trademark name for an information-rich type of matrix or barcode. Of course, the transactions themselves still get recorded on the blockchain.

Multicurrency wallets

Many alternative currencies, or altcoins, are not supported by a broker exchange, trading exchange, or any other exchange from the standpoint of being able to choose to leave your coins there. Most high-profile exchanges, the safer ones usually, only allow trading in better-known altcoins. For the rest of the altcoins, you have no choice and will have to select a wallet, likely a multicurrency wallet.

A *multicurrency* wallet does exactly what it sounds like — it holds an assortment of select alternative currencies. Though the selection isn't endless, you do get value for money with multicurrency wallets because they're convenient, secure, and generally well supported. They also come in the classic categories of desktop, online, and mobile.

Desktop multicurrency wallets

Jaxx is a multiplatform and multicurrency wallet that installs on your desktop computer or smartphone. Jaxx works on the Windows, Mac, Linux, Android, and iOS platforms. It supports about 15 cryptocurrencies. Exodus is another multicurrency desktop wallet that allows you to exchange coins within the wallet itself through its proprietary exchange.

Online multicurrency wallets

Coinbase is a very large and well-known exchange that provides an online platform, not just for trading digital currency, but also for storing your digital currency. (We discuss exchanges that provide this capability earlier in this chapter.) In Canada, Coinsquare is a large equivalent to Coinbase and provides storage capacity as well. You can always leave your coins behind at the exchange if you're comfortable with its advertised security posture. However, we don't recommend keeping all of it there.

Other online multicurrency wallets include Copay, a cloud-based and secured Bitcoin wallet. GreenAddress likewise advertises high online security from hacking and supports multiple currencies. Cryptonator is yet another online cryptocurrency wallet you may want to check out.

Mobile wallets

Popular mobile wallets for iOS that can be used on your iPhone or iPad include Bread, Jaxx, Xapo, and Mycelium. All are very functional wallets that work with your smartphone and support a wide range of different cryptocurrencies.

A very popular mobile-only wallet for Android is Coinomi, which supports over 200 different digital currencies operating on various blockchains. Other mobile wallets for Android include Airbitz, GreenAddress, Celery, Blockchain Wallet, Ledger Nano S, and MyEtherWallet. Mycelium and Bread also support Android.

Will that be hot or cold?

You can also think of wallets as hot or cold. *Hot* wallets are connected online to the Internet; cold wallets are not. Both are designed for different purposes, so many people have both. Hot wallets are like checking accounts; cold wallets are more like savings accounts. You would want to hold a smaller amount of digital currency in a hot wallet so you can conveniently buy things or perform quick but small trades. But leading storage practices suggest that you should keep the majority of your digital currency in a cold wallet.

Another leading practice is to receive money through your hot wallet first, as this is the least prone to transfer errors. Digital exchanges like Canada's Coinsquare, Poloniex, Kraken, and Bittrex are considered to be hot wallets, because your funds are held in their facilities and on their servers. It's acceptable to hold some portion of your digital currency in these more established companies.

A cold wallet, remember, is a hardware wallet that is really just a physical device that's kept offline but can be connected to a computer and online as needed. There are two popular brands: the Trezor and Ledger Nano S.

Hot wallets are easier to use, access, and set up. They tend to accept more tokens. Cold storage is more secure but handles fewer types of digital currencies — and the devices cost you money, as USB sticks cost you money. Check out Trezor and Ledger Nano S to see which coins are supported.

TIP

Some wallets, like Copay and Armory, enable you to execute transactions with multiple signatures. They require the permission of another user or users before a transaction can be executed.

Brain wallet

A *brain wallet* asks you to memorize a mnemonic recovery phrase. Essentially, the digital currency can be considered to be held in your memory. However, if you forget the recovery phrase, the digital coins *are lost forever*. A brain wallet is created by brain wallet software that generates a mnemonic seed you're asked to memorize.

WARNING

Use rigorous security measures with any of the wallets described in this chapter. Regardless of which wallet you use, losing your private keys will expose you to a loss of your digital currency. There is no way to recover coins lost to hackers. Be careful out there.

Final Thoughts

We want to emphasize once again that investing in Bitcoin and other cryptocurrencies, at this stage in their development, is a form of pure speculation. Speculation is separate and distinct from investing, the latter being the fundamental and dominant theme of this book. Digital currencies remain one of the riskiest and most speculative areas you can invest in. While they share similarities with stocks and exchange-traded funds, they are neither of those.

Our overall advice to you is to invest only a small amount of money; or just watch cryptocurrencies and simply be aware of them for now. Any investment should represent an amount you can afford to lose. They should represent a small speculative position in an aggressive portfolio. They are not conducive to conservative, mildly aggressive, or typical portfolios. Invest only money you are prepared to lose (or win big). Digital currencies should not be invested in by novices or the faint of heart.

A picture truly is worth a thousand words to support our advice to you. Take particular note of the speculative bubble that has occurred in cryptocurrencies, as shown in Figure 19-3.

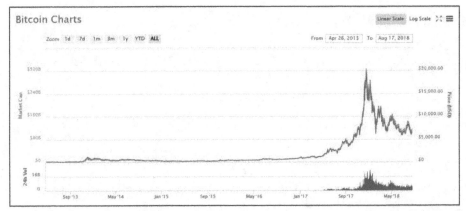

Courtesy of Coinmarketcap.com

FIGURE 19-3: Bitcoin chart courtesy of Coinmarketcap. com.

WARNING

Finally, consider the security challenges associated with digital currencies. If you're not careful and don't follow our advice about security and wallets throughout this chapter, you can inadvertently delete or misplace your Bitcoins or other cryptocurrencies as they are virtual, not physical in nature. Once a cryptocurrency digital file is lost, it is gone forever. Being secure also means being watchful for hacking. Very little of value is safe on the internet. Just ask banks, credit card companies, and even the Pentagon, who have all been hacked despite their strong security postures.

Chapter **20**

Skullduggery: Looking at Insider Activity

I magine that you're boarding a cruise ship, ready to enjoy a hard-earned vacation. As you merrily walk up the plank, you notice that the ship's captain and crew are charging out of the vessel, flailing their arms, and screaming at the top of their lungs. Some are even jumping into the water below. Pop quiz: Would you get on that ship? You get double credit if you can also explain why (or why not).

What does this scenario have to do with stock investing? Plenty. The behaviour of the people running the boat gives you important clues about the near-term prospects for the boat. Similarly, the actions of company insiders can provide important clues into the near-term prospects for their company.

Company insiders are key managers or investors in the company. Insiders include the president of the company, chief financial officer, chief risk officer, or other managing executive. An insider can also be someone who owns a large stake in the company or someone on the board of directors. In any case, insiders usually have a great bird's-eye view of what's going on with the company and a good idea of how well (or how poorly) the company is doing.

In this chapter, we describe different kinds of insider activities, such as insider buying, insider selling, corporate stock buybacks, and stock splits. We also show you how to keep track of these activities with the help of a few resources.

REMEMBER

Keep tabs on what insiders are doing, because their buy/sell transactions tend to have a strong correlation to the near-term movement of their company's stock. However, don't buy or sell stock only because you heard that some insider did. Use the information on insider trading to confirm your own good sense in buying or selling stock. Insider trading sometimes can be a great precursor to a significant move that you can profit from if you know what to look for. Many shrewd investors have made their profits (or avoided losses) by tracking the stock trading activity of insiders.

Tracking U.S. Insider Trading

Fortunately, we live in an age of disclosure and the Internet. Insiders who buy or sell stock in American companies must file reports that document their trading activity with the U.S. Securities and Exchange Commission (SEC), which makes the documents available to the public. You can view these documents on the SEC's website, which maintains a filings database (www.sec.gov). Just click "Filings." Some of the most useful documents you can view there include the following:

>> **Form 3:** This form is the initial statement that insiders provide. They must file Form 3 within ten days of obtaining insider status. An insider files this report even if he hasn't made a purchase yet; the report establishes the insider's status.

>> **Form 4:** This document shows the insider's activity, such as a change in the insider's position as a stockholder, how many shares the person bought and sold, or other relevant changes. Any activity in a particular month must be reported on Form 4 by the tenth day of the following month.

>> **Form 5:** This annual report covers transactions that are small and not required on Form 4, such as minor, internal transfers of stock.

>> **Form 144:** This form serves as the public declaration by an insider of the intention to sell restricted stock — stock that the insider was awarded, or received from the company as compensation, or bought as a term of employment. Insiders must hold restricted stock for at least one year before they can sell it. After an insider decides to sell, she files Form 144 and then must sell within 90 days or submit a new Form 144. The insider must file the form on or before the stock's sale date. When the sale is finalized, the insider is then required to file Form 4.

TIP

Companies are required to make public the documents that track their trading activity. The SEC's website offers limited access to these documents, but for greater access, check out one of the many websites that report insider trading data, such as www.marketwatch.com and www.bloomberg.com.

TECHNICAL STUFF

The SEC has enacted the short-swing profit rule to protect the investing public. This rule prevents insiders from quickly buying the stock that they just sold at a profit. The insider must wait at least six months before buying it again. The SEC created this rule to prevent insiders from using their privileged knowledge to make an unfair profit quickly, before the investing public can react. The rule also applies if an insider sells stock — he can't sell it at a higher price within a six-month period.

Checking Out Canadian Insider Trading

Canadian insider trading information isn't generated in the same way that you see in the States. Insiders in the U.S. complete long, detailed forms. In Canada, we have just an electronic listing, or table, of key insider trading information:

>> Who traded shares?

>> What is the person's relationship to the company?

>> How many shares were traded, and at what price?

>> When did the trades occur?

>> Where does the person reside?

The answers to these questions can be readily accessed — but the most important question isn't even asked: Why? Why did the insider sell the shares? Although no way exists for you to know for sure, the fact that the insider sold, especially if it was lots of shares, is something you need to be alert to. We discuss questions such as these in more detail later in this chapter.

You can access the public documents of companies listed on a Canadian exchange at the System for Electronic Disclosure by Insiders (SEDI) website at www.sedi.ca. This site is maintained by the Canadian Securities Administrators, a self-regulatory body. Click the Help icon to allow you to get more comfortable using the more advanced features of this useful online tool.

Here's a primer on how you launch a basic query from the SEDI website:

1. **Click the Access Public Filings link.**

   A new screen appears.

2. **Click the View Summary Reports link.**

   You are taken to a new page with specific search instructions listed at the top. Near the bottom of the same page, you are given four options for insider trading searches:

   - Insider transaction detail filters: These allow you to refine your search for even more precise results.

   - Issuer report history: The system provides a list and description of events (like annual meetings and special votes for mergers, new board members, and so on) for a Canadian company.

   - Insider information by issuer: This search lists all insiders and their holdings.

   - Weekly summary: This option provides you with all recent insider trading information for a Canadian company or issuer (of stock).

TIP

We recommend that you select the bread-and-butter weekly summary option. The other three options require you to input more detailed criteria pertaining to insider trade activity.

You can download reports (in PDF file format) for one-, two-, and three-week periods. These insider activity summaries are presented alphabetically by company name.

TIP

In SEDI, you can also click the View Insider Information link to search by insider, or click the View Issuer Information link to view the details of the insiders of a stock issuer, or company.

Looking at Insider Transactions

The classic phrase "Actions speak louder than words" was probably coined for insider trading. Insiders are in the know, and keeping a watchful eye on their transactions — both buying and selling their company's stock — can provide you with useful investing information. But insider buying and insider selling can be as different as day and night; insider buying is simple, while insider selling can be complicated. In the following sections, we present both sides of insider trading.

Breaking down insider buying

Insider buying is usually an unambiguous signal about how an insider feels about his company. After all, the primary reason that all investors buy stock is that they expect it to do well. If one insider is buying stock, that's generally not a monumental event. But if several or more insiders are buying, those purchases should certainly catch your attention.

Insider buying is generally a positive omen and beneficial for the stock's price. Also, when insiders buy stock, less stock is available to the public. If the investing public meets this decreased supply with increased demand, the stock price rises. Keep these factors in mind when analyzing insider buying:

>> **Identify who's buying the stock.** The CEO is buying 5,000 shares. Is that reason enough for you to jump in? Maybe. After all, the CEO certainly knows how well the company is doing. But what if that CEO is just starting her new position? What if before this purchase she had no stock in the company at all? Maybe the stock is part of her employment package, offered to encourage her to align her interests with shareholders (that is, to motivate her to do her best to raise stock prices).

REMEMBER

The fact that a new company executive is making her first stock purchase isn't as strong a signal urging you to buy as the fact that a long-time CEO is doubling her holdings. Also, if large numbers of insiders are buying, that sends a stronger signal than if a single insider is buying.

>> **See how much is being bought.** In the preceding example, the CEO bought 5,000 shares, which is a lot of stock no matter how you count it. But is it enough for you to base an investment decision on? Maybe, but a closer look may reveal more. If she already owned 1 million shares at the time of the purchase, then buying 5,000 additional shares wouldn't be such an exciting indicator of a pending stock rise. In this case, 5,000 shares is a small incremental move that doesn't offer much to get excited about.

However, what if this particular insider has owned only 5,000 shares for the past three years and is now buying 1 million shares? Now that should arouse your interest! Usually, a massive purchase tells you that particular insider has strong feelings about the company's prospects and that she's making a huge increase in her share of stock ownership. Still, a purchase of 1 million shares by the CEO may not be as strong a signal as ten insiders buying 100,000 shares each. Again, if only one person is buying, that may or may not be a strong indication of an impending rise. However, if lots of different people are buying, consider it a fantastic indication.

An insider purchase of any kind is a positive sign, but it's always more significant when a greater number of insiders are making purchases. "The more the merrier!" is a good rule for judging insider buying. All these individuals have their own, unique perspectives on the company and its prospects. Mass buying indicates mass optimism for the company's future. If the treasurer, the president, the vice president of sales, and several other key players are putting their wealth on the line and investing it in a company they know intimately, that's a good sign for your stock investment as well.

>> **Notice the timing of the purchase.** The timing of insider stock purchases is important as well. If we tell you that five insiders bought stock at various points last year, you may say, "Hmm." But if we tell you that all five people bought substantial chunks of stock at the same time and right before earnings season, that should make you say, "HMMMMM!"

Picking up tips from insider selling

Insider stock buying is rarely negative — it either bodes well for the stock or is a neutral event at worst. But how about insider selling? When an insider sells his stock, the event can be either neutral or negative. Insider selling is usually a little tougher than insider buying to figure out, because insiders may have many different motivations to sell stock that have nothing to do with the company's future prospects. Just because the president of the company is selling 5,000 shares from his personal portfolio doesn't necessarily mean you should sell, too.

Insiders may sell their stock for a couple reasons: They may think that the company won't be doing well in the near future — a negative sign for you — or they may simply need the money for a variety of personal reasons that have nothing to do with the company's potential. Some typical reasons why insiders may sell stock include the following:

>> **To diversify their holdings:** If an insider's portfolio is heavily weighted with one company's stock, a financial advisor may suggest that she balance her portfolio by selling some of that company's stock and purchasing other securities.

>> **To finance personal emergencies:** Sometimes an insider needs money for personal medical, legal, or family reasons.

>> **To buy a home or make another major purchase:** An insider may need the money to make a down payment, or perhaps to buy something outright without having to take out a loan.

REMEMBER

How do you find out about the details regarding insider stock selling? Although insiders must report their pertinent stock sales and purchases to the SEC or through SEDI, the information isn't always revealing. As a general rule, consider the following questions when analyzing insider selling:

>> **How many insiders are selling?** If only one insider is selling, that single transaction doesn't give you enough information to act on. However, if many insiders are selling, you should see a red flag. Check out any news or information that's currently available by going to websites such as www.marketwatch.com, www.sec.gov, www.sedi.ca, and ca.finance.yahoo.com (and other sources listed in Appendix A).

>> **Are the sales showing a pattern or unusual activity?** If one insider sold some stock last month, that sale alone isn't that significant an event. However, if ten insiders have each made multiple sales in the past few months, those sales are cause for concern. See whether any new developments at the company are potentially negative. If massive insider selling has recently occurred and you don't know why, consider putting a stop-loss order on your stock immediately. We cover stop-loss orders more fully in Chapter 17.

>> **How much stock is being sold?** If a CEO sells 5,000 shares of stock but still retains 100,000 shares, that's not a big deal. But if the CEO sells all or most of his holdings, that's a possible negative. Check to see whether other company executives have also sold stock.

>> **Do outside events or analyst reports seem coincidental with the sale of the stock?** Sometimes, an influential analyst may issue a report warning about a company's prospects. If the company's management pooh-poohs the report but most of them are bailing out anyway (selling their stock), you may want to do the same. Frequently, when insiders know that damaging information is forthcoming, they sell the stock before it takes a dip.

Similarly, if the company's management issues positive public statements or reports that contradict their own behaviour (they're selling their stock holdings), the SEC may investigate to see whether the company is doing anything that may require a penalty (the SEC regularly tracks insider sales). Unfortunately, in Canada, provincial securities regulators are relatively lax in oversight and enforcement, so be a bit more careful with Canadian listings in the context of corporate skullduggery.

Considering Corporate Stock Buybacks

When you read the financial pages or watch the financial shows on TV, you sometimes hear that a company is buying its own stock. The announcement may be something like, "SuperBucks Corp. has announced that it will spend $2 billion dollars to buy back its own stock." Why would a company do that, and what does that mean to you if you own the stock or are considering buying it?

When companies buy back their own stock, they're generally indicating that they believe their stock is undervalued and that it has the potential to rise. If a company shows strong fundamentals (for example, a good financial condition and increasing sales and earnings; refer to Chapter 11 for details about accounting) and it's buying more of its own stock, it's worth investigating — it may make a great addition to your portfolio.

Just because a company announces a stock buyback doesn't always mean that one will happen. The announcement itself is meant to stir interest in the stock and cause the price to rise. The stock buyback may be only an opportunity for insiders to sell stock, or it may be needed for executive compensation — recruiting and retaining competent management are positive uses of money.

The following sections present some common reasons a company may buy back its shares from investors, as well as some ideas on the negative effects of stock buybacks.

WARNING

If you see that a company is buying back its stock while most of the insiders are selling their personal shares, that's not a good sign. It may not necessarily be a bad sign, but it's not a positive sign. Play it safe and invest elsewhere.

Understanding why a company buys back shares

You bought this book because you're looking at buying stocks, but individuals aren't alone in the stock-buying universe. No, we don't just mean that exchange-traded funds, pensions, and other entities are buyers; we mean the companies behind the stocks are buyers (and sellers), too. Why would a public company buy stock — especially its own?

Boosting earnings per share

By simply buying back its own shares from stockholders, a company can increase its earnings per share without actually earning extra money (see Chapter 11 and Appendix B for more on earnings per share). Sound like a magician's trick? Well, it is, kind of. A corporate stock buyback is a financial sleight of hand that investors should be aware of. Here's how it works: Noware Earnings, Inc. (NEI), has 10 million shares outstanding, and it's expected to net earnings of $10 million for the fourth quarter. NEI's earnings per share (EPS) would be $1 per share. So far, so good. But what happens if NEI buys 2 million of its own shares? Total shares outstanding shrink to 8 million. The new EPS becomes $1.25 — the stock buyback artificially boosts the earnings per share by 25 percent!

REMEMBER

The important point to keep in mind about stock buybacks is that actual company earnings don't change — no fundamental changes occur in company management or operations — so the increase in EPS can be misleading. But the marketplace can be obsessive about earnings, and because earnings are the lifeblood of any company, an earnings boost, even if it's cosmetic, can also boost the stock price.

If you watch a company's price-to-earnings ratio (refer to Chapter 11), you know that increased earnings usually mean an eventual increase in the stock price. Additionally, a stock buyback affects supply and demand. With less available stock in the market, demand necessarily sends the stock price upward.

REMEMBER

Whenever a company makes a major purchase, such as buying back its own stock, think about how the company is paying for it and whether it seems like a good use of the company's purchasing power. In general, companies buy their stock for the same reasons any investor buys stock — they believe that the stock is a good investment and will appreciate in time. Companies generally pay for a stock buyback in one of two basic ways: funds from operations or borrowed money. Both methods have a downside. For more details, see the section "Exploring the downside of buybacks," later in this chapter.

Beating back a takeover bid

Suppose you read in the financial pages that Company X is doing a hostile takeover of Company Z. A hostile takeover doesn't mean that Company X sends storm troopers armed with mace to Company Z's headquarters to trounce its management. All a hostile takeover means is that X wants to buy enough shares of Z's stock to effectively control Z (and Z is unhappy about being owned or controlled by X). Because buying and selling stock happens in a public market or exchange, companies can buy each other's stock. Sometimes, the target company prefers not to be acquired, in which case it may buy back shares of its own stock to give it a measure of protection against unwanted moves by interested companies.

REMEMBER

Takeover concerns generally prompt interest in the investing public, driving the stock price upward and benefiting current stockholders.

Exploring the downside of buybacks

As beneficial as stock buybacks can be, they have to be paid for, and this expense has consequences. When a company uses funds from operations for the stock buyback, less money is available for other activities, such as upgrading technology, making improvements, or doing research and development. A company faces even greater dangers when it uses debt to finance a stock buyback. If the company uses borrowed funds, not only does it have less borrowing power for other uses, but it also has to pay back the borrowed funds with interest, thus lowering earnings figures.

REMEMBER

In general, any misuse of money, such as using debt to buy back stock, affects a company's ability to grow its sales and earnings — two measures that need to maintain upward mobility to keep stock prices rising.

Say that Noware Earnings, Inc. (NEI), typically pays an annual dividend of 25 cents per share of stock and wants to buy back shares, which are currently at $10 each, with borrowed money with a 9 percent interest rate. If NEI buys back 2 million shares, it won't have to pay out $500,000 in dividends (2 million × 25 cents). That's money saved. However, NEI has to pay interest on the $20 million it borrowed ($10 per share × 2 million shares) to buy back the shares. The interest totals $1.8 million (9 percent of $20 million), and the net result from this rudimentary example is that NEI sees an outflow of $1.3 million (the difference between the interest paid out and the dividends savings).

Using debt to finance a stock buyback needs to make economic sense — it needs to strengthen the company's financial position and be done preferably in a low-interest rate environment like we have today. Perhaps NEI could have used the stock buyback money toward a better purpose, such as modernizing equipment or paying for a new marketing campaign. Because debt interest ultimately decreases earnings, companies must be careful when using debt to buy back their stock.

Stock Splits: Nothing to Go Bananas Over

Frequently, management teams decide to do a stock split. A stock split is the exchange of existing shares of stock for new shares from the same company. Stock splits don't increase or decrease the company's capitalization; they just change the number of shares available in the market and the per-share price.

Typically, a company may announce that it's doing a 2-for-1 stock split. For example, a company may have 10 million shares outstanding, with a market price of $40 each. In a 2-for-1 split, the company then has 20 million shares (the share total doubles), but the market price is adjusted to $20 (the share price is halved). Companies do other splits, such as a 3-for-2 or 4-for-1, but 2-for-1 is the most common split.

The following sections present the two basic types of splits: ordinary stock splits and reverse stock splits.

TIP

Qualifying for a stock split is similar to qualifying to receive a dividend — you must be listed as a stockholder as of the date of record. Keep good records regarding your stock splits in case you need to calculate capital gains for Canadian tax purposes. (For information on the date of record, refer to Chapter 6. See Chapter 21 for tax information.)

Ordinary stock splits

An ordinary stock split — when the number of stock shares increases — is the kind investors usually hear about. If you own 100 shares of Dublin, Inc., stock (at $60 per share) and the company announces a stock split, what happens? If you own the stock in certificate form, you receive in the mail a stock certificate for 100 more shares. Now, before you cheer over how your money just doubled, check the stock's new price. Each share is adjusted to a $30 value. In effect, your total dollar holdings of the stock are equal in either case, both before ($60 × 100 shares = $600) and after ($30 × 200 shares = $600) the stock split.

REMEMBER

An ordinary stock split is primarily a neutral event, so why does a company bother to do it? The most common reason is that management believes the stock is too expensive, so it wants to lower the stock price to make the stock more affordable and therefore more attractive to new investors. Studies have shown that stock splits frequently precede a rise in the stock price. Although stock splits are considered a non-event in and of themselves, many stock experts see them as bullish signals because of the interest they generate among the investing public.

Reverse stock splits

A reverse stock split usually occurs when a company's management wants to raise the price of its stock. Just as ordinary splits can occur when management believes the price is too expensive, a reverse stock split means the company feels that the stock's price is too cheap. If a stock's price looks too low, that may discourage interest by individual or institutional investors (such as exchange-traded and mutual funds). Management wants to drum up more interest in the stock for the benefit of shareholders (some of whom are probably insiders).

A reverse split can best be explained with an example. TuCheep, Inc. (TCI), is selling at $2 per share on the Nasdaq. At that rock-bottom price, the investing public may ignore it. So TCI announces a 10-for-1 reverse stock split. Now what? If a stockholder had 100 shares at $2 (the old shares), the stockholder now owns 10 shares at $20.

WARNING

Technically, a reverse split is considered a neutral event. However, just as investors may infer positive expectations from an ordinary stock split, they may have negative expectations from a reverse split because a reverse split tends to occur for negative reasons. One definitive negative reason for a reverse split is if the company's stock is threatened to be delisted. If a stock is on a major exchange and the price falls below $1, the stock will face delisting (basically getting removed from a mainstream exchange like the Nasdaq and being banished to the pink sheets, a place reserved mostly for penny stocks). A reverse split may be used to ward off such an event.

TECHNICAL STUFF

If, in the event of a stock split, you end up with an odd number of shares, the company doesn't produce a fractional share. Instead, you get a cheque or a credit for the cash equivalent.

Chapter **21**

'Cause I'm the Tax Man

How much tax does investment income draw? Yup, you guessed it — it depends! (We hate it when people say that, too!)

Different forms of income attract different levels of taxation. For example, relative to other types of investment income, interest income draws the most punishing tax. Things get a bit better with dividend income, where the Canada Revenue Agency (CRA) taxes you but may also give you a tax credit to cushion the blow. With capital gains, the CRA hits you with only half a blow — only a fraction of your gains or losses are included in, or deducted from, your income. And then there's the other investment-related stuff, like real estate investment trusts, which add more murkiness to the CRA's arsenal of rules. We explore these and other tax-related issues in this chapter. Hey, without the smoke and mirrors, accountants would starve!

Before cutting into the nitty-gritty stuff, however, we set the stage with an overview that will help you deal more easily with the many tax rules that are associated with investment income. In fact, since our last edition there have been quite a few significant changes in tax rules, deduction limits, and tax credit rates that have both a far reach and high impact for many stock investors. Knowing the tax rules for investment income is a critical first step in tax planning, if your objective is to minimize your taxes. We trust that at the end of this chapter, you'll realize what we have come to realize: most of the rules, and their associated tax planning tips, are more manageable than they look!

Interest Income

Interest income is taxable in full in the year in which it's received. No deductions or credits are associated with interest income, other than any small expenses incurred to actually earn interest, like bank fees. Bank accounts, GICs, term deposits, mortgages receivable, and bonds are some of the financial instruments out there that produce interest income.

The CRA wants your interest income so much that, for interest income on compound-interest obligations obtained in 1990 or later, interest has to be reported on an annual accrual basis from the investment's anniversary date. That means you report it as though you have received interest even if you haven't. Providers of investment vehicles (like banks that provide GICs) are required by law to send their clients annual information slips (T5 – Statement of Investment Income) reporting interest, dividends, and other forms of investment income.

WARNING

Some interest-bearing investments have their own unique reporting methods. These investments include annuity contracts, investments bought at a discount to face value, stripped bonds, Canada Savings Bonds, and indexed debt obligations. For Treasury bills for example, the difference between the purchase cost and the selling price is generally deemed to be interest. Consider these nuances when making investment and tax planning decisions; they can have a major impact on your taxes payable. Check out these and other current tax law requirements at the CRA's website (www.cra-arc.gc.ca).

REMEMBER

One big change since our last edition is that Canada Savings Bonds (CSBs) are no longer available for purchase as of November 2017. Any bonds you already own are guaranteed and continue to earn interest until maturity or redemption, whichever comes first.

TIP

It's a good idea to keep bonds inside a registered account like a RRSP, RRIF, or TFSA. Interest is taxed at a high rate, and the bookkeeping, which is a nuisance, is avoided if bonds are inside a registered account. We discuss registered accounts later in this chapter.

Dividend Income

Compared to interest income, any eligible dividends you receive from a Canadian corporation are subject to preferential tax rates. Eligible dividends are typically captured automatically on your T5. They are taxed at a lower rate because of the availability of a dividend tax credit. This dividend tax credit is available to you because the corporation has already paid tax on the earnings when it distributed them as dividends to you. In this way, the CRA guards against double taxation.

Dividend income received from foreign companies — before any withholding tax is held back — is taxed at the same full tax rates as interest income. There is no gross-up and dividend tax credit treatment (see the section "Grossed out," later in this chapter). The absence of a dividend tax credit makes sense because the CRA doesn't tax foreign corporations, so there is no double taxation issue in the first place.

Dividends included in your tax return are converted to Canadian dollars, of course. However, a foreign tax credit is available for any foreign taxes that are withheld. So foreign dividends are taxed more like interest instead of like dividends from Canadian companies.

If dividends from Canadian and foreign corporations were received inside your RRSP, tax on this income is deferred. When you finally withdraw money from your RRSP, it will be fully taxable as regular income. That's because inside RRSPs, investment income loses its nature and comes in only one flavour — high-tax vanilla. Inside RRSPs, you also lose the tax advantage of applying the dividend or foreign tax credit. Again, we'll deal with RRSP strategies later in this chapter.

There are also financial animals called *capital gains dividends,* which are distributions that may come from Canadian mutual funds, ETFs, and REITS. For REITS, any dividend payments made by the REIT are taxed to the unitholder as ordinary income, unless they're considered qualified dividends, in which case they're taxed as capital gains. Your T5 slip sorts this out for you, so don't worry. For capital gains dividends, just realize that one half of the capital gain distributed will be taxable on your tax return.

REMEMBER

Distributions made by Canadian ETFs can take on many forms as well in the eyes of the CRA. They can be one or a combination of Canadian dividends eligible for dividend tax credit treatment; capital gains (only 50 percent taxable) return of capital (not taxable, but triggers a reduction of the adjusted cost base); other income (100 percent taxable); and foreign income (100 percent taxable). Your T5 usually comes to the rescue and will indicate the split.

REMEMBER

Any distributions you receive from foreign ETFs as a Canadian are usually treated as foreign dividends, which are 100 percent taxable. When distributions from U.S. ETFs are categorized as capital gains or return of capital for U.S. taxpayers, they're still fully taxable in the hands of Canadian taxpayers.

Grossed out

If you received dividends from a taxable Canadian corporation, you must gross the dividends up by 38 percent (that is, multiply them by 1.38) and then include that grossed-up amount in your taxable income. Hey! That's not fair! But wait — the federal dividend tax credit we mentioned previously (or 15.02 percent of the grossed-up eligible dividend) reduces your federal income tax payable. Provincial tax credits are available, too. Okay, that's better.

TECHNICAL STUFF

Provinces now have their own dividend tax credit, similar to the federal credit. Previously, provincial tax was calculated as a simple percentage of the federal tax after the federal dividend tax credit was applied.

Stock dividends and splits

A stock dividend is a dividend that a corporation pays by issuing shares instead of cash. Stock dividends are generally considered to be ordinary taxable dividends and are treated as such. The amount of the dividend you include in taxable income — your share of the increase in paid-up capital — also represents the cost of your new shares for future sales as well as capital gain or loss calculations.

Stock splits — where you get more shares without any change in the total dollar value of those shares — are not taxable. You gained or lost nothing from an economic or a tax standpoint.

TIP

When you get your T3 (Statement of Trust Income Allocations and Designations) or T5 tax slip showing, among other things, your annual dividend income (including any stock dividend values), you'll see that there are boxes that contain both the actual dividends and the taxable amount of dividends paid. Be careful to include only the taxable amount of dividends on your tax return.

Capital Gains and Losses

A capital gain occurs when you sell or otherwise dispose of a capital property for more than what you paid for it — technically, the CRA refers to this cost as the adjusted cost base because they may sometimes require you to adjust your original cost. However, we'll keep things simple and leave special rules about costs out of the picture for now. Just keep in mind that capital gains are reduced by any disposition costs incurred, such as brokers' commissions.

Unlike ordinary income such as salary or interest, only 50 percent of the capital gain that you make outside of your RRSP is included in your taxable income. This is called a taxable capital gain, and this portion of the total capital gain is taxed in the year of the sale. If you suffer a capital loss — where your costs exceed your proceeds — the 50 percent allowable portion should first be used to offset any taxable capital gains that may exist in the same year. The allowable capital loss cannot be used to reduce other income except under special circumstances such as death. Any unused allowable capital loss can be carried back up to three years, or carried forward indefinitely, but only to reduce any future taxable capital gains.

WARNING

Keep in mind that just because you didn't receive any proceeds from a sale, that doesn't always mean that you have no capital gain or loss to report. A special scenario can play out when you gift shares or other capital property to family members. In such cases, the CRA may deem you to have received fair-market-value consideration at the time of the gift (or a sale for less than fair market value). The amount of cash actually changing hands is irrelevant to the CRA.

Superficial losses

The CRA has certain rules concerning superficial losses. A superficial loss occurs if you execute a transaction (like a sale or other transfer of investments) that creates a loss while you, or a related person, keep or quickly regain control of the same (or identical) property that created the loss in the first place. The CRA applies the superficial loss provision beginning 30 calendar days before and ending 30 calendar days after the disposition of a property. In other words, no fancy footwork (such as the manipulation of the timing or ownership of losses) is permitted a month before or after the sale.

Foreign Exchange Gains and Losses

When foreign investment property such as stocks and other investment assets are sold, the gain for Canada Revenue Agency (CRA) purposes is calculated by converting the net proceeds into Canadian dollars. The CRA simplifies the process for stocks by allowing you to use an average rate that your discount broker provides, and which you use to convert the value of foreign currency into Canadian dollars. The foreign exchange gain or loss on the disposition is, of course, independent of the calculated gain or loss on sale of the property.

The CRA's tax treatment of the foreign currency gain or loss as either income (100 percent taxable or deductible) or as capital (50 percent taxable and any loss being deductible only against capital gains) typically takes on the attributes and character of the investment asset generating the gain/loss in the first place.

TIP

The CRA provides two avenues for the relief of double taxation that can arise with foreign investments, including stocks and other financial instruments. The first is the foreign tax credit and, in certain circumstances, a second is a deduction from income for income taxes actually paid in a foreign country. Also, Canada is party to international tax treaties with many countries to mitigate double taxation.

Deferred-Income Tax Shelters and Plans

Deferred-income plans are designed to let you earn investment income and, at the same time, defer paying tax for as long as the investments and income stay inside the plan. Deferring investment income to a time when your tax rate will likely be lower reduces your tax obligation. RRSPs even go a step further and provide a tax deduction, within CRA limits, for the contributions you make. The following sections explore RRSPs and other deferred-income plans. You'll find out how you can use these plans strategically to maximize your investment returns. But before you can implement tax strategy and planning in this area, you first have to understand how these plans actually work.

Registered Retirement Savings Plans (RRSPs)

RRSPs are registered savings plans that let you contribute cash or eligible investments for future use — usually for retirement. You can open several different RRSP accounts, and you can passively or actively invest in each one in different ways with different investments, such as GICs, stocks, or mutual funds. You can contribute to an RRSP, subject to certain rules, up to and including the year that you turn 71 years old.

Because RRSP contributions lower your taxable income, you save tax immediately. Keep in mind, however, that RRSP withdrawals trigger an income inclusion for the year — even if the full amount withdrawn is reinstated into the plan later in that same year. Also bear in mind that while you can pay RRSP-related administrative fees outside of your plan, they aren't tax-deductible.

RRSP contribution limits

Your allowable RRSP contribution for the current year is the lower of

>> 18 percent of your *earned income* from the previous year or;

>> The maximum annual contribution *limit* (see below) for the taxation year *less*;

>> Any company sponsored pension plan contributions (the pension adjustment indicated on your T4 slip).

Earned income limits

For most Canadians, earned income for RRSP purposes is the amount indicated in Box 14 on T4 slips. Additionally, earned income includes self-employment income, disability payments under the Canada Pension Plan (CPP) or Quebec Pension Plan (QPP), net rental income, alimony or separation allowances received, royalties, and supplementary unemployment benefit plan payments (not Employment Insurance, or EI).

But earned income is reduced by current-year losses from self-employment or an active partnership, current-year rental losses, and deductible alimony and maintenance payments.

TIP

In the context of the earned income calculation that determines your RRSP contribution room, dividends and other investment income are not considered by the CRA to represent earned income. Other income streams that also do not qualify as earned income include Old Age Security, Registered Retirement Income Funds, CPP/QPP, retiring allowances, and taxable capital gains. Therefore, they don't boost RRSP contribution room for you.

Dollar limits

Annual RRSP contributions can't be greater than $26,230 in 2018 with limits likely changing thereafter. Because "thereafter" may not be longer than the next annual federal budget, you can check out CRA's website at www.cra-arc.gc.ca for changes to deduction limits.

Also be sure to check out the notice of assessment you receive from the CRA after filing your prior year's tax return. There, you can find your RRSP contribution limits for the current tax year. Contributions have to be made within 60 days of the calendar year-end for them to be deductible for the previous tax year. Bear in mind that unused RRSP limits that have accumulated since 1991 can be carried forward.

Spousal Registered Retirement Savings Plans

Many investors have their own RRSP and also open a spouse or common-law partner's RRSP. Spousal contributions are deemed by the CRA to be the recipient spouse/common-law partner's property. Spousal contributions reduce the contributor's RRSP limit, but they don't impact the recipient spouse's contribution limits for his or her own RRSP. The key here is that as the contributor, you get the benefit of the deduction! Also, with a spousal RRSP, your tax savings may be maximized in the future because spousal RRSP contributions can provide you and your spouse with the opportunity to balance out retirement income and reduce your combined future taxes. The higher-income spouse that contributes gets a nice tax break. The lower-income spouse can withdraw those funds at a later time and pay little or no tax. It's a win-win, unless you divorce!

WARNING

Be mindful, however, that withdrawals from a spousal plan may be taxable in your hands if spousal contributions were made in either the year of the withdrawal or within the two preceding years.

Self-directed RRSPs

Self-directed RRSPs are popular with Canadians who wish to hold and manage individual stocks in their RRSP. Another reason many stock investors set up a self-directed RRSP is to capitalize on the absence of foreign-content limits (the same as for non-self-directed RRSPs) by exploring stocks traded on stock exchanges outside of Canada while still getting a tax deduction.

A self-directed RRSP provides a greater selection of investment options than a regular RRSP. That's the key difference between the two choices. They are available through discount and full-service brokerage firms. These plans are designed for Canadians who wish to personally control and manage the assets residing in their plan. Like for non-self-directed RRSPs, the annual administration fee and commissions that you pay aren't tax deductible.

The list of what you can throw into a self-directed RRSP plan, over and above stocks, includes the following:

>> Bank deposit accounts and investment certificates

>> Federal, provincial, and municipal bonds and debentures (debt instruments that pay interest)

- » Mortgages and mortgage-backed securities

- » Mutual funds, REITS, and ETFs

- » Limited partnerships and income trusts

- » Rights and warrants of corporations listed on Canadian stock exchanges

- » Savings bonds

- » Treasury bills

As for foreign stocks, they also have to be listed as a designated stock exchange to qualify for a self-directed RRSP. Check out www.fin.gc.ca/act/fim-imf/dse-bvd-eng.asp for a current list that includes some of the Asian exchanges we discuss in Chapter 14.

Retirement allowances

You can transfer retiring allowances (like severance packages and accumulated attendance credits) directly into your RRSP, subject to certain limits and rules. For years of service from 1989 to 1995, inclusive, the contribution limit is $2,000 per year of service. For those years before 1989, an additional $1,500 can be contributed (for a potential total of $3,500 per year) for each year of service that you didn't have a pension plan. For years of service from 1996 and on, you can transfer the balance to an RRSP as long as you have contribution room. However, for any balance remaining, you can't carry forward these unused RRSP contributions to future periods.

Locked-in RRSPs

When employees leave their workplaces, they may have a choice of either receiving a pension at retirement or transferring the commuted value of their pensions to another plan. Under strict Canadian law, the commuted value can't be immediately paid out directly to the individual. Instead, the transferred commuted (actuarially calculated) value is either placed directly into another company pension plan or in a locked-in retirement account (LIRA), also referred to as a locked-in RRSP. Both are essentially the same thing.

With a regular RRSP, you can make a withdrawal at any time. With a locked-in RRSP, early withdrawals can't typically be made. Furthermore, when you retire as early as age 55, or as late as age 69, the locked-in RRSP cash can be applied to purchase a life annuity or a life income fund (ask your tax advisor if one of these is a route you should consider). You may not be able to transfer funds into an RRIF (discussed later in this chapter). However, Ontario and other residents are now an exception and may be able to transfer the proceeds of locked-in RRSPs into a locked-in RRIF. This is another complex area beyond the scope of this book, so discuss it with your tax advisor when appropriate.

Tax-Free Savings Accounts (TFSAs)

A Tax-Free Savings Account (TFSA) is an investment vehicle where investment income within the account (such as dividends, capital gains, or interest) isn't taxed, even when you withdraw that income. This means your investments can grow a bit more rapidly within a TFSA than in a taxable account.

For a TFSA, the annual contribution limit is $5,500 for the 2018 tax year. You can also carry forward any unused contribution room indefinitely. In fact, if you do not currently have a TFSA, you could open one today and contribute a catch up instant maximum of $57,500, the cumulative limit as of 2018! (Check out the CRA's web site at www.canada.ca/en/revenue-agency.html for cumulative limit rules for a given future year.) The CRA reports your TFSA contribution room to you annually in the same way it reports your RRSP room.

Unlike with RRSPs, you don't have to have earned income to contribute to a TFSA. However, you *don't* get a tax deduction for contributing to a TFSA. This is a key distinction. In a TFSA, you can withdraw money at any time and your withdrawals are tax-free. Although dividends or capital gains from stock investing aren't taxable, you maybe subject to foreign tax on any foreign investment income.

From a cash flow management standpoint, you can also recontribute the amounts you withdrew at anytime after the year of withdrawal. For example, if you contributed $5,500 in February 2017 and then in November 2017 you withdrew $3,000, your maximum 2018 TFSA contribution allowed by the CRA is $8,500. The $8,500 is the sum of your $5,500 limit for 2018 we mention earlier plus the $3,000 you withdrew in November 2017.

TIP

Ask your financial or tax advisor to help you decide whether a RRSP, a TFSA, or a combination of both is the way to go. Your advisor will assess your investment goals, tax situation, and financial condition to help you make the right decision. Robo-advisors, which we discuss in Chapter 7, also help you at a basic level to optimize your investment portfolio for tax purposes.

Registered Retirement Income Funds (RRIFs)

You have until December 31 of the year when you turn 71 to terminate your RRSP account. You have three options when you terminate your RRSP:

>> **Withdraw the RRSP funds.** The total of lump-sum cash withdrawn is included in your annual taxable income. Ouch!

>> **Transfer your RRSP into an RRIF.** An RRIF is like an RRSP because the RRIF's funds and income earned stay untaxed until they are withdrawn. You can exercise control over investment decisions. However, you must withdraw a minimum amount from the plan each year, based on your age or the age of a younger spouse or common-law partner. The minimum amount to be withdrawn, based on a percentage of the value of your RRIF and rates of depletion set by the government, increases each year until age 94. At that time, the amounts become set at 20 percent annually until the plan is depleted.

>> **Buy an annuity providing a regular income for a set period of time.** This may include your lifetime, the combined lifetimes of you and your spouse or common-law partner, a set period, or a combination of these time frames. The choices are wide open. No part of the RRSP will be taxed immediately on this type of transfer. The tax kicks in when the annuity payments begin to be received.

Take note that you can withdraw amounts over and above the minimum, although any excess amounts withdrawn will also become taxable in that year.

There's a catch

If you have an RRSP or other tax shelter, you have a few obligations. You are required to identify any tax-sheltered investment deductions and to disclose the shelter identification number on your tax return. The folks who sold you their tax shelter products should provide you with the required filing forms and associated details, like the amount of the deduction.

REMEMBER

Also be aware of the fact that you face a number of special rules regarding tax-shelter deductions, which can result in alternative minimum tax (AMT), or be exposed to at-risk rules, where you aren't allowed to write off more than the cost base of your investment. Consult your tax advisor for advice about this complex area.

Invest Inside or Outside Your RRSP?

At the outset of this chapter, we point out that the money you make on your investments draws different effective rates of tax, depending on the type of income you receive from the investment. Recall that income you generate from your investments held outside of your RRSP will be taxed differently if it's interest income, dividends, or capital gains. But the variables and choices don't end there.

You can choose to earn investment income either inside or outside of an RRSP — each option has different tax implications and other consequences. This is where it pays off for you to understand the tax treatment of various sources of investment income. This knowledge will make it easier to decide which investments should be in a tax-advantaged plan such as an RRSP, and which investments should be held outside of an RRSP. No one-size-fits-all formula applies here, only rules that can be carefully plugged into your personal financial objectives.

Things to Remember: Recap

You may recall that, in general, fixed-income investments such as GICs and bonds generate regular interest income, while stocks may generate capital gains and, in certain cases, dividends. You may also recall that a capital gain is the profit realized when a capital property like a stock is sold. For example, if you purchase a stock for $30 and sell it for $45, your capital gain is $15.

REMEMBER

To contrast again, interest income is taxable even if it has not been paid out. Also, capital gains are taxed at a more merciful 50 percent. Dividends, an altogether different kind of animal, entitle you to a dividend tax credit that lowers your effective tax on dividends. Interest income is taxable at relatively high rates, but if a GIC or bond is held inside your RRSP, any tax on interest earned is deferred until you withdraw it. Keep these principles in mind.

Capital gains are the key focus of most stock investors, so the taxation of capital gains and treatment of capital losses are important considerations. The current capital gains inclusion rate is 50 percent, so only one-half of any capital gains you generate outside your RRSP will be subject to tax in the year of the sale. For instance, if you invested $15,000 in stocks outside your RRSP and later sold the stocks for $25,000, only $5,000 of this income (50 percent of the $10,000 capital gain) would be taxable in the year of sale. But if you realized that capital gain inside your RRSP, the full amount of the capital gain would be taxable when you withdraw it from your RRSP. You lose the tax benefit of the 50 percent exclusion from taxable income. However, you would defer the tax up until the time you withdrew the money from your plan. Also bear in mind that you'll likely be in a lower tax bracket in your retirement years than you are in currently. As you can see, there is no clear solution.

Things to consider

Here's a recap of issues, some conflicting, for you to consider applying to your personal situation:

>> Deferring tax through an RRSP is great, but many Canadians value the immediate tax deductions a lot more. Sure, tax-smart investing outside of an RRSP may not defer tax, but it can help you to reduce it.

>> RRSP withdrawals are fully taxable. Withdrawals from your non-RRSP account may be taxed at preferential rates, saving you money.

>> Consider your current tax deduction available where you have contribution room. Your immediate tax savings can be invested. Investing outside of an RRSP doesn't afford you this instant benefit.

>> Income splitting — shifting taxable income from the hands of one family member who pays tax at a high rate to another who pays tax at a lower rate — can be accomplished with spousal RRSPs. Income splitting outside of an RRSP is administratively more tedious.

>> An RRSP instills disciplined investing. The annual contribution deadline compels many Canadians to contribute at least something into the plan before they run out of time for that year.

Ways to look at the RRSP debate

A popular view is that keeping investments that generate interest income outside of your RRSP may not be best because interest income is more heavily taxed. If you hold investments inside your RRSP, your interest returns will be higher because your income is temporarily sheltered from tax. But capital gains and dividends, on the other hand, are taxed at preferential rates. You may want to hold investments generating capital gains and dividends outside of your RRSP.

No one right answer exists; everyone has different personal and financial objectives. But seeking the advice of a financial or tax planner will likely help you to arrive at the best decision.

Mutual Funds

A mutual fund allocates its income to the unitholders, who then report the income as capital gains, dividends, foreign income, or other income. Regardless of source, when you sell units of mutual fund trusts or shares of mutual fund corporations, you may realize a capital gain. Again, the beneficial tax treatment of capital gains and dividends is lost if they are received within an RRSP. Funds often reinvest distributions to unitholders as new shares of the fund. Here, though you don't see the cash, you'll still be taxed on the income distributed. That's why you may have received a tax slip even though you saw no cash.

Oil, Gas, and Mineral Stock Investments

The CRA offers tax incentives to encourage Canadians to invest capital to aid in the exploration and development of oil, gas, and minerals. These incentives are provided through limited partnerships, flow-through shares, joint ventures, and royalty trust units. By going through these risky avenues, you may be able to deduct certain exploration expenses.

Joint ventures and limited partnerships are a lot alike, except for the fact that at-risk rules don't apply to the former. Flow-through shares enable companies to forgo certain income tax deductions that they could have claimed and to pass them on to investors — the deductions flow through to you. (Because many junior exploration companies can't generate a regular taxable income, they aren't able to use their tax deductions, anyway.) Flow-through-share investor deductions typically lower the cost base of the shares to nil. This decrease can ultimately result in a tax-preferential capital gain when the shares are sold.

Also take note that the CRA permits a temporary nonrefundable investment tax credit to be claimed. The rate is 15 percent in order to cover certain Canadian mineral exploration and other expenses to create a flow-through share structure. Furthermore, the government also provides tax incentives regarding the availability of flow-through shares for Canadian investors in certain renewable energy and energy conservation projects. In this way, the government makes these shares more attractive for people to buy.

Check out the suitability of these tax-advantaged, but risky, mechanisms with your investment or tax advisor before proceeding. As you can see, the rules are tight, complex, and well beyond the scope of this book.

TIP

As an added incentive to seek professional advice when your tax situation gets complicated, you can deduct fees (but not commissions) for advice you get about the purchase, sale, and administration of shares and certain other securities.

5

The Part of Tens

Get tips on picking good stocks.

Find out how to make money in a bear market.

Check out tried and true investments and strategies.

Chapter **22**

Ten Indicators of a Great Stock

In a book like this, the goal would be good to identify the Holy Grail of stock investing . . . *the* stock . . . the kind of stock that, if stocks were people, then Apple, General Electric, Proctor & Gamble, Royal Bank of Canada, and Microsoft would be peasants compared to this king. Yeah, that's the kind of stock that would be the Grand Pooh-Bah of your portfolio! Well, hold your horses.

That stock is likely in heaven's stock market right now, and you have to be firmly planted on terra firma. If you have a stock that has all the following features, back up the truck and get as much as you can (and let us know so that we can do the same!).

Seriously, we doubt that you'll find a stock with all ten hallmarks described in this chapter, but a stock with even half of them is a super-solid choice. Get a stock with as many hallmarks as possible and you likely have a winner.

The Company Has Rising Profits

The very essence of a successful company is its ability to make a profit. In fact, profit is the single most important financial element of a company. We can even make the case that profit is the single most important element of a successful economy. Without profit, a company goes out of business. If a business closes its doors, private jobs vanish. In turn, taxes don't get paid. This means that the Canadian or provincial government can't function and pay its workers and those who are dependent on public assistance. Sorry for veering away from the company's main hallmark, but understanding the importance of profit is vital.

REMEMBER

Profit is what is left after expenses are deducted from sales. When a company manages its expenses well, profits will grow. For info on the numbers measuring a company's success, look at Chapters 6 and 11 as well as Appendix B.

The Company Has Rising Sales

Looking at the total sales of a company is referred to as analyzing the *top-line numbers*. Of course, that's because when you're looking at net income (gross sales minus total expenses), you're looking at the bottom line.

A company (or analysts) can play games with many numbers on an income statement; there are a dozen different ways to look at earnings. Earnings are the heart and soul of a company, but the top line gives you an unmistakable and clear number to look at. The total sales (or gross sales or gross revenue) number for a company is harder to fudge.

TIP

It's easy for an investor — especially a novice investor — to look at sales for a company for a particular year and see whether it's doing better or worse than in the prior year. Reviewing three years of sales gives you a good overall gauge of the company's success.

Granted, some years are bad for everyone, so don't expect a company's sales to go up every year like a rocket. Sometimes success is relative; a company with sales down 5 percent is doing fine if every other company in that industry has sales down much more.

Suffice it to say that when a company's total sales are rising, that's a positive sign. The company can overcome other potential issues (such as paying off debt or sudden expenses) much more easily and can pave the way for long-term success.

Check out Appendix B for ways to look at sales and do your own top-line analysis.

The Company Has Low Liabilities

All things being equal, we would rather have a company with relatively low debt than one with high debt. Too much debt will kill an otherwise good company. Debt can consume you, and as you read this, debt is consuming many countries across the globe.

Because a company with low debt has borrowing power, it can take advantage of opportunities such as taking over a rival or acquiring a company that offers an added technology to help propel current or future profit growth.

Notice that we didn't say a company with no debt. Don't get us wrong — a company with no debt or little in the way of liabilities is a solid company. But in an environment where you can borrow at historically low rates, it pays to take on some debt and use it wisely with an eye on value-for-money. In other words, if a company can borrow at, say, 3 percent and put it to use to yield a profit of 5 percent or more, why not?

Secondly, notice that we are talking about liabilities. It isn't always conventional debt that may sink a company. What if that company is simply spending more money than it's bringing in? Liabilities or "total liabilities" takes into account everything that a company is obligated to pay, whether it's a long-term bond (long-term debt), paying workers, or the water bill. Current expenses should be more than covered by current income, but you don't want to accumulate long-term debt, which means a drain on future income.

Also, in some industries, the liabilities can take a form that isn't typically conventional debt or monthly expenses. We read the recent industry report that some very large banks and stock brokerage firms have huge positions in *derivatives*, which are complicated financial instruments that can easily turn into crushing debt that could sink a bank. In our research, for example, we found one Wall Street broker that had total derivatives of a whopping $35 trillion, even though its net worth on its balance sheet was only $104 billion.

The point is that one of the hallmarks of a successful company is to keep liabilities low and manageable. You find a company's debt in its financial statements (such as the balance sheet). There's more about debt in Chapter 11.

TIP

To discover some good parameters of acceptable debt, look at the company's financial ratios on debt to assets. Get the scoop about this in Appendix B.

The Stock Is at a Bargain Price

Price and value are two different concepts, and they aren't interchangeable. A low price isn't synonymous with getting a bargain. Just as you want the most for your money when you shop, you want to get the most for your money in stock investing.

You can look at the value of a company in several ways, but the first thing we look at is the price-to-earnings ratio (P/E ratio). It attempts to connect the price of the company's stock to the company's net profits quoted on a per share basis. For example, if a company has a price of $15 per share and the earnings are $1 per share, then the P/E ratio is 15.

REMEMBER

Generally speaking, a P/E ratio of 15 or less is a good value, especially if the other numbers work out positively (for example, profits and sales are rising, as we note earlier in this chapter). When the economy is in the dumps and stock prices are down, P/E ratios of 10 or lower are even better. Conversely, if the economy is booming, then higher P/E ratios are acceptable.

P/E ratios in the teens or better (lower) make us comfortable. However, someone else might bristle at that and consider P/E ratios of 25 or even 50 acceptable. Then again, at those levels (or higher), you're no longer talking about a bargain.

WARNING

Too many investors see no problem with buying stocks that have no P/E ratio. These stocks may have the P (price of the stock), but they have no E (earnings). If you invest in a company that has losses instead of earnings, then to me you aren't an investor; you're a speculator.

Investing in a company that is losing money is making a bet, and more importantly, it isn't a bargain at all. (However, when you find a company that is losing money, it could be a good shorting opportunity; see Chapter 17 for details.)

A stock may also be a bargain if its market value is at or below its *book value* (the actual accounting value of net assets for the company). You can find out more about book value in Chapter 11.

Dividends Are Growing

Long-term investing is where the true payoff is for today's investors. But before you start staring at your calendar and dreaming of future profits, take a look at the company's current dividend picture.

Dividends are the long-term investor's best friend. Wouldn't it be great if after a few years of owning that stock, you received total dividends that actually dwarfed what your original investment was? That's more common than you know! We've calculated the history of accumulated dividends for a given stock, and it doesn't take as long as you think to get your original investment amount back (counting cumulated dividends). We know some people who bought dividend-paying stocks during a bear market (when stock prices are very low) and got their original investment back after eight to ten years (depending on the stock and its dividend growth, of course).

Dividend growth also carries with it the potential growth of the stock itself. A consistently rising dividend is a positive sign for the stock price. The investing public sees that a growing dividend is a powerful and tangible sign of the company's current and future financial health.

A company may be able to fudge earnings and other soft or malleable figures, but when a dividend is paid, that's hard proof that the company is succeeding with its net profit. Given that, just review the long-term stock chart (say five years or longer) of a consistent dividend-paying company, and 99 times out of 100, that stock price is zigzagging upward in a similar pattern.

We discuss dividends and dividend-growing stocks in Chapter 9. For exchange-traded funds (ETFs) that have dividend stocks in their portfolios, see Chapter 5 and 9. Lastly, check out resources that include dividend investing strategies in Appendix A.

The Market Is Growing

In this context, when we say that the market is growing, we mean the market of consumers for a given product. If more and more people are buying widgets (remember those?) and the sales of widgets keep growing, that bodes well for companies that sell (or service) widgets.

Take a look at demographics and market data and use this information to further filter your investing choices. You could run a great company, but if your fortunes are made when a million folks buy from you, and next year that number shrinks to 800,000, and the year after that it shrinks again, what will happen to your fortunes?

Consider this example: If you have a successful company that is selling something to seniors and the market data tells you that the number of seniors is expanding relentlessly for the foreseeable future, then this rising tide (demographics) will certainly lift that particular boat (your stock). Find out more about market growth using the resources in Appendix A.

The Company Is in a Field with a High Barrier to Entry

If you run a company that offers a product or service that is easy to compete with, building up a strong and viable business will be more difficult for you; you'll need to do something different and better.

Maybe you have a great technology, or a patented system, or superior marketing prowess, or a way to make what you're selling both cheaper and faster than your competition. Maybe you have a strong brand that has endured for decades.

A *high barrier to entry* simply means that companies that compete with you will have a tough time overcoming your advantage. This gives you the power to grow and leave your competition in the dust.

Here's an example: Coca-Cola (KO) positioned and branded itself for decades as the top soda with a secret recipe for its soda. In spite of imitators and competitors, it's still dominant today — more than a century after its founding. The company's soda is still on kitchen tables and in picnic baskets, and its shareholders are still being refreshed with stock splits and dividend increases.

To find resources that can help you learn about the advantages and characteristics of stocks with a high barrier to entry, check out Appendix A.

The Company Has a Low Political Profile

Politics: Just the thought of it makes us wince. Political discussions may be great at cocktail parties and perhaps fun to watch as your relatives go at it, but we think that flying below the political radar is a good thing for companies. Why?

We live in times that are politically sensitive (we don't think that is a good thing). All too often, politics affects the fortunes of companies and by extension the portfolios of investors. Yes, sometimes politics can favour a company (through backroom deals and such), but politics is a double-edged sword that can ruin a company.

History shows us that companies that are politically targeted either directly or by association (by being in an unpopular industry) can suffer. There was a time that holding tobacco companies in your portfolio was the equivalent of garlic to a vampire.

All things being equal, we would rather hold a stock in a popular industry or a nondescript industry than one that attracts undue (negative) attention.

The Stock Is Optionable

REMEMBER

An *optionable stock* (which has call and put options available on it) means that you have added ways to profit from it (or the ability to minimize potential losses). Options give a stockholder ways to enhance gains or yield added revenue.

Say you do in fact find the perfect stock, and you truly load up and buy as many shares as you can lay your hands on, but you don't have any more money to buy another batch of shares.

Fortunately, you notice that the stock is optionable and see that you can speculate by buying a call option that allows you to be bullish on 100 shares with a fraction of the cash needed to actually buy 100 shares. As the stock soars, you're able to take profits by cashing out the call option without having to touch the stock position at all.

Now, with your stock at nosebleed levels, you're getting a little nervous that this stock is possibly at an unsustainable level, so you decide to buy some put options to protect your unrealized gains from your stock. When your stock does experience a correction, you cash out your put with an enviable gain. With the stock down, you decide to take the proceeds from your put option–realized gains and buy more of the stock at favorable prices.

Options (both the call and the put in this scenario) give you the ability to bank more gains from the same great stock. Find out more about options in the book *High-Level Investing For Dummies* (published by Wiley).

The Stock Is Benefiting from Favorable Megatrends

A *megatrend* is a trend that affects an unusually large segment of the marketplace and may have added benefits and/or pitfalls for buyers and sellers of a given set of products and services. A good example of a megatrend is "the aging of North America"; the United States and Canada has more than 90 million people who are getting ready for retirement as they reach and surpass the age of 65 (although some assume a larger number when they include folks who are over 50). Those companies that provide services and products for senior citizens would have greater opportunities to sell more of what they provide and would then be a good consideration for investors.

REMEMBER

When megatrends are with you, you can even have a mediocre stock but end up with extraordinary gains. In fact, even a "bad stock" will rise sharply if it's swept up in a rally pushed by a powerful megatrend. Of course, a bad stock won't have staying power (the stock will eventually go down if the underlying company is losing money or struggling), so stick to quality stocks to truly optimize the long-term benefits that a megatrend can provide.

The problem is that when a stock has little substance behind it (the company is losing money, growing debt, and so on), its up move will be temporary, and the stock price will tend to reverse in an ugly pullback. Just ask anyone who bought a failing dot-com stock about two decades ago (that's right — that guy softly sobbing in the corner). The rising-tide-lifts-all-boats idea is a powerful one, and when you have a great company that will only benefit from this type of scenario, your stock price will go higher and higher.

Find out more about megatrends and other factors in the big picture in Chapters 13 and 15.

Chapter **23**

Ten Ways to Profit in a Bear Market

Bear markets are brutal when they hit. Ask any stock investor who was fully invested in stocks during 1973–1975, 2000–2002, or 2008. You relieve the pain from the carnage by vigorously pulling your lower lip up and over your forehead to shield your eyes from the ugliness. Fortunately, bear markets tend to be much shorter than bull markets, and if you're properly diversified, you can get through without much damage.

For nimble and quick investors, bear markets can provide opportunities to boost your portfolio and lay the groundwork for more long-term wealth-building. Here are ten ways to make bear markets very bear-able (and profitable).

Find Good Stocks to Buy

In a bear market, the stocks of both good and bad companies tend to go down. But bad stocks tend to stay down (or head into the dustbin of stock history if the underlying companies go bankrupt), while good stocks recover and get back on the growth track.

REMEMBER

For the investor, the strategy is clear. If the stock of a good, profitable company goes down, that presents a buying opportunity. Translation: Good stuff is on sale! Here's where some basic research yields some diamonds in the rough. When you find companies with good sales and profits and a good growth outlook (get some guidance from Chapter 8) and then you use some key ratios (such as the price-to-earnings ratio and others covered in Appendix B), you can uncover a great stock at a bargain price (thanks to that bear market).

Many forget that some of the greatest investors in history (such as Warren Buffett and John Templeton) have used bear markets to buy companies when their stocks fell to bargain levels. Why not you?

Hunt for Dividends

A dividend comes from a company's net income, while the stock's price is dictated by buying and selling in the stock market. If the stock's price goes down because of selling yet the company is strong, still earning a profit, and still paying a dividend, it becomes a good buying opportunity for those seeking dividend income.

Say you have a $50 stock of a great company, and it has a $2.50 annual dividend. That means that you're getting a dividend yield of 5 percent ($2.50 divided by $50 is a percentage yield of 5 percent). Say that it's a brutal bear market and the stock price falls to $25 per share. In that case, the dividend yield would be much higher. If the stock is at $25 and the dividend is at $2.50, the dividend yield would be 10 percent because $2.50 is 10 percent of $25.

For more about investing for dividend income, check out Chapter 9.

Unearth Gems with Bond Ratings

As a bear market unfolds, the tough economic environment is like the tide that rolls back from the surf and reveals who still has swim trunks on and who doesn't. A bear market usually occurs in tough economic times, and it reveals who has too much debt to deal with and who is doing a good job of managing their debt.

This is where the bond rating becomes valuable (or is it invaluable?). The *bond rating* is a widely viewed snapshot of a company's creditworthiness. The rating is assigned by an independent bond rating agency (such as Moody's, DBRS, or Standard & Poor's). A rating of AAA is the highest rating available and signifies that the agency believes that the company has achieved the highest level of creditworthiness and is therefore the least risky to invest in (in terms of buying its bonds). The ratings of AAA, AA, and A are considered "investment-grade," whereas ratings that are lower (such as in the Bs and Cs or worse) indicate poor creditworthiness (risky).

TIP

If the economy is in bad shape (recession or worse) and stocks have been battered, and if you see a stock whose company has a bond rating of AAA, that may be a good buy! Flip to Chapter 9 for more information about bond ratings.

Rotate Your Sectors

Using exchange-traded funds (ETFs) with your stocks can be a good way to add diversification and use a sector rotation approach. Different sectors perform well during different times of the ebb and flow of the economic or business cycle.

When the economy is roaring along and growing, companies that offer big-ticket items such as autos, machinery, high technology, home improvement, and similar large purchases tend to do very well, and so do their stocks (these are referred to as *cyclical stocks*). Sectors that represent cyclical stocks include manufacturing and consumer discretionary. Basically, stocks of companies that sell big-ticket items or "wants" do well when the economy is growing and doing well.

However, when the economy looks like it's sputtering and entering a recession, then it pays to switch to *defensive stocks* tied to human need, such as food and beverage (in the consumer staples sector), utilities, and the like.

For skittish investors, consumer staples and related defensive sectors are the place to be during an economic recession and a bearish stock market. Aggressive investors that like to be contrarians may see battered sectors as a buying opportunity, anticipating that those stocks will rally significantly as the economy returns to a growth path and a new bull market in stocks.

The bottom line is that rotating into sectors that will subsequently benefit from the next expected turn in the economy's ebb and flow has been worth considering for many investors. How about you? See Chapter 13 for the scoop on sectors.

Go Short on Bad Stocks

Bear markets may be tough for good stocks, but they're brutal to bad stocks. When bad stocks go down, they can keep falling and give you an opportunity to profit when they decline further.

When a bad stock (the underlying company is losing money, getting over-indebted, and so on) goes down, the stock often goes into a more severe decline as more and more investors look into it and discover the company's shaky finances. Many folks would short the stock and profit when it continues plunging (we cover the mechanics of how to go short in Chapter 17).

WARNING

Going short is a risky way to bet on a stock going down. If you're wrong and the stock goes up, you have the potential for unlimited losses. A better way to specu-late on a stock falling is to buy long-dated put options, which gives you the poten-tial to profit if you're right (that the stock will fall) but limits your losses if you're wrong. We describe put options later in this chapter.

Carefully Use Margin

We typically don't use margin, but if you use it wisely, it's a powerful tool. Using it to acquire dividend-paying stocks after they've corrected can be a great tactic. *Margin* is using borrowed funds from your broker to buy securities (also referred to as a *margin loan*). Keep in mind that when you employ margin, you do add an element of speculation to the mix. Buying 100 shares of a dividend-paying stock with 100 percent of your own money is a great way to invest, but buying the same stock with margin adds risk to the situation. Chapter 17 goes into greater detail about the uses and risks of margin.

WARNING

Notice the phrases "after they've corrected" and "dividend-paying stock." Both phrases are intended to give you a better approach to your margin strategy. You would hate to use margin before the stock corrected or declined because the brokerage firm wants you to have enough "stock collateral," so to speak. Using margin at the wrong time (when the stock is high and it subsequently falls) can be hazardous, but using margin to buy the stock after a significant fall is much less risky.

Buy a Call Option

A *call option* is a bet that a particular asset (such as a stock or an ETF) will rise in value in the short term. Buying call options is about speculating, not investing. We say this because a call option is a derivative, and it has a finite shelf life; it can expire worthless if you're not careful.

The good part of a call option is that it can be inexpensive to buy and tends to be a very cheap vehicle at the bottom (bear market) of the stock market. This is where your contrarian side can kick in. If the stock price has been hammered but the company is in good shape (solid sales, profits, and so on), betting on a rebound for the company's stock can be profitable.

Say the stock price for DEF, Inc., is at $23 per share. Consider buying a call option with a strike price of $25 that has a long-term expiration such as a year or longer. (In a call option, the *strike price* is the agreed-upon price at which the call buyer has the option but not the obligation to buy the underlying stock or ETF). Doing this means that you're betting the stock will go up and meet or surpass the price of $25. If DEF goes to, say, $28 per share, then your call option could easily go up 100 percent or more in value and net you a tidy profit. Of course, if DEF stays down and doesn't approach $25, then the call option will lose value. If DEF's stock price doesn't go to $25 during the entire time of the life of the call option, then the call option could expire worthless. Fortunately, the option didn't cost that much money, so you probably didn't lose much in the worst-case scenario. Depending on the strike price and the shelf life of the option, an option can cost as little as under $100.

REMEMBER

Options are a form of speculating, not investing. With investing, time is on your side. But with options, time is against you because options have a finite life and can expire worthless.

Write a Covered Call Option

When you own a stock, especially an optionable stock, you have the ability to generate extra income from that position. The most obvious way to generate income from the stock (besides dividends) is to write a covered call option.

Writing a *covered call* means that you're selling a call option against a stock you own; in other words, you accept an obligation to sell your stock to the buyer (or holder) of the call that you wrote at a specified price if the stock rises and meets or exceeds the strike price. In exchange, you receive income (referred to as the *option premium*). If the stock doesn't rise to the option's specified price during the life of the option (an option has a diminishing shelf life and an expiration date), then you're able to keep both your stock and the income from doing (writing) the call option.

Writing covered call options is a relatively safe way to boost the yield on your stock position by up to 5 percent, 7 percent, and even more than 10 percent depending on market conditions. Keep in mind, though, that the downside of writing a covered call is that you may be obligated to sell your stock at the option's specified price (referred to as the *strike price*), and you forgo the opportunity to make gains above that specified price. But done right, a covered call option can be a virtually risk-free strategy.

Write a Put Option to Generate Income

Writing a *put option* obligates you (the put writer) to buy 100 shares of a stock (or ETF) at a specific price during the period of time the option is active. If a stock you'd like to buy just fell and you're interested in buying it, consider instead writing a put option on that same stock.

The put option provides you income (called the *premium*) while it obligates you to buy the underlying stock at the option's agreed-upon price (called the *strike price*). But because you want to buy the stock anyway at the option's strike price, it's fine, and you get paid to do it too (the premium). Writing put options is a great way to generate income at the bottom of a bear market. The only "risk" is that you may have to buy a stock you like. Cool!

Be Patient

REMEMBER

If you're going to retire ten years from now (or more), a bear market shouldn't make you sweat. Good stocks come out of bear markets, and they're usually ready for the subsequent bull market. So don't be so quick to get out of a stock. Just keep monitoring the company for its vital statistics (growing sales and profits and so on), and if the company looks fine, then hang on. Keep collecting your dividend and hold the stock as it zigzags into the long-term horizon.

Chapter **24**

Ten Investments and Strategies

We think that stock investing is indeed an essential part of an overall wealth-building program, but we think that reminders about the other pieces of the puzzle are important so that you have a complete financial picture (nice wrap-up, right?). In today's financial markets, hedging is an important accompaniment to your stock-investing pursuits. Hedging can take a variety of forms, but the point is to have vehicles that help you diversify and protect you against the potential downside of pure stock investing. The ten strategies in this chapter are good accompaniments to your stock investing pursuits.

Gold

Gold (and we mean the physical bullion) is important for all investors in today's times. Gold has been a store of value for centuries, and it outlives paper assets. It's also in Canada's DNA as well since we have dozens of large Canadian companies mining it. Virtually all paper assets (stocks, bonds, currencies, and so on) have counter-party risk — something that physical gold does not.

What do we mean by counter-party risk? The value of a paper investment is directly tied to the promise or performance of the counter-party; a *counter-party* is the entity that makes the promise or is tied to the performance. A stock is only as good as the performance of the underlying company. A bond's value depends on the counter-party (issuer) to make good on its promise to pay back principal and interest. The value of currency (such as dollars or euros) depends on the issuing government's ability to manage the currency to keep it from losing value (for example, the currency's value falls when inflation rises). In short, a paper security is only as good as the quality of the promisor.

REMEMBER

Physical gold bullion (coins or bars) is one of the few investments that doesn't have counter-party risk the way that stocks, exchange-traded funds (ETFs), and other paper investments do. Acquire some to truly diversify away from the risks of paper investments.

Nonstock ETFs

Stocks are good, and they're an important part of any long-term portfolio, but your brokerage account gives you the ability to buy other securities to diversify away from general stock market risks. Good diversification means that you (hopefully) add quality positions to hedge the risks that may be present in the rest of your portfolio.

REMEMBER

The stock market usually doesn't move in lockstep with other markets (such as some currencies and precious metals), and it's a good idea to consider adding some of these other markets by using exchange-traded funds (ETFs). Some nonstock ETFs can be in areas such as energy, precious metals, and currencies. Check out Chapter 5 for the scoop.

Inverse ETFs

Exchange-traded funds (ETFs) are a great companion to your stock investing pursuits, partly because different objectives can be established very easily right in your stock brokerage account. ETFs can be a good part of a diversified portfolio. But let us add another wrinkle to the mix: inverse ETFs. An inverse ETF is just what it sounds like: It acts inversely to what it corresponds to. For example, if you get an inverse ETF on the S&P 500, that particular inverse ETF will go up if the S&P 500 index goes down, and vice versa.

In other words, if the S&P 500 goes down, the inverse ETF will go up accordingly. Of course, if the S&P 500 goes up, that inverse ETF will go down. You get the picture.

TIP

The Canadian ETF market has a few inverse ETFs, although nowhere near as many as in the U.S. There are inverse ETFs on many stock vehicles ranging from major market indexes (such as the S&P 500 and the Dow) all the way to specific sectors (such as financial stocks or technology). The same sources that we provide on ETFs in Chapter 5 and in Appendix A provide information and guidance on inverse ETFs, and we certainly hope you discuss this type of security with an investing professional or someone you trust. The bottom line is that an inverse ETF can be a good way to hedge against severe recessions or extended bear markets.

Covered Call Options

Writing a covered call option is a great strategy for generating income from a current stock position (or positions) in your portfolio. A *call option* is a vehicle that gives the call buyer the right (but not the obligation) to buy a particular stock at a given price during a limited time frame (call options expire). The buyer pays what's called the *premium* to the call seller (referred to as the *call writer*). The call writer receives the premium as income but in return is obligated to sell the stock to the buyer at the agreed-upon price (called the *strike price*) if called upon to do so during the life of the option. The call option is typically a speculative vehicle for those who are buying them, but in this case we specifically refer to writing a covered call option.

Covered call writing is a conservative way to make extra cash from just about any listed stock of which you own at least 100 shares. Whether your stock has a dividend or not, this could boost income by 5 percent or more.

Put Options

A *put option* is a bet that a stock or ETF will fall in price. If you see the fortunes of a company going down, a put option is a great way to make a profit by speculating that the stock will go down. Many use puts to speculate for a profit, while others use put options as a hedging vehicle or a form of "portfolio insurance."

TIP

If you're holding a stock for the long term but you're concerned about it in the short term, consider using a put option on that stock. You're not hoping the stock goes down; you're merely using a form of protection for your stock holding. If the stock goes down, the put option will rise in value. What some investors do is then cash out the put option at a profit and use the proceeds to buy more shares of that stock because the stock's price is lower and possibly a buying opportunity.

Tangibles

Hold on to your hat. We're about to tell you to get stuff that will make you think that your authors will soon wear tinfoil hats. But we're serious. Consider beefing up your pantry, along with other tangibles that are related to the world of human necessities. Look . . . the reason you own stocks is to help you deal with human necessities in the future (fund your retirement, buy food, pay utilities, and so forth). But the economy is so fragile right now that difficulties in acquiring necessities (food, water, medicines, and so on) could happen at any time. Let's face it — when folks panic, they do all sorts of things (besides panic-selling their stocks à la 2008).

REMEMBER

When times are good, we tell folks to have emergency funds someplace safe, such as a bank savings account. But when times look as bad as they have in recent years (trending toward potentially more difficult times), it's better to be prepared. We personally keep extra essentials on hand (nonperishable food, water, candles, and other items that are necessities during difficult times). Even the U.S. government encourages this practice with websites such as www.ready.gov.

Cash

Cash in the form of savings or an amount parked in a secure money market fund is part of your arsenal for overall financial well-being. As a direct investment, it's good in a deflationary environment and very bad in an inflationary environment, but that's not why we mention it here. We mention it because investors need cash on the sidelines for a variety of reasons: chief among those reasons are short-term emergencies and as capital for buying opportunities. Chapter 2 has more on the topic of having cash on hand (such as in an emergency fund).

Motif Investing

Starting with only a few hundred bucks, you can have a theme-based portfolio that can augment your portfolio of individual stocks. *Motif investing* is a relatively new twist on investing (or speculating if you choose a risky motif). It gives you the convenience of investing in a pre-structured portfolio that's designed to do well given a particular expected event, trend, or worldview that will unfold.

If you believe, for example, that interest rates will rise, you can with a single motif have a basket of stocks that would optimally benefit from that event. If you believe that inflation will rear its ugly head, then you can consider a motif that intends to benefit from that outcome.

TIP

The major decision on a motif is not necessarily the motif itself but on your particular worldview or expectations going forward. What do you expect in the coming months or years? If there's one positive (or negative) trend that you're fairly certain will unfold and you're not sure how to profit from it through a single stock or fund, then take a look at motif investing. It may just be your cup of tea . . . or coffee (heck, there may even be a motif on tea and coffee). Find out more about motif investing at www.motifinvesting.com (but you could've guessed that).

Bearish Exchange-Traded Funds

Did you know that as recently as in 2016, about 25 world stock markets were down by double-digit percentages? Fortunately, the U.S. stock market had a relatively good year, although the Canadian stock market continued to struggle. And by the time you read this in 2018 (or later), a possibility of a sharp correction still looms due to general economic weakness, unsustainable debt, and global economic and financial difficulties. What should investors do given that possible event?

Investors can do plenty of things, both before and during tumultuous market times. If you're invested in quality stocks, then you shouldn't panic, especially if you have a long-term outlook. But hedging to a small extent can be a good consideration. In other words, why not consider a vehicle that will benefit in the event of a downturn in the stock market?

Exchange-traded funds (ETFs) are a good companion vehicle in your stock portfolio, and their versatility can become part of your overall strategy. If you believe that the stock market is or soon will be in difficult times, then consider a bearish stock market ETF. A bearish (or inverse) stock ETF is designed to go up when stocks go down. If stocks go down 5 percent, then the bearish ETF goes up by a similar inverse percentage (in this case, 5 percent).

TIP

What some investors do with bearish ETFs is cash them out when the market plunges and then take the proceeds to buy more of their favorite stocks (which presumably are cheaper given the market's move down). Tactics such as this mean you keep your portfolio growing for the long term while playing it safe during short-term market difficulties. Flip to Chapter 5 for general information on ETFs.

Dividend Yield Exchange-Traded Funds

The movement of stock prices can certainly be puzzling at times. Because they're subject to buying and selling orders, their movement may not always be logical or predictable, especially in the short term (and we mean *especially*). There is, however, one aspect of stocks that is much more logical and predictable: dividends.

Strong, profitable companies that have consistently raised their dividends in the past tend to reliably keep doing so in the future. Many companies have raised their dividends, or at the very least kept paying them, year-in and year-out, through good times and bad. Dividends are paid out from the company's net earnings (or net profit), so dividends also tend to act as a barometer gauging the company's financial health, which basically boils down to profitability.

Finding good dividend-paying stocks isn't hard; we describe them in Chapter 9. You can also find them with the stock-screening tools we cover in Chapter 16. However, investing in a strong basket of dividend-paying stocks by checking out dividend yield ETFs can be a good idea. A *dividend yield ETF* selects a basket of stocks based on the criteria of dividends — how consistently they're paid and continuously raised. They make it easy to include dividend-payers in your portfolio with a single purchase. We cover ETFs in more detail in Chapter 5.

Appendixes

Appendix A

Resources for Stock Investors

Getting and staying informed are ongoing priorities for stock investors. The lists in this appendix represent some of the best Canadian and American information resources available.

Financial Planning Sources

To find a financial planner to help you with your general financial needs, contact the following organizations:

» **Advocis** (www.advocis.ca): Advocis is a member-based association of financial advisors and planners in Canada. It is the voice of Canada's financial gurus who must also follow a professional code of conduct. It serves Canadian financial advisors, their clients, and website visitors.

» **Investments & Wealth Institute** (http://investmentsandwealth.org/ learning): Primarily geared to U.S. investment advisor accreditation, this is also a provider of advanced financial education inviting members in Canada, Australia, the U.K., Asia, and other countries to take advantage of the Institute's live conferences, online courses, and leading publications.

» **RRSP.org** (www.rrsp.org): A Canadian website providing online financial planning advice about RRSPs. You can also browse their reviews of Canadian and U.S. investment books and a list of articles dealing with many financial planning and investment matters.

The Language of Investing

>> **Investing for Beginners** (beginnersinvest.about.com): This site offers good basic information for novice investors.

>> **Investopedia** (www.investopedia.com): An excellent site with plenty of information on investing for beginning and intermediate investors.

>> **Investor Words** (www.investorwords.com): One of the most comprehensive sites on the Internet for beginning and intermediate investors for learning words and phrases unique to the financial world.

>> *Standard & Poor's Dictionary of Financial Terms* by Virginia B. Morris and Kenneth M. Morris (Lightbulb Press): A nicely laid out A-to-Z publication for investors mystified by financial terms. It explains the important investing terms you come across every day.

Textual Investment Resources

Stock investing success isn't an event; it's a process. The periodicals and magazines listed here (along with their websites) have offered many years of guidance and information for investors, and they're still top-notch. The books provide much wisdom that's either timeless or timely (covering problems and concerns every investor should be aware of now).

Periodicals and magazines

>> *ADVICE For Investors* (http://AdviceForInvestors.com)

>> *Barron's* (online.barrons.com)

>> *Canadian MoneySaver* (www.canadianmoneysaver.ca)

>> *Forbes* magazine (www.forbes.com)

>> *Investing.com* (www.investing.com)

>> *Investor's Business Daily* (www.investors.com)

>> *Kiplinger's Personal Finance* magazine (www.kiplinger.com)

>> *Money* magazine (www.money.cnn.com)

>> *MoneySense* (www.moneysense.ca)

>> *The Wall Street Journal* (www.wsj.com)

Books

>> *Common Stocks and Uncommon Profits and Other Writings* by Philip A. Fisher (Wiley, 2003): Although the book is from 2003, the information and guidance are still valuable for today's investors.

>> *Elliott Wave Principle: Key to Market Behavior Elliott Wave Principle: Key to Market Behavior,* **11th Edition** by A. J. Frost and Robert R. Prechter (New Classics Library): Robert Prechter, a leading technician, has had some very accurate forecasts about the stock market and the general economy.

>> *Forbes Guide to the Markets: Becoming a Savvy Investor* by Marc M. Groz (Wiley, 2009): A solid investing guide from the folks at *Forbes*.

>> *Fundamental Analysis For Dummies* by Matt Krantz (Wiley, 2016): A worthwhile book for serious investors. The author "drills down" into the financials of a company, which any serious investor would need to know.

>> *How to Pick Stocks Like Warren Buffett: Profiting from the Bargain Hunting Strategies of the World's Greatest Value Investor* by Timothy Vick (McGraw-Hill Professional, 2000): When you're investing, it's good to see what accomplished investors like Warren Buffett do, and this book explains his approach well.

>> *The Intelligent Investor: The Classic Text on Value Investing* by Benjamin Graham (HarperCollins, 2006): This is a classic investing book that was great when it was published and is very relevant in today's tumultuous stock market.

>> *Security Analysis: The Classic 1951 Edition* by Benjamin Graham and David L. Dodd (McGraw-Hill, 2004): A classic. Investors in this uncertain age should acquaint themselves with the basics.

>> *Standard & Poor's Stock Reports* (www.netadvantage.standardandpoors.com): Ask your reference librarian about this excellent reference source, which gives one-page summaries on the major companies and has detailed financial reports on all major companies listed on the NYSE, Nasdaq, and the Toronto Stock Exchange.

>> *The Wall Street Journal Guide to Understanding Money and Investing* by Kenneth M. Morris and Virginia B. Morris (Lightbulb Press, 2004): This is a neat little book that offers a good overview of investing.

>> *Value Investing in Asia: The Definitive Guide to Investing in Asia* by Stanley Lim and Cheong Mun Hong (Wiley Finance, 2017): A gateway for both new and experienced investors seeking practical reference to new opportunities in Asian markets while addressing key challenges unique to Asian investing.

Special books of interest to stock investors

>> *The Coming Bond Market Collapse: How to Survive the Demise of the U.S. Debt Market* by Michael G. Pento (Wiley, 2013): The global bond market is a huge bubble that will send shockwaves through stock markets and economies; Pento tells you why and what to do.

>> *The ETF Book: All You Need to Know About Exchange-Traded Funds* by Richard A. Ferri (Wiley, 2009): Considering the marketplace, ETFs are better choices than stocks for some investors, and this book does a good job of explaining them.

>> *Hot Commodities: How Anyone Can Invest Profitably in the World's Best Market* by Jim Rogers (Random House, 2007): The cornerstone of "human need" investing includes commodities, provides great insights.

>> *The Money Bubble* by James Turk and John Rubino (DollarCollapse Press, 2014): These are epic times as historic currency bubbles and crises unfold with serious consequences for stocks and other aspects of the financial picture. Offers great guidance for enhancing financial safety.

Investing Websites

How can any serious investor ignore the Internet? You can't, and you shouldn't. The following are among the best information sources available.

General investing websites

>> **BNN Bloomberg** (www.bnnbloomberg.ca)

>> **Canoe Money** (http://www.canoe.ca/Canoe/Money/)

>> **CNN Money** (www.money.cnn.com)

>> **Financial Sense** (www.financialsense.com)

>> *Forbes* (www.forbes.com)

>> **Invest Wisely: Advice From Your Securities Industry Regulators** (www.sec.gov/investor/pubs/inws.htm)

>> **Investing.com** (www.investing.com)

>> **MarketWatch** (www.marketwatch.com)

Stock investing websites

» **AllStocks.com** (www.allstocks.com)

» **Benzinga** (www.benzinga.com)

» **Canadian Securities Institute** (www.csi.ca)

» **CNBC** (www.cnbc.com)

» **Morningstar Canada** (www2.morningstar.ca)

» **Standard and Poor's** (www.standardandpoors.com)

» **Stockhouse** (www.stockhouse.com)

» **Yahoo! Finance Canada** (http://ca.finance.yahoo.com)

» **Yahoo! Finance** (www.finance.yahoo.com)

Digital currency investing websites

These websites cover digital currencies. There are articles, blogs, price data, charts, technical analyses, and predictions about where the cryptocurrency ecosystem is heading. It's hard to get bored with these websites!

» **Bitcoin.com** (http://news.bitcoin.com)

» **Bitcoin Exchange Guide b** (http://bitcoinexchangeguide.com)

» **Bitcoin Magazine** (http://bitcoinmagazine.com)

» **CCN** (www.ccn.com)

» **Coindesk** (www.coindesk.com)

» **Coinforum.ca** (http://coinforum.ca)

» **Coinnoob** (www.coinnoob.com)

» **Coin Telegraph** (http://cointelegraph.com)

» **Cryptocurrency Facts** (www.cryptocurrencyfacts.com)

» **Crypto Potato** (www.cryptopotato.com)

» **NewsBTC** (www.newsbtc.com)

» **Stockhouse** (www.stockhouse.com/markets/cryptocurrency)

» **The Bitcoin News** (www.thebitcoinnews.com)

» **99 Bitcoins** (http://99bitcoins.com)

Asian stock investing websites

» **China Economic Net** (http://en.ce.cn/Markets)

» **Fundsupermart.com** (www.fundsupermart.com)

» **Investor Relations Asia Pacific** (www.irasia.com)

Cannabis investing websites

» **Invest In MJ** (www.investinmj.com)

» **MarijuanaStocks.com** (www.marijuanastocks.com)

» **Stockhouse** (www.stockhouse.com/news/trending/cannabis_69303)

» **The Marijuana Index** (www.marijuanaindex.com/stock-quotes/canadian-marijuana-index)

Stock investing blogs

These blogs offer a wealth of opinions and insights from experts on investing to round out your research (you may even find some articles from us).

» **Minyanville** (www.minyanville.com)

» **Seeking Alpha** (www.seekingalpha.com)

» **StockTwits** (www.stocktwits.com)

» **StreetAuthority** (www.streetauthority.com)

Other useful blogs for stock investors

» **Feedspot** (https://blog.feedspot.com/canadian_investment_blogs): This website refers you to many Canadian investment blogs.

» **HoweStreet** (www.howestreet.com)

» **King World News** (www.kingworldnews.com)

» **Market Sanity** (www.marketsanity.com)

» **Mish's Global Economic Trend Analysis** (www.themaven.net/mishtalk)

» **Zero Hedge** (www.zerohedge.com)

Investor Associations and Organizations

>> **Canadian Securities Administrators** (www.securities-administrators.ca): An association of provincial and territorial securities regulators in Canada with an aim to improve harmonization among regulators.

>> **Canadian Society of Technical Analysts** (www.csta.org)

>> **Investment Funds Institute of Canada** (www.ific.ca): An association dedicated to enhancing the integrity and growth of its member companies. It also provides information useful to stock investors.

>> **Investment Industry Regulatory Organization of Canada** (www.iiroc.ca): Sets investment and regulatory standards for the securities industry, but it has limited powers and isn't fully independent.

>> **Ontario Securities Commission** (www.osc.gov.on.ca): A securities regulator that is often criticized for not being as aggressive against noncompliance as U.S. securities regulators are.

>> **SEDAR** (www.sedar.com)

Stock Exchanges

>> **Toronto Stock Exchange** (www.tmx.com): The main stock exchange in Canada and where you'll find many Canadian company listings.

>> **Chicago Board Options Exchange** (www.cboe.com and http://cfe.cboe.com/cfe-products/xbt-cboe-bitcoin-futures): The CBOE is an options exchange, and the CBOE options learning center has lots of information about how options can enhance your stock investing. It also permits trading in Bitcoin futures.

>> **Nasdaq** (www.nasdaq.com): The main site for Nasdaq. You'll find lots of information and guidance for stock investors here.

>> **New York Stock Exchange/Euronext** (www.nyse.com): The NYSE's site has a wealth of information for stock investors.

>> **OTC Bulletin Board** (www.otcbb.com): If you decide to research small cap stocks, this is the site to go to for data and research on small publicly traded companies.

Finding Brokers

These offer an extensive list of brokers and sources to help you evaluate them so you can do your own shopping.

Choosing brokers

>> **Reviews.com** (www.reviews.com/online-stock-trading): This site provides reviews in many categories, including stock brokerage firms.

>> **Stock Brokers** (www.stockbrokers.com): Tracks and reviews brokers.

Brokers

>> **BMO InvestorLine** (www.bmoinvestorline.com)

>> **CIBC Investor's Edge** (www.investorsedge.cibc.com)

>> **Disnat Direct** (www.disnat.com)

>> **HSBC InvestDirect** (http://invest.hsbc.ca)

>> **National Bank Direct Brokerage** (http://w3.nbdb.ca)

>> **QTrade Investor** (www.qtrade.ca/investor)

>> **Questrade** (http://questrade.com)

>> **RBC Direct Investing** (www.rbcdirectinvesting.com)

>> **Scotiabank iTrade Canada** (www.scotiabank.com/itrade)

>> **TD Waterhouse Canada** (www.tdwaterhouse.ca)

Fee-Based Investment Sources

These are fee-based subscription services. Many of them also offer excellent (and free) email newsletters tracking the stock market and related news.

>> **Adviceforinvestors.com** (www.adviceforinvestors.com)

>> **The Bull & Bear** (www.thebullandbear.com)

>> **The Daily Reckoning, Agora Publishing** (www.dailyreckoning.com)

>> **Elliott Wave International** (www.elliottwave.com)

>> **InvestorPlace** (www.investorplace.com)

>> **The Motley Fool** (www.fool.com)

>> **Weiss Research's Money and Markets** (www.moneyandmarkets.com)

Exchange-Traded Funds

>> **ETF Database** (www.etfdb.com)

>> **ETF Trends** (www.etftrends.com)

>> **ETFguide** (http://etfguide.com)

>> **Stock-Encyclopedia.com** (http://etf.stock-encyclopedia.com/category/etfs-listed-in-canada.html): Also check out its home page (http://etf.stock-encyclopedia.com) for investing by themes.

Sources for Analysis

The following sources give you the chance to look a little deeper at some critical aspects regarding stock analysis. Whether it's earnings estimates and insider selling or a more insightful look at a particular industry, these sources are among our favorites.

Earnings and earnings estimates

>> **Earnings Whispers** (www.earningswhispers.com)

>> **Thomson Reuters** (www.thomsonreuters.com)

>> **Yahoo's Stock Research Center** (biz.yahoo.com/r/)

>> **Zacks Investment Research** (www.zacks.com)

Sector and industry analysis

>> **Hoover's** (www.hoovers.com)

>> **MarketWatch** (www.marketwatch.com)

>> **Standard & Poor's** (www.standardandpoors.com)

Stock indexes

Note: If these direct links don't work, search for indexes from the sites' home pages. Also, keep in mind that many of the resources in this appendix offer extensive information on indexes (such as MarketWatch and Yahoo! Finance).

>> **Dow Jones Indexes** (www.djindexes.com)

>> **Investopedia's tutorial on indexes** (www.investopedia.com/university/indexes)

>> **Reuters' list of indexes** (www.reuters.com/finance/markets/indices)

Factors that affect market value

Understanding basic economics is so vital to making your investment decisions that we had to include this section. These great sources have helped us understand the big picture and what ultimately affects the stock market.

Economics and politics

>> **Canada NewsWire** (www.newswire.ca)

>> **Federal Reserve Board** (www.federalreserve.gov)

>> **Financial Sense** (www.financialsense.com)

>> **Grandfather Economic Report** (www.grandfathereconomicreport.com)

>> **Moody's Analytics** (www.economy.com)

Technical analysis

>> **Big Charts** (www.bigcharts.com)

>> **Elliott Wave International** www.elliottwave.com

>> **Stock Technical Analysis** (www.stockta.com)

>> **StockCharts.com** (www.stockcharts.com)

Insider trading

>> **SEC Info** (www.secinfo.com)

>> **Securities and Exchange Commission** (www.sec.gov)

>> **SEDI** (www.sedi.ca)

>> **StreetInsider** (www.streetinsider.com)

Tax Benefits and Obligations

>> **Canada Revenue Agency** (www.cra-arc.gc.ca)

>> **Cantax** (www.cantax.com)

>> **H&R Block** (www.hrblock.ca)

>> **Intuit Canada** (www.intuit.ca)

Fraud

>> **Canadian Investor Protection Fund** (www.cipf.ca): The CIPF may be able to help you recover losses, within limits, if a CIPF-member investment dealer becomes insolvent.

>> **National Consumers League's Fraud Center** (www.fraud.org)

>> **North American Securities Administrators Association** (www.nasaa.org)

>> **Securities and Exchange Commission** (www.sec.gov): The U.S. government agency that regulates the securities industry.

Appendix B

Financial Ratios

Considering how many financial catastrophes have occurred in recent years (and continue to occur), doing your homework on the financial health of your stock choices is more important than ever. This appendix is your go-to when considering stocks for your portfolio. It lists the most common ratios that investors should be aware of and use. A solid company doesn't have to pass all these ratio tests with flying colours, but at a minimum, it should comfortably pass the ones regarding profitability and solvency:

>> **Profitability:** Is the company making money? Is it making more or less than it did in the prior period? Are sales growing? Are profits growing? You can answer these questions by looking at return on equity, return on assets, and common size ratio (income statement).

>> **Solvency:** Is the company keeping debts and other liabilities under control? Are its assets growing? Is the company's net equity (or net worth or stockholders' equity) growing? You can answer these questions by looking at the quick ratio, debt to net equity, and working capital.

REMEMBER

While you examine ratios, keep these points in mind:

>> Not every company and/or industry is the same. A ratio that seems dubious in one industry may be just fine in another. Investigate and check out the norms in that particular industry. (Chapter 13 has more details.)

>> A single ratio isn't enough to base your investment decision on. Look at several ratios covering the major aspects of the company's finances.

>> Look at two or more years of the company's numbers to judge whether the most recent ratio is better, worse, or unchanged from the previous year. Ratios can give you early warning signs regarding the company's prospects. (Chapter 11 has details on two important documents that list a company's numbers — the balance sheet and the income statement.)

Liquidity Ratios

Liquidity is the ability to quickly turn assets into cash. Liquid assets are simply assets that are easy to convert to cash. Real estate, for example, is certainly an asset, but it's not liquid because converting it to cash can take weeks, months, or even years. Current assets such as chequing accounts, savings accounts, marketable securities, accounts receivable, and inventory are much easier to sell or convert to cash in a short period of time.

Paying bills or immediate debt takes liquidity. Liquidity ratios help you understand a company's ability to pay its current liabilities. The most common liquidity ratios are the current ratio and the quick ratio; the numbers to calculate them are located on the balance sheet.

Current ratio

The current ratio is the most commonly used liquidity ratio. It answers the question, "Does the company have enough financial cushion to meet its current bills?" It's calculated as follows:

Current ratio = Total current assets ÷ Total current liabilities

If Schmocky Corp. (SHM) has $60,000 in current assets and $20,000 in current liabilities, the current ratio is 3, meaning the company has $3 of current assets for each dollar of current liabilities. As a general rule, a current ratio of 2 or more is desirable.

WARNING

A current ratio of less than 1 is a red flag that the company may have a cash crunch that could cause financial problems. Although many companies strive to get the current ratio to equal 1, we like to see a higher ratio (in the range of 1–3) to keep a cash cushion in case the economy slows down.

Quick ratio

The quick ratio is frequently referred to as the "acid test" ratio. It's a little more stringent than the current ratio in that you calculate it without inventory. We'll use the current ratio example discussed in the preceding section. What if half of the assets are inventory ($30,000 in this case)? Now what? First, here's the formula for the quick ratio:

Quick ratio = (Current assets less inventory) ÷ Current liabilities

In the example, the quick ratio for SHM is 1.5 ($60,000 minus $30,000 equals $30,000, which is then divided by $20,000). In other words, the company has $1.50 of "quick" liquid assets for each dollar of current liabilities. This amount is okay. Quick liquid assets include any money in the bank, marketable securities, and accounts receivable. If quick liquid assets at the very least equal or exceed total current liabilities, that amount is considered adequate.

The acid test that this ratio reflects is embodied in the question, "Can the company pay its bills when times are tough?" If the company can't sell its goods (inventory), can it still meet its short-term liabilities? Watch the accounts receivable as well. If the economy is entering rough times, you want to make sure that the company's customers are paying invoices on a timely basis.

Operating Ratios

Operating ratios essentially measure a company's efficiency. "How is the company managing its resources?" is a question commonly answered with operating ratios. If, for example, a company sells products, does it have too much inventory? If it does, that could impair the company's operations. The following sections present common operating ratios.

Return on equity (ROE)

Equity is the amount left from total assets after you account for total liabilities. (This can also be considered a profitability ratio.) Net equity (aka shareholders' equity, stockholders' equity, or net worth) is the bottom line on the company's balance sheet, both geographically and figuratively:

Return on equity (ROE) = Net income ÷ Net equity

The net income (from the company's income statement) is simply the total income less total expenses. Net income that isn't spent or used up increases the company's net equity. Looking at net income is a great way to see whether the company's management is doing a good job growing the business. You can check this out by looking at the net equity from both the most recent balance sheet and the one from a year earlier. Ask whether the current net equity is higher or lower than the year before. If higher, by what percentage?

For example, if SHM's net equity is $40,000 and its net income is $10,000, its ROE is a robust 25 percent (net income of $10,000 divided by net equity of $40,000).

The higher the ROE, the better. An ROE that exceeds 10 percent (for simplicity's sake) is good (especially in a slow and struggling economy). Use the ROE in conjunction with the ROA ratio in the following section to get a fuller picture of a company's activity.

Return on assets (ROA)

The return on assets (ROA) may seem similar to the ROE in the preceding section, but it actually gives a perspective that completes the picture when coupled with the ROE. The formula for figuring out the ROA is

Return on assets = Net income + Total assets

The ROA reflects the relationship between a company's profit and the assets used to generate that profit. If SHM makes a profit of $10,000 and has total assets of $100,000, the ROA is 10 percent. This percentage should be as high as possible, but it will generally be less than the ROE.

WARNING

Say that a company has an ROE of 25 percent but an ROA of only 5 percent. Is that good? It sounds okay, but a problem may exist. An ROA that's much lower than the ROE indicates that the higher ROE may have been generated by something other than total assets — debt! The use of debt can be a leverage to maximize the ROE, but if the ROA doesn't show a similar percentage of efficiency, then the company may have incurred too much debt. In that case, investors should be aware that this situation can cause problems (see the section "Solvency Ratios," later in this appendix). Better ROA than DOA!

Sales-to-receivables ratio (SR)

The sales-to-receivables ratio (SR) gives investors a clue into a company's ability to manage what customers owe it. This ratio uses data from both the income statement (sales) and the balance sheet (accounts receivable, or AR):

Sales-to-receivables ratio = Sales + Receivables

Say you have the following data for SHM:

Sales in 2017 are $75,000. On 12/31/17, receivables stood at $25,000.

Sales in 2018 are $80,000. On 12/31/18, receivables stood at $50,000.

Now you can figure out that sales went up 6.6 percent (sales in 2018 are $5,000 higher than 2017 and $5,000 is 6.6 percent of $75,000), but receivables went up 100 percent (the $25,000 in 2017 doubled to $50,000, which is a move up of

100 percent)! In 2017, the SR was 3 ($75,000/$25,000). But the SR in 2018 sank to 1.6 ($80,000 divided by $50,000), or was nearly cut in half. Yes, sales increased, but the company's ability to collect money due from customers fell dramatically. This is important to note because what good is selling more when you can't get the money (get repayment on the sales)? From a cash flow point of view, the company's financial situation deteriorated.

Solvency Ratios

Solvency just means that a company isn't overwhelmed by its liabilities. Insolvency means "Oops! Too late." You get the point. Solvency ratios have never been more important than they are now because the Canadian economy is currently carrying so much debt. Solvency ratios look at the relationship between what a company owns and what it owes. Companies that fail to generate sufficient cash are exposed to the risk of becoming insolvent. The following sections discuss two of the primary solvency ratios.

Debt-to-net-equity ratio

The debt-to-net-equity ratio indicates how dependent the company is on debt. It tells you how much the company owes and how much it owns:

Debt-to-net-equity ratio = Total liabilities ÷ Net equity

If SHM has $100,000 in debt and $50,000 in net equity, the debt-to-net equity ratio is 2. The company has $2 of debt to every dollar of net equity. In this case, what the company owes is twice the amount of what it owns.

WARNING

Whenever a company's debt-to-net-equity ratio exceeds 1 (as in the example), that isn't generally good. In fact, the higher the number, the more negative the situation. If the number is too high and the company isn't generating enough income to cover the debt, the business runs the risk of bankruptcy.

Working capital

Technically, working capital isn't a ratio, but it does belong to the list of things that serious investors look at. Working capital measures a company's current assets in relation to its current liabilities. It's a simple equation:

Working capital = Total current assets − Total current liabilities

Does the company have enough to cover current bills? You can formulate a useful ratio. If current assets are $25,000 and liabilities are $25,000, that's a 1-to-1 ratio — cutting it close. Current assets should be at least 50 percent higher than current liabilities to have enough cushion to pay bills and have money for other purposes. Preferably, the ratio should be 2 to 1 or higher.

Common Size Ratios

Common size ratios offer simple comparisons. You have common size ratios for both the balance sheet (where you compare total assets) and the income statement (where you compare total sales):

>> To get a common size ratio from a balance sheet, the total assets figure is assigned 100 percent. Every other item on the balance sheet is represented as a percentage of total assets. Total assets equal 100 percent. All other items equal a percentage of the total assets. For example, if SHM has total assets of $10,000 and debt of $3,000, then debt equals 30 percent (debt divided by total assets, or $3,000 ÷ $10,000, or 30 percent).

>> To get a common size ratio from an income statement (or profit and loss statement), you compare total sales. Total sales equal 100 percent. All other items equal a percentage of the total sales. For example, if SHM has $50,000 in total sales and a net profit of $8,000, you know that profit equals 16 percent of total sales ($8,000 ÷ $50,000, or 16 percent).

Keep in mind the following points with common size ratios:

>> Net profit: What percentage of sales is it? What was it last year? How about the year before? What percentage of increases (or decreases) is the company experiencing?

>> Expenses: Are total expenses in line with the previous year? Are any expenses going out of line?

>> Net equity: Is this item higher or lower than the year before?

>> Debt: Is this item higher or lower than the year before?

Common size ratios are used to compare the company's financial data not only with prior balance sheets and income statements but also with other companies in the same industry. You want to make sure that the company is not only doing better historically but also as a competitor in the industry.

Valuation Ratios

Understanding the value of a stock is very important for stock investors. The quickest and most efficient way to judge the value of a company is to look at valuation ratios. The type of value that you deal with throughout this book is the market value (essentially the price of the company's stock). You hope to buy it at one price and sell it later at a higher price — that's the name of the game. But what's the best way to determine whether what you're paying for now is a bargain or is fair market value? How do you know whether your stock investment is undervalued or overvalued? The valuation ratios in the following sections can help you answer these questions. In fact, they're the same ratios that value investors have used with great success for many years.

Price-to-earnings ratio (P/E)

The price-to-earnings ratio (P/E) can double as a profitability ratio because it's a common barometer of value that many investors and analysts look at. Chapter 11 covers this, but it's such a critical ratio, we also include it here:

P/E ratio = Price (per share) ÷ Earnings (per share)

For example, if SHM's stock price per share is $10 and the earnings per share are $1, the P/E ratio is 10 (10 divided by 1).

REMEMBER

The P/E ratio tells you if you're paying too much for the company's earnings. Value investors find this to be very important:

>> Generally, the lower the P/E ratio, the better (from a financial strength point of view). Frequently, a low P/E ratio indicates that the stock is undervalued, especially if the company's sales are growing and the industry is also growing. But you may occasionally encounter a situation where the stock price is falling faster than the company's earnings, which would also generate a low P/E. And if the company has too much debt and the industry is struggling, then a low P/E may indicate that the company is in trouble. Use the P/E as part of your analysis along with other factors (such as debt, for instance) to get a more complete picture.

A company with a P/E ratio significantly higher than its industry average is a red flag that its stock price is too high (or that it's growing faster than its competitors). If the industry's P/E ratio is typically in the range of 10–12 and you're evaluating a stock whose P/E ratio is around 20, then you may want to consider avoiding it. A company's P/E ratio needs to be not only taken in context with its industry peers but also based on its year-over-year performance.

>> Don't invest in a company with no P/E ratio (it has a stock price, but the company experienced recurring losses). Such a stock may be good for a speculator's portfolio but not for your retirement account.

>> Any stock with a P/E ratio higher than 40 should be considered a speculation and not an investment. Frequently, a high P/E ratio indicates that the stock is overvalued.

TIP

When you buy a company, you're really buying its power to make money. In essence, you're buying its earnings. Paying for a stock that's priced at 10 to 20 times earnings is a conservative strategy that has served investors well for nearly a century. Make sure the company is priced fairly and use the P/E ratio with other measures of value (such as the ratios in this appendix).

Price-to-sales ratio (P/S)

The price-to-sales ratio (P/S) helps to answer the question, "Am I paying too much for the company's stock based on the company's sales?" This is a useful valuation ratio that we recommend using as a companion tool with the company's P/E ratio (see the preceding section). You calculate it as follows:

P/S = Stock price (per share) ÷ Total sales (per share)

This ratio can be quoted on a per-share basis or on an aggregate basis. For example, if a company's market value (or market capitalization) is $1 billion and annual sales are also $1 billion, the P/S is 1. If the market value in this example is $2 billion and annual sales are $1 billion, then the P/S is 2. Or, if the share price is $76 and the total sales per share are $38, the P/S is 2 — you arrive at the same ratio whether you calculate on a per-share or aggregate basis. For investors trying to make sure that they're not paying too much for the stock, the general rule is that the lower the P/S, the better. Stocks with a P/S of 2 or lower are considered undervalued.

WARNING

Be hesitant about buying a stock with a P/S greater than 5. If you buy a stock with a P/S of 5, you're paying $5 for each dollar of sales — not a bargain.

Price-to-book ratio (P/B)

The price-to-book ratio (P/B) compares a company's market value to its accounting (or book) value. The book value refers to the company's net equity (assets minus liabilities). The company's market value is usually dictated by external factors such as supply and demand in the stock market. The book value is indicative of the company's internal operations. Value investors see the P/B as another way of valuing the company to determine whether they're paying too much for the stock. The formula is

Price-to-book ratio (P/B) = Market value ÷ Book value

An alternate method is to calculate the ratio on a per-share basis, which yields the same ratio. If the company's stock price is $20 and the book value (per share) is $15, then the P/B is 1.33. The company's market value is 33 percent higher than its book value. Investors seeking an undervalued stock like to see the market value as close as possible to (or even better, below) the book value.

REMEMBER

Keep in mind that the P/B may vary depending on the industry and other factors. Also, judging a company solely on book value may be misleading because many companies have assets that aren't adequately reflected in the book value. Software companies are a good example. Intellectual properties, such as copyrights and trademarks, are valuable yet aren't fully covered in book value. Just bear in mind that, generally, the lower the market value is in relation to the book value, the better for you (especially if the company has strong earnings and the outlook for the industry is positive).

Index

I

icons, explained, 3
identifying trends, 159–160
IDEX (website), 306
illiquid investments, 18
income
  about, 139
  defined, 87
  dividend, 343–344
  interest, 342–343
  investing for. *See* income
    stocks
  tallying your, 26
income and expense statement.
  See income statement
income investing, 47–49
income investor, defined, 99
income mutual funds, 143
income statement
  about, 131–132
  common size ratios from, 396
  evaluating, 178, 184–189, 199
income stocks
  about, 140–144
  advantages of, 141–142
  analyzing, 144–149
  assessing your needs, 144–145
  bond rating, 148–149
  disadvantages of, 142–144
  diversifying, 149
  dividends/dividend rates, 140
  DRPs, 141
  payout ratio, 147–148
  real estate investment trusts
    (REITs), 150–152
  royalty trusts, 152
  types of investors for, 141
  utilities, 149–150
  yield of, 48–49, 145–147
Incredible Charts (website), 153
independence, of industries, 215

indexes, 77–80, 287
indicators
  about, 167
  Bollinger bands, 171
  crossovers, 170
  divergence, 170
  future, 228
  moving average, 168–170
  moving average convergence/
    divergence (MACD), 170
  oscillators, 171
  Relative Strength Index
    (RSI), 168
industries. *See also specific*
  industries
  about, 209–210
  categories of, 211–212
  categories of, in Yahoo!
    Finance, 260
  choosing, 211–216
  compared with sectors,
    210–211
  evaluating dependence of, 215
  evaluating growth in, 129,
    214–215
  evaluating leading companies
    in, 215
  government action and, 216
  outlining, 216–221
  sources for analysis of, 388
industry research, 92
inflation, 142–143, 254
inflation risk, 58
information gathering
  about, 83–84
  accounting basics, 86–87
  dividends, 99–101
  economics basics, 86, 87–90
  financial news, 91–94
  investment tips, 101–102
  stock exchanges, 84–86
  stock tables, 94–99

Initial Coin Offering (ICO), 303,
  311–312
innovators, 215
insider activity
  about, 329–330
  Canadian insider trading,
    331–332
  corporate stock buybacks,
    335–338
  insider transactions, 332–335
  stock splits, 338–340
  U.S. insider trading, 330–331
insider buying, 132, 333–334
insider reports, 203
insider selling, 334–335
insider trading
  Canadian, 331–332
  sources for, 389
  U.S., 330–331
insider transactions, 332–335
institutional buying, 133
institutional stockbrokers, 104
insurance, needs for, 66
The Intelligent Investor: The
  Classic Text on Value
  Investing (Graham), 381
Interactive Brokers Canada, 236
interest, 43, 47
interest income, 342–343
interest rate risk, 53–56
interest-rate sensitivity, of
  income stocks, 142
intermediate-term investing, 45
intermediate-term trend, 161
International Federation
  of Technical Analysis
  (website), 153
Internet, using for research, 207
intrinsic value, 177–178
Intuit Canada (website), 389
inventory, evaluating, 181
inverse ETFs, 372–373

S

About the Authors

Andrew Dagys, CPA, CMA, is a best-selling author who has written and co-authored more than a dozen books, mostly about investing, personal finance, and technology. Andrew has contributed columns to major Canadian publications. He is also a frequently quoted author in many of Canada's daily news publications, including The Globe and Mail, National Post and Toronto Star. He has appeared on several national news broadcasts to offer his insights on the Canadian and global investment landscapes. Andrew considers writing books, in collaboration with talented publishing and editorial partners, to be one of life's most truly amazing experiences!

Andrew enjoys actively serving his community in the not-for-profit sector. He lives in Toronto with his wife, Dawn-Ava, and their three children — Brendan, Megan, and Jordan. He looks forward to your comments and can be reached at andrew.dagys@gmail.com.

Paul Mladjenovic, CFP, is a certified financial planner practitioner, writer, and public speaker. His business, PM Financial Services, has helped people with financial and business concerns since 1981. In 1985, he achieved his CFP designation. Since 1983, Paul has taught thousands of budding investors through popular national seminars such as "The $50 Wealthbuilder" and "Stock Investing Like a Pro." Paul has been quoted or referenced by many media outlets, including Bloomberg, MarketWatch, Comcast, CNBC, and a variety of financial and business publications and websites. As an author, he has written the books *The Unofficial Guide to Picking Stocks* (Wiley, 2000) and *Zero-Cost Marketing* (Todd Publications, 1995). In recent years, Paul accurately forecast many economic events, such as the rise of gold, the decline of the U.S. dollar, and the housing crisis. He edits the financial newsletter Prosperity Alert, available at no charge at www.prosperitynetwork.net. Paul's personal website can be found at www.mladjenovic.blogspot.ca.

Dedication

Andrew dedicates this book to his beloved wife, Dawn-Ava, and their three children Brendan, Megan, and Jordan. He thanks God daily for them all and for all of life's blessings. He commends Canadians like you with the courage to invest wisely in the face of a challenging and rapidly changing world.

Paul dedicates this book to his beloved Fran, Adam, and Joshua and his loving, supportive family — he thanks God for you. He also dedicates this book to the millions of investors who deserve more knowledge and information to achieve lasting prosperity.

Author's Acknowledgments

Andrew thanks Tracy Boggier, a visionary who provided him with yet another opportunity to co-author this fifth edition and who recognized the exciting changes in the investment landscape as a story that needed to be told. He also thanks Corbin Collins, his very talented project and copy editor, for his insights and guidance. He is a professional who sees both the importance of details as well as their place in the bigger picture. Even as he was preparing to get married, Corbin was dedicated to making this title the best it could be and was an absolute pleasure to work with. I was lucky to have him as a partner in writing this book.

Andrew also thanks his technical editor, Bruce Curwood, for his ongoing quest for factual accuracy. This is the second time that Bruce contributed to this work, and his contributions were very valuable. He is a talented in-vestment industry expert, and Andrew is grateful for his involvement.

Additional thanks go to all the dedicated people at Wiley who work hard behind the scenes.

Paul's technical editor, Juli Erhart-Graves, is a great financial pro whom he appreciates. She made sure his logic is sound and his facts are straight. Paul's gratitude again goes out to the Wiley editorial department.

Fran Lipa Zyenska, Paul appreciates your great support during the writing and updating of this book. It's not always easy dealing with the world, but with you by his side, he knows that God has indeed blessed him. Te amo!

Lastly, Andrew and Paul want to personally acknowledge you, the reader. Over the years, you've made the For Dummies books what they are today. Your devotion to these wonderful books helped build a foundation that played a big part in the creation of this book and many more yet to come. Thank you!

Publisher's Acknowledgments

Senior Acquisitions Editor: Tracy Boggier

Editor: Corbin Collins

Technical Editor: Bruce Curwood

Production Editor: Magesh Elangovan

Cover Photo: © Lester Balajadia/Shutterstock; Canadian flag © alexsl/iStock.com